EARL R. WASSERMAN

ELH Essays for
EARL R. WASSERMAN

Edited by
Ronald Paulson and Arnold Stein

THE JOHNS HOPKINS UNIVERSITY PRESS
Baltimore and London

Copyright © 1974, 1976 by The Johns Hopkins University Press

All rights reserved. No part of this book may be
reproduced or transmitted in any form or by any means,
electronic or mechanical, including photocopying,
recording, xerography, or any information storage and
retrieval system, without permission in writing
from the publisher.

"The Context of Dryden's *Absalom and Achitophel*," by Thomas E. Maresca,
appeared in expanded form in his *Epic to Novel* (Columbus: Ohio State
University Press, 1974).

Manufactured in the United States of America.

The Johns Hopkins University Press, Baltimore, Maryland 21218
The Johns Hopkins University Press Ltd., London

Library of Congress Catalog Card Number 75-36934
ISBN 0-8018-1815-x

PR
14
.E43
1976

Library of Congress Cataloging in Publication data
will be found on the last printed page of this book.

CONTENTS

Preface   vii

The Simplicity of Hogarth's *Industry and Idleness*   1
RONALD PAULSON

Experience as History: Shelley's Venice, Turner's Carthage   31
KARL KROEBER

The Context of Dryden's *Absalom and Achitophel*   50
THOMAS E. MARESCA

Images of Samuel Johnson   69
W. K. WIMSATT

Reflections on the Letter: The Reconciliation of Distance and Presence in *Pamela*   85
ROY ROUSSEL

Nature Spiritualized: Aspects of Anti-Newtonianism   110
A. J. KUHN

Swift's Satire: Rules of the Game   123
ROBERT C. ELLIOTT

Christopher Smart's *Magnificat*: Toward a Theory of Representation   139
GEOFFREY H. HARTMAN

Narrative and History   165
J. HILLIS MILLER

The Constant Couple: Farquhar's Four-Plays-in-One   184
JACKSON I. COPE

Coopers Hill: The Manifesto of Parliamentary Royalism, 1641   201
JOHN M. WALLACE

A Note on Wittgenstein and Literary Criticism   248
M. H. ABRAMS

Most Holy Forms of Thought: Some Observations on Blake and Language   262
  ROBERT F. GLECKNER

The Moralized Song: Some Renaissance Themes in Pope   285
  KATHLEEN WILLIAMS

The Role of Improvisation in *Corinne*   309
  GEORGES POULET

The Problem of *Amelia*: Hume, Barrow, and the Conversion of Captain Booth   320
  MARTIN C. BATTESTIN

The Socialization of Catherine Morland   356
  AVROM FLEISHMAN

Characteristics of Dryden's Prose   375
  ALAN ROPER

Bibliography of Books and Articles by Earl R. Wasserman   400

PREFACE

Earl R. Wasserman began his association with *ELH* in 1942, serving first as editor and then as senior editor until his death in March 1973. The following essays, written by friends, colleagues, and former students, were presented to honor his memory. They appeared in the 1974 Fall and Winter issues of *ELH*, Volume 41, Numbers 3 and 4.

Earl Wasserman's accomplishments were many and admirable. They speak and will speak for themselves. But one attribute, not on the record, may be named for those who know only the rigor of mind and critical discernment that characterized his scholarship. During a lifetime of enlarging and disciplining his own imagination and that of others, he maintained—toward new work, new directions, and the first stirrings of promise in the young—that authentic intellectual openness which reflects the magnanimous correspondence of literary scholarship with the greatness of its subject.

THE SIMPLICITY OF HOGARTH'S
INDUSTRY AND IDLENESS

BY RONALD PAULSON

The twelve plates of *Industry and Idleness,* which Hogarth published in 1747, tell of two apprentices whose stories are as simple as their names: Francis Goodchild and Tom Idle.[1] In Plate 1 Goodchild directs the thread on his loom as he directs his life by the *Prentice's Guide* and the ballads of *Dick Whittington* and *The London Prentice* toward the Whittingtonian goal of mayorship. Tom Idle dozes, relinquishing control of his spindle; his *Prentice's Guide* is tattered and discarded on the floor and his only models are the ballad of *Moll Flanders,* beer, and tobacco. Light from the window shines in on Goodchild, and in the margin of his side of the plate are the mace of the City of London, an alderman's gold chain, and the sword of state. But Idle, asleep, is away from the light, and along his border are whip, fetters, and a rope, and across the room from him retribution enters in the form of his chastising master. The contrast between industry and idleness and their consequences, in fact the whole story, is summed up in this first plate.

But we have eleven more plates built on the same contrasts. Plates 2 to 9 are structured in pairs, with Goodchild's action followed by Idle's. 2 and 3 contrast their piety: Goodchild inside the church, accompanied by his master's daughter, with light falling on him again, and Idle, outside, with bad company, gambling on the sabbath, suspended over an open grave, among skulls and bones, and with nothing over him but the threatening shape of a beadle replacing that of his master.

Plate 4 shows Goodchild inside his master's counting house, with the master pointing to the shop, saying in effect: " The shop is all yours: I entrust you with the management of it." The

[1] The plates are reproduced in Ronald Paulson, *Hogarth's Graphic Works* (New Haven and London, 1965; revised ed., 1970), II, pls. 180-91, and elsewhere.

church is followed by the counting house, obedience to his heavenly master by obedience to his earthly master. In Plate 5 Idle has forfeited his indentures—perhaps as a result of his un-apprentice-like doings on the sabbath, perhaps of his own free will. But his indentures are floating away in the water; he has betrayed first his heavenly and then his earthly master, and he is now outdoors and exposed to the elements. Instead of being in the solid, comfortable, protective shop, he floats precariously on a choppy sea, accompanied by the figure of his widowed mother, a sad reminder of conscience and duty. As the master points to the shop, which is now Goodchild's, so a sailor points to Idle's immediate and eventual destinations, the ship and the gallows; as the master rests his hand on Goodchild's shoulder, so does a sailor on Idle's, but to show him the cat-o'-nine tails and indicate the misery he will suffer on shipboard. Idle defiantly responds with the cuckold's sign directed at his tormentors, but almost equally at his poor mother. Nooses hang at the side of the boat: they have now moved inside the print.

In 6 Goodchild has married his master's daughter and become his partner (the order of the names, " Goodchild & West," implies the master's retirement). In the morning sunshine Goodchild leans out of his window to pay the serenading musicians, while in 7 Idle is in bed with a prostitute, with stolen earrings, a watch, and a pistol at the ready. Unlike Goodchild's solid brick house, this is a dilapidated garret with fallen plaster, gaping holes in the floor, a crumbling chimney, and broken utensils. Goodchild's door is open, a gesture of charity; Idle's is bolted shut, and as usual he is lying on a bed. The sound of music pleases Goodchild; the noise of the cat and rat terrifies Idle, reminding him of the hostile outside world.

In Plate 8 Goodchild, now sheriff, is at an official banquet, and a constituent appears at the door with a petition for him; in 9 Idle is among brawling, thieving hoodlums in a night-cellar, being betrayed by the girl he was in bed with in Plate 7, accompanied by the same character with the eye-patch and striped cap he gambled with in Plate 3 when he should have been in church. A constable, directed by the treacherous girl, enters to arrest him. And the hangman's noose is again materialized within the picture, hanging from the ceiling.

In 10 the two apprentices are brought together once more: Idle begging for mercy, Goodchild regretfully passing judgment; Idle, who until now has always been asleep or nearly recumbent (though never relaxed), cowers before Goodchild, his bent form contrasted with the strong unbending verticals of the pillars, the wall, the desk, and Goodchild's own torso. Finally, in 11 and 12 the order of contrast is reversed, and first Idle is shown on his way to the gallows and then Goodchild on his way to the Guildhall to be inaugurated as Lord Mayor: Idle outside, exposed, under a cloudy sky, with a Methodist minister exhorting him to repent; Goodchild under a clear sky, inside a coach, accompanied by dignitaries, with the sword of state (now materialized within the picture) showing at the coach window.

I

When *Industry and Idleness* appeared it must have looked very different from Hogarth's earlier series. The prints were smaller, in a cruder style, with the visual image much simpler. The complex reading structure of allusions, puns (both visual and verbal), parallels and contrasts, that reached a climax of intricacy in *Marriage à la Mode* (1745), is replaced by the simple pattern of a morality—right and wrong, reward and punishment, action and consequence, strengthened by the stark blacks and whites of the design. For the greys are largely absent visually as well as morally: the earlier plates were reproductive engravings which imitated the minutest shades of texture in an oil painting. These plates are simply penny prints, with the art-historical context ostentatiously rejected by the turn to a popular twelve-plate cycle with Biblical mottos at bottom, title at top, and emblematic borders. No longer are connoisseurs of painting or readers of the English and Roman Augustans directly addressed, but rather the people who went to puppet shows and morality plays at Bartholomew Fair and knew their Bible. The audience, for the first time, coincides with the subject of the prints. The *Harlot's* and *Rake's Progress* were obviously not addressed to harlots and rakes but to an audience that could meditate with detachment on such representative types. But *Industry and Idleness* is addressed— in both form and content—to apprentices, and though it was the master who bought the prints, he hung them for his apprentices' enlightenment or gave them sets of their own as Christmas presents. And the master himself was, of course, an ex-apprentice.

I hope that my initial description of the plates has at least shown Hogarth's ingenuity of elaboration to be still active. Idle's decline, for example, is not haphazard. Like writers on idleness from Bunyan to Samuel Johnson, Hogarth begins with sleep, a pursuit of dreams of ease and Moll Flanders, which has caused Idle to drop his spindle as Christian's sleep on Mount Difficulty caused him to drop his heavenly ticket. The second stage is to extend idleness to acedia or spiritual sloth; and thence to the escape from labor that takes him to sea; which leads to the final stages, illustrating the justification of the Church fathers for making idleness one of the capital sins. It produces an occasion for sin—any sin that, to use Dr. Johnson's phrase, will take " firm possession of the mind . . . when it is found empty and unoccupied." [2] Here the void of idleness is filled with thievery and illicit lust, and the final stage is the punishment, first private (betrayal) and then public (hanging).

All of this elaboration, however, is on the basic contrast of Goodchild and Idle: control and negligence, piety and basphemy, good company and bad, giving and taking, respect and contempt, wife and prostitute, loyalty and betrayal, prosperity and poverty, social and anti-social behavior, with beyond all this the contrast of the reason and the unreason, the directed and the undirected, order-security and chaos-danger. For the first time, Hogarth has produced a *hero*, a normative counter to oppose the foolish Harlot or Rake, his usual protagonist, who embodied qualities of both good and evil, freedom and compulsion. If complexity is the keynote of the earlier cycles, simplicity is the ostensible keynote here.

Hogarth turned to a more popular audience because in addressing them he could use simpler, more elemental forms and emotions than were available to him in sophisticated art. He was trying one more way of getting away from the stereotypes of contemporary academic art, while responding to the disparagement of rococo art and too difficult reading structures. The pleasure of the imagination which, in Addison's words, " is but opening the Eye and the scene enters " is precisely the one Hogarth

---

[2] *Rambler* No. 85, 8 Jan. 1751: the intellect then " will embrace any thing, however absurd or criminal, rather than be wholly without an object."

addresses himself to satisfy in *Industry and Idleness*—and in various ways in his subsequent work, practical and theoretical. The intricate patterns of light and shade that led the eye about in the earlier cycles, never allowing more than momentary rest, forcing one to *read*, are replaced by a simple, immediately-graspable gestalt. Before, the death of the Rake might be expressed through echoes of the statues of Melancholy and Raving Madness over the portal of Bedlam and—including the figures around him— by the echoes of a Pietà. But in *Industry and Idleness* the system of analogy on which the earlier series were founded is absent. The shapes are only expressive in themselves: not because the Apollo Belvedere has that pose, but because there is something inherently (or in the "cartoonist's armoury" of popular graphic convention) [3] straight and unbending in Goodchild's pose and something servile, cringing, and dishonest in Idle's.

Since this is a morality, the pattern is based on *This* vs. *That*. The opposition of Idle vs. Industrious Apprentice is emphasized, for example, by placing Idle on the left of the picture and Goodchild on the right, whether they appear together or alone. We come to expect on the left the irregular, flattened visage of Idle and on the right the regular good looks of Goodchild, and inevitably recall, " He shall set the sheep on His right hand but the goats on the left " (Matt. 25:33). Then we notice that Idle is always kept out in open spaces or in a crumbling tenement, unprotected and unsafe, while Goodchild is shown within solid, well-built architectural structures. Most obviously, the mottos, which appear under every design, emphasize the stark pattern of contrast and causality in the prints. They are mostly from Proverbs, whose verses are verbally equivalent to the visual structure Hogarth has constructed: " The soul of the sluggard desireth, and hath nothing; but the soul of the diligent shall be made fat " (13:14) — a structure of *this* against *that*, or of *this* will produce *that*. And many of the proverbs were, like this one, concerned with industry vs. idleness.[4] Leviticus, the next favorite source of mottos, carries

---

[3] See Gombrich, "The Cartoonist's Armoury" in *Meditations on a Hobby Horse* (London, 1963), pp. 127-42.

[4] See also Proverbs 12:24, 27; 19:24; 20:4. It should be noted that the scriptural passages were said to have been chosen for Hogarth by his friend the Rev. Arnold King (according to Dr. Ducarel, reported in *Genuine Works of William Hogarth*, I [1809], 138). This may simply mean that King found the passages Hogarth wanted or

the related structure, if you do *this*, then you will be punished (or rewarded) *thus* and *thus* and *thus*, to an extreme of rigor.

However, one might well ask whether this further reaction against sophisticated academic art has not taken Hogarth full circle and returned him to a work reducible to the simplest sort of topos, against which he had originally reacted in the *Harlot's Progress*? Has he not begun with the topos of industry's reward and idleness' punishment and illustrated it naively? There is a primitive, elemental strength here—what Alexander Gerard would have praised as "purity"[5]—that is most impressive, but is there not also a sacrifice?

The time has come to look more closely at those large simple oppositions we have taken in "at one blow."[6] I have said that in every case the idle apprentice is kept to the left side of the plate, the industrious to the right, as goats separated from sheep. With this pattern of expectation established, however, we may notice—or perhaps only sense—that in every one of the plates in which Goodchild appears alone, on the right, there is also something on the left. This is a repoussoir figure that helps to stabilize the composition, but also leads the viewer's eye into it, establishing its depth: the ugly old pew-opener in 2, the carbuncular-nosed porter in 4, the grotesque beggar in 6, the gormandizing citizens in 8, and the lascivious and drunken revellers around the grandstand in 12. I think Plate 4 tells us what we are to make of this pattern: the porter, intruding from the outside world, is paralleled by his equally ill-favored dog in dispute with the bristling cat who stands on the platform with Goodchild and his master. In other words, the other apprentice is a silent presence even when the subject is his opposite. The viewer's habit of left-right association with Idle and Goodchild leads him (assisted by the related shapes) to see the left-hand figure as another denizen of Idle's gross world, which Goodchild cannot escape even in the safety of

---

that he pointed out appropriate passages which Hogarth then arranged for the effect he desired by editing and placing. But there is no reason to think that Hogarth was not thoroughly familiar with the Bible himself.

[5] Gerard, *Essay on Taste* (1759), pp. 50-51: when the imitation of virtue is "pure and unmixed, we cannot question, that the whole pleasure of the sentiment produced, is owing to it alone."

[6] Sir Joshua Reynolds, Discourse VIII, in *Discourses*, ed. Robert R. Wark (San Marino, 1959), p. 146.

the counting house, and the contention between these worlds is an aesthetic one, now of beauty vs. ugliness.[7]

In the Idle plates there is no repoussoir figure—no one to anchor the composition down on either side, so that he always appears to be floating over a gulf. Because he is himself on the left, the emptiness of the right side is all the more emphatic.

The final plates, however, change all this. In Plates 8 and 9, though still toward the right and left respectively, Goodchild and Idle are moving closer to the center than in the earlier plates. And in the last two plates the order has been reversed, and Idle comes first; moreover, while the two apprentices are shown proceeding in opposite directions, they have been moved to exactly the same position to the left of center, and both seem suspended now above the mass of crowd. They are, different as their fates (and the skeletons and cornucopias in their margins), located spatially at the same spot.

The motto under this last plate is "Length of days is in her right hand and in her left hand Riches and Honour" (Proverbs 3:16), which in the light of the earlier plates draws attention to the left-right pattern while at the same time minimizing the difference. *Both* long life and riches and honor are things that Goodchild has gained and Idle lost. As it happens, since the general view (following Matthew 25:33 and other texts)[8] was that left= evil and right=good, it was just this text from Proverbs failing to distinguish between them that the preachers and exegetes fastened upon for debate.[9]

One inference is that so much emphasis on contrasting values in plate after plate ends by drawing attention to underlying

---

[7] Left stands not only for sin, but for misfortune, malformation, ugliness. Among the many variations on the left-right opposition, see the poem by Callimachus in which Apollo explains his posture: "In the left hand I carry the bow because I am slower to chastise mortals, but the Graces in the right hand, as I am always disposed to distribute pleasant things." See Rudolf Pfeiffer, "The Image of the Delian Apollo and Apolline Ethics," *Journal of the Warburg and Courtauld Institutes*, 15 (1952), 20-32.

[8] E.g., Ecclesiastes 10:2; Isaiah 9:20; Jonah 4:11 suggests undifferentiation.

[9] See e.g., Cornelius à Lapide and the *Biblia Critica*. The old prejudice against the left side had begun to break down in the sixteenth and seventeenth centuries, especially with the location of the heart (and presumably the Sacred Heart). See Vladimir Gurewich, "Observations on the Iconography of the Wound in Christ's Side, with special Reference to its Position," *Journal of the Warburg and Courtauld Institutes*, 20 (1957), 358-62; and "Rubens and the Wound in Christ's Side," *ibid.*, 26 (1963), 358.

parallels. Take the crowds that surround both apprentices. The contrast was initially between crowd and isolation: in 6 the crowd is celebrating Goodchild; in 7 there is no crowd around poor solitary Idle. But two musicians in Goodchild's crowd are squabbling, the dog's face is sad and downcast, and the celebration itself is for hire (and by its shapes and placement on the left is associated with Idle). In 8, 9, and 10 both apprentices are surrounded by ugly, greedy, self-interested folk, distinguished mainly by the respectability of the group having dinner with Goodchild. The crowds in 11 and 12 are initially contrasted: the one watching Idle is shabby, fighting, crying (his mother), stealing, and immoral, presided over by Mother Douglas the bawd; the crowd watching Goodchild is cheering, more prosperous, presided over by the Prince of Wales. But both consist largely of drunken, celebrating, out of control people, including bruisers with sticks (though they are wielded only in 11). But can we say that the people at Tyburn came to watch Idle die, while the people in the City came to wish Goodchild well, and their drunkenness and lechery and disorder only reflect this joy? We must if we carry out the contrast. Or is the point the parallel: that the genteel and the ungenteel amount to the same, as in a sense do the roads to Tyburn and to the Guildhall? For these are not the contrasted crowds of *Beer Street* and *Gin Lane*, any more than Tom Idle is the murderer Tom Nero of *The Four Stages of Cruelty*. Recall the old saying: The crowd that cheers him at his coronation would cheer as lustily at his execution. Hogarth may have reversed the order of Plates 11 and 12 and moved both apprentices to the same position on the two plates in order to suggest something about the interchangeability of the fates of the two apprentices.

Disquieting thoughts also arise if we consider the large contrasts of spatial relationships that recur throughout the plates. The perspective itself is very odd: in the first plate the two apprentices are placed within separate perspective systems, Idle's loom having a different vanishing point from Goodchild's, and the room itself having yet a third. The effect is to set up two alien systems of reference, and this fits with the fact we have noticed that Idle's scenes tend to be open while Goodchild's are closed, the one outside ordinary perspective systems altogether, while the other is rigidly constructed along the lines of a perspective box.

At the beginning both apprentices are entirely enclosed in a room, overshadowed and further enclosed by their looms. Goodchild in effect never leaves the closed room; visually his world is fixed within the perspective-defined and closed spaces of a box, hedged in by a labyrinth of pews, covered and safe; he never ventures out of an enclosure, but remains careful, comfortable, and protected. His final residence is so safe that a row of fire buckets hangs from the ceiling, an indication that the building is insured by the Sun Fire Office. But Idle, compared to Goodchild, is unlocated, unfixed, and his world is open and uncovered. Though the open door of Goodchild's house is contrasted with Idle's barricaded door (Plates 6 and 7), Goodchild himself is within his house, just protruding his head and arm through a window, while Idle, trying to close himself in, utterly fails: the gaping holes in the floor, the propped and rickety door, the collapsing bed, and the chimney through which rats and cats race show that his room is anything but closed. Idle's is an unprotected, unordered world of liberty but of temptations and dangers as well, with the threat of some sort of retribution always hanging over him and a chasm yawning beneath his feet. Once the choice is made between idleness and industry, outside all is hostile and fearful; inside is religion, shrewd business sense, money, a wife, status, and order.

Only in Plate 10 is he finally caught within the sturdy architectural world of Goodchild, which ends within the loomlike framework of the triple gallows of Tyburn. Meanwhile Goodchild too is receding. The expressively exaggerated perspective of the City banquet (Plate 8) emphasizes the giant guzzlers in the foreground against the tiny figure of Goodchild, so diminished as to hint that he may have gained the office of Sheriff at the expense of his individuality. In his next appearance his face is shielded behind his hand, and in the last obscured within a closed coach. The parallel is unmistakable between the Anglican clergyman in his covered coach (vs. the Methodist preacher uncovered, helping Idle in his last moments) and Goodchild in his covered coach, guarded by the sword of state.

Read in the context of Hogarth's earlier work, these spatial relationships carry associations that cannot be dismissed. Outdoors was initially associated by him with freedom and one's natural self, an association sanctioned by Addison in the *Spectator* and confirmed in the year of *Industry and Idleness*' publication by William Gilpin in his *Dialogue upon the Gardens at Stowe*. As the Harlot declined, her room, her container, shrank until in the last plate she was enclosed in a coffin, and much the same was true of the Rake. The Distressed Poet (1736) was cut off from his wife and the world of unpaid bills and unfed babies by the heavy architectural lines of the alcove in which he sequestered himself to write his poem " On Riches." The Enraged Musician (1741) has enclosed himself in his house, visible through his window (rather like Goodchild in Plate 6), trying to order the lively noise-makers outside in the street who are disturbing him. Hogarth has begun to develop another meaning inherent in the closed room: its comfort and security. These qualities were present in the dark, overfurnished room of the Harlot's keeper, but in *Industry and Idleness* they are associated with a protagonist who does not come to grief. It is the ostensible hero of the series, the respectable man who spends his life in metaphoric prison cells, while the bad man remains out in the open. There *is* no prison cell in this series concerning a real criminal—it is only implied by the gap between the scenes of courtroom and gallows. So the ambiguous contrast of the idle and industrious apprentices relies on the one being unprotected, out in the open, vulnerable to both criminals and the law; the other always enclosed, and with the associations from the earlier works a feeling of counter-movement against the purely schematic pull of the series begins to be felt. For the world of ordered, rigid architectural shapes in *Industry and Idleness* is also the world of the contrasted plates, of vice and virtue, of left and right, and this is the orderly world of Goodchild, which is increasingly impinged upon by Idle's world of undifferentiation and chaos.

Let us now look more closely at the emblematic structure of image and motto in which Hogarth couches his plates. The proverbs, I said, emphasize the simple pattern of contrast and causality in the prints. But they also, for the viewer who was familiar with Hogarth's earlier print series, carried a particular meaning. These readers would notice that all but one of the mottos are from the Old Testament, and remember Hogarth's use of Old Testament stories in his *Harlot's Progress*: where Uzzah shown being struck down for trying to steady the Ark of the Covenant and Abraham about to sacrifice Issac were used to support a theme concerning strict justice vs. mercy. When the magistrate approached the unsuspecting Harlot in Plate 3 of that series, the composition was very like Plate 1 of *Industry and Idleness*, except that above on the wall Hogarth placed the admonitory print of *Abraham sacrificing Isaac*. As it happens, the single New Testament motto used, for Plate 4, is from the parable of the talents (Matt. 25: 14-30), one of the very few places in the New Testament where an "unprofitable servant" meets an Old Testament punishment, being cast "into outer darkness."

I see no reason to doubt that his viewers from the trading class were thoroughly familiar with Proverbs, Leviticus, Psalms, and the parables of Christ—as much so as the connoisseurs had been with the classical myths and the traditional iconography of western art. How far the merchants saw into Hogarth's use of the Biblical context is, of course, another matter; the "Men of greater Penetration" who had followed his earlier prints would also know the Biblical contexts, the complexity of which depends on the "penetration" of the reader.[9a] At its simplest, as in Plate 4, a motto alludes to the "good and faithful servant," and the reader naturally infers the other half of the story, the "wicked and slothful servant" who hid his one talent in the ground; and "A virtuous woman is a crown to her husband" in Plate 6 is completed by: "but she that maketh ashamed is as rottenness in his bones" (Proverbs 12: 4). The contrast of good and bad women is already implicit then in Plate 6, and so in Plate 7, where the other "wife" (Idle's whore) appears, Hogarth can proceed to Idle's fear and quote, "the sound of a shaken leaf shall chase him" (Leviticus 26: 36).

But often the surrounding verses or the whole chapter from which the motto is taken gives it a context that virtually tells the story of the plate.[10] The chapter of Leviticus from which "the sound of a shaken leaf shall chase him" is taken, about the perils

---

[9a] The reference is to Addison's *Spectator* No. 315, and to the double meaning—a "plain literal Sense" and a "hidden Meaning"—of epic allegory. "The Story should be such as an ordinary Reader may acquiesce in, whatever Natural, Moral or Political Truth may be discovered in it by Men of greater Penetration." Hogarth makes his position clear in *Boys Peeping at Nature*, the subscription ticket for his first series, *A Harlot's Progress* (1732): the lifting of the skirt is an allusion to the veil of allegory by which the poet traditionally protected the truth he was conveying, keeping it from being debased by contact with the multitude.

[10] Plate 2 uses Psalm 119, v. 97, but verses 97-104 all apply to the Industrious

of sloth, is a horrible sequence of action-consequence structures with consequence heaped upon consequence: "And if ye walk contrary unto me, and will not hearken unto me; I will bring seven times more plagues upon you according to your sins."

At yet other times the motto is twisted to Hogarth's purpose by the context of the plate itself. In Plate 8 the motto becomes, to say the least, ambiguous: " With all thy getting get understanding. Exalt her & she shall promote thee: she shall bring thee to honour when thou dost Embrace her " (Proverbs 4: 7-8). Most noticeably, the feminine pronoun in the context of Proverbs Chapter 4 refers to Wisdom. But Hogarth has omitted the referent (his quotation should accordingly refer to Understanding, which however he has not honored with capitalization), and so in the context of the plate and the two immediately preceding Goodchild plates, " her " and " she " apparently apply to the only familiar " she " present, the wife who sits next to Goodchild on the dais: " Exalt her & she shall promote thee "—marry her and she will get you her father's business; " she shall bring thee to honour when thou dost Embrace her "—not the spiritual but the physical embrace (which Hogarth *does* capitalize) that has brought him to honor. The word " getting " in " with all thy *getting* get understanding " sounds, in the light of all those London politicians busy gorging themselves, like a necessary admonition.

Hogarthian irony is at work here; and this interaction of motto and image draws us back to Plate 2. (Remember that the plates would have all been visible at the same time as they hung on a wall.) That motto, " Oh how I love thy Law it is my meditation all the day " (Psalm 119: 97), raises the question, settled in Plate 8, of whether " love " and " thy Law " that is to be Goodchild's meditation all the day refer to God or to the master's daughter, who stands next to him. Then when Goodchild next appears in Plate 4 in his master's counting house, what are we to make of the almanac emblem of Opportunity taking Time by the forelock? Plate 4 itself refers to his industry in the shop, but the daughter is so emphasized in the surrounding plates that, as we look back from Plate 8, she is another strong contender for the role of Opportunity.

Apprentice and fill in the story. So too in Plate 3 the " judgment " referred to in Proverbs 10: 29 is in fact for sloth.

The motto of Plate 11 sums up Idle's fear and desolation as he goes to his death and concludes: " Then they shall call upon God, but he will not answer." Hogarth has changed "me," which refers to Wisdom (the speaker in both the surrounding verses), to God. In the verse before, Wisdom is responding to the fool who did not heed her words: " I also will laugh at your calamity; I will mock when your fear cometh." The chapter ends, " But whoso hearkeneth unto me shall dwell safely, and shall be quiet from fear of evil." In the final motto of Plate 12 it is still Wisdom who is speaking, explaining that the " merchandize " of wisdom (v. 14) is " more precious than rubies " (v. 15), making it clear that wisdom is what leads to this end. This follows all the proverbs that say if you honour the Lord, " so shall thy barns be filled with plenty, and thy presses shall burst out with new wine " (v. 10), as they do here. The motto itself (v. 16), " Length of days is in her right hand; and in her left hand riches and honor," is followed by " Her ways are ways of pleasantness, and all her paths are peace " (v. 17), and a bit later by " Keep sound wisdom and discretion " (v. 21). The reiterated " her " of course applies to Wisdom in the Biblical context, but we recall those earlier " hers " in the plates' context. The consequences are spelled out: longevity and riches and honor; Goodchild is not being hanged, he is rich, and he is mayor of London. Proverbs is full of wisdom about industry and idleness, about the prudent man and the foolish, the righteous and the wicked; and Hogarth pointedly omits the last category, the moral, leaving the emphasis on the prudential, though introducing the name of God as a synonymn for Wisdom. Good and evil are only alluded to in the characters who affect the two protagonists.

So much for the mottos. The images themselves derive from popular graphic art rather than from the emblematic tradition. Were we to go to Ripa's *Iconologia* to see how Idleness was represented, we would find that it is " an old Hag cloth'd in Rags " with her head bound about with a black cloth. As Ripa explains the significance of this hieroglyphic, she is " *old,* because at that Age, Strength and Activity to work, begin to fail; her Rags denote that Idleness produces Proverty; the black Cloth about her Head signifies her senseless Thoughts." Now it is significant historically that Hogarth does not employ the hieroglyphic—the veiled—symbol for Idleness, but rather the unlearned, the probable representation, simply a young man dozing over his loom.[11] But it is equally characteristic of him that, with his primary meaning established in this way, he also introduces the emblematic figure, with its traditional but enigmatic meaning; for the old lady, the black cloth bound about her head in widow's weeds, first introduced as the pew-keeper in Plate 2, by the fifth plate is Idle's mother; and the idleness of old age, weakness, and helplessness is contrasted with the wilfull idleness of youth. This is not, of course, merely a gathering of both kinds of iconography to complicate meaning; real idleness is in the natural representation, not in the enigmatic—the poor mother industriously follows her son step by step to the gallows, not seeking handouts but trying to help him.

A few learned, but widely-known emblems do appear in the plates of *Industry and Idleness*. Goodchild's covering his eyes in Plate 10 is an allusion to Blind Justice, who, not a respecter of persons, cannot recognize favors or friends.[12] Goodchild, assuming the pose, is the one who *alludes* to Blind Justice, yet in its immediate context, this pose prevents him from seeing Idle's treacherous girl friend bribing the clerk and the man with the eye-patch (who lured Idle into crime) taking his oath illegally with his left hand as he swears away Idle's life. (Behind, the weapons being held up form a caduceus, emblem of Mercury the thief.) The motto under Goodchild, Leviticus 19:15, deals with blind justice (" ye shall do no unrighteousness in judgment "), but the verses preceding are about stealing and lying with an admonition " ye shall not swear by my name falsely " as the one-eyed man is doing.[13] The verse following the motto is about tale-bearers and those who " stand against the blood of thy neighbor," and the next two admonish one not to " rebuke thy neighbor ": " Thou shalt not avenge . . . but thou shalt love thy neighbor as thyself." Though far less direct, this interaction of image, motto, and context is saying very much what the print of *Abraham sacrificing*

[11] In the popular tradition there are many instances of graphic representations of the sin of idleness by a sleeping man.

[12] See Ripa, *Iconologia* (1709 ed.), no. 118; but no source book is necessary for so basic an emblem. Cf. Hogarth's use of the Justice figure in *Paul before felix Burlesqued*.

[13] Verse 12, and also " shalt not curse the deaf, nor put a stumbling-block before the blind, but shalt fear thy God. . . ." Psalm 9:11, under Idle, has to do with his own ensnaring; he is paying the penalty for his friends, who here betray him.

Isaac said on the Harlot's wall as Justice Gonson and his constables approached to seize the poor girl.

The reader is drawn back to Plate 8 and the statue holding a dagger in a niche on the wall, whom Hogarth's City audience, from Lord Mayor down to apprentice, would have recognized as Sir William Walworth, the Lord Mayor who without warning struck down Wat Tyler— a sudden blow that saved the king, as perhaps Goodchild strikes down Idle.[14] The message is that the idle, who have sunk into crime, get what they deserve; the bribery and lying *are* justice, according to the Old Testament injunction " an eye for an eye "; Idle has loafed, cheated, robbed, and must expect equal treatment. But implicit also is the sense that justice is cruel and that the legal system is quick, almost unthinking (like Walworth's blow), but not perfect—for one guilty man apprehended, many escape. The wicked, the temptors and corruptors, continue to flourish, and Goodchild's world is one in which he not only cannot rid himself of the Idles but must overlook bonds of friendship, the crimes of his own subordinates, and the guzzling grossness of his colleagues.

Goodchild's world of enclosed architectural spaces is further clearly delimited as the City of London, of which he becomes sheriff and the mayor. The porter in Plate 4 wears the badge of the City, the almanac with Time seizing Opportunity by the forelock is a " London Almanac," Walworth was a London mayor and his dagger became part of its escutcheon, and the insignia of London's mayor appears in the margins.[15] Hogarth goes far beyond the necessary when in Plate 6 he ignores the impossible distance and the scale to reproduce the inscription on the London Fire Monument indicating that this " Protestant City " was once burned as

---

[14] The dagger is also an attribute of Severity (see Ripa, added in 1645 edition [Venice], p. 568).

[15] The ballad of Dick Whittington, Lord Mayor of London, in Plate 1 is one of these references. The Whittington ballad activates the cat who appears, most noticeably again in 4, representing the Counting House and the master and Goodchild against the intrusion of those types of the outside world associated with Idle. Note that his cat, and not Whittington himself, was the hero of the story: the cat acted, and Whittington's virtue was his ability to take Opportunity by the forelock on these occasions. In Plate 7 the cat by his rush down the chimney after the mouse is a terror to Idle and perhaps a reminder of the feat of Whittington's cat, who brought him prosperity precisely by devouring the rats that destroyed the cargo of his master's ship. To judge by these scenes, the cat in Plate 1 is a Whittingtonian cat too, trying in vain to awaken the sleeping apprentice and make him into as much a Whittington as Goodchild.

the result of a Catholic plot. To some extent he may be suggesting something ironic about the danger to be feared by London from a Tom Idle (cf. the fire buckets in the scene of his condemnation), but mainly he is establishing that the values represented here are Protestant ones (it was Defoe who in *The Complete English Tradesman* called idleness the sin against the Holy Ghost).

This inscription, I believe, tells us something about how the "veil of allegory" operates in these popular prints. The City fathers (on down to the City apprentices) probably still believed—and certainly preserved—the inscription; but anyone with detachment knew by this time that it was a Protestant myth, and may have recalled Pope's lines about "London's column pointing to the skies, / Like a tall bully, lifts the head, and lyes."[16] As Pope uses the Monument (in his "Epistle to Bathurst") to place Sir Balaam in a particular economic and moral code of Protestant capitalism, so Hogarth uses it to locate not only Goodchild but the audience to whom he is directly addressing himself and their assumptions about industry and idleness. The "men of greater penetration" are certainly a smaller group now—smaller perhaps than ever before—and yet they are the objective men who will be able to place both industry and idleness in relation to Protestant and other systems of values, and perhaps even remember that the sin of the "wicked and slothful servant" who hid his one talent was (as his master put it) not "to have put money to the exchanger," so that at "my coming I should have received mine own with usury." The large, popular audience to which he turns for his "ordinary reader" offers him a way into simpler, more basic images, but also into a parochialism which he is careful to define.

II

The elaborate play with the emotions and the active involvement of the different audiences may perhaps be subsumed under a very English and contemporary use of irony. The discrepancy between the City-merchant view and the larger, more inclusive view, like that between Fielding's prejudiced and understanding

---

[16] Pope, "Epistle to Bathurst" (1732), ll. 339-40. The inscription was erased in James II's reign, restored in William III's, and not finally removed until 1831. See also Addison's *Freeholder* No. 47 (1 June 1716) in which a visiting Tory from the country looks down from the Monument and mistakes the surrounding warehouses for meeting houses. With its references to Catholics, however, the inscription might also have had a certain topical relevance a year or so after the Rebellion of '45.

readers in *Tom Jones*, is related to the larger Augustan reliance on irony, or in general saying (or showing) one thing and meaning another. Such an ironic structure can act as an instrument of metaphysical knowledge, evoking the power of thought, or it can induce confusion and uncertainty in the reader, or both. Hogarth is in fact setting up stereotypes of popular thought and art in order to scrutinize them as well as draw upon their undeniable vigor.

One can imagine some of the authoritarian commands couched as adages that were in his mind, doubtless to be heard any day walking through the City: " The better gamester the worse man. What else is it to dance but to play the fool? So much money so much credit. He hath not wherewithal to buy a halter to hang himself."[17] The contemporary Protestant feeling about idleness, expressed so staunchly by Defoe, found its most popular expression in the apprentice's guides, a popular sub-literary form that flourished in great abundance throughout the 1730s. These works, which achieved an apotheosis of a sort in George Lillo's play, *The London Merchant* (1731), habitually contrasted the industrious and idle apprentices, the latter demonstrating " the fatal Consequence of his Neglect " of his duty to God and his master, " with Regard both to his *temporal* and *eternal* Happiness."[18] The idle apprentice was assured that even reading, " or any Amusement, however laudable at *proper* Times," carried on during " the Hours of Business " " would be directly robbing " the master. Even someone who accompanies an apprentice in his delinquence " knows he contributes to a Robbery at the same time," for the master is being " defrauded of his Apprentice's Time."[19]

In his *Apprentice's Vade Mecum* (1734) Samuel Richardson virtually outlines the scenario for *Industry and Idleness* (in terms, however, available in almost any apprentice's guide) : " how naturally, as it were Step by Step, Swearing, Cursing, Profaneness, Drunkenness, Whoredom, Theft, Murder, and the Gallows, succeed one another! " Indeed, he concludes with the dangerous lure of fashion for idle apprentices:

---

[17] These adages were copied down by Sir Isaac Newton as a lad; quoted, Frank Manuel, *A Portrait of Isaac Newton* (Cambridge, Mass., 1968), p. 58. " Almost all the statements are negations," Manuel remarks, " admonitions, prohibitions."

[18] Part of the title of *The Apprentice's Faithful Monitor*, advertised in *The London Magazine*, II (Oct. 1733), 534.

[19] Samuel Richardson, *The Apprentice's Vade Mecum* (1734), pp. 27, 8-9.

I wish, to complete the Ridicule, and shame such Foplings into Reformation, the ingenious Mr. *Hogarth* would finish the Portrait.[20]

Which, in a sense, Hogarth did: but unlike Richardson (and Lillo), he did not allow his apprentice to proceed from theft to murder. He added also a rather aristocratic awareness, which had more in common with Fielding than with Richardson, of the master's vested interest, his concern with profits, concealed under warnings to idle apprentices.[21]

Hogarth prejudiced the case against industry from the start by choosing as his illustration the profession of weaving. Contemporary sources on the weavers all emphasize that it was the poorest paying of London trades for the weavers themselves, with the supply usually exceeding the demand, and Englishmen being discharged for the cheaper labor of women, children, and Irishmen. There were bloody riots in 1736 against the Irish interlopers, and the trade was known for its violence. Only the masters prospered, and the pamphlets emphasize the frequency with which the master weaver's children (sons as well as daughters) marry other weavers in order to perpetuate the family business.[22]

The undermining of the industry half of industry vs. idleness brings into question the whole pattern (and assumption) of choice itself. Elsewhere I have referred to Hogarth's use of the Choice of Hercules topos in his earlier works;[23] in fact Hercules' choice, as Prodicus explained it, was essentially between industry and idleness, between the difficult way and the easy or pleasurable. In *A Harlot's Progress* Hogarth reversed the roles of rational in-

---

[20] *Ibid.*, pp. 33-35. Richardson is connecting delinquent apprentices with Hogarth's theme (expressed in the 1730s in the Harlot and the Rake) of the young man or woman who emulates fashion and comes to grief. Fashionable dress and other luxuries such as gambling lift "up the young Man's Mind far above his Condition as an Apprentice." After a long description of apprentices aping the fashion, Richardson concludes with his charge to Hogarth. And Hogarth does begin with both apprentices and their models—Whittington and Moll Flanders—and ends with the logical consequences of such emulation.

[21] Criminal biography, an important segment of the popular fiction produced for an audience of shopkeepers, their servants and apprentices, habitually romanticizes the "flamboyant independence of the highwayman because it is unreal enough to serve as a pleasant fantasy which has no direct relevance," but whenever an apprentice strays he is condemned in no uncertain terms and pursued to a grim end. See John J. Richetti, *Popular Fiction before Richardson* (Oxford, 1969), p. 56.

[22] See M. Dorothy George, *London in the Eighteenth Century* (London, 1966), pp. 181-87.

[23] See Paulson, *Hogarth: His Life, Art, and Times* (New Haven, 1971), I, 271-77.

dustry and irrational idleness and blurred the distinction between them by making the clergyman's industry his place-seeking and the bawd's idleness her vigorous persuasion to employment of the young girl. It is the girl's lackadaisical attention to her employment that gets her discharged by her keeper and apprehended by the police. The distinction is not, Hogarth is saying, an easy one to make. But idleness is what leads the merchant's son away from his business to the life of an aristocratic rake. The series concerning Goodchild and Idle, then, builds on the most basic and elemental of Hogarth's earlier structures, materializing both paths of the journey, and making the original choice explicitly one of industry and idleness. We would appear to be at the bottom of the matter, concerned with pure choice; but if we think the choice is being made by the apprentices, we are clearly mistaken: it is being made by the readers, and it is not so simple as the readers are at first led to believe.

As I have tried to show, on one level at least the structure of choice itself is emphasized until it is seen as something that oversimplifies the complexity of real life. If this is done much more sharply than in *A Harlot's Progress*, it may be because although the Choice of Hercules was throughout the half-century a part of every schoolboy's, every educated man's, consciousness, the interest seems to have become intense in the 1740s. To take only one example, Joseph Spence, in his *Polymetis* (1747), published Robert Lowth's poem, " The Choice of Hercules," and preceded it with an essay on the subject.[24] There " can be no virtue without choice " is his message. Spence is a good example of a contemporary who looks back to antiquity and sees choice between *virtus*

[24] Lowth's " The Choice of Hercules " appeared anonymously in *Polymetis* in 1747 and was reprinted in Dodsley's *Collection of Poems* in 1748 and in the same year in the *Preceptor: Containing a General Course of Education . . . for . . . Advancing the Instruction of Youth* (1748). Handel put Lowth's verses, adapted by Morell, to music in 1750 as *The Choice of Hercules* (publ. 1751). For other examples see: William Shenstone, *The Judgment of Hercules* (verse, 1741); John Baillie, *An Essay on the Sublime* (1747), p. 15, in which he says Prodicus' parable is "universally allow'd noble and sublime "; John Gilbert Cooper in *Dodsley's Museum* (1746), II, 48-49; Peter Laying, *The Judgment of Hercules, Imitated . . . from Prodicus* (Eton, 1748); [Thomas Cooke of Braintree], *The Tryal of Hercules, an Ode on Glory, Virtue, and Pleasure* (1752); and translations by William Duncombe (1745) and Spence, in *Moralities: or, Essays, Letters, Fables, and Translations* (1753), by "Sir Harry Beaumont." Maurice Greene (whom Hogarth discusses in a well-known anecdote) set a *Judgment of Hercules* to music (*Apollo Society Collection* of 1740), and John Stanley also produced a musical setting in the 1740s.

and *voluptas* as the basic pattern not only in Prodicus and Cebes, but in Philostratus, Silvius Italicus, Horace, and Ovid; he adduces Ulysses' choice between Circe and Penelope, Paris' between the goddesses (which Hogarth used in *Rake,* Plate 2), Aeneas' between Dido and Latium, Persius' between *avaritia* and *luxuria,* and Lucian's between Eloquence and Sculpture.

All of this evidence contributes to a general tendency of the age, " to simplify morality into a decision between opposing alternatives," as E. R. Wasserman has put it.[25] There certainly seems to have been a general assumption that human happiness was attainable if the right choice was made between clearly defined alternatives, especially between *virtus* and *voluptas* or *luxuria.* As a study of eighteenth-century gardens, poetry, and prose demonstrates, " everything is bipolar, not multiple; reality is made up of opposites "—whether structured into a choice or resolved into a *concordia discors.*[26]

Hogarth repeatedly uses the bipolar choice in order to show its inadequacy: earlier in his career because of the forces internal and external on contemporary man, and now because of the very structure of choice itself. It is only the final example of his awareness—perhaps the great Hogarthian insight—that his age has inherited and molded itself on a system of cultural formulae, reaching from old master paintings to an *Apprentice's Vade Mecum,* that simplify and create order.

Hogarth must also have been aware of the poems written in the 1740s that questioned the oversimplification of choice. A straightforward case was Akenside's use of Shaftesbury's account of the Choice of Hercules in his *Pleasures of Imagination,* Book II (1744). Here the goddesses of Virtue and Pleasure are regarded not as antagonists but as supplementary companions, " the shining pair," while a third figure, the son of Nemesis, is introduced as antagonist of both."[27] A much less straightforward and more interesting case was James Thomson's *Castle of Indolence,* which

---

[25] " Johnson's 'Rasselas': Implicit Contexts," *Journal of English and Germanic Philology,* forthcoming.

[26] *Ibid.*

[27] *Pleasures of Imagination,* II, 11. 381ff. A. O. Aldridge, who pointed this out, interprets the passage to mean that "the path of virtue is at the same time the path of pleasure and that one way cannot be attained without the other," a view "less stoic and severe than Shaftesbury's" ("The Eclecticism of Mark Akenside's *The Pleasures of Imagination,*" *Journal of the History of Ideas,* 5 (1944), 312-13).

though not published until 1748 had been in various stages of composition since the early 1740s. In the first canto the wizard Indolence tempts weary passers-by in search of refreshment into his castle with the enchantments of euphoria and narcotic dreams, seductively described; in the second canto the Knight of Arts and Industry frees them. But as was well known, the stanzas began as Thomson's self-defense against his friends' chiding of his own notorious indolence, and his attitude toward the subject was decidedly ambivalent.[28]

Hogarth and Thomson were in circles that impinged at more than one point; their mutual friend, Joseph Mitchell (whom Hogarth had known as early as 1731), had written an ironic poem called *The Charms of Indolence* in 1722, in which indolence equals dulness.[29] Another close friend, Thomas Morell was, we know, aware of *The Castle of Indolence* as early as 1742 when he wrote verses on it.[30] Even if Hogarth did not know of the poem directly from Thomson, he would have known of it from Morell, who later assisted Handel with a libretto on the subject of the Choice of Hercules. Thomson, who includes dulness, inertia, and sluggishness (idleness) in his meaning of indolence, is actually concerned with a refined hedonism, a cultivation of the choicest pleasures on the one hand, and a virtuous and philosophic retirement on the other. The ambiguity with which he plays depends on awareness of both the shopkeeper's idleness as "the devil's cushion" or his couch or pillow [31] and the gentleman's sense of " the sweetness of being idle " *(Inertia dulcedo)*, or " Dolce far niente " or " Vis inertiae " and other well-known catch phrases.[32]

---

[28] Patrick Murdock, "Life of Thomson," in *The Works* (1762), I, xiv; and cf. Johnson's "Life of Thomson" in *Lives of the Poets*, III, 297. Johnson himself projected a *Palace of Sloth—a Vision* (*Life*, IV, 382n.).

[29] *Poems on Several Occasions* (1729), I, 55. In 1731 Mitchell had published *Three Poetical Epistles*, one of which was to and in praise of Hogarth. In 1740 Hogarth etched a ticket for Mallet and Thomson's *Masque of Alfred*. His roots went back originally to Scotland, and he was a friend of both Ramsays, father and son, and a supporter of the Scots prime minister Bute.

[30] These verses have been dated 1742; see A. D. McKillop, introduction to James Thomson, *The Castle of Indolence and Other Poems* (Lawrence, Kansas, 1961), pp. 6-8.

[31] Thomas Adams, *Works* (1630), pp. 197; Alexander Ross, *The History of the World* (1652), preface, attributing this to the Church Fathers; and James Howell, *Parly of Beasts* (1660), p. 134.

[32] Tacitus, *Agricola*, sec. 3; Pliny the Younger, *Epistles*, Bk. viii, epist. 9. Also cited were Scipio Africanus, "I am never less idle than when I have nothing to do" (Nunquam se minus otiosum, quam cum otiosus) or Atilius, "It is better to be idle than busy

Idle's attempt to escape from duty by going to sea or onto the highway is a rough parody of the classical retirement theme; recalling Indolence's argument that if you withdraw with him you will avoid all "the Filthy Fray, / Where the Soul sowrs, and gradual Rancour grows, / Imbitter'd more from peevish Day to Day." Despite his conclusion in favor of the Knight of Industry, Thomson is well aware of the lovely ambiguity in classical references to *otium*—peace, leisure, or idleness—as in Virgil's close of his fourth *Georgic* when he remarks that at the very time when Augustus was winning victories in battle and giving laws to the Roman people,

> illo Vergilium me tempore dulcis alebat
> Parthenope studiis florentem ignobilis oti,
> carmina qui lusi pastorum audax-que iuventa,
> Tityre, te patulae cecini sub tegmine fagi.

(sweet Parthenope cared for me, Virgil, happy in my studies of ignoble idleness, who once played at shepherd songs and bold in the season of youth sang of thee, Tityrus, under the shade of spreading beech.)

This is idleness in that it avoids *negotium*, but peace and leisure in that it produced Virgil's *Pastorals*.

The same readers who were the "men of greater penetration" in the matter of epic allegory were these men of cultivated aristocratic values who would remember that the Golden Age was, after all, the time of pleasure and virtuous idleness, unmotivated by ambition or paltry desires for gain, and replaced by the love of profit in the Iron Age; from the Renaissance pastoral they would recall that the ideal of *otium*, vs. *negotium*, preferred leisure for contemplation and intellectual pleasure over vulgar money-grubbing.

But something more was at stake, for indolence, as the motto to Thomson's first canto suggests, was part of the Country Party's polemic against luxury, which (according to their formulation) derives from excessive commercial prosperity and political corruption, made possible by the new Walpolian finance. Bolingbroke, the chief of propaganda for the Opposition in the 1730s, indicts the "sloth" of the idle harpies (financiers) and the "luxury" of all classes consequent to corruption and commerce. Thom-

---

about nothing" (Apothegm, quoted Cicero, *De Officiis*, Bk. III, chap. 1, sec. 1; Atilius, quoted Pliny, *Epistles*, Bk. I, epist. 9). For yet other examples of praiseworthy *otium*, see Masenius, *Speculum in imaginum veritatis occultae* (1664 ed.), p. 189.

son picks up both Bolingbroke's emphasis and, from further back, Shaftesbury's description of the psychological traits of the indolent, and places indolence in a specifically political context.[33]

In turn, he attaches the unsatisfactory connotations of "industry" to those of "indolence": the merchants of the City are now "idly busy." This stage is developed more fully by John Brown in his *Estimate of the Manners and Morals of the Time*. Though not published until 1757, Brown's views were very much a part of the arguments of the 1740s and may have been known to Hogarth, who was a personal friend. Brown argues that we should try to stop industry at the second level of its development, because at its third and final level it produces luxury, effeminacy, and indolence among most classes, especially the nobility, and avarice among the merchants. At moments Thomson too admits that commercial prosperity leads to universal indolence, which in this sense lies at both the beginning and the end of the commercial cycle. Primitive man is slothful; industry arouses him; but beyond a certain point it results in universal luxury, and so further indolence, and along the way the merchants who bring prosperity through industry generate avarice.[34]

This is what industry has led to in Plate 6 and the following plates of *Industry and Idleness*. Goodchild's industry has produced another kind of idleness—eating and drinking or sitting in state (besides, of course, the responsibilities of a magistrate); in fact, as Goodchild's industry pays off, Idle's idleness gives way to a kind of frantic industry of stealing and vending. Industry produces idleness, and idleness leads to industry, and both in this way tend toward further undifferentiation.

Not many years after *Industry and Idleness* appeared, Samuel

---

[33] For Thomson, see also *Spring*, 11. 275-308; *Autumn*, 11. 56-106; *Liberty*, V, 381-88; III, 370-82 and 404 ff. For Shaftesbury, see *Characteristicks* (6th ed., 1737), II, 133-34, 155, 160. Addison had attempted to apply Shaftesbury's indictment of "indolence" to the idle, dog-feeding gentry (*Spectator* Nos. 55, 115). For Bolingbroke, see "On Luxury," in *Works* (Philadelphia, 1841), I, 474 ff.; *Remarks on the History of England*, Letter V, *Works*, I, 324; Letter XIV, p. 375. For the general background, see McKillop's introduction to *Castle of Indolence*, p. 2; Isaac Kramnick, *Bolingbroke and his Circle* (Cambridge, Mass., 1968), pp. 199, 247-48.

[34] See Brown, *Enquiry*, I, 151-61, 173-74, 184-85, 217. Something of the paradox behind Hogarth's plates can be sensed reading Francis Hutcheson on the use of wealth: too much money leads to sloth and contempt for our fellow creatures, while poverty produces humility and industry (*Essay on the Nature and Conduct of the Passions and Affections*, 3rd ed., 1742, pp. 195-96).

Johnson published *Rasselas* (1759), a tale which poses a similar "choice of life" and comes to a similar conclusion about the nature of choice:

> Those conditions which flatter hope and attract desire, are so constituted, that, as we approach one, we recede from another. These are goods so opposed that we cannot seize both, but, by too much prudence, may pass between them at too great a distance to reach either.

No man, the characters in *Rasselas* learn, "can, at the same time, fill his cup from the source and from the mouth of the Nile." [35] Driven by the hunger of imagination, man will choose the mouth only to desire the source, and once at the source only desire the mouth again. There is no possibility of choosing one over the other, nor of a happy median between the extremes, nor of having a *concordia discors* of both. And so one's choice is finally a matter of indifference: the industrious apprentice will envy the idle as much as the idle will envy the industrious, which is one way of explaining what happens when Hogarth sets about drawing the progresses of these antithetical apprentices.

Although there are no Biblical mottos to point the way, the real moral context of *Industry and Idleness* is less Proverbs—which is another constricting form like the choice between opposites—than Ecclesiastes, and the famous series of fruitless alternatives beginning "To every thing there is a season" which ends: "What profit hath he that worketh in that wherein he laboreth?" [36] The success of labor shows the Industrious Apprentice getting more riches, power, and honor (2:4-11) but ends: "Then I looked on all the works that my hands had wrought, and on the labor that I had labored to do: and, behold, all was vanity and vexation of spirit, and there was no profit under the sun."

III

With this awareness of the views of Hogarth's personal friends, Thomson and Morell and Johnson, we move a step closer to defining the complex effect involved in an experiencing of *Industry and Idleness* in 1747.

The Spectator, from which Hogarth drew so much of the com-

---

[35] *Rasselas,* ed. G. B. Hill (Oxford, 1887), pp. 107-08.
[36] Ecclesiastes 3:9; commentary, Cornelius à Lapide, p. 215.

monplace wisdom of his age, saw in idleness a potential for both good and evil—for good if one can only know how to be idle without slipping into vice or folly. For idleness is at the heart of the new aesthetic Addison is explaining in these essays on the Pleasures of the Imagination: an aesthetic enjoyment gained by merely opening the eyes and eschewing the time-consuming labor of reason and exegesis.[37] But *The Spectator* also carried a sense of the terms that touched Hogarth's own case: in No. 83, characterizing the different schools of painting, Addison uses Industry to personify the Dutch School. "His Figures were wonderfully laboured; if he drew the Portraiture of a Man, he did not omit a single Hair in his Face; if the Figure of a Ship, there was not a Rope among the Tackle that escaped him." Hogarth's detractors called him a laborious Dutch painter, and in the late 1740s he was trying to extricate himself from the shadow of Rembrandt and the Dutch School by returning more self-consciously to the simplified compositions of Raphael. It is worth speculating on the extent to which the characterization of the Dutch School by Addison (and by others like Jonathan Richardson) was in his mind when he embodied Industry in Francis Goodchild. Hogarth perhaps associated with the word, not only money-making and success, but also the Dutch School's laboriousness and mere mechanical ingenuity.[38]

Johnson is, of course, the best-known example of an eighteenth-century idler, and the agony he suffered all his life from idleness led to many strong expressions of detestation together with some signs of ambivalence.[39] His moral horror of idleness in his prayers, his *Dictionary*, his essays, and his conversation is well known.

[37] See *Spectator*, No. 411.

[38] Thomson's Knight of Industry and Art works hard at the plough and loom, and also "To solace then these rougher tools he tried / To touch the kindling canvas into life; / With nature his creating pencil vied— / With nature joyous at the mimic strife. . . ." (II, xiii).

[39] His trouble, as Boswell defined it, was "the listless torpor of doing nothing," the "dismal inertness of disposition" (*Life of Johnson*, ed. G. B. Hill, I, 56). In Johnson's own experience industry and idleness, as contraries, were associated with his two early friends, the industrious Edward Cave and the idle but endearing Richard Savage; and his remarks from time to time contain something of the ambivalence he showed in his *Life of Mr. Richard Savage* (1744). For his remarks on Cave, see his biographical sketch in *Gentleman's Magazine*, 24 (Feb. 1754). For the general subject, see W. J. Bate, *Achievement of Samuel Johnson* (New York, 1955; 1961 ed.), pp. 9-10; and Arieh Sachs, *Passionate Intelligence: Imagination and Reason in the Work of Samuel Johnson* (Baltimore, 1967), pp. 12-14, 54-65.

Idleness extends for him from "laziness, sloth, sluggishness, aversion from labor" to "barrenness, worthlessness," and ultimately "unreasonableness, want of judgment, foolishness, madness."[40] He uses it as his contemporaries did in a large way to cover a general area of unreason which sucks down the rational part of man that knows he must work and produce.[41]

But, as his indulgent attitude toward that idler Richard Savage shows, his feelings about idleness were sometimes affectionate and humorous. They emerge in the persona of an Idler he adapted for his eponymous periodical (1758), who equates idleness with "peace," the end to which the "busy" are striving; for "Every man is, or hopes to be, an Idler" (No. 1). And therefore, he adds, there is "no appellation by which a writer can better denote his kindred to the human species." He is quite serious when he argues that man is not basically either a reasonable or laughing animal, as he has been called, but an idle animal. Man is the only animal "that does by others what he might do himself, or sacrifices duty or pleasure to the love of ease." Moreover, having withdrawn from competition, he is the only man with "no rivals or enemies. The man of business forgets him; the man of enterprise despises him...."[42]

Hogarth himself, in *Industry and Idleness*, has replaced the two levels of readability with a conscious level on which the ordinary

[40] *Dictionary* (1755): sense 1 is "Laziness; sloth; sluggishness; aversion from labour" (with South's sermon cited, "*idleness* is both itself a great sin, and the cause of many more"); sense 6 is "barrenness; worthlessness," and no. 7 is "Unreasonableness; want of judgment; foolishness; madness," and his quotation is from Bacon's *War with Spain*: "There is no heat of affection but is joined with some *idleness* of the brain." In his periodicals, he comes down hardest in *Rambler*, No. 85, 8 Jan. 1751; see also Nos. 67 (6 Nov. 1750) and 155 (10 Sept. 1751).

[41] See Michel Foucault, *Madness and Civilization* (New York, 1965), which has shown the centrality of idleness within the general category of unreason used in this period to cover the poor, unemployed, and insane.

[42] The complexity of his, and perhaps Hogarth's, attitude may be suggested in a letter in which he explains why we delay those things we most desire to accomplish: "What we think of importance we wish to do well, to do anything well, requires time, and what requires time commonly finds us too idle or too busy to undertake it. To be idle is not the best excuse, though if a man studies his own reformation it is the best reason he can allege to himself, both because it is commonly true, and because it contains no fallacy, for every man that thinks he is idle condemns himself and has therefore a chance to endeavour amendment, but the busy mortal has often his own commendation, even when he engages himself in trifles only to put the thoughts of more important duties out of his mind, or to gain an excuse to his own heart for omitting them" (*Letters*, ed. R. W. Chapman [Oxford, 1952], no. 29).

viewer would sympathize with industry and abhor idleness, and another in which comparison as well as contrast exists. I suppose we might conclude that he is simply repeating his own pattern, addressing himself to one audience that settles for the contrasts, and a more sophisticated one that has followed his works since *Boys peeping at Nature* and sees beneath the veil to subtler, more ironic meanings. But in this case the subtlety does not reach to further distinctions so much as to undifferentiation. The primary process, which does not distinguish between opposites, allowing all firm boundaries to melt in a free chaotic mingling of forms, is brought into play by both author and audience.

We have now come very close to the artist himself. For contemporaries—those who knew him or even his London-wide reputation—would have perceived an obvious parallel between the industrious apprentice and Hogarth himself who married his " master's " daughter and succeeded to his business (so to speak),[43] continuing his efforts as an English history painter, carrying on his art academy, and defending his reputation as an artist long after his death. But surely one would also have noticed that there is no resemblance whatever between Hogarth's and Goodchild's idealized face—his handsome, bland, almost sheeplike features. One recalls the look of self-satisfaction on his face, the heartlessly academic poses he assumes, the affected manner in which he holds his cup (perhaps trying to emulate the manners of the West End) in Plate 6. It is perhaps significant that Hogarth originally called him *William* Goodchild but, thinking better of it, changed his name to Francis.[44]

[43] Hogarth was, of course, only figuratively apprenticed to Thornhill, though for him this would have been the real apprenticeship, the official one to Ellis Gamble's illusory one. It should be remembered that Richardson, the author of the *Apprentice's Vade Mecum*, also like Goodchild married his master's daughter; indeed, he married two master's daughters, a second after his first wife died. For the Hogarth background, see Paulson, *Hogarth*, I.

[44] This appears in Hogarth's list of the plates on the back of a first sketch for Plate 10 (BM). It is also interesting to note that among these jottings he originally included an explicit reference to *The London Merchant*: Idle's name was to have been Barnwell. The choice of Barnwell may also indicate something of the ambivalence of his own feelings, for in *The London Merchant* Barnwell is, in the last act with his punishment about to be carried out, forgiven by all the other characters, including the master he has betrayed. Among other literary sources, Fielding's *Jonathan Wild* (1743) presented the bad and good merchant prototypes that might have lodged in Hogarth's mind: Heartfree is made a merchant in order to set off Wild, the criminal " merchant." And finally, it is interesting that Hogarth knew a City merchant named Goodchild,

It is, on the contrary, Tom Idle's face that resembles Hogarth's own puggish, plebeian profile, which can be seen in *The Gate of Calais* (another personally-oriented work of a year later), or in his self-portrait of a few years later, or in Roubiliac's bust.[45]

Whether for purposes of self-irony to balance the saccharine self-portrait of Goodchild, or at some less conscious level, Hogarth has introduced his opposite. Perhaps it is simply Plato's "generation of opposites," which W. J. Bate has described sensitively in relation to Johnson:

> Psychologically, this may be described as the tendency of the mind to react defensively against what another part of it is reacting toward. While it loves, it also resists; while it says yes, it generates a no; while going in one direction, it finds itself sensing the attractions of another. So "labour and rest, hurry and retirement," and all other opposites, said Johnson, "endear each other."[46]

Being so successful, working so hard, doing his own engraving continually, makes a "habitual dislike," as Johnson called it, steal into any occupation. And yet one side of Hogarth plainly sought, as he put it a few years later in his autobiographical notes, his "pleasure" as well as his "studies." Looking back on his time as an apprentice, both in silver engraving and in painting at Vanderbank's academy, he emphasized his idleness, saying that he required a technique "most suitable to my situation and idle disposition"; the mnemonic system he hit upon for recording his ideas was useful because it allowed him "to make use of whatever my Idleness would suffer me to become possest of."[47] Though perhaps written with tongue-in-cheek, "idleness" is one of the key words he applies to himself in those years. It sounds very much as if there is a self-portrait included in Tom Idle, hinting at that aspect of Hogarth that kept him from finishing his own apprenticeship, liked to go wenching or on "peregrinations," was

---

who was with him a governor of St. Bartholomew's Hospital in the 1730s and 40s. Unfortunately, nothing is known of him except his attendance at board meetings.

[45] *Gate of Calais* painting is in the Tate, engraving published August 1748; Roubiliac's bust is in the National Portrait Gallery, London. The strange muffled shape of Idle's mother, repeated from print to print, which we have seen recalls the symbol idleness, bears a disconcerting resemblance to the single portrait Hogarth painted of his own mother, hooded and in mourning attire, which must have hung in his house (now private collection).

[46] Bate, *Achievement of Samuel Johnson*, p. 154.

[47] *Autobiographical Notes*, in *Analysis*, ed. Burke, pp. 201, 208, 209, 211, etc.; also p. 195

deluded by illusions of ease and grandeur, and, perhaps, unconsciously associated the creative act (as opposed to the successful businessman's practice) with punishment and death.[48]

One way to put our conclusion is that Hogarth's sympathy embraced both apprentices, both value systems. Another is to say that *Industry and Idleness* marks the end for Hogarth of a long-standing dichotomy of concentration and distraction in the Harlots and Rakes who will not fulfill their given calling but are distracted to the lives of ladies and rakes; vs. the implied ideal of the concentration of those who achieve identity and happiness by total absorption into a profession or calling. The one involves shifting, unstable role-playing; the other a fixity that balances happiness with security. Take Plate 2 of *A Rake's Progress* where the Rake is drawn in all directions by the group of individually-concentrated professional men, each completely absorbed in his own particular role. Ultimately Hogarth shows us Idle who simply exchanges one role for another, and his opposite Goodchild, who is all concentration and abrogates the sense of difference.

A third way is to conclude that a private meaning has been introduced that was perhaps also present in the *Harlot*, perhaps even in *Marriage à la Mode* (with its emphasis on clandestine marriages), but which did not alter or even contradict the straight —the popular—meaning in those works. Hogarth is changing the audience ratio in *Industry and Idleness*, increasing the number of general readers and reducing the readers of greater penetration, until at times they may be only one or two people, and he has also begun to widen the discrepancy between their two meanings—meanings no longer supporting but nearly contradictory. *Industry and Idleness* is in more ways than one a turning point for Hogarth. Thereafter his works become in general more publicly accessible, but at the same time more personal, more private. There is a clear movement away from readability toward expressive form, but in fact that is the addition of new modes of communication, whose end is again meditation. Within the large simple contrasts complete understanding requires also a knowledge of the painter's own oeuvre, and even of his personal life, past and present. Moreover, the reaction against common-

[48] To confirm that Hogarth was capable of a personal irony concerning his own marriage to his master's daughter, see Paulson, *Hogarth*, II, 274.

places of meaning, with which he began his career, far from mellowing, has led him now to present a staring commonplace—so staring that most viewers will give it their unthinking assent—and then so subtly, or perhaps I should say cynically, undercut it that the reader can come to no solution or final moral judgment.

What is effected incidentally is the planing away of distinctions until a moral structure has been virtually transformed into an aesthetic one. That this was an undercurrent earlier in Hogarth's career can be seen by comparing the moral contrasts of the *Harlot* and *Rake* with the largely aesthetic ones of *The Enraged Musician*. *Industry and Idleness*, which appears to be all morality, transforms Tom Idle into a figure not altogether unrelated to the one William Gilpin discusses somewhat later in his account of the Picturesque:

> In a moral view, the industrious mechanic is a more pleasing object, than the loitering peasant. But in a picturesque light, it is otherwise. The arts of industry are rejected; and even idleness, if I may speak, adds dignity to a character. Thus the lazy cowherd resting on his pole; or the peasant lolling on a rock, may be allowed in the grandest scenes; while the laborious mechanic, with his implements of labour, would be repulsed.[49]

Gilpin's scenes require men doing "for what in real life they are despised—loitering idly about, without employment."[50] He is also, of course, talking about the draining of meaning out of moral emblems: with the industrious and idle apprentices, so too the ass as emblem of dull, meaningless, stupid labor is replaced by the shaggy-coated beast, who, Gilpin informs us, is preferable to smooth-coated horses, as a bearded is to a smooth-cheeked man, because roughness is a picturesque element. When morality is removed, and iconographical (to a large extent moral) meaning is drained, one result is the Picturesque.

The Johns Hopkins University

---

[49] Gilpin, *Observations, relative to Picturesque Beauty . . . particularly Mountains, and Lakes of Cumberland, and Westmoreland* (1786), II, 44.
[50] "Instructions for Examining Landscape," pp. 17-18 (MS., Fitzwilliam Museum, Cambridge).

EXPERIENCE AS HISTORY:
SHELLEY'S VENICE, TURNER'S CARTHAGE

BY KARL KROEBER

The thesis of the large study of which this essay is a part is that " Romantic " sensibility (dominating European art between 1770 and 1870) is alien to " modern " sensibility, because the Romantic identifies individual experience with historical process, whereas to the modern " experience " and history are antithetical. To understand the Romantic sensibility we have to turn from its artifices readily misinterpreted to suit our apocalyptic yearnings toward something for us distasteful, what the Romantics specially admired. We are repelled, for example, even by the title of the painting J. W. M. Turner considered his masterpiece, which he hoped to have permanently exhibited between two pictures by Claude Lorrain: *Dido Building Carthage; or the Rise of the Carthaginian Empire—1st Book of Virgil's Aeneid*.[1] Sympathetic to Turner's harbingers of abstractionism, we gag on his narrative illustrations of literary historical texts. Analogously, we are dismayed when Shelley " describes " Venice in stereotyped phrases evoking not so much what the poet sees as what he imagines the city to have been and what it may become.

>Sun-girt City, thou hast been
>Ocean's child, and then his queen;
>Now is come a darker day,

[1] The two Claudes were *Sea Port* and *The Mill*: see Graham Reynolds, *Turner* (New York: Abrams, n.d.) p. 94. Reynolds provides the best general introduction to Turner's work, but a penetrating recent study is *Color in Turner* by John Gage (New York and Washington: Praeger, 1969). Although the standard biography is that of A. J. Finberg, *The Life of J. M. W. Turner* (London: Oxford, 2nd ed. 1961), Jack Lindsay, *J. M. W. Turner: A Critical Biography* (London: Cory, Adams, Mackay, 1966) is original and stimulating, as are the interpretations in Lawrence Gowing, *Turner: Imagination and Reality* (New York: Museum of Modern Art, 1966). The best collection of reproductions of Turner's work will be found in John Rothenstein and Martin Butlin, *Turner* (London: Heineman, 1964), Martin Butlin, *Turner's Watercolors* (London: Radcliffe and Barrie, 1962), and Gerald Wilkinson, *Turner's Early Sketchbooks* (London: Radcliffe and Barrie, 1972). Ruskin's extensive writing on Turner is still valuable.

> And thou soon must be his prey,
> If the power that raised thee here
> Hallow so thy watery bier.
> A less drear ruin then than now,
> With thy conquest-branded brow
> Stooping to the slave of slaves
> From thy throne, among the waves
> Wilt thou be, when the sea-mew
> Flies, as once before it flew,
> O'er thine isles depopulate,
> And all is in its ancient state,
> Save where many a palace gate
> With green sea-flowers overgrown
> Like a rock of Ocean's own,
> Topples o'er the abandoned sea
> As the tides change sullenly.
> The fisher on his watery way,
> Wandering at the close of day,
> Will spread his sail and seize his oar
> Till he pass the gloomy shore,
> Lest thy dead should, from their sleep
> Bursting o'er the starlight deep,
> Lead a rapid masque of death
> O'er the waters of his path.[2]

Most modern readers explain their distress at such a passage by faulting Shelley's language as conventional and generalized: "gloomy shore," "drear ruin," "conquest-branded brow," "masque of death." But displaying interrelations between natural

---

[2] Ll. 115-41, "Lines Written Among the Euganean Hills"; this citation, like all others in this essay, is from the text of *Percy Bysshe Shelley: Selected Poetry*, ed. Neville Rogers (Boston: Houghton-Mifflin, 1968), checked against G. M. Matthews' corrected edition of the *Poetical Works,* ed. Thomas Hutchinson (London: Oxford, 2nd. ed. 1970), and those passages reproduced by Judith Chernaik, *The Lyrics of Shelley* (Cleveland and London: Case Western Reserve Press, 1972). Mrs. Chernaik's commentaries, pp. 61-74 and 168-75, and Donald H. Reiman, "Structure, Symbol, and Theme in 'Lines Written Among the Euganean Hills,'" *PMLA,* 76 (1962), 404-13, are invaluable. My criticism is indebted as well to Carl Woodring's commentary in *Politics in English Romantic Poetry* (Cambridge, Mass: Harvard University Press, 1970), pp. 259-62, and to Earl Wasserman, *Shelley: A Critical Reading* (Baltimore, Johns Hopkins Press, 1971), pp. 197-203. My greatest debt to Professor Wasserman, however, is several private conversations of cheerful disagreement with him shortly before his untimely death. On "non-referentiality" in Shelley's description, one may consult my essay discussing Wordsworth's fondness for "contrary-to-fact" constructions in the very face of the facts, "'Home at Grasmere': Ecological Holiness," *PMLA* 89 (1974), 132-141, esp. p. 139. My thinking on these matters of style has been influenced by my colleague, Professor Michael Riffaterre; see, for example, his "Interpretation and Descriptive Poetry: A Reading of Wordsworth's 'Yew Trees,'" *New Literary History,* 4 (1972-73), 229-56.

and historical time and compromising images of immediate perception by references to a remote past and envisagements of an uncertain future, Shelley escapes the concrete singularity of diction we think essential to poetry. He attains, instead, remarkable fluidity. In six lines Venice is not merely personified but had been child, was queen, is fallen, must become ocean's prey—if, oddly, her corpse should so be sanctified by the power that long before had raised her from nothingness. Different periods and conditions succeed one another to form not a picture but a process—how Venice has changed, is changing, may change, e.g., "A less drear ruin then than now."

Shelley's language directs our attention less to objects than to systems—historical, artistic, linguistic. In the third line quoted above, " darker day " is a visual absurdity, effective so far as its physical inapplicability verifies its metaphoric appropriateness—its power to evoke a slavery-darkness-prison-death stereotype. By interplaying verbal and visual, Shelley establishes an " historical " structure, individualizing a *moment*. The present, for Venice and for the poet perceiving the city, is created not alone by immediate sensations, what *is*, but also by reference to what is not, to what may be, which recalls, even as it differs from, what had been. We're made aware of Venice less as a place than as an historical phenomenon, rising from unpeopled marshes to the glorious mercantilism of city-sea bridal only to decline, perhaps finally, into a superstition-haunted natural cenotaph.

The city as historical phenomenon is appropriately evoked by stereotyped language reminding us of conventions, especially the history of the art to which the poem contributes, the aesthetic *langue* of the poet's *parole*. Shelley draws upon two traditions, one of descriptive meditation, usually upon ruins, focused by the " ubi sunt " theme, and the other of " prospect " landscape description. The latter looks " forward " and the former " back," and " The Euganean Hills " depicts a beautiful prospect Shelley sees and a beautiful past he remembers—and what he *foresees*. Imagining the triumphant past, he can envisage a desolate horror that may in time be realized within the beauty perceptible before him. The poet's foresight is the obverse of his historical imagination, a power to see what *is* in the perspective of what now *is not*, either " no longer " or " not yet." If only at the end of the poem's second line do most readers discover that what had seemed an " actual " description in line one is metaphoric, the surprise prepares for the poem's continual interchanging of literal-visual with metaphoric-verbal. The interchange depends on time shiftings. The possibility of an island "healing Paradise" in the poem's concluding lines then seems appropriate because we have been conditioned to the poet's vision as an interfusing of visible and visionary, perceptible *is*, reconstructed *was*, envisioned *might be*. From the perspective of what Venice is, the city's past glory has become unreal; from the perspective of that free, glorious past, the present Venice, the city the poet looks upon, is unreal. Likewise, from the point of view of the present, the city's future is only an uncertain dream, but from the vantage point of that time, the present city may appear only a superstition-haunted half-memory.

Analogously, interpolated lines 169-205 in praise of Byron exploit Shelley's friend for another kind of historical perspective. The poet's fellow-exile and European celebrity conjoins not only the history of England to that of Venice and the history of British literature to Mediterranean literatures, but also Shelley's sad private history to the sad history of post-Napoleonic Europe. That Shelley is not indulging a personal eccentricity by interconnecting personal experience with cultural history is indicated by *Dido Building Carthage*. Turner wants us to see his specific accomplishment as part of an historical development. He wished his picture to be hung between paintings by Claude so that we might see his work (as I believe Shelley desired us to read his poem) as commenting on current events through its role in its art's history. To these Romantics, the autonomy of art was not reduced but enhanced when thus doubly participating in history.

If Turner's painting, first exhibited in 1816, strikes us as academic, we forget how topical was the founding of a great maritime empire at the moment of Napoleon's overthrow and the emergence of seafaring Britain as Europe's chief power. Turner's picture engages us in a temporal dialectic. The absurd title tells us that Turner painted not "Carthage" but Carthage as depicted in Virgil's *Aeneid*, the principal literary continuity between classical antiquity and later Western civilization. In painting a scene from the *Aeneid* (which *he* doubtless read in Dryden's seventeenth-century translation), Turner reaffirmed the vitality of a major historical continuity, as is illustrated by at least one detail. Even if the figures on the frieze of the building to the right are not easy to discriminate, the frieze recalls a compelling passage in Book One, that in which Aeneas sees a bas relief of scenes from the Trojan War, including episodes of his own heroism. Turner's picture adds another dimension to an historical self-consciousness introduced into the epic tradition by Virgil. Turner shows the founding of the Carthaginian Empire, obliterated two centuries before Virgil recreated it in his celebration of Imperial Rome, a Rome vanished for a milennium and a half when Turner reconstructed the ambitious Phoenician beginning. To overlook Turner's comment upon imperialism would be as narrow-minded as repudiating the cogency of his observation: the British Empire is no more. But Turner's prophecy, at the moment of the Empire's burgeoning, is not an abstract, metaphysical, apocalyptic one. He foresees the British Empire vanishing into a continuity of history. His visionariness is historical.

To understand it, we may look into the tradition in which it originated and which it transformed in emerging, because the late neo-classical aesthetic is in some respects congenial to the modern sensibility, especially in America. The display of Benjamin West's *The Death of General Wolfe*, painted in 1771, initiated the first popular exhibition of the British Royal Academy. The painting confirmed the colonial West's position as a leading painter in England when the graphic arts flourished in a culture traditionally more hospitable to literary enterprise. Sir Joshua Reynolds' comment upon *The Death of Wolfe* was prophetic: "Mr. West has conquered! I foresee that this picture will not only become one of the most popular but will occasion a revolution in art." [3]

[3] The quotation, like others by or about West cited in my text, is from James Thomas Flexner, *America's Old Masters* (New York: Dover, Riverside edition, 1967), pp. 19-97. Reynolds' comment appears on p. 66. On West worth consultation (besides Rosenblum's studies, cited below) are Grose Evans, *Benjamin West and the Taste of his Times* (Carbondale: Southern Illinois Press, 1959), and Charles Mitchell, "Benjamin West's 'Death of General Wolfe' and the Popular History Piece" in *England and the Mediterranean Tradition,* ed. Warburg and Courtauld Institutes (London: Oxford, 1945), pp. 179-92. Mitchell observes the possible unreliability of Galt's reporting of Reynolds' words, and credits West with an adapting of classical and religious aesthetics to new feelings of nationalistic patriotism. On the Royal Academy, see Sidney C. Hutchinson, *The History of the Royal Academy,* 1768-1968 (London: Thames and Hudson, 1968). The success of English painting is to a degree attributable to the Academy, established by a monarch shrewd enough unobtrusively to secure a "control over its private affairs that has descended in turn to each of his successors and has never been relaxed"; see William T. Whitley, *Artists and Their Friends in England 1700-1799* (New York and London: Blom, re-issue, 1968, orig. 1928), 2 vols, I, 251.

West was the man to give European neo-classicism a turn. The son of a Pennsylvania Quaker tavern-keeper, he had no formal instruction in drawing until he was an adult and already celebrated as a painter. His shrewdness is illustrated by his arrival in Rome. When the twenty-one-year-old "American Raphael" appeared there in 1759, he was mistaken by Cardinal Albani, the blind dictator of Roman connoisseurship, for an Indian. After the swarthy Cardinal had been persuaded that West was as "fair" as himself, the American was conducted by a curious crowd to see the Apollo Belvedere, then thought perfect classical art. "My God," cried West, "how like a Mohawk warrior!" After momentary consternation, the Italians acclaimed the comment, as was appropriate, with the star of Rousseau and the image of the Noble Savage ascendent among European intellectuals who wouldn't have known a Mohawk from a Mojave.[4]

To understand the revolutionary quality of West's *Death of Wolfe* a dozen years later, one must remember that the usual historical paintings of the time depicted all heroes in the dress of classical antiquity, in toga and sandals. West was historically specific for several reasons, one of which may have been that the subject recalled his place of origin, the new world. Unlike European painters (Zoffany, Hodges) who adapted figures and scenes of exotic places to neo-classic forms, West adapted the later neo-classic style to his natively "exotic" vision. Compositionally, *The Death of Wolfe* is late neo-classical in foregrounding a group of figures brought together by death. In the art of the 1750s and 1760s death is a preferred theme.[5] Living change, transition, process are not this style's delight. It aims for a conclusive statement, a finished period—a decline and final fall.

A premise underlying this art of variousness confined, what Paulson calls the circle of response, was belief in a common human

---

[4] I have drawn on the account by Flexner, pp. 19-22, his source probably being John Galt, *The Life and Studies of Benjamin West*, on whose reliability, see Mitchell. The story is retold by Robert Rosenblum, "The Dawn of British Romantic Painting" in *The Varied Pattern: Studies in the Eighteenth Century*, ed. Peter Hughes and David Williams (Toronto: A. M. Hackett, 1971), pp. 189-210.

[5] Consult the important article by Ronald Paulson, "The Pictorial Circuit and Related Structures in Eighteenth-Century England" in *The Varied Pattern*, pp. 165-87, especially pp. 186-87. Rosenblum, p. 199, points out that West repeated the compositional pattern of *Wolfe* in pictures of the death of Epaminondas and Chevalier Bayard. Mitchell discusses these adaptations of classic form at length, being especially helpful in defining shifts in taste for historical costuming (pp. 181-82).

nature: all men are alike.[6] The noblest expression of this faith in human uniformity is no work of art but the constitution of the United States of America. And it was this premise that was challenged by Romantic exoticism, local color, primitivism, and admiration for folk cultures. West, a frontiersman invading European salons, in himself embodies the Romantic "revolution," which in part evolved from later neo-classicism, claiming to "return to nature," but in fact introducing a new concept of nature. Notice West's defense of his picture's truth.

The event to be commemorated took place on the thirteenth of September 1759, in a region of the world unknown to the Greeks and Romans, and at a period of time when no such nations, nor heroes in their costumes, any longer existed.... The same truth that guides the pen of the historian should govern the pencil of the painter.... I want to mark the date, the place, and the parties engaged in the event.[7]

West is as far from the a-historicity of the medieval-early-Renaissance art which depicted, say, Greek heroes in fourteenth-century Italian dress, as from late-Renaissance idealizations of modern generals in the garb of Pericles. West, almost accidentally, introduced into art historical diacriticalness. Specifying time and place of his subject so contrastively, by implication he distinguished his subject from the time and place of the painter. He opened a field of possible discrimination between event depicted and event of depiction. Within forty years, Turner, wanting his *Carthage* displayed alongside Claude's paintings of a century and half earlier, was exploiting the distinction in a fashion that must have startled West.

But Turner developed a practice whose beginnings we see in West, some of whose predecessors had depicted historical figures in classical costume because they believed in the unchanging uni-

---

[6] Montesquieu, for example: "Since men have had the same passions at all time, the causes [of historical events] are always the same." Or Hume: "Would you know the sentiments, inclinations, course of life of the Greeks and Romans? Study well the temper and actions of the French and English: you cannot be much mistaken." An eloquent appeal for recognizing the progress of historical thinking during the eighteenth century is to be found in the fifth chapter of Ernst Cassirer, *The Philosophy of the Enlightenment,* trans. Koelln and Pettegrove (Princeton: Princeton University Press, 1951).

[7] Flexner, p. 65. Mitchell, p. 189, points out that by 1771 the subject of Wolfe's death was not, as it had been for Penny eight years earlier, "hot news," and that it was the historicity rather than the contemporaneity of West's picture which impressed the first viewers.

formity of human nature. If, as Hume and Montesquieu affirmed, there was no essential difference between modern French and English and ancient Greeks and Romans, representing historical contingencies of costume, furniture, and locale would have been to trivialize art. And it is these neo-classicists' disdain for historical contingency which makes them today perhaps more congenial than their Romantic successors. Admirers of Samuel Beckett or of Jackson Pollock find little of interest in historical art. Philosophers, anthropologists, psychologists, and linguists seeking structures, timeless models of thought, language, mind, and culture, can have scant patience with historical individualization. Our faith in the validity of computable alternatives provided by electronic mechanisms accords with neo-classic faith in a mechanical rationalism. Our " structure " parallels their " consistency of human nature." Then and now history hardly matters.

For Romantics, history does matter, and one can perceive a Romantic tendency in West's art. Admittedly, the arrangement of the figures in *The Death of Wolfe* echoes a Pietà, and the Indian in the foreground is in a Poussinesque position.[8] Yet his alert but comfortable pose contrasts with the sagging body of the general and the uptight uprightness of his subordinates, whose distress is conveyed by conventionalized gestures and facial distortions. The Indian surely is inscrutable. And the " accurate " costuming of the soldiers is impressive because played off against the nakedness of this anonymous, enigmatic native, who appears to be observing not a hero but merely the leader of an alien and perhaps overdressed people. No wonder the celebrated actor David Garrick, like many Englishmen, felt West had portrayed Wolfe with insufficient patriotism. To the applause of a crowd in front of the painting, Garrick assumed a posture and expression which he felt was truer to what must have been Wolfe's actual behaviour, how he must have looked and acted at the moment of his heroic death.[9]

That Garrick's performance raises important issues can be illustrated by a contrast of West's picture with one no actor could have performed before. Turner's *Snowstorm: Hannibal and His*

---

[8] On these and other debts of West see Mitchell, Paulson, and Rosenblum, *passim*.

[9] Flexner, pp. 66-67. Jean Starobinski, *The Invention of Liberty 1700-1789* (Geneva: Skira, 1964), points out that " artists were free to ignore the particular kinds of passion drawn by Le Brun, but they could not escape from the general obligation of giving visual form to a typology of the passions " (p. 135). The typology, of course, reinforced the sense of " appropriateness."

Army Crossing the Alps.[10] Detailed contrast is difficult, because Turner's picture is so obscure. The snowstorm, recreating one Turner had walked through in Yorkshire in 1810, confuses our vision. Turner's titular figure—in contrast to West's Wolfe, who dominates the Plains of Abraham outside Quebec—is as elusive for the viewer as he was for the Romans. And so much is happening in Turner's picture that we scarcely know how to order our perceptions. Whereas West's figures only watch Wolfe die, Turner's die, kill, save themselves, march, fall, stagger on, encourage some comrades, abandon others. To Turner, as later to Tolstoy, " history " is a confused struggle of many people. History is a dubious process involving multiple and uncontrollable contingencies, of which not the least important is weather. The winter of 1812, the year Turner's *Hannibal* was exhibited, destroyed Napoleon, in fact, and in *War and Peace*: some of Tolstoy's scenes of the French retreat are much like Turner's painting. Thomas Carlyle's Romantic history of the French Revolution, published in 1837, is packed with meteorological descriptions. Edward Gibbon almost never mentions the weather in his pre-Revolutionary *Decline and Fall*. Meteorology is minor in *The Death of Wolfe* but dominant in *Hannibal*. Of course, art historians are correct to say that Turner seized on the snowstorm to emphasize parabolic, curving forms that revolutionized the simpler geometric patterns giving structure to neo-classic art. But Turner's revolution was conceptual as well as perceptual, metaphysical as well as technical. Gifted with Carlyle's linguistic flamboyance and knowledge of mathematics, he would have argued, as no neoclassicist could, with the sage of Craigenputtock that history's pattern is not circular but Hyperbolic-Asymptotic.[11]

[10] Besides Gage, see Lindsay, pp. 123-39. I am indebted to Donald H. Reiman for calling my attention to a striking illustration of the England-Carthage comparison: " England is the modern Carthage: the love of gold, ' the last corruption of man,' pervades the whole state from the centre to the extremities." Letter of Thomas L. Peacock to E. T. Hookham, November 28, 1808, in *The Works of Thomas Love Peacock*, Haliford Edition, ed. H. F. B. Brett-Smith and C. E. Jones (rpt. New York, AMS, 1967), vol. VIII, 162. There is reason to think Turner's *Hannibal* to be indebted to a lost painting of Robert Cozens.

[11] Carlyle so defined history in " On History Again " in 1833. Turner's literary source, Goldsmith's *History of Rome*, emphasizes Hannibal's genius rather than the fortitude of his troops: " nothing was capable of subduing the courage of the Carthaginian general." When an avalanche blocked the army: " It was then that despair appeared in every face but Hannibal's."

Less mathematically, for the Romantic artist, history and nature are infinitely equivocal. Turner exploits ambiguities West barely introduced. Wolfe's death is heroic; but the Indian watching shadows his heroism by foreshadowing a different perspective. Turner seizes an event *intrinsically* doubtful, especially in 1812. Was Hannibal's invasion of Italy an heroic act, or the wilful recklessness of a power-hungry barbarian? Were the sufferings of the Carthaginian army deserved, or glorious sacrifices? Was Rome's ultimate victory affirmation of the value of its austere virtue? Or did Rome's witless strength destroy the inspiration of individualistic genius? By 1812 a Napoleon-Hannibal analogy was not original, but its meaning was still disputable.

Hannibal Crossing the Alps displays a passage, an event in process, and part of the larger process of a Punic war—the middle one of three. These Alpine sufferings led to Hannibal's most memorable triumphs. There is light ahead; the elephant's trunk points toward the bright warmth of Italy beyond the stormy pass. Yet even the brightness is ambiguous. Hannibal's successful battles in Italy did not lead to victory over Rome. The light at the end of these tunnel-like vortices embodies *The Fallacies of Hope*, the title of a long poem Turner worked at for years and which, beginning with this picture, provided epigraphs for many of his chief canvases.[12]

There can be fallacies of hope because Turner, unlike his predecessors in the sublime style, passes beyond the self-contained episode, perceiving experience as process. Hannibal's crossing of the Alps implies both a past and a future, and implies them with all the confusion of cause and consequence, motivation and result entering into any historical event understood as a complex of multiple sequences. The key unit for neo-classic historians is the epitomizing occurrence, the episode revealing with rationalized clarity the pattern in which historical meaning resides. For the Romantic

---

[12] Gage and Reynolds have pertinent comments on the relation of Turner's strange poetry to his painting, and there is a worthwhile study by Jerrold Ziff, "J. M. W. Turner on Poetry and Painting," *Studies in Romanticism*, 3 (1964), pp. 193-215. The verse is most readily available in the not quite satisfactory collection *The Sunset Ship*, ed. Jack Lindsay (London: Scorpion Press, 1966), which should be read in conjunction with T. S. R. Boase, "Shipwrecks in England Romantic Painting," *Journal of the* Turner on Poetry and Painting," *Studies in Romanticism*, 3 (1964), 193-215. The Window and the Storm-tossed Boat: Iconography of Romanticism," *Art Bulletin*, 37 (1955), 281-90.

artist like Turner, significance is not to be so confidently *measured* —it is evaluated by the more relativistic quality of intensity. Turner's technical development was toward increased blurriness and disintegration of outlines, because he more and more directly painted light. As Ruskin observed, shadow alone creates distinct outlines. If one compares the work of John Martin, a near-contemporary of Turner who carried on earlier conceptions of sublimity, one notices Martin's distinctness of line, concentration on shadows. Martin's " sublime effect " is principally a matter of scale. Tiny man stands against towering mountain, profound chasm, or grandiose edifice of antiquity. Even a vast crowd is composed of individually little people. Turner moved away from this measured grandeur into the perceptual haziness and conceptual equivocations of intense luminosity.[13]

The movement carries Turner beyond the historicity of practitioners of a simpler sublimity such as Martin. Ruins, for example, were used throughout the latter half of the eighteenth century as a dramatic measure of time. Byron still so used them in *Childe Harold*. But in Byron's poem the sombre ancientness of ruins is counterpointed by the intense personal immediacy of the poet's experience of their antiquity.[14] A parallel dialectic appears in

---

[13] The best study of sublime theorizing is still Samuel H. Monk, *The Sublime* (Ann Arbor: University of Michigan press, 1935, rpt. 1960). Notable also is Geoffrey Grigson, " Painters of the Abyss," *Architectural Review*, 108 (1950), 215-20. On Turner and luminosity, see Gage *passim*, but especially his discussion of the later " Carthaginian " painting of *Regulus*, pp. 143-45, leading to his argument that Turner knew and imitated the passage from " The Euganean Hills " I have quoted, which had been published separately as " Venice " by S. C. Hall in his *Book of Gems* in 1838— see Gage, pp. 146-47 and notes 87-90, p. 260.

We need an aesthetic study of the " mob " or the " crowd " in Romantic art. In another essay I compare Carlyle's representation of mobs in *The French Revolution* with some of Turner's painting of " masses." By participating in a crowd, a human being becomes something other than an individual, and though this may entail a loss of humanness, it could be argued that a mob is uniquely human because created by the surrender of qualities of individuality no creature other than man possesses to give up. This line of thought enables one to pursue Paulson's suggestion that in painting of the late neo-classic period " history was interpreted as largely the variety of gestures and facial expressions of response to a central action " (p. 171). For Romantics like Turner, the dialectic which creates " history" out of interplay between individual and multitude is more intricate, but it derives from the " circuit " Paulson describes. See also Edgar Wind, " The Revolution in History Painting," *Journal of the Warburg Institute*, 2 (1938-39), 116-37; and Robert Rosenblum, *Transformations in Late Eighteenth-Century Art* (Princeton: Princeton University Press, 1967), pp. 34ff.

[14] It is Byron's experiential intensity which differentiates his " ruin " poetry (especially in *Childe Harold*) from that of most of his predecessors. For Byron ruins

Turner's art, which shows us, for instance, ancient Carthage instead of ruined, not yet built. Similarly, *Hannibal* involves us in a snowstorm, in which, nevertheless, we see an elephant among mountains, infallible signal of a unique ancient event. The Romantic artist of history feels acutely his separation from the experience in which he would have us participate, of the time dividing event depicted from depiction of event.

The resultant dialectic is obvious in Carlyle's *French Revolution*, where it is expressed by movements back and forth between past and present tenses, modes of the historical and experiential. The same interplay appears in a subtler and more significant form in *War and Peace*'s oscillating between history and fiction. Tolstoy exploits a complexity introduced by Walter Scott, whose fiction we have been told, " made history come alive." Yet as early as *Waverley*, Scott defends introductory " historical " chapters as essential to his fictive story, incomprehensible, he insists, unless we understand its context of actual history.[15] For him, only history can make fiction live. Our difficulty in understanding the purpose of this Romantic dialectic is perhaps best defined by our bewilderment at the Romantics' tendency to combine " experience " with " omniscience." Percy Lubbock lamenting Tolstoy's failure to organize *War and Peace* around a restricted, Jamesan point of view illustrates the twentieth-century tendency to identify subjectivity and experientiality. A bothersome feature for us in " Lines Written Among the Euganean Hills " is the poem's failure in consistent subjectivity. For our taste, too much impersonal history intrudes. But for Shelley, the immediate experience, what he sees from the hill, would not be complete (nor accurately represented) did not his imagination encompass within his sensory perceptions the history (past and future) invisibly *in* his perceiving. *What* he sees is valuable in part because it embodies powers of historical culture, powers determining *how* he sees. For

are *not* only monuments of "lost significance," as Starobinski correctly observes that they are for Neo-classic artists—see *The Invention of Liberty*, p. 180.

[15] *Waverley*, Chapter Five: " I beg pardon . . . for plaguing . . . so long with old-fashioned politics. . . . ; The truth is, I cannot promise . . . that this story should be intelligible, not to say probable, without it." For the modern view succinctly stated, contrast J. Hillis Miller, *Poets of Reality* (Cambridge, Mass: Harvard University Press, 1965), p. 4: " The development of fiction from Jane Austen to Conrad and James is a gradual exploration of the fact that for modern man nothing exists except as it is seen by someone viewing the world from his own perspective."

Shelley, "imagination" includes history of imagination. Most of his *Defence of Poetry* is devoted to that history. Because of that history, his poem expresses an equivocal " vision," referring both to sensory perception and to what cannot be sensorily perceived. The equivocation finds a graphic analogue in Turner's *Hannibal*, wherein it is difficult to see what is happening, because the painting accurately represents how in fact we see in a snowstorm—none too clearly.

The quality of *Hannibal* depends, as Ruskin observed, in part upon Turner's precision in depicting a snowstorm. And Shelley's accuracy about autumnal sunrise at the Venetian latitude contributes to his poem's success. Snowstorm and sunrise are available to many, not just the artist. But critics today tend to talk about experience without referring to such actual experiences, and this is why " experience " has become a jargon term. It was not some seventy years ago, when it was first used to define the innovativeness of Romantic artists by G. K. Chesterton. He argued that the juxtaposition in Palgrave's *Golden Treasury* of Goldsmith's " When lovely woman stops to folly " and Burns's " Ye banks and braes of bonnie Doon " represented an enormous revolution, the overthrow of the idea of the poet's " absolute capacity," his right and duty, in my terms, to evaluate behavior.

... two poems on exactly the same subject ... the whole difference ... that Goldsmith's words are spoken *about* a certain situation, and Burns's words are spoken *in* that situation.... there comes a bitter and confounding cry out of the very heart of the situation itself. ... no one ... but a person who knew something of the inside of agony would have introduced that touch of the rage of the mourner against the chattering frivolity of nature ... [the] poet in his absolute capacity is defied ... by this new method of ... the songs of experience.[16]

Notable is Chesterton's point about Burns's " rage ... against the chattering frivolity of nature." Applying his personal experience, the critic observes a Romantic is not necessarily a lover of nature. The Romantics needed nature. Their predecessors, representing behavior rather than experience, had not. A forceful analysis of the distinction between behavior and experience is R. D. Laing's,[17] but if modern psychology is objectionable, one

---

[16] G. K. Chesterton, *Robert Browning* (London: Macmillan, 1957, orig. 1903), pp. 168-70.
[17] For example, R. D. Laing, *The Politics of Experience* (New York: Ballantine, 1968), p. 18: " I see your behaviour. You see my behaviour. But I do not and never

can imagine Garrick trying to improve on Turner's *Hannibal* as he had on West's *Wolfe*. What, after all, could the actor do about the snowstorm? Turner's protagonist is so inseparable from his situation that we may even overlook him. Chesterton observes that by adopting the girl's point of view Burns enters into the *situation* Goldsmith had only spoken about. Burns is Romantic, I'd suggest, because for him experience is more a matter of "situation" than of subjective viewpoint. Turner's *Hannibal* may be called a "painting of experience" not so much because of its subjectivity, but because it is a view from inside a situation conceived of as a transient combination of contingent circumstances, in short, as an historical event.

Today we may miss the distinction between Burns's poem and Goldsmith's because we're accustomed to songs of experience expressing perspectives rather than historical situations. But the distinction is radical. Goldsmith, like Benjamin West, depicts visible behaviour. Garrick perhaps objected to West's representation of Wolfe because the artist departed from behavior, allowing the General's features to betray something of an experience of death not appropriate to his public martyrdom. And the perfection of Goldsmith's lyric springs from the poem's unfailing exclusion of experiential elements. Goldsmith articulates with total clarity a pattern of appropriate behavior.[18] Behavior is open to evaluations of appropriateness, concord or discord with publicly accepted standards. Experience, never as controllable, never can be so evaluated; in this respect it may be termed inherently equivocal, even indeterminate. Experience is only self-validating.

The Romantic sensibility, unlike the neo-classic or modern, is often satisfied by engagement with this intrinsic uncertainty of experience. Keats's "Ode to a Nightingale" ends with the characteristic Romantic mark of punctuation, a question mark: "Do I wake or sleep?" Modern critics worry the question, seldom considering that for Keats a question might be the best ending for

have and never will see your *experience* of me. Just as you cannot 'see' my experience of you.... Experience is man's invisibility to man."

[18] In an art focused on behavior, anything other than the human is irrelevant. It is Turner and Burns who provide us with mountain, storm, bird, and river, "nature," that is, the non-human. This proves not that Romantics disvalued the human, only that they sought the humanity of "invisible" experience. Paulson touches on the issue from a different angle, pointing out that West, though working in a tradition drawing on sources as remote as Alberti's *Della pittura,* represents something new in "the passions": "the mourners' very grief now expresses their alienation ... the emphasis is on the responses of the periphery, which has lost touch with its center" (p. 187).

his experience, that the proper validation of what has happened to him is an equivoque. Were he not now uncertain, he would not fully have experienced (or not fully have reported) his situation in the darkening garden listening to the nightingale's song. Perhaps more difficult for us are Romantic poems (of which "The Euganean Hills" is one) ending not with a question but an hypothesis, a recognizedly provisional affirmation, a flight of fancy, a tone shift, some movement rounding off but not resolving the experience. Even a philosophic statement, such as closes Keats' "Grecian Urn," may not for a Romantic do away with the incertitude of experience but, instead, may mark it off to protect its equivocalness. Characteristic of the Romantic sensibility is desire *not* to transcend the experiential by a turn to some metaphysical certainty, some "deeper" structure, some archetypal pattern explaining, justifying, or giving supermundane sanction to its intrinsic indeterminacy.

To live in history is to live in uncertainty. *Our* determination to find apocalypse everywhere in Romantic art is misleading. The error, however, reveals a difference between ourselves and our Romantic predecessors. It is the modern sensibility that craves more than experience, the craving betraying an ontological insecurity. Ontological security may have come easier to Romantics because they identified history and experience, and regarded reality as a complex of temporal processes, necessarily constantly changing. If they engaged in such processes, they felt attuned to actuality, participating in essential being. Turner's readiness to move from a "literary-narrative" canvas to a "color beginning" and back, and, even more, his endeavor to fuse both modes in later canvases, graphically illustrates this kind of confidence, a confidence shared by Shelley, even though of all British Romantic artists he was probably the most idealistic, the most "Platonic" in the general sense of that term. He was certainly the most articulate necessitarian of the lot. And there can be no denying his later faith in an unchanging "One," something beyond the mutable world of appearances. Even so, Shelley can find experience intrinsically meaningful because historical, and he can believe that nothing exists except as it is perceived without becoming a modern fanatic of perspectivism.

His attitude is a source of his poetry's special uncongeniality to modern taste. By our standards, "The Euganean Hills" is too long. A minor lyric, it contains nearly as many lines as Eliot's

Wasteland. Shelley does not epitomize. He recounts the progress of an autumnal day from dawn to evenfall to portray sequentialities of human affairs as related to but distinct from—as visible in contrast against even though blending with—sequences of the physical cosmos. Nature and history are both temporal in essence, both are rhythmic, but the cyclic irreversibility of the former, for instance, is not an inescapable feature of the latter. If "Freedom should awake" in Venice,

> Thou and all thy sister band
> Might adorn this sunny land,
> Twining memories of old time
> With new virtues more sublime. (156-59)

Cultural decay is not inevitable in the same sense in which sunset is the inevitable consequence of dawn. The metaphor of the natural cycle which dominates early twentieth-century visions of history (not only Spengler's but also Joyce's and Yeats's) Shelley distrusts. Yet awareness that all things human, from civilizations to private sensations, are of and in time, and, therefore, impermanent, is conveyed by both details and total movement of his lyric, particularly his use of the diurnal progress to structure its central portion. This ambiguity creates much of the poem's overt emotionality, tempting us to characterize it as either optimistic or pessimistic. It is both, but in the poem joy and misery, despair and hope, do not so much balance as interact: one becomes the other. The dramatic confrontations we would prefer Shelley melts into something like a narrative process. In the process is lost most of the irony we like, the irony which discovers the permanent beneath the transient, the timeless within phenomenal change, a certainty precluding the possible alternative futures Shelley envisions so equivocally.

In the "Euganean Hills" we are asked to adopt more than the poet's physical viewpoint, and are offered the perspective created by his still incomplete personal history, the course of life which momentarily makes the volcanic hilltop in the "waveless plain of Lombardy" an "island" for the poet, a temporary refuge from misery. This respite as a flowering isle in the voyage of Shelley's life across a sea of agony (perhaps leading to a paradisal isle and perhaps to bones and skull bleaching on a desolate shore) is like, yet dissimilar to, what he sees. So perceiver and perceived can also function as metaphors of one another. Venice, literally an island in the Adriatic and metaphorically one in the Lombard plain, embodies part of the agony, the agony of history, through which the poet voyages. Simultaneously, the city recalls past glory and suggests a possibly glorious future, and, therefore, may also be one of the flowering isles for which he yearns. We are presented not so much an ironic opposition of appearance to reality as an interpenetrative process by which (actually or potentially) one becomes the other. The gleaming towers of Venice are in fact

> Sepulchres, where human forms,
> Like pollution-nourished worms,
> To the corpse of greatness cling.

But from this grim reality (and what could be worse than "pollution-nourished"?) new grace and virtue may come, just as Tyranny trampling out learning's spark in Padua has fed the flame of "antique" liberty now springing to life in many lands. In this temporalized vision there is little place for the condensed dramatics of the epiphanic mode.[19] Even the climactic moment keeps us in the realm of time, with a thirty-four line sentence whose molten grammar reveals no transcendent reality but the fluid interpenetrativeness of all phenomena upon which

> Noon descends ...
> Mingling light and fragrance, far
> From the curved horizon's bound
> To the point of Heaven's profound,
> . . . .
> Pointing from this hoary tower
> In the windless air; . . .
> And the Alps, whose snows are spread
> High between the clouds and sun;
> And of living things each one;
> And my spirit which so long
> Darkened this swift stream of song,—
> Interpenetrated lie
> By the glory of the sky:
> Be it love, light, harmony,
> Odour, or the soul of all

---

[19] At this point I find Wasserman's reading unpersuasive but exemplary of the modern point of view. "The poet's moment of noon ... is a timeless moment," even though it is, Wasserman admits, "his historical revelation." For modern critics it is inconceivable that a climactic experience should not transcend time: "the unifying noontime radiance endows the poet with his own personal experience of perfection, his eternal moment of absolute illumination, his insight into eternity and into the unity of which he is a part" (p. 200). I believe "eternal moment" is imported by the modern critic, and that Shelley strives to recreate a vision in and of time.

> Which from Heaven like dew doth fall,
> Or the mind which feeds this verse
> Peopling the lone universe. (ll. 285-319)

All of Shelley's elegant prose testifies that the syntactic dissolutions of this passage are deliberate; the grammatical fluidity is a linguistic equivalent to the blurring interpenetrations of color by which Turner dissolved to recreate the geometrical structuring of neo-classic painting. Organization through conventionalized separations, the organization which *is* syntax, Shelley's language tries to overcome, so as to recreate the flowing simultaneity which is *now*, this particular ensemble of impressions emerging out of what has gone before and shaping itself into an unfolding future. Analogously, Turner renders the specificity of experiential process by freeing colors from the separateness created by conventionalized representational outlining. Interpenetration is essential for the Romantic, who individuates not by alienation and opposition, not by segregating one thing from another, but by depicting *how* they conjoin and interfuse.[20] For him, the experiential process can be realized only in an art made up itself of transformational activities—as is suggested by the last five lines of the preceding quotation.

Well, is it love or light or odor, we tend to ask of Shelley, who will not give us the discriminative answer we desire. He finds unifying significance in the sheer interactivity of diverse phenomena—including diffusion of his verse into an Italian landscape in which natural and cultural have blended, are blending, will blend, which we would perceive inadequately were we to see it as only one or the other.[21] Our anti-historical vision obscures for us the possibility of such temporalized interpenetration as an individualizing mode. Shelley's Euganean hill is *not* the still point of a turning world, but the opposite, a *now*, a complex ensemble of sensation which is meaningful only because involving past and future. To the contrary, *Four Quartets* is about time and can

---

[20] Mrs. Chernaik observes that "throughout the poem the relationship between scene and the thought it occasions is complex" (p. 62). To my mind the chief complexity is that to some degree the thought also "occasions" the scene. To Shelley, because the mind quite literally "feeds" verse, the poet can people the lone, companionless universe.

[21] Careful critics have noticed shiftings within metaphors: "the 'green isle' is not only a physical refuge but a moment of time, a metaphor for the poet's day . . . the moment is but an interlude; it passes with the day, and the poet resumes his original metaphor" (Chernaik, p. 65 and p. 71). See Woodring, p. 261, on the Lombard cities as dancing graces *and* chained slaves.

employ succinctly abstract language referring *to* time because Eliot's poem focuses on eternity. It does not render the temporal process of experience. It is not *in* time, as Shelley's poem is. Even Yeats, admirer of Shelley, presents us a golden bird singing "Of what is past, *or* passing, *or* to come," not their interactions, and in "Byzantium." The same city for Shelley, significantly, was Constantinople, in "the poem of *Hellas*, written at the suggestion of events of the moment . . . wrought upon the curtain of futurity, which falls upon the unfinished scene . . ." [22]

Archibald MacLeish speaks for modern sensibility when he claims a poem should only *be*, only exist statically. So does Auden observing that "poetry makes nothing happen." For Shelley, to the contrary, "all things exist as they are perceived," and the poet reorients the world by apprehending in it what does not yet exist in it, revealing "the gigantic shadows of futurity" within the luminous indeterminacy of present events. By perceiving the not-yet-perceptible the poet may determine what will be perceived. Turner could not philosophize as ingeniously as Shelley, but he seems to have acted on the same principle, enriching our visual powers and extending the potency of art by depicting what is difficult to see. For the Romatics, only through art can men make anything happen. It is imagination that enables us to participate creatively in the processes of life.

Columbia University

---

[22] Preface to *Hellas*, Rogers, p. 274. The conception of open-ended art implied by Shelley has recently attracted much attention. "His poems," remarks Mrs. Chernaik, move "toward possibility, toward questions, rather than demonstrating or reaffirming doctrine" (p. 62). Her words are almost identical to those used by Larry J. Swingle, "On Reading Romantic Poetry," *PMLA*, 86 (1971), 974-81, to describe the fundamental philosophical direction of Romantic poetry, which "offers questions, exposes problems, uncovers data. It casts doubt upon supposed certainties, and it suggests possible new directions for thought. Romantic poetry stirs the mind—but then it leaves the mind in that uneasy condition. . . . In reading Romantic poetry, one is perhaps tempted to ask: What is the poetry telling us? But usually one's question should rather be: What is the poetry asking us?" (p. 980).

I suggest consideration of Turner's art helps us to understand how and why Romantic art functions in this fashion, though I realize as J. R. Watson has observed, that "large-scale comparisons between Turner and individual romantic poets cannot be made," and that with an artist so variously gifted we can note at best that "certain pictures connect with certain poets." Yet, Watson adds, Turner's art includes "many of the emotions and attitudes we associate with romanticism . . . however varied our discrimination of romanticisms may be, in England, they are united in the work of Turner"; see "Turner and the Romantic Poets," *Encounters*, ed. John Dixon Hunt (New York: Norton, 1971), pp. 96-123, p. 121.

THE CONTEXT OF DRYDEN'S *ABSALOM AND ACHITOPHEL*

BY THOMAS E. MARESCA

With very few exceptions, Dryden's *Absalom and Achitophel* maintains a narrative integrity that few political allegories ever reach; its fable (in our terms, its vehicle) achieves a kind of autonomy which renders it complete and satisfying in itself and perfectly transparent as a metaphor for other things. These very qualities hide the real achievement of the fable of *Absalom and Achitophel* by cloaking it with an inevitability which it by no means possesses. We have been sufficiently reminded of the frequency with which seventeenth-century political writers compared Charles to David to accept without demur the appropriateness of the biblical tale to the English situation. If we remember piously that Dryden has really reversed the roles of the biblical Absalom and Achitophel, the fact does little to alter our acceptance of Dryden's fable as a *donnée* rather than an *aperçu*, a fiction. Yet the imaginative reordering of history, both Jewish and English, constitutes the excellence of Dryden's poem, and the "fabulous" (in the root sense) nature of Dryden's narrative makes it so inevitable a vehicle of his meaning. This is the aspect of *Absalom and Achitophel* I would like to explore in this paper.

In general terms, the most significant change Dryden has made in the biblical narrative lies in his radical transformation of its temporal and conceptual contexts, both of which he wrenches into a rich ambiguity. To clarify this, we shall have to examine the much-worked-over opening lines of the poem:

> In pious times, e'r Priest-craft did begin,
> Before *Polygamy* was made a sin;
> When man, on many, multiply'd his kind,
> E'r one to one was, cursedly, confind:
> When Nature prompted, and no law deny'd
> Promiscuous use of Concubine and Bride;
> Then, *Israel's* Monarch, after Heaven's own heart,
> His vigorous warmth did, variously, impart

> To Wives and Slaves: And, wide as his Command,
> Scatter'd his Maker's Image through the Land. (1-10)[1]

Let us put aside at the outset the idea that this passage serves only as a witty justification for or palliation of Charles' promiscuity; that is certainly true, but I doubt that Dryden needed ten lines for only that. The passage establishes an explicit temporal and conceptual context for the whole poem, a context which the remainder of the poem will treat with the same irony and ambiguity that Dryden provides for the biblical narrative on which the poem as whole is based. " Pious times, e'r Priest-craft did begin " were technically the patriarchal period before the establishing of the Levitical priesthood, the period between God's covenant with Abraham and the more explicitly codified covenant established with the people of Israel through Moses.[2] Obviously, chronological difficulties present themselves from the beginning: the biblical David did not live in those pious times, and Dryden's " Before *Polygamy* was made a sin " ignores the pointed injunction of Deuteronomy 17:17 that kings should not multiply horses, wives, or concubines. Indeed, before the end of this same first verse paragraph Dryden also indicates that priest-craft of some sort already had begun:

> Gods they had tri'd of every shape and size
> That God-smiths could produce, or Priests devise.... (49-50)

Later sections of the poem of course confirm this fact:

> This set the Heathen Priesthood in a flame,
> For Priests of all Religions are the same.... (98-99)
> Hot *Levites* Headed these; who pul'd before
> From th' *Ark*, which in the Judges days they bore,
> Resum'd their Cant, and with a Zealous Cry,
> Pursu'd their old belov'd Theocracy. (519-22)

The solution to these apparent contradictions can be found in careful consideration of the first lines of the poem. " Pious times " contrast with those after priesthood began. Priesthood itself Dryden associates with the institution of law and consequently of sin: polygamy is *made* a sin; man is cursedly confined; laws deny na-

---

[1] The text quoted is that of James Kinsley, *The Poems of John Dryden* (Oxford, 1958).

[2] Barbara Lewalski's " The Scope and Function of Biblical Allusion in *Absalom and Achitophel*," ELN, 3 (1965-66), 29-35, also deals with some of this material, and I am indebted to her article for several suggestions. For this particular point, see p. 30.

ture's promptings. The conception of law herein contained, particularly the conception of the law of Moses, would have been quite familiar to Dryden's audience, since it is St. Paul's conception of the nature and function of the Mosaic law as he lengthily argues it in the Epistle to the Romans. Here is a brief extract of his argument:

> What shall we say then? Is the law sin? God forbid. Nay, I had not known sin, but by the law: for I had not known lust, except the law has said, Thou shalt not covet. But sin, taking occasion by the commandment, wrought in me all manner of concupiscence. For without the law sin was dead. For I was alive without the law once: but when the commandment came, sin revived, and I died. (7:7-9)

Dryden's appropriation of this conception at the beginning of his poem forces a revaluation, a relocation of the conceptual context in which we understand David. By placing him firmly in "pious times," Dryden leads us to see him as sharing the same sort of direct relationship to God as the patriarchs and Moses possessed; the language of the opening lines, with their emphasis on David as the monarch "after Heaven's own heart" (7), reinforces this. In fact, Dryden depicts David's sexuality as analogous to God's own creativity: it is his maker's image, not his own, that he scatters through the land.[3] Dryden here exploits a distinction familiar to his readers as the difference between the dominion of law, as exemplified by the Mosaic code, and the dominion of grace, as established by the crucifixion of Christ.[4] The pivotal point which allows him to turn this neat inversion is the traditional conception of David as a type of Christ, a conception which Achitophel recalls for us at a crucial point in the poem (416) and which Dryden obviously exploits as a careful counterpoint to the dominion of grace his conspirators and Levites—and English puritans—hope to attain. David lives under the dominion of grace, in a kind of golden world where what nature prompts is after God's own heart: he embodies the conception of the divinely appointed king to whom law is irrelevant, who founds his dominion in God's will, in grace, and in his literal and metaphoric paternity of his people. David's own comments, at the end of the poem, make quite explicit this dichotomy between the dominion of law and the dominion of

---

[3] The implicit image of the scattering of seed the rest of the poem capitalizes upon by linking it with the parable (Matthew 13:1-12) as in lines 194-95.

[4] See the Epistle to the Romans, 5:12-21.

grace, and argue moreover that in rejecting him his rebels reject grace itself and demand the rigor of the law—which as St. Paul says, is death.

> Law they require, let Law then shew her Face;
> They could not be content to look on Grace,
> Her hinder parts, but with a daring Eye
> To tempt the terror of her Front, and Dye. (1006-09)

And these lines also complete the conception of David as a patriarchal king possessing direct access to the deity by their overt allusion to Moses' vision of the hinder parts of God, whose face no man can look upon and live (Exodus 33:18-23).

Into this context Dryden has fitted the action of *Absalom and Achitophel*. All of his rebels oppose not just kingship, but grace; monarchy and divinity are at least parallel and probably interchangeable terms. "No King could govern, nor no God could please" (48) the Jews; they are called "a Headstrong, Moody, Murmuring race" who try, not the limits of law, but "th' extent and stretch of grace" (45-46). David becomes in their minds "An Idoll Monarch which their hands had made" (64), and they think to "melt him to that Golden Calf, a State" (66). Achitophel's temptation of Absalom adopts the form of the satanic temptation of Christ because it is simultaneously a temptation from grace, from filial devotion, and from political loyalty. But Achitophel and the other rebels do not reject the grounds of David's authority; rather, they seek to imitate them. Achitophel thus tempts Absalom to accept the role of Messiah, to falsely assume the guise of a bringer of the new and full dispensation of grace. The "Hot *Levites*" who head the "*Solymaean* Rout" parody exactly the basis of David's reign:

> Hot *Levites* Headed these; who pul'd before
> From th' *Ark*, which in the Judges days they bore,
> Resum'd their Cant, and with a Zealous Cry,
> Pursu'd their old belov'd Theocracy.
> Where Sanhedrin and Priest inslav'd the Nation,
> And justifi'd their Spoils by Inspiration;
> For who so fit for Reign as *Aaron's* Race,
> If once Dominion they could found in Grace? (519-26)

Shimei, "who Heavens Annointed dar'd to Curse" (584), grotesquely parodies Christ's promise of abiding grace:

> When two or three were gather'd to declaim

> Against the Monarch of *Jerusalem*,
> *Shimei* was always in the midst of them. (601-06; cf. Matthew 18:20)

Corah too, among all his other accomplishments, manages a travesty of Christ: Dryden applies to him the imagery of the brazen serpent set up in the desert to preserve the Israelites (633-35)—the image, of course, was traditionally accepted as a type of the crucifixion of Christ. All of these distortions of the true reign of grace simply repeat in David's kingdom the same sort of satanic parody of God's dominion that Milton described in *Paradise Lost*; the devil's party constantly tries to reproduce God's power, and constantly lapses into vulgar burlesque.

Within the overall framework of the dichotomy between the dominion of law and the dominion of grace, the opening lines of the poem establish a subsidiary dialectic of grace, law and nature. Nature prompts, and no law denies " Promiscuous use of Concubine and Bride " (5-6). While in Absalom alone " twas Natural to please " (28), still " His motions " were " all accompanied with grace; / And Paradise was open'd in his face " (29-30). And the Jews, though minimally bound by law, still " led their wild desires to Woods and Caves, / And thought that all but Savages were Slaves " (55-56). This threefold battery of themes, grace, law, and nature, governs the ideological progression of the poem: " Religion, Common-wealth, and Liberty " (292) form, as Achitophel says, the general cry.

This dialectic operates in the poem in curious and often paradoxical ways. For David, to follow nature is to follow grace; at nature's prompting he scatters his maker's image through the land. His " native mercy " (939) Absalom admits is " God's beloved Attribute " (328). Yet even for him conflict occurs, especially when law and justice enter the case:

> If my young *Samson* will pretend a Call
> To shake the Column, let him share the Fall:
> But oh that yet he would repent and live!
> How easie 'tis for Parents to forgive!
> With how few Tears a Pardon might be won
> From Nature, pleading for a Darling Son! (955-60)

Dryden presents David as torn between two natures, between the king's two bodies, if you will: [5] as man, he grieves for his wayward

---
[5] See Ernst Kantorowicz, *The King's Two Bodies* (Princeton, 1957). Kantorowicz's

son; as king, he punishes his wayward subject. The beginning of the poem schematizes this paradox of kingship brilliantly. Initially, "Godlike *David*" (14), prompted by nature, scattered his maker's image through the land. The lines immediately following transform the procreative process from the semi-divine imparting of warmth it had been to a more earthy and natural—in a lesser sense —husbandry through an extended farming-seed metaphor. At the end of this, Dryden for the first time introduces Absalom and offers the following rationale for his physical beauty:

> Whether, inspir'd by some diviner Lust,
> His Father got him with a greater Gust;
> Or that his Conscious destiny made way
> By manly beauty to Imperiall sway. (19-22)

The contrast between Absalom's "manly beauty" and David's eminence as "*Israel's* Monarch, after Heaven's own heart" (7) explains itself, while the concise oxymoron "diviner Lust" sums up both David's dilemma and what is wrong with Absalom's conception. Dryden then makes of Absalom a baser—a more natural —version of David; he too follows nature, and his motions are "all accompanied with grace" (29), but what David and the reader see in him is not his maker's image, but rather

> With secret Joy, indulgent *David* view'd
> His Youthful Image in his Son renew'd.... (31-32)

Absalom bears the image of David as man, not of David as king; he is, as was the Duke of Monmouth, a *natural* son, an illegitimate —born according to the order of nature rather than the order of law or grace. Dryden needs nowhere to stress either the irony of the unnatural conduct of this natural son or the paradox that the illegitimate should call for law.

Flawed human nature, as epitomized in the poem by Absalom, provides the possibility for the disruption of the dominion of grace in David's kingdom, just as it did in the garden:

> But, when to Sin our byast Nature leans,
> The careful Devil is still at hand with means;
> And providently Pimps for ill desires. (79-81)

The brief paradox of the devil's providential pimping reminds us of the overarching dominion of divine law and grace within which

contention that the doctrine of the king's two bodies developed out of the theology of the mystical body of Christ seems to me to have genuine relevance to Dryden's poem.

human nature acts out its "ill desires"; it recalls an ultimate law, nature, and grace which are not in conflict but are in fact identical —but in the world of fallen nature, these are only hints. More immediately apparent in this world is the "natural Instinct" by which the Jews every twenty years rebel (218-19). Achitophel appeals shrewdly to this baser nature when he urges Absalom to set aside filial regard for David—

> Nor let his Love Enchant your generous Mind;
> 'Tis Natures trick to Propagate her Kind.
> Our fond begetters, who would never dye,
> Love but themselves in their Posterity. (423-26)—

and again when he urges him to open rebellion:

> Resolve on Death, or Conquest by the Sword.
> Which for no less a Stake than Life, you Draw;
> And Self-defence is Natures Eldest Law. (456-58)

And I presume Dryden refers ironically to this same nature when he ends Achitophel's speech with "He said, And this Advice above the rest, / With *Absalom's* Mild nature suited best" (477-78). Yet even within this generally sinful context paradox occurs, and this same "byast Nature" also works to ironic good among the poem's Villains:

> But far more numerous was the herd of such,
> Who think too little, and who talk too much.
> These, out of meer instinct, they knew not why,
> Ador'd their fathers God, and Property:
> And, by the same blind benefit of Fate,
> The Devil and the *Jebusite* did hate:
> Born to be sav'd, even in their own despight;
> Because they could not help believing right. (533-40)

Dryden focusses all of these paradoxes in his disquisition on the social contract, where he raises a whole series of questions about the nature of governor and governed and the scope of law (753-810). Men are naturally prone to rebellion against both kings and god; but isn't something to be said for their natural rights, "their Native sway" (760)? May kings abrogate law? If not, are kings only trustees? If so, how can any man claim any natural right other than what can be defended by brute power? The result of such a process must be a Hobbesian state of nature "where all have Right to all" (794), and that is anarchy. Alteration of existing social structures always ends that way:

> To change Foundations, cast the Frame anew,
> Is work for Rebels who base Ends Pursue:
> At once Divine and Humane Laws controul;
> And mend the Parts by ruine of the Whole. (805-08)

Dryden has carefully suppressed overt mention of grace from this argument to present fully the dilemma into which unaided nature and merely human law lead; as Dryden argues it, the political problem of the one and the many is unresolvable in human terms.

The poem, however, does offer a solution to this problem in terms of its major metaphor. *Absalom and Achitophel* contains an image cluster which sums up fully all the ramifications of this dialectic of grace, law, and nature: the relations of fathers and sons, the metaphors of paternity and sonship, offer the key to the totality of the poem. The poem specifically labels kings as " the Godheads Images" (792) and consistently describes David in particular as " Godlike." The beginning of the poem explicitly links David and God through David's sexual potency: the " vigorous warmth " he indiscriminately imparts makes him the sun of the human world, analogous to the creative warmth of the sun in the physical universe and the overflowing being of God in the metaphysical. David the King and God the Father stand in almost one-to-one relation to each other, and this analogous relationship provides the resolution of the problem of government. Dryden signals us that this is the case when, near the beginning of his discussion of the problem of government, he makes choosing heirs for monarchs and decreeing for God parallel and almost cognate acts (758). He undercuts his own question about the contractual nature of kingship by referring to it as a " resuming Cov'nant " (767), and so linking it with God's covenant with the Israelites and implying the consequent parallel between God's dominion and the king's—and since the poem has argued from the very beginning that David's kingship constitutes the dominion of grace, this necessarily implies also that David's authority is as irrevocable as God's. Dryden clinches his argument by appeal to Adam's sin, a stock argument of the theorists of patriarchal government: [6]

---

[6] See especially Sir Robert Filmer's *Patriarcha*, ed. Peter Laslett (Oxford, 1949), pp. 57-60 and 74-78. *Patriarcha* was published in 1680 after circulating in manuscript for many years; obviously it was brought out as a document in support of the royalist cause.

> If those who gave the Scepter, coud not tye
> By their own deed their own Posterity,
> How then coud *Adam* bind his future Race?
> How coud his forfeit on mankind take place?
> Or how coud heavenly Justice damn us all,
> Who nere consented to our Fathers fall? (769-74)

Dryden's rhetorical questions amalgamate all three areas of the poem's dialectic and convict the rebels of the heresy of challenging divine justice. Adam's simple status as the natural father of the human race nullifies all questions of the people's "Native sway" (760): they have none, since it was all vested in him as the father of human nature. His rebellion against the kingship of God is symbolically reenacted in the poem in the temptation and fall of Absalom, an act which, like Adam's, will once again bring mankind under the dominion of law and death until the second Adam can restore the dominion of grace. David thus stands in the poem as God's vice-regent, king by divine right and patriarchal descent— a fact even Achitophel admits in his sneering reference to David's "Successive Title, Long, and Dark, / Drawn from the Mouldy Rolls of *Noah's Ark*" (301-02). Dryden's whole argument throughout this section of the poem draws heavily upon the patriarchal theorists and constantly employs their language. He states the basic problem in terms of the rights of fathers and sons:

> What shall we think! can people give away
> Both for themselves and Sons, their Native sway? (759-60)

And his citation of Adam uses the same terms of reference—tying posterity, binding one's future race, consenting to our father's fall (769-74). His subsequent critique of the problem of individual rights in a democracy follows quite closely the arguments of Sir Robert Filmer's *Patriarcha* and other similar tracts.[7] His implicit conclusion is inescapable: David exercises authority just as does a father in his family or God in the universe. Rebellion against him equals apostacy from God—setting up the golden calf of a state (66). Logically then, when "Godlike *David*" speaks at the end of the poem, "His Train their Maker in their Master hear" (938), and the paternal, creative David of the opening lines brings

---

[7] See Filmer, pp. 81-82. It is also worth pointing out, as Filmer does, that the seventeenth century believed that the duty of obedience to magistrates and kings was biblically enjoined by the fourth commandment, "Honor thy father and thy mother."

forth one more image of his maker in the land. And equally logically, the final lines of the poem harmonize grace, law, and nature in the restoration of " Godlike *David* " as " Lawfull Lord " presiding over " a Series of new time " (1026-31); Dryden alludes to the supposedly messianic eclogue, with its promise of the birth of the wonder child, the restoration of a golden world, and the reestablishment of the reign of justice and grace. The end of the poem fulfills its beginning; David's kingship and paternity are transformed into symbols of the re-establishment of universal order and the undoing of Adam's fall. The paradise which was metaphorically opened in Absalom's face (30) reaches its fulfillment in the advent of the second Adam who is to be born of David's line; the dominion of grace his rebels mistakenly seek through the son of his mortal body will be established by the son of his divine body.

Given the paramount importance of the idea of paternity in this scheme, the sort of son produced becomes a major index of the rightness or wrongness, the morality or immorality, of the father and his activities. The poem juxtaposes and contrasts the sons of its various actors for the purpose of illustrating the presence of proper hierarchical order or the absence of it. The comely Absalom, ambiguously graceful, starkly contrasts with the ugly, unformed progeny of Achitophel, the physical image of his father's mind:

> ... that unfeather'd, two leg'd thing, a Son:
> Got, while his Soul did hudled Notions try;
> And born a shapeless Lump, like Anarchy. (170-72)

Immediately after presenting the essentially patriarchal argument about government which we have already discussed, Dryden illustrates it by his encomium of Barzillai's son, who fulfilled all parts of the parallel duties " of Subject and of Son " (836). Such acceptance and fulfillment of the obligations of a hierarchical and patriarchal state produce another, metaphoric, image of the maker:

> Oh Narrow Circle, but of Pow'r Divine,
> Scanted in Space, but perfect in thy Line! (838-39)

This encomium of Barzillai's son thus forms an integral unit in the poem's imagistic structure, point by point damning Absalom for his dereliction of the duties " of Subject and of Son." David himself places this image in its most important perspective when he refers to his rebellious subjects as Jacob and Esau:

> True, they petition me t'approve their Choise,
> But *Esau's* Hands suite ill with *Jacob's Voice*. (981-82)

Jacob, the younger son and inferior by the order of nature, achieved priority according to the order of grace; as Bishop Hall expressed it, "Esau got the right of nature, Jacob of grace."[8] These two sons, contending for a paternal blessing, sum up the image of sonship in the poem: nature and grace struggle for dominion, nature with Esau's hands, simple power and bodily strength, grace with Jacob's voice, reason and prayer.

Dryden characterizes all of the poem's Esaus by marked physical descriptions; this process makes them primarily corporeal, while leaving the poem's Jacobs relatively untouched by the taint of fallen bodily nature. *Absalom and Achitophel*'s villains exist in our imaginations primarily as physical entities—"that unfeather'd, two Leg'd thing," Achitophel's son (170); Achitophel himself,

> A fiery Soul, which working out its way,
> Fretted the Pigmy Body to decay:
> And o'r informed the Tenement of Clay (156-58);

Corah;

> Sunk were his Eyes, his Voyce was harsh and loud,
> Sure signs he neither Cholerick was, nor Proud:
> His long Chin prov'd his Wit; his Saintlike Grace
> A Church Vermilion, and a *Moses's Face* . . . (646-49);

and even "The well hung *Balaam*" (574). Corporeal imagery marks all the rebels and their activities, dragging them down from the realm of spirit they would usurp to the world of matter, much as Satan's rebellion in *Paradise Lost* degraded him to the material form of the serpent. Images of eating and of food particularly abound in the poem, frequently in semi-blasphemous contexts. Jewish rabbis and Jebusites agree that it is their duty "T'espouse his Cause by whom they eat and drink" (107). The plot itself is "swallow'd in the Mass, unchew'd and Crude" (113). Dryden describes the beliefs of the Jebusites as follows:

> Th' *Egyptian* Rites the *Jebusites* imbrac'd;
> Where Gods were recommended by their Tast.

---

[8] *The Works of Joseph Hall, D.D.,* 12 vols. (Oxford, 1837), I, 41. Some reference to Jacob and Esau may also appear in lines 405-06, "His Right, for Sums of necessary Gold, / Shall first be Pawn'd, and afterwards by Sold. . . ." In general, Dryden seems to have drawn many ideas and some phrases from Hall's various *Contemplations on the Old Testament:* compare *Absalom and Achitophel* 1030-31 and *Hall,* I, 106, for instance.

> Such savory Deities must needs be good,
> As serv'd at once for Worship and for Food. (118-21)

Nadab, in addition to canting, "made new porridge for the Paschal Lamb" (576). Dryden even uses such imagery negatively, and paradoxically corporealizes even his most abstemious villain, Shimei:

> And, that his nobel Stile he might refine,
> No *Rechabite* more shund the fumes of Wine.
> Chast were his Cellars, and his Shrieval Board
> The Grossness of a City Feast abhor'd:
> His Cooks, with long disuse, their Trade forgot;
> Cool was his Kitchen, tho his Brains were hot. (616-21)

This whole image pattern culminates in Absalom's offering himself to the mob:

> Th' admiring Croud are dazled with surprize,
> And on his goodly person feed their eyes.... (686-87)

Naturally enough, Dryden also metamorphoses his speech into one more meal: his words are "More slow than Hybla drops, and far more sweet" (697). But the final transformation of the image, and its ideological climax in the poem, occur in David's speech: the process of corporealization to which the rebels have all been subjected here reaches its nadir in a symbolic cannibalism:

> Against themselves their Witnesses will Swear,
> Till Viper-like their Mother Plot they tear:
> And suck for Nutriment that bloody gore
> Which was their Principle of Life before. (1012-15)

Dryden binds his rebels together with still other material links; an ubiquitous pattern of references to blood, humors, lakes, and seas ties leaders and mob together in a common allegiance to the moon which governs the motions of all such changeable bodies.

> For, govern'd by the *Moon,* the giddy *Jews*
> Tread the same track when she the Prime renews:
> And once in twenty Years, their Scribes Record,
> By natural Instinct they change their Lord. (216-19)

Zimri, "in the course of one revolving Moon, / Was Chymist, Fidler, States-Man, and Buffoon" (549-50). Sanhedrins and crowds are "Infected with this publick Lunacy" (788): both lack stability; they flow to the mark and run faster out (786). Achitophel hopes that David's power, "thus ebbing out, might be Drawn to the dregs of a Democracy" (226-27). But the most important use of the image occurs quite early in the poem; it links Absalom even then with the fickle mob and sets up a loose parallel between his warm excess in murdering Amnon and the people's feverish propensity to rebellion. Absalom's "warm excesses" (37), Dryden tells us, "Were constru'd Youth that purg'd by boyling o'r" (38). He shortly after employs the analogy of the human body and the body politic to apply this same image, in much greater detail, to the consequences of the Popish Plot in the mob:

> This Plot, which fail'd for want of common Sense,
> Had yet a deep and dangerous Consequence:
> For, as when raging Fevers boyl the Blood,
> The standing Lake soon floats into a Flood;
> And every hostile Humour, which before
> Slept quiet in its Channels, bubbles o'r:
> So, several Factions from this first Ferment,
> Work up to Foam, and threat the Government. (134-41)

This last use of the image once again forces a more serious revaluation of Absalom's excesses, and at the same time degrades him by linking him with the mob in a common subservience to passion and irrationality, to the lowest common denominators of human nature. All of these images of food, eating, and humors achieve a common effect in the poem: they constitute the symbolic enactment, in the moral and individual realm, of the public rebellion. They debase the image of his maker that David bears by reducing that image in the individual and in society to a mere physical effigy—they are, if you will, simply other versions of the golden calf to which the rebels would reduce David.

As opposed to the striking corporeality of the rebels, David and his party seem somewhat ethereal. Dryden employs no physical description whatever in his catalog of the royalists, and his opening encomium of Barzillai's sainted and angelic son casts a protective cloak of spirituality and immateriality over all the members of the group. Indeed, Dryden does not even have the royalists *do* very much; in contrast to the rebels who slide, rush, ebb, flow, etc., the royalists merely stand and speak—thereby making a minor but effective imagistic point about stability and motion that David will capitalize upon in the very final lines of his speech

(1018-25). But speech itself figures as the most important attribute of David's followers—honest speech as opposed to Achitophel's lies, rational argument as opposed to the rebel's propaganda, poetry as opposed to the fictions of Corah, Jacob's voice vs. Esau's hands. This whole final section of the poem, from line 811 to the end, centers itself upon the right use of language as a criterion of loyalty, intelligence, and morality. The poem climaxes in David's speech precisely because only the enunciation of clear truth can conclude such a parade of lies and misrepresentations as the rebels have enacted. In a precisely parallel way, Dryden at this point in the poem begins emphasizing the fictive and artificial nature of *Absalom and Achitophel* itself, reminding us that it *is* a poem and exploiting the paradox of discovering truth through falsehood and fiction. The personality of the poet, as a kind of magical recorder of praise or blame for all future time, appears at the very beginning of this section; speaking of David's friends, Dryden says

> Yet some there were, ev'n in the worst of days,
> Some let me name, and Naming is to praise. (815-16)

He sustains this emphasis on the personal role of the poet and his personal involvement in his fiction all through the section on Barzillai and Barzillai's son:

> His Eldest Hope, with every Grace adorn'd,
> By me (so Heav'n will have it) always Mourn'd,
> And always honour'd.... (831-33)

The apostrophe to the dead hero, beginning at line 838 with " Oh Narrow Circle, . . ." continues this tone, allowing us to hear the narrator's personal grief paradoxically set within the artificial framework of formal eulogy—a point which is reinforced by the poet's address to his muse and reference to what he has just spoken as " this Verse / To hang on her departed Patron's Hearse " (858-59). Barzillai himself Dryden praises for his discrimination and generosity in honoring " The Fighting Warriour, and Recording Muse " (828). He similarly commands " Him of the Western dome " for sense and eloquence (868-69), and pointedly adds the following:

> The Prophets Sons by such example led,
> To Learning and to Loyalty were bred:

> For *Colleges* on bounteous Kings depend,
> And never Rebell was to Arts a friend. (870-73)

Dryden likewise distinguishes Adriel as " the Muses friend, / Himself a Muse " (877-78). He lauds Jotham for his ability " To move Assemblies " (844) and Amiel for his skill in leading the Sanhedrin—

> So dexterous was he in the Crown's defence,
> So form'd to speak a Loyal Nation's Sense,
> That as their band was *Israel's* Tribes in small,
> So fit was he to represent them all. (904-07)

Dryden's long satiric portrait of Corah offers the best perspective from which to view this concern with language, since Corah commits the poem's greatest perversion of words. Dryden contrasts him tellingly with St. Stephen, who bore witness to the truth with his life; the bilingual pun on martyr and witness enables him somewhat less than covertly to warn Corah of the fate that awaits him:

> Who ever ask'd the Witnesses high race,
> Whose Oath with Martyrdom did *Stephen* grace? (642-43)

And again, later in the passage:

> Let *Israels* foes suspect his heav'nly call,
> And rashly judge his Writ Apocryphal;
> Our Laws for such affronts have forfeits made:
> He takes his life, who takes away his trade. (664-67)

But other aspects of Stephen's story serve Dryden's purposes as well: certainly the fact that the protomartyr was brought to trial in the first place by the suborned testimony of false witnesses bears heavily on Dryden's irony here. In another way too Stephen provides a norm against which to judge Corah: he enjoys a vision of Christ in glory (Acts 7:55-56) which Corah's lies grossly parody—

> Some future Truths are mingled in his Book;
> But, where the witness faild, the Prophet Spoke:
> Some things like Visionary flights appear;
> The Spirit caught him up, the Lord knows where.... (654-57)

Dryden's mention of Corah's " *Moses's* Face " (649) and Stephen's actual citation of Moses in his defense provide further clues to the significance of this passage. Stephen described Moses as a precursor of Christ, and as such he has already appeared in

Absalom and Achitophel; Achitophel initially hailed Absalom as the Jews' " second *Moses, whose extended Wand / Divides the Seas, and shews the promis'd Land* " (234-35). Moses as the leader of the exodus from Egypt has of course been subliminally present in the poem from the first mention of the golden calf in line 66, or perhaps even from the first line of the poem, with its implicit reference to the founding of the Levitical priesthood under Moses' direction. However that may be, the figure of Moses as a divinely appointed ruler having direct access to the deity has operated up to this point in the poem as a minor analog to David. Here Dryden chooses to make this analog explicit and important. The final lines of the passage on Shimei, which immediately precede the portrait of Corah, start the process in motion:

> And *Moses's* Laws he held in more account,
> For forty days of Fasting in the Mount. (628-29)

The fact of God's dispensing law to the Israelites obviously has in itself considerable importance to *Absalom and Achitophel,* but I want to concentrate for the moment upon the idea of Moses' vision of God on the mount, since Corah bears a parodic version of the outward effects of that vision in his " *Moses's* Face ":

> And it came to pass, when Moses came down from mount Sinai with the two tables of testimony in Moses' hand, when he came down from the mount, that Moses wist not that the skin of his face shone while he talked with him. (Exodus 34:29)

Corah too has his visions, but they sound oddly more like St. Paul's than Moses': " the Spirit caught him up, the Lord knows where " (657). The line recalls St. Paul's famous account in II Corinthians:

> I knew a man in Christ above fourteen years ago, (whether in the body, I cannot tell; or whether out of the body, I cannot tell: God knoweth;) such an one was caught up to the third heaven. And I knew such a man, (whether in the body or out of the body, I cannot tell: God knoweth;) How that he was caught up into paradise, and heard unspeakable words, which it is not lawful for a man to utter. (12:2-4)

And there, I think, we have the crux of the matter: he " heard unspeakable words, which it is not lawful for a man to utter." Corah debases that vision with his imaginary plots and malicious lies: he perjures himself, quite literally speaking " words, which it is not lawful for a man to utter." Dryden's description of him as the brazen serpent raised in the desert continues and completes the travesty: Corah, like Absalom, plays false prophet, false Moses, false Messiah. He leads not to the dominion of grace which the brazen serpent tokens, but only to the same sort of parody of it that Absalom and Achitophel offer, and ultimately to the oblivion from which he rose. Corah, as a " *Levite* " and one of " Godalmightys Gentlemen " (644-45), pursues what Dryden has earlier described as " their old belov'd Theocracy " (522),

> Where Sanhedrin and Priest inslav'd the Nation,
> And justifi'd their Spoils by Inspiration. . . . (523-24)

The parody is perfect and complete, for the biblical Corah—also a Levite—rebelled against Moses for precisely the same reasons:

And they gathered themselves together against Moses and against Aaron, and said unto them, Ye take too much upon you, seeing all the congregation are holy, every one of them, and the Lord is among them: wherefore then lift ye up yourselves above the congregation of the Lord. (Numbers 16:3)

Needless to say, the predictive value of historical allusion would warn this Corah about the exemplary punishments God visits upon those who challenge his appointed rulers, even in the name of grace.

Dryden draws Corah as a total hypocrite, one who perverts the offices of priest, prophet, and witness to his own ends by base lies. His first couplet of direct address to Corah—

> Yet, *Corah,* thou shalt from Oblivion pass;
> Erect thy self thou Monumental Brass . . . (632-33) —

seems to me to recall the famous opening of the last ode of Horace's third book, " Exegi monumentum aere perennius . . . I have built a monument more lasting than brass. . . ."[9] The conception of Corah as anti-poet, as one who uses language to deceive and disorder, contrasts coherently in the poem with the emphasis Dryden will later place, and which we have already partially discussed, upon himself as poet: opposed to Corah stands, as loyal member of the king's party, the king's poet laureate (more accurately, and more to the point, the historiographer royal), who employs words to impose order, who uses fictions only for their inherent truth. Corah's lies constitute another debased image of the maker; Dryden, as a lesser maker in his own right, creates a true image

---

[9] Dryden's reference to Corah's obscure birth parallels Horace's own mention in the ode of the obscurity of his own birth.

of reality. So too does David, when he promises the speedy advent of law:

> Law they require, let Law then shew her Face;
> They could not be content to look on Grace
> Her hinder parts, but with a daring Eye
> To tempt the terror of her Front, and Dye.
> By their own arts tis Righteously decreed,
> Those dire Artificers of Death shall bleed.
> Against themselves their Witnesses will Swear
> Till Viper-like their Mother Plot they tear:
> And suck for Nutriment that bloody gore
> Which was their Principle of Life before. (1006-15)

His reference to the hinder parts of grace returns us to Moses' vision on the mount of the glory of God; now David, like Moses, acts as the bringer of divine law to men who have fallen from grace to depraved nature. In " Viper-like their Mother Plot they tear " we see the inevitable end to which unaided nature leads, as well as the end of that part of the paternal and filial images of the poem: nature can only turn upon itself; it can never rise above itself to law or grace, both of which are the free dispensations of God and his anointed kings. But the reference to the hinder parts of grace implies more than this. If David is now functioning properly as an intermediary between God and man, as the second Moses Achitophel claimed Absalom to be, then he is not merely imposing law upon his unruly subjects, but offering them access to grace as well—that is, at the very moment when the operations of grace seem about to be suspended in the face of the " curst Effects of necessary Law " (1003), God and David paradoxically offer fresh gifts of grace. David stands as a hinge between the two great dispensations, that of law in Moses and that of grace in Christ. The dominion of law contains, in embryo, the dominion of grace. What Moses saw on the mount when he viewed the hinder parts of God most biblical commentators of Dryden's time agreed upon: he saw an image of the glory of God—the Schechinah some called it, others the Word, others Christ.[10] But it amounts to the same thing: at the moment of receiving the law, which brings death, Moses received a vision of the grace which brings life and of which he himself served as a type. That image of God's glory which he

---

[10] See for instance the commentary of Simon Patrick on the passage: *A Commentary upon the Historical Books of the Old Testament,* 5th edition, 2 vols., (London, 1694).

saw David here reproduces in himself and in his speech, using words as the agent of the divine will to create an image of the divine justice and mercy, just as the poet Dryden employs words to create yet another image of divine providence and just as the divine Word himself *is* that justice and mercy. And God himself guarantees the veracity of these images and words—not just by his consenting nod and thunder, but in the " Series of new time " (1028) which here begins. These new times will witness the divine birth, as Virgil's fourth eclogue tells us: " iam nova progenies caelo demittitur alto " (iv.7). The event there described Dryden and his audience knew to be the birth of Christ, the advent of the dominion of grace, the incarnation of the Word. That entrance of the eternal Word into human time establishes both the historicity and the essential truth of Dryden's fiction. It confirms the validity of God's own poem, which is creation in general and David in particular, and provides the ground for the human maker John Dryden's partial image of that creation. *Absalom and Achitophel* goes full circle, and " Godlike *David* " at the end of the poem is once more reproducing his maker's image in the land. Even the metaphor of paternity is restored to honor through the divine paternity and the divine sonship which will flow from David's line. Language too is restored after the abuse heaped on it by Absalom, Achitophel, and Corah: in the laconic " He said " which concludes David's speech, to which " Th'Almighty, nodding, gave Consent " (1026), and in the birth of the Word lie the restitution of all words and the vindication of all poetry—including this present fiction— as a true image of reality.

State University of New York at Stony Brook

IMAGES OF SAMUEL JOHNSON *

BY W. K. WIMSATT

Like all Johnsoniana ... [Sir John Hawkins's *Life of Samuel Johnson*] leaves us with an increased respect for both Johnson and Boswell. For Boswell, because he is so incomparably the best of the reporters: for Johnson, because he comes so unmistakably through them all. How many other men in all history have this double reality—real to our intellect (we believe him to be historical), but also as real to our imagination as Mr. Pickwick or Mr. Woodhouse?

—C. S. Lewis, review of *Hawkins's Life of Johnson*, edited by B. H. Davis, *The Sunday Telegraph*, 1 April 1962.

I

About thirteen years ago I wrote an essay entitled "The Fact Imagined: James Boswell." The title meant for me that Boswell deliberately encountered " fact " in the simplest sense, was faithful to facts and even pursued them with a degree of mania, but that he had a way of responding to mere facts so as to invest them with a kind of hyperactuality and heightened import. He was a visionary of the real. This was true of his way of experiencing and reporting his own life, and in a special way of his experiencing that very special part of his life the literary hero Samuel Johnson. Boswell's Johnson is a Johnson who really sounds like the author of the writings we ascribe to him.

Professor F. A. Pottle had written some earlier accounts of Boswell's memory and his imagination. Boswell's "imagination" is essentially Professor Pottle's domain. He has restated and expanded his thesis elegantly and persuasively in a very recent essay.[1] Recently also, at the Indiana Conference on Biography as

---

* A shorter version of this paper was read at the meeting of the Modern Language Association of America at Chicago in 1971.

[1] Professor Pottle advises me that Claude Colleer Abbott was probably the first to credit Boswell with " imagination "—in a lecture delivered on 25 October 1945. See his *Boswell* (The Literary and Philosophical Society of Newcastle upon Tyne, 1946), pp. 21-22. Pottle used the term and concept independently in the essay " The

an Art, in 1967, Professor Ralph W. Rader, flourishing an elaborate quasi-Aristotelian apparatus of justification, has celebrated Boswell's construction of the "monumental" Johnson; Rader argues with a thoroughness and insistence that go far toward inviting a comparison between Boswell and DeFoe or Fielding. Professor Philip Daghlian, the editor of the Indiana Conference papers, drops the laconic remark that the "monumental" Johnson is not the only permissible image.[2]

A literary theorist of the Parisian structuralist school, Tzvetan Todorov, in the foreword of his recent book on the poetics of prose fiction (*Poétique de la prose*), invokes the language of the detective story to express a fancy that writing a critical study is inevitably a kind of retracing one's own steps in a return to the scene of a crime. The modest purpose of the present paper is to resume the now well-established theme of Boswell's biographical achievement—but mainly by the method of contrast. To get on with this paper I have had to assume that the image of Johnson created by Boswell in his *Life of Johnson* and recently celebrated by such writers as Professor Pottle and Professor Rader is a familiar one.

We are in an especially good position to talk about Boswell's Johnson through the circumstance that Johnson was the cynosure of so many other observers and reporters. He was the subject of at least seven biographical sketches during his lifetime and of at least seven others within about ten years after his death. And these minor accounts have recently had their book about them [3]—as earlier in the present century they were noticed in an essay by Walter Raleigh. It is only fair to say of these beginnings in the construction of the image of Johnson that they are far from ignorant or inept. The sketch of his moral and literary character

Life of Boswell," *Yale Review*, 35 (March 1946), 445-60. See other statements by him in "The Power of Memory in Boswell and Scott," *Essays on the Eighteenth Century, Presented to David Nichol Smith* (Oxford, 1954), pp. 185-87; *Boswell's London Journal, 1762-1763* (New York, 1950), pp. 12-14; *James Boswell, The Earlier Years, 1740-1769* (New York, 1966), p. 88 (in imaginative power Boswell was "the peer of Scott and Dickens"); and most recently, "The *Life of Johnson*: Art and Authenticity," *Twentieth Century Interpretations of Boswell's Life of Johnson* (Englewood Cliffs, N. J., 1970), pp. 67, 72.

[2] *Essays in Eighteenth Century Biography*, ed. Philip B. Daghlian (Bloomington, Indiana, 1968).

[3] Robert E. Kelley and O. M. Brack, Jr., *Samuel Johnson's Early Biographers* (Iowa City, 1971).

which appears first in *Baker's Companion to the Playhouse* (1764) and receives expansions mainly in Reed's *Biographica Dramatica* (1782) shows some remarkable, if largely abstract, anticipations of Boswellian themes and attitudes.

We know that the first full-length biography of Johnson was written not by Boswell but by Sir John Hawkins. Hawkins too has had his recent celebrator and his abridged edition,[4] and he can give us some special instruction in the want of the biographical imagination. This dour magistrate and historian of music survives as a biographer in virtue of earnest purpose, authority, information, and a scrupulous regard for the truth. His weakness appears not in any such "dark uncharitable cast" as Boswell imputes to him, but in a generally pedestrian and wandering style and, here and there, in the magisterial tone of his remarks upon some of Johnson's irregular habits—his "unmanly thirst for tea," his love of tavern society, his indiscriminate generosity, or, as C. S. Lewis has put it, his "vulnerability by compassion." And Hawkins differs from Boswell in one *prima facie* respect of first importance—the fact that although he knew Johnson pretty well from the early years in London (c. 1749) until his death, he recorded only a few snatches of Johnson's incomparable conversation.

Recording Johnson's conversation was, we know, an active cult among his friends and even among lesser acquaintances. One of the books published just after his death was entitled *Dr. Johnson's Table Talk* (1785), and William Cooke's *Life* of Johnson published two weeks after his death included "Johnsoniana; or, a selection of . . . Bon-mots, Observations &c." In addition to Boswell, at least seven other members of Johnson's circle participated in the cult with distinction. And it is these conversationalists chiefly who challenge our attention, and two of them especially, both females.

In 1941 appeared Professor James L. Clifford's vastly entertaining biography *Hester Lynch Piozzi (Mrs. Thrale)*, and in 1942 Katharine Balderston's edition in two volumes of the exuberant lady's diary for thirty-four years, 1776-1810, *Thraliana*. These monuments, together with the review article of the biography by F. A. Pottle and Charles H. Bennett in *Modern Philology* for May

[4] Bertram H. Davis, *Johnson Before Boswell, A Study of Sir John Hawkins' Life of Samuel Johnson* (New Haven, 1957); John Hawkins, *The Life of Samuel Johnson, LL.D.*, ed. Bertram H. Davis (New York, 1961).

1942 may be said to have settled, beyond the likelihood or need of further dialectic, the issue of literal veracity between Boswell and Mrs. Thrale-Piozzi. *Thraliana* was the only source book which the lady had with her on her Italian travels in 1785.[5] From this she quarried more than half of her rivalrous *Anecdotes of the Late Samuel Johnson, LL.D. during the Last Twenty Years of his Life*, published in 1786, about six months after Boswell's *Hebrides Tour*.[6] The rest was a liberal memory. It was a book for the hour; it met an eager audience and went through four editions in a little over a month. It was scarcely an accident of the hour. Rather, as Miss Balderston argues,[7] Mrs. Piozzi's whole life had prepared her for the opportunity. She had nursed literary ambitions. She had been collecting *Johnsoniana* for eight years before she began her entries in *Thraliana* in 1776. Since 1773 or thereabouts, she had been hinting an intention to write some memorial of Johnson.

"Every variety of freedom," writes the meticulous Miss Balderston, "was taken by Mrs. Piozzi with the original record. She expanded, contracted, telescoped, confused the time sequence, changed general statements into specific ones and specific into general, invented occasions for conversations floating in a vacuum, transferred speeches from one person to another, and repeatedly gave in the form of direct quotation from Johnson statements for which there is no hint at all in her diary." [8] Miss Balderston adds, what is no doubt true enough, "Mrs. Piozzi's standards were those of her age." She adds also, what Pottle and Bennett in 1942 were already busy rebutting, that "Boswell himself, in a lesser degree, was guilty of most of the [same] peccadilloes." [9] Boswell's regard for the literal fact, I believe we may safely assert, was of a different order. His standards were not those of his age. He engaged in a kind of manic pursuit of the facts which would set a standard for the most scrupulous biographers of later ages. Literal veracity, however, is only an adjunct—though possibly for Boswell it was a needed adjunct—of the kind of imaginative veracity which is my theme in this paper.

A more puzzling distinction perhaps confronts us in the un-

---

[5] Mary Hyde, *The Impossible Friendship, Boswell and Mrs. Thrale* (Cambridge, Mass., 1972), pp. 96-99.
[6] Her manuscript was completed before she read the *Tour* (p. 99).
[7] *Thraliana*, I, xii-xiv, xix-xx. Cf. Hyde, p. 29.
[8] *Thraliana*, I, xxiii-xxiv.
[9] *Thraliana*, I, xxviii.

doubted personal greatness, the force of character and the social brilliance, of the lady who ran the household and salon at Southwark and Streatham, who bore the stolid brewer's children and his infidelities, who soothed twenty years of the radically wretched life of a retired sage lexicographer, who had the heart and the head to contend against that sage, against her own daughters, the world of the Blues, and all the rules of caste—as she wooed and wedded her second husband, the Italian music master of her choice. All this, so vividly realized in Professor Clifford's biography, cannot be in the least doubt. Beyond question she was an extraordinary woman. The evidence for this, let us remember too, is not entirely in her own autobiographical jottings and letters, numerous and varied as these are. The evidence for Mrs. Thrale-Piozzi the personality converges from many directions, and one of these is Johnson himself, in his letters to her, with which she moved ahead of Boswell when she published them in 1788.

She had given Johnson a life which he could not find in the masculine world of his London haunts; he had given her his own great person, as resident intellectual, the center and prompter of her salon. Thus we ought not to be surprised that he had shown her some sides of his character which he did not, perhaps even could not, show Boswell. On her publishing Johnson's letters to her, Boswell enters in his *Journal* the record of his disappointment "in having a proof" of Johnson's "fawning on a woman whom he did not esteem."[10] The easiest revelations to identify come under the head of tenderness and a certain elephantine playfulness in teasing the female. Another theme might have been Johnson's concealed dark fear of insanity and perhaps certain strongly disguised psychic drives which Freud might be more capable than a literary scholar in exploring—the locked chamber at Streatham, the message sent out in French, the whip (?) and the padlock. Miss Balderston advances the evidence discreetly in an essay apart from her edition of *Thraliana*.[11]

An impressive woman, a woman in most respects unusually gifted, enjoys unusually intimate, tender, and mutually benevolent

[10] *Private Papers of James Boswell from Malahide Castle*, XVII, 74, quoted by Frederick A. Pottle and Charles H. Bennett in *Modern Philology*, 39 (May, 1942), 424, n. 4.
[11] "Johnson's Vile Melancholy," in *The Age of Johnson, Essays Presented* to Chauncey Brewster Tinker (New Haven, 1949), pp. 5-10.

relations with an extraordinary man. She sees various sides of him that his male friends see far less of. She records anecdotes of his manners and conversation. We might well expect to discover here some perceptions of extraordinary profundity and interest. Miss Balderston indeed goes so far as to claim that "the image of Johnson which emerges ... is a living one, and in the larger sense a truthful one. It is the same Johnson who moves with such Titanic vigour through the pages of Boswell. . . ."[12] Here the aspect of devotion in the scholar is dominant. It is my own notion that if we turn from the acknowledged Mrs. Thrale, the eminent historical figure, to her portrayal of Johnson in her *Anecdotes*, what we encounter is grotesque, even shocking. We encounter Mrs. Thrale-Piozzi looking inward, to memory, trying to catch her impressions and recollections in a deliberate tissue of words—Mrs. Piozzi in short trying to be a writer. She wrote other chattery, middling books, her two volumes of *Observations and Reflections Made in the Course of a Journey through France, Italy, and Germany*, 1789; the two volumes of her *British Synonymy*, 1794. Boswell took Johnson to the Hebrides in 1773. The result was not only Johnson's *Journey to the Western Islands of Scotland*, a survey of Highland social and economic life which has retained its authority and interest to this day, but Boswell's *Hebrides Tour*, " one of the finest travel books ever written."[13] The Thrales took Johnson to North Wales in the year after the Hebrides and to Paris the year after that—the literary results of each trip were negligible. On rereading this paper (in proof), I realize that my comparison applies more justly to Mrs. Thrale and Boswell as impresarios than as writers. " There was a coarseness in her fibre," says Virginia Woolf, " and a commonness in her vision that explains why as an observer she was so greatly inferior to Boswell."[14]

Mrs. Piozzi's *Anecdotes of Samuel Johnson* is a decidedly middling book, if not worse. This is not an uncommon fate. It is what befalls many of us, most of us, when we try to put ourselves, or any segment of what we have experienced, into public words. A literary imagination is precisely that which we are able to accom-

---

[12] *Thraliana*, I, xxviii.

[13] See the appreciation by M. J. C. Hodgart, *Samuel Johnson and His Times* (London, 1962), pp. 85-87; and Mary Lascelles, ed. *A Journey to the Western Islands of Scotland* (New Haven, 1971), p. xv.

[14] *The Moment and Other Essays* (New York, 1948), p. 55, a review of Clifford.

plish in words. It is not the same as our moral character, our business sense, or our social expertise. Boswell, a man of moral character in one or two ways much inferior to Mrs. Thrale's, had literary imagination. He had professional skill in the construction of a narrative and the styling of its parts. She did not.

The erudition of Mr. Johnson proved his genius; for he had not acquired it by long or profound study: nor can I think those characters the greatest which have most learning driven into their heads, any more than I can persuade myself to consider the river Jensica as superior to the Nile, because the first receives near seventy tributary streams in the course of its unmarked progress to the sea, while the great parent of African plenty, flowing from an almost invisible source, and unenriched by any extraneous waters, except eleven nameless rivers, pours his majestic torrents into the ocean by seven celebrated mouths.[15]

At the age of two years Mr. Johnson was brought up to London by his mother, to be touched by Queen Anne for the scrophulous evil, which terribly afflicted his childhood, and left such marks as greatly disfigured a countenance naturally harsh and rugged, beside doing irreparable damage to the auricular organs, which never could perform their functions since I knew him.[16]

Though he was attentive to the peace of children in general, no man had a stronger contempt than he for such parents as openly profess that they cannot govern their children. "How (says he) is an army governed? Such people, for the most part, multiply prohibitions till obedience becomes impossible, and authority appears absurd; and never suspect that they tease their family, their friends, and themselves, only because conversation runs low, and something must be said." [17]

"Poor people's children, dear Lady (said he), never respect them: I did not respect my own mother, though I loved her: and one day, when in anger she called me a puppy, I asked her if she knew what they called a puppy's mother." [18]

I exhibit the first of these passages as an instance of Mrs. Thrale-Piozzi's frivolous attitude toward learning and her talent for beautiful euphuisms; the second as a moment of more than Johnsonian philosophic diction; the third to show a curious effect of *non sequitur* (or garbling?) in Johnson's quoted discourse;

---

[15] *Anecdotes of Samuel Johnson,* ed. S. C. Roberts (Cambridge at the University Press, 1932), p. 4.
[16] *Anecdotes,* pp. 9-10.
[17] *Anecdotes,* pp. 19-20.
[18] *Anecdotes,* p. 154.

and the fourth for its harshness. Here are some varied cold strains, coming early in the *Anecdotes*, each in its own way extreme, even an oddity. Collectively, they put us on notice what kind of world we enter.

It is true that she has given us a handful of lantern slides and texts of some of Johnson's occasional verses which we are very glad to have, and for these she has enjoyed ample celebration by the Johnsonian annotators and essayists. One of the most discerning of these is Walter Raleigh, but it is he who, while praising the lady, notices also how much of the meaning of Johnson's conversations depended on the setting of circumstance which only Boswell has been careful to preserve. Partly through the average brevity of her anecdotes, partly through their random order, partly through the miscellaneous intrusions of her own personality, the general impression is that of a farrago of trifles—or, as she herself says, " a piece of motley Mosaic work." [19]

Mrs. Thrale-Piozzi proceeds from moment to moment of her *Anecdotes* by very loose principles of association (one thing reminds her of another) or often apparently by no principle at all. One result is a high degree of thematic dispersal and repetitiveness. We hear repeatedly (somewhat monotonously) that Johnson was a tremendous conversationalist, and that conversation was his only happiness, but that he despised exaggeration and demonstration, whether of happiness or of sorrow, pessimism or optimism; he disliked all cant, hyperbole, prating, unprofitable " chat " about solemn subjects; next to conversation, he loved travelling and was scornful of the dangers supposedly incident to it; he defended children against their parents, and poor people against the world; he was chronically charitable and loved the company of the low and mean. Those are some of the main motifs, things Mrs. Thrale has learned in eighteen years of her converse with Johnson. (At two places she laments her many lost opportunities to record their conversations. She despised one way of doing this which she said she had witnessed in her own house, a trick of writing down his words even as he was speaking.) But beyond all else that she attempts to recall in her *Anecdotes*, runs the theme of what she calls his " roughness," " harshness," " asperity," or " coarseness," the savage polemic spirit which had become the settled habit of

---

[19] *Anecdotes*, p. 154.

his conversation in his later years. He is prompt to give and prompt to take offense—easily, suddenly, and violently angered. Sometimes he repents or regrets. But in general his talk is arrogant, and his silence supercilious. Mrs. Thrale experiences " horror " or " disgust." He says very contemptuous things of the female sex. (A favorite way of bullying the female is to find fault with her dress—send her back upstairs to change.) One page in every five or six of the *Anecdotes* is embellished with illustrations and reflections upon such themes. The illustrations are convincing.

"I would advise you, Sir (said he with a cold sneer), never to relate this story again: you really can scarce imagine how *very poor* a figure you make in the telling of it." [20]

"Do not forget dear Dick Sir, said I, as he went out of the coach: he turned back, stood still two minutes on the carriage-step—"When I have written my letter for Dick, I may hang myself, mayn't I?"—and turned away in a very ill humour indeed.[21]

"*Sit down, Sir!*" [22]

Mr. Johnson did not like any one who said they were happy, or who said any one else was so. . . . "If your sister-in-law is really the contented being she professes herself Sir (said he), her life gives the lie to every research of humanity; for she is happy without health, without beauty, without money, and without understanding." [23]

The creature displayed before us in such passages as we have been quoting, looming behind other repellent odds and ends, and wreathed in the girlish graces of the lady's style, has little inner principle except that of savage neurosis. He is an assemblage of grotesque features and gesticulations. Perhaps at best he deserves the label affixed by a recent *Hudson Review* essay entitled " The Ogre at the Feast of Life." [24] He bears somewhat the same relation to Boswell's Johnson as Falstaff by the Queen's command in *The Merry Wives* bears to the companion of the Prince at the Boar's Head Tavern; or as caricatures of Johnson by Rowlandson bear to portraits by Johnson's friend Sir Joshua. He may be laughably agitated in trivial ways. But he is not really lively or lifelike. As Mrs. Thrale creates no coherent Johnson of her own, her clutter

[20] *Anecdotes*, p. 91.
[21] *Anecdotes*, p. 126.
[22] *Anecdotes*, p. 188.
[23] *Anecdotes*, p. 181.
[24] Marvin Mudrick, *Hudson Review*, 23 (Summer, 1970), 278-92.

of anecdotes must be referred to Boswell. We measure the figure she gives us inevitably by Boswell.*

If we assume that, as seems likely, all of Mrs. Thrale-Piozzi's anecdotes represent more or less faithfully some Johnsonian episode (either actually experienced by her or known by hearsay), we may say that she participated too simply in the mania of her age for anecdote, and that, even in her inaccuracies, she was a victim of an inadequate theory of narration expounded more than once in her hearing by Johnson himself, who, in reiterating his doctrine that a story, to be interesting, must be true, did not usually distinguish between the literal truth of a particular event and the general or symbolic truth of its human significance. He did not enjoy (as Irving Babbitt has argued), or at least he did not confess to, an adequate notion of the truth of fiction.

The phlegmatic glutton Henry Thrale was the steadying influence that made possible the relation between the spirited lady and the suffering sage. When Thrale was gone, that relation deteriorated rapidly. The closing pages of her *Anecdotes* are torn with her conflicting memories. She was writing, as Professor Clifford observes, in haste to publish, at a distance from some of her records, and with the double purpose of becoming famous as a biographer and of justifying her later treatment of Johnson. She vibrates between reiterated expressions of piety to the memory of the best and greatest man she has ever known and angry recollections of the escalating bad temper and irrationality of his closing years. She will say that she saw Johnson only in a tranquil uniform state, a " mere *candlelight*,"[25] and she will illustrate his manners with the examples we have quoted above. She will say on one page [26] that no man ever required fewer ministrations for his comfort, and ten pages later she will pour out a torrent of resentment in the recital of his exorbitant demands.

When there was nobody to restrain his dislikes, it was extremely difficult to find anybody with whom he could converse, without living always on the verge of a quarrel. . . . I . . . found it convenient, for every reason of health, peace, and pecuniary circumstance, to retire to Bath,

---

* On rereading, I conclude that my treatment of Mrs. Thrale's *Anecdotes* has been on the whole somewhat over simple and too severe. For a more sympathetic interpretation I recommend the essay by Virginia Woolf cited below in my last paragraph.

[25] *Anecdotes*, p. 157.
[26] *Anecdotes*, p. 176.

where I knew Mr. Johnson would not follow me, and where I could for that reason command some little portion of time for my own use; a thing impossible while I remained at Streatham or at London, as my hours, carriage, and servants had long been at his command, who would not rise in the morning till twelve o'clock perhaps, and oblige me to make breakfast for him till the bell rung for dinner, though much displeased if the toilet was neglected, and though much of the time we passed together was spent in blaming or deriding, very justly, my neglect of economy, and waste of that money which might make many families happy.

Veneration for his virtue, reverence for his talents, delight in his conversation, and habitual endurance of a yoke my husband first put upon me ... made me go on so long with Mr. Johnson; but the perpetual confinement I will own to have been terrifying in the first years of our friendship, and irksome in the last.[27]

In a rude hodge-podge way, Mrs. Thrale-Piozzi may have been trying to do what Boswell had done in the *Hebrides Tour*—that is, give a dramatized portrait of Johnson, an interesting chiaroscuro or truthful rounding of opposite traits. Both she and Boswell elicited cries of outrage from the polite part of the London audience —even from friends like Burke and Dr. Burney. Professor Clifford thinks that she came somewhat short of Boswell in artistry—but that in our present age of psychologized biography we ought to find her style amusing. Still it is no light undertaking to put the disgusting and the admirable (and values intermediate to these) together in one artistically satisfactory composition. As an American critic of our time (Mr. J. C. Ransom, himself a not un-Johnsonian figure) has said, contraries are not reconciled simply by being got into the same poem.

James Boswell was more fortunate than Mrs. Thrale in his sex and in geographical distance from Johnson. He was both more fortunate and more skillful in the caliber of the conversationalists in whose company he characteristically recorded Johnson, and in the whole devoted aim of his relation with the great man. For Boswell, Johnson remained a steady beacon to the end. Boswell's Journal of their jaunt to Oxford, only six months before Johnson's death, is written in the eager, cheerful style of the great years. Mrs. Thrale had labored under circumstances unfavorable to a biographer; as chatelaine and hostess, her interest was to preserve concord and decorum. Boswell was a talented provocateur of con-

[27] *Anecdotes,* pp. 185-87.

versation and debate. The relation between Boswell and Johnson was reciprocally beneficial for biography. As Professor Tinker long ago pointed out,[28] there is a sense in which the personal power of Johnson created his biographer Boswell—just as surely as there is a sense in which Boswell created Johnson.

To get on with this paper (as I have said at the start), I have had to assume that the image of Johnson created by Boswell and in our day celebrated notably by Professor Pottle and Professor Rader is a familiar one. The following example from Boswell's record of the year 1773 is chosen for insertion here because of its parallel to motifs we have just been considering. In that year it fell to the lot of Mrs. James Boswell to play the temporary role of a Northern Mrs. Thrale. Boswell and Johnson arrived in Edinburgh after their Hebrides Tour on the 9th of November. Boswell almost immediately had to take up his work during the mornings before the Court of Session. But Johnson stayed on for ten days more of breakfasts, dinners, teas, and suppers, receiving the homage of the Edinburgh literati. "On the mornings when he breakfasted at my house," wrote Boswell in the *Tour,* "he had from ten o'clock till one or two a constant levee of various persons. . . . My wife was so good as to devote the greater part of the morning to the endlesss task of pouring out tea for my friend and his visitors." On his return to London, Johnson wrote back, announcing his safe arrival and remarking: "I know Mrs. Boswell wished me well to go." Boswell inserts the letter in the *Life* and, with characteristic naivete, adds a note: "In this he showed a very acute penetration. My wife paid him the most assiduous and respectful attention while he was our guest; so that I wonder how he discovered her wishing for his departure. The truth is, that his irregular hours and uncouth habits, such as turning the candles with their heads downwards, when they did not burn bright enough, and letting the wax drop upon the carpet, could not but be disagreeable to a lady . . . and what was very natural to a female mind, she thought he had too much influence over her husband." [29]

---

[28] *Dr. Johnson and Fanny Burney* (New York, 1911), pp. xxxvii-xxxviii.

[29] *Boswell's Journal of A Tour to the Hebrides,* ed. Frederick A. Pottle and Charles H. Bennett (New York, 1936), pp. 385-86; *Boswell for the Defence,* ed. William K. Wimsatt and Frederick A. Pottle (London, 1960), p. 205; *Boswell's Life of Johnson,* ed. G. B. Hill and L. F. Powell (Oxford, 1934), II, 268.

II

What of that other guest member of the Streatham household, Mrs. Thrale's attendant nympth, Fanny Burney? Let us touch her gently. Unlike Mrs. Thrale, she would be present in London to bear the anguish of a day-by-day, sometimes hour-by-hour, awareness of Johnson's prolonged final illness. She had literary imagination, she was a writer (as Mrs. Thrale was not). Before her deep entrancement in late youth by the Johnsonian prose model, she produced her one good novel of manners, *Evelina*. She kept a far better journal than Mrs. Thrale, both at her father's house in Leicester Fields and at Streatham. Professor Tinker has pronounced the judgment that her early diaries contain her supreme stylistic and imaginative achievements.[30] *Dr. Johnson and Fanny Burney*, a book extracted from her several memorials by Tinker in 1911, is a volume about one tenth larger than Mrs. Thrale-Piozzi's *Anecdotes*. Fanny Burney did not revise or rearrange her journal for the public of her day. She wrote for " Nobody," as she says, for her own girlish and whimsical self, or for two of her sisters —often with aspirations and graces of the semifictional sort. The record of her Johnsonian years has been substantially published, despite some mutilations inflicted by the prudently aging Madame D'Arblay and some deletions by her early editors. Even some of her more painful notations of Johnson's violence have recently been exhumed from the Berg Collection by Joyce Hemlow.[31] The account that she gives of the Streatham Johnson is far better dramatized than Mrs. Thrale's; it is centered in a far more realizable figure. Professor Tinker thought her superior to Boswell in dramatic sketching. The scene in which Johnson is quizzed by the Streathamites about the kitchen arrangements at Bolt Court [32] is indeed equal if not superior in sustained finesse to anything in Boswell. Still Miss Burney gives us characteristically a picture of an excited little girl being cuddled by an affectionate, if frightful-looking old bear. She admired his playfulness, his " fun," his " comical humour," and his " love of nonsense." [33] We have her own testimony, recorded during the years when she was keeper of

---

[30] *Dr. Johnson and Fanny Burney*, pp. xix-xx.

[31] " Dr. Johnson and Fanny Burney—Some Additions to the Record " in *Johnsonian Studies*, ed. Magdi Wahba (Cairo, 1962), pp. 184-87.

[32] *Dr. Johnson and Fanny Burney*, pp. xxi, 63-71.

[33] *Diary and Letters of Madame D'Arblay*, ed. Austin Dobson, I (London, 1904), 211; letter to Samuel Crisp, March, 1779.

the robes to Queen Charlotte, that Boswell waited in vain upon her outside Windsor Castle. "We have seen him long enough upon stilts. . . . Grave Sam, and Great Sam, and solemn Sam, and learned Sam. . . . Now I want to entwine a wreath of the graces across his brow; I want to show him as gay Sam, agreeable Sam, pleasant Sam; so you must help me with some of his beautiful billets to yourself." [34]

She had been not quite twenty-five when she first saw Johnson, as he was brought to the Burney home by Mrs. Thrale.

He is tall and stout; but stoops terribly; he is almost bent double. His mouth is almost continually opening and shutting, as if he were chewing. He has a strange method of frequently twirling his fingers, and twisting his hands. His body is in continual agitation, *see-sawing* up and down; his feet are never a moment quiet; in short, his whole person is in *perpetual motion*.[35]

About a year and a half later, Fanny Burney was carried to Streatham on the wave of her semi-anonymous success with *Evelina*. As she becomes domesticated there and experiences the conversation of great persons, her journal speeds up somewhat and crowds in more information, usually in less complete pictures. Still it continues a good journal, and a chronological narrative (even though she was careless of dates).

"Miss Burney," said Mrs. Thrale, "is fond of the *Vicar of Wakefield:* and so am I;—don't you like it, sir?"
"No, madam, it is very faulty; there is nothing of real life in it, and very little of nature. It is a mere fanciful performance."
He then seated himself upon a sofa, and calling to me, said, "Come,—Evelina,—come and sit by me."
I obeyed; and he took me almost in his arms,—that is, one of his arms, for one would go three times, at least, round me,—and, half-laughing, half-serious, he charged me to "be a good girl!" [36]

III

I am moved to insert here as a tailpiece a passage from Boswell's *Hebrides Journal,* which is none the worse because I have alluded to it once before.[37] It gives both Boswell and Johnson an obvious

[34] *Dr. Johnson and Fanny Burney,* p. 202; October 1790.
[35] *Dr. Johnson and Fanny Burney,* pp. 2-3; 27 March 1777.
[36] *Dr. Johnson and Fanny Burney,* p. 38.
[37] "The Fact Imagined: James Boswell" in *Hateful Contraries* (University of Kentucky Press, 1965), p. 170.

advantage in that they are recorded in a situation where Mrs. Thrale and Burney would have had to be much more like the equestrian Celia Fiennes [38] in order to have followed them.

Sunday 12 September. It was a fine day. . . . All the family walked down to the shore to see us depart. . . . Raasay himself went with us in a large boat with eight oars, built in his island. So did worthy Malcolm. So did Mr. Donald Macqueen. Dr. MacLeod, two of Raasay's sons, and their tutor. . . . We spoke of death. Mr. Johnson gave us a short discourse worth any sermon, saying that the reflections of some men as to dying easily were idle talk. . . . "No wise man will be contented to die if he thinks he is to go into a state of punishment. Nay, no wise man will be contented to die if he thinks he is to fall into annihilation. For however bad any man's existence may be, every man would rather have it than not exist at all. No, there is no rational principle by which a man can be contented, but a trust in the mercy of God, through the merits of Jesus Christ." All this delivered with manly eloquence in a boat on the sea, upon a fine autumn Sunday morning, while everyone listened with a comfortable air of satisfaction and complacency, had a most pleasing effect upon my mind. . . . We came into the harbour of Portree, which is a large and good one. There was lying in it a vessel to carry off the emigrants. . . . We approached her, and she hoisted her colours.[39]

It occurs to me that in the context of the present day, I am likely to be censured for sexism, or the implication that the feminine intelligence *per se* fell short of an adequate response to the majestic sage. It is likely I may be charged with taking revenge upon both Mrs. Thrale and Burney for some acid sketches that they wrote of Boswell in action. It is true that I might have said something about the relatively weak prose portraits of Johnson by his male friends the painter Sir Joshua or the learned scholar Bishop Percy. Yet I found these less instructive. And on the other hand, it is true that in the early part of our century, another lady, Virginia Woolf, in a vignette to be found in her *Second Common Reader*, has accurately lifted materials from both Mrs. Thrale and Burney and has heightened them to a degree where they shimmer brightly as fictive imagination; it is a Johnsonian scene before which the male scholar happily bows in homage. I will be content to argue that the ladies of Johnson's own time were not his destined best portrayers. The few who were his intimates were no doubt among

---

[38] Author of *Through England on a Side-Saddle*, 1688. See Elizabeth W. Manwaring, *Italian Landscape in Eighteenth Century England* (London, 1927), p. 6.
[39] *Boswell's Journal of a Tour to the Hebrides* (1936), pp. 153-56.

the most gifted of the time. Yet they were too, in large part, what the men of their time wished them to be, and what they themselves no doubt wished to be. Let us not omit to mention Henry Thrale's favorite the beautiful Miss Sophia Streatfield, who combined a knowledge of Greek with the gift of being able to weep at will, and more prettily than any other woman, and who sometimes obliged the company with a demonstration.[40] We must add, however, that both the men and the women of the company would laugh at her immoderately—something that is not always mentioned when this anecdote from Miss Burney's *Diary* is retailed. Even the most characteristic flower of a culture is likely to find its critics within that culture. And sometimes both flower and critic inhabit the same person. The mind of an age is a tree with at least three blackbirds in it.

Yale University

---

[40] *Diary and Letters of Madame D'Arblay*, ed. Austin Dobson, I (London, 1904), 210, 237-41.

REFLECTIONS ON THE LETTER: THE RECONCILIATION OF DISTANCE AND PRESENCE IN *PAMELA*

BY ROY ROUSSEL

> Who would not choose, when necessary absence ... deprive her of the person of her charming friend, to have a delight in retiring to her closet, and there, by pen and ink, continue, and, as I may say, perpetuate, the ever agreeable and innocent pleasures that flow from social love, from hearts united by the same laudable ties?
>
> . . . . .
>
> . . . . .
>
> Who then shall decline the converse of the pen? The pen that makes distance, presence; and brings back to sweet remembrance all the delights of presence; which makes even presence but body, while absence becomes the soul. . . .[1]

I

For Richardson, familiar letters are the product of a paradoxical double movement in the writer's consciousness. On the one hand, they are the result of an act of retirement in which the writer closets himself from the world. Written "either morning or evening, before needful avocations take place, or after they have been answered" (L, III, 247), the letter is composed in the solitude of the self alone and speaks for the almost obsessive need for privacy that Richardson shares with many of his characters. "The pen," he writes, "is jealous of company. It expects, as I may say, to engross the writer's whole self; everybody allows the writer to withdraw: it disdains company; and will have the entire attention" (L, III, 247).

Yet if letters and letter-writing reflect the writer's withdrawal from the "company" of others, it is not a withdrawal which implies the writer's independence from the world around him.

---

[1] *The Correspondence of Samuel Richardson* (New York, 1966), III, 244-46. All references to Richardson's letters are to this edition.

Richardson's letters lack the meditative quality of a mind reflecting on itself which his emphasis on withdrawal might suggest. They are, instead, letters in the true sense of the word; that is, they are written to someone. Even the most didactic of them are not monologues. On the contrary they are extremely conversational; filled with comments and questions which invoke the response of a reader who is there not simply as an excuse for writing but as a full and immediate presence.

The withdrawal of the writer, then, is balanced by a seemingly contradictory movement which carries him to an intimate union with another. If he conceals himself from the company of those around him, it is only to reveal himself in a letter which " will shew soul and meaning " (L, III, 252) and which is " indicative, generally beyond the power of disguise, of the mind of the writer " (L, III, 244). If he disengages himself from " needful avocations " (L. III, 247) it is only to fill the resulting void with " the ever agreeable and innocent pleasures that flow from social love, from hearts united " (L, 244-45).

The letter is the form in which character manifests itself in Richardson's fiction, and the tension between presence and absence, company and retirement, implicit in his conception of the letter defines an equivalent tension in his conception of human nature. For Pamela and B, this tension is at the center of the conflict between love and society which informs their story.

II

" .... Wise Providence
Does various parts for various minds dispense:
The *meanest slaves,* or those who *hedge* and *ditch,*
Are useful, by their sweat, to feed the *rich.*
The *rich,* in due return, impart their store;
Which comfortably feeds the lab'ring *poor.*
Nor let the *rich* the *lowest slave* disdain:
He's *equally* a *link* of Nature's *chain*:
Labours to the *same end,* joins in *one view;*
And *both alike* the *will divine* pursue. . . ."[2]

This passage, which Pamela cites in an attack on Lady Davers' pride, suggests that Richardson saw society as a divinely ordained

[2] Samuel Richardson, *Pamela* (New York, 1958), p. 272. All references to *Pamela* are to this edition.

structure in which each individual, in fulfilling his " part," fulfills as well his duty to his fellow man and to God. What is important, however, is less the presence of this traditional image of society than the particular tonality it takes on in the novel, and as a key to this tonality the poem is somewhat deceptive. The poem suggests that a reciprocity exists between classes which balances their separation so that each " Labours to the *same end,* joins in *one view.*" With the possible exception of Pamela's comments on the duties of her role as B's wife, however, there is little of this sense of communion in the novel. There is little feeling that not only roles but the whole structure of social conventions mediates between people in a positive way.

Instead, Richardson concentrates on the way in which a man's " part " in society allows him to separate himself from others. One of the words which appear obsessively in *Pamela* is the word " distance," and one of its important uses is to define the relation between different classes. His jest, Pamela tells B, " is not a jest that becomes the distance between a master and a servant " (P, 29) to which Mrs. Jervis replies " don't be so pert to his honour: you should know your distance " (P, 29), and Pamela answers, " It is very difficult to keep one's distance to the greatest of men, when they won't keep it themselves to their meanest servants " (P, 30). Altogether, the term " distance " or some variation of it is used in this context 16 times in the first 50 pages, a frequency which suggests how important this separation is for Richardson and how it overshadows any reciprocity which might exist between classes.

In both *Pamela* and *Clarissa,* however, Richardson uses distance in another way. According to Pamela the most important lesson taught to her by Mr. B's mother was to " *keep the men at a distance* " (P, 210). Lady Davers advises Pamela in a like manner to " keep the fellows at a distance " (P, 8) and Mr. B asks Mrs. Jervis if Pamela " kept the men at a distance " (P, 11). In these instances " distance " functions to define the clear area which modesty or privacy requires, and the duality of this key term suggests that for Richardson the structure of society—not just the order of classes but the whole system of usages and manners—is important precisely because it serves to protect the self from any outside intrusion. This protective function of social forms is particularly apparent in *Clarissa.* Here Lovelace's need to " open my whole soul "[3] to Clarissa makes him an enemy not only of the distance between them—" I cannot bear to be kept at this distance from you " (C, II, 375), he tells her—but also of the social properties which Clarissa, " a *lover of forms*" (C, II, 245), uses to create this distance. " Had she not thus kept me at arm's length," he writes, " had she not denied me those innocent liberties which our sex, from step to step, aspire to; could I but have gained access to her in her hours of heedlessness and dishabille [for full dress creates dignity, augments consciousness, and compels distance] we had been familiarized to each other long ago " (C, II, 341). The relation between Clarissa and Lovelace, however, is only a reflection of that between Pamela and B. It is clear that when B complains to Pamela during their first meeting in the summer-house that " you always fly me when I come near you " (P, 15) and she replies, " It does not become your poor servant to stay in your presence, sir, without your business required it; and I hope I shall always know my place " (P, 15-16), her implicit assertion of " the distance that fortune made between us " (P, 17) is less the abstract statement of a social ideology than a deeply felt need to enforce a protective separation between them.

Because the forms of society maintain a distance between its members, men are able to exist at ease with one another in Richardson's world. Without these forms, they would be subject continuously to the fearful uneasiness which assails Pamela after her mistress dies and she no longer has a clearly defined role in the world of B's Bedfordshire estate. But these forms are not sufficient; if they were, there would be no novel *Pamela*. The novel begins with the emergence of another force at the center of the ordered image of society we find in its pages. This force is love. It is love which precipitates the action of *Pamela*, for if it is true that the novel begins at the moment when Pamela's position in B's household is made ambivalent, this is so only because the death of his mother allows all of B's latent feeling toward Pamela to crystalize.

Love is the emergence of a need to be present to another and to be confirmed by another in an immediate way. It is born in the isolation of a self distanced from others in the same way the writer's movement toward union with his correspondent is born in the soli-

---

[3] Samuel Richardson, *Clarissa* (New York, 1932), II, 375. All references to *Clarissa* are to this edition.

tude created by his need for privacy, by his withdrawal from company. The movement of love, too, seeks to transcend this separation. For this reason Richardson always associates it with a loss of rational control, with a loss, in other words, of a sense of independent and self-contained existence, and with the lover's desire to negate the distance on which this existence had been founded. The birth of the violent force of love at the center of a self so frail, so neuralgically sensitive, that it could not bear the closeness of another is the great mystery in Richardson's world, and his characters experience its presence as the presence of an unknown force which leaves them " vexed and confused " (P, 17) at their own actions. " But love is not a voluntary thing," Pamela writes, "*Love*, did I say?—But come, I hope not:—At least it is not, I hope, gone so far as to make me *very* uneasy: For I know not *how* it came, nor *when* it began; but crept, crept it has like a thief, upon me; and before I knew what was the matter, it looked like love " (P, 260).

III

It is with the birth of love that Richardson's characters confront the full demands of selfhood. Born from the struggle between privacy and desire, they can achieve completion only insofar as they can resolve this tension. Such a tension is at the center of both Pamela's and B's experience in the novel, but because love comes most violently to B, it is his story which best testifies to its acuteness in Richardson's world.

The fact that we see B through the eyes of Pamela and, consequently, see him primarily as an aggressor, obscures the references which suggest that a certain defensive privacy has played an important part in his life. Until he met Pamela, Mr. B was a man who was " averse to matrimony upon any terms " (P, 437). His initial objections to marrying Pamela have less to do with his class consciousness than they do with his general aversion to marriage and the involvement it implies. He cannot " endure," he tells Pamela, " the thought of marriage, even with a person of equal or superior degree to myself " (P, 223), and it is clear that before his encounter with Pamela, B is a man in whom the need for union with another has lain dormant, one who has lived at a comfortable remove from those around him.

Mr. B's self-sufficient privacy ends during his meeting with Pamela in the summer-house early in the novel: "I do own to you," he is to tell Pamela later, "that I love you with a purer flame than ever I knew in my whole life; a flame to which I was a stranger; and which commenced for you in the garden" (P, 279). The most immediate effect of this new force in B's life is the destruction of that control on which his previous independence had been based. This scene begins with B presenting himself to Pamela in his role as her master whose "business does require" (P, 16) Pamela's presence. B established this role, however, only to discover himself forced by the "purer flame" (P, 279) of love to abandon it. It is important to understand that when he seizes Pamela and violates both literally and figuratively the distance between them, he is not acting with the cynical callousness of a rake. At this moment, Pamela remarks, B looks "I don't know how; wildly, I thought" (P, 16), and B later says to Mrs. Jervis that he was "bewitched by her . . . to be freer than became me" (P, 29). Instead, as these passages make clear, he is caught in the sudden flood of an emotion which, in carrying him toward an intimacy with Pamela, negates the separateness which is the foundation of his old self.

The movement of B in this scene from reserved master to lover, a movement which characterizes so many of the encounters between B and Pamela, defines again the tension between two opposing concepts of the self. More than this, however, B's experience here reveals why it is that the self's commitment to privacy and distance is not simply swept away by the emergence of love. It explains why B struggles so hard in the summer-house to regain control and, in telling Pamela that "I own I have demeaned myself; but it was only to try you" (P, 17), to reassert himself in his protective role as master. The reason for this is simple. When B is seized by love and forced to violate the distance between himself and Pamela, he is forced as well to reveal himself to her. One of the words which constantly appear in opposition to distance in the novel is the word "expose." "And so I am to be exposed" (P, 24), B remarks when he discovers Pamela has told Mrs. Jervis about their encounter in the summer-house. "You may well be ashamed," he tells Pamela later, ". . . after your noise and nonsense, and exposing me as you have done" (P, 28). Again, he complains, " I have pert saucy answers from you, besides exposing me by your letters " (P, 71).[4]

To be exposed is to be humiliated, it is to demean yourself. But even more, it is to be delivered into the power of another. In Richardson's world, as in the world of Restoration Comedy, access to another brings with it the possession of his identity. The uneasiness which Richardson exhibits toward love derives from the fact that love forces you to reveal yourself, and, therefore, deliver yourself, to another. It is this fact that is behind B's sense that he has been " robbed " (P, 55) by Pamela, as well as behind the feeling we have that because he is in Pamela's power, the roles of master and servant have been reversed. " O how poor and mean must those actions be," writes Pamela, " and how little must they make the best of gentlemen look, when they offer such things as are unworthy of themselves, and put it into the power of their inferiors to be greater than they! " (P, 17).

Richardson's sense of the dangers of exposing oneself to others is revealed in a special way in his correspondence with Lady Bradshaigh. Under the assumed name of Belfour, Lady Bradshaigh had written him to plead for a happy ending to *Clarissa*. During the exchange of letters which followed, she was able to maintain this pseudonym for over a year, and, although their relationship was casual, Richardson was unable to live comfortably with the sense that he was known by Lady Bradshaigh in a way that he did not know her. His letters are filled with intense and repetitious complaints that her refusal to acknowledge her true identity is founded in a " wantoness of power " (L, IV, 318, 343), that she is a " lover of power " (L, IV, 339), and that she is making him " one of her diversions " (L, IV, 321). His feelings that her knowledge of him gave her a power which he did not share were intensified when, in what she later confessed was " a desire to see you, without being known " (L, IV, 376), she persuades him to take Sunday afternoon walks in Hyde Park on the promise of meeting him there. It is a promise which, of course, she did not keep, and Richardson writes bitterly that he would never have appeared " could I have imagined that hating a crowd, a gay

---

[4] B is afraid of Pamela's ability to expose him to others, but such an ability obviously presupposes that she has some special access to him. See for example his request to Pamela after their engagement not to " expose me any more than is necessary for your justification " (P, 259).

crowd especially, it was expected that I walk up and down the Mall, exposing myself, as I may say, to the observation of a lady whom I have never had the honour to see" (L, IV, 371).

Not only Richardson's letters to Lady Bradshaigh, but the tenor of much of his correspondence remind us how much the tension in *Pamela* between exposure and concealment, distance and involvement, was a part of his own life. Richardson's interest in the novel was certainly centered on Pamela, but it is equally true that his heart was in some way with B and that B's situation of being exposed was one he understood fully. More than this, however, these letters give us an insight into the logic of the fear of exposure in Richardson's world. Despite the most obvious implications of Richardson's emphasis on privacy, it is clear from the extremely abstract quality exposure has both in his work and in his letters to Lady Bradshaigh that it would be a mistake to associate his fear of exposure with any idea that the self in Richardson is defined by something hidden and concrete, such as a secret. Lady Bradshaigh does not know any actual secret concerning Richardson, for example, nor does Pamela know anything about B which makes her a real danger to him. Even when Pamela convinces Parson Williams to tell Sir Simon about her kidnapping his only reaction is to say, "He hurts no family by this" (P, 138). The fear of exposure in both Richardson and his characters is not founded on the practical consequences of revelation. Instead, this fear and the shyness with which it is associated seem to result from another cause. In the beginning, his characters are defined by a role which distances them from others. Defined by this distance, they are defined by the nothingness which surrounds them rather than by their substantial relation to something or someone outside themselves. Since they lack such a concrete relation and the positive sense of self it would provide, their experience of their self is an experience of something ephemeral. Faced with the intuition of their own insubstantiality, they seem to be attempting by their shyness to conceal this insubstantiality from others.

The exposure which accompanies love is not a threat, then, because it delivers to the beloved the kind of pre-existing self which could be associated with a secret that the beloved had discovered. Instead, in Richardson love itself constitutes at the center of the lover's ephemerality a new and more substantial self-awareness. It is a self-awareness, however, whose only source is paradoxically the relationship which love has established between the lover and the beloved. Richardson's lovers exist for themselves more intensely after the birth of love, but the new intensity of their awareness is curiously alienated because its source lies outside them. After the awakening of his love for Pamela, B is defined by the new "shapes" (P, 44) into which love has transformed him. But these shapes are only the forms of his love for Pamela. In the same way, when Lovelace asks Clarissa to "take me to yourself, mould me as you please ... give me your own impression" (C, II, 80), he is not delivering his self to her so much as he is asking her to constitute this self for him in a new way.

The fear of exposure in Richardson must be read in this context. This fear grows from the recognition that, with the advent of love, the very form of the lover's new self will be determined by another. The term "expose" expresses both the character's initial experience of love as a rupture of the bounds of his privacy, a rupture which allows the beloved to shape him in this way, and his recognition that because the beloved is now the ground of his self he must continue to remain open to her. Exposure is accompanied by fear in Richardson because, in the world of his novels, this is not a reciprocal relationship. In the beginning, B feels himself defined by Pamela, yet he does not serve in an equivalent way as the ground of her self. It is because Pamela maintains her independence while serving as the source of B's self-awareness that he feels possessed by her.

Since love threatens such a possession by another, its appearance is not a blessed relief from solitude but a trauma. Torn between the need for involvement with Pamela and the necessity for some kind of protective separation which this need makes even more acute, B finds himself literally at the center of a war between love and distance. "He then took me in his arms," Pamela writes, "and presently pushed me from him. Mrs. Jervis, said he, take the little witch from me; I can neither bear, nor forbear her— (Strange words these!)—But stay; you shan't go!;—Yet begone! —No, come back again" (P, 53-54). The story of B and Pamela is the story of his attempts to resolve those opposing claims.

IV

The most obvious course open to B is for him to turn his back on love, to allow Pamela to return home and to live at his former distance from those around him. Such a strategy is suggested by B's periodic attempts to reassert his role as master as well as by the time when he is actually on the point of allowing her to leave. Yet we never feel this is a real alternative for B; we never feel that once their relationship is opened it can be abandoned by either. Although Richardson's characters first experience love as something alien to their former lives, it is the manifestation of a need so fundamental that, once awakened, it cannot be lain to rest.

If B cannot banish love then he must come to terms with it. To do this, he must somehow redress the balance of power which exists between himself and Pamela. Power over another, however, is a function, as we have seen, of one's ability to gain access to the other's consciousness. Pamela's power over B lies in the access to him which his love for her creates. This imbalance can be equalized only if B can somehow achieve an equivalent access to Pamela's consciousness.

It is the desire for such an equality which is behind even the most physical of B's advances toward Pamela. B's actual attacks on her—the scenes in the summer-house and her room, her kidnapping and near rape—are the first and most basic expression of that movement toward another which comes with the birth of love. As such, they are not intended to neutralize Pamela's threat to B by reducing her to the level of an object. Instead, they attempt, in B's own words to Pamela, to "frighten you from your reservedness" (P, 82). These attacks are efforts to unveil Pamela's self through an act of violence equivalent in effect to the action of love on B's own sense of discrete selfhood; efforts which, if successful, would leave Pamela exposed to B in the same way he is exposed to her.

B's attempt to come to know Pamela through the immediate and forceful destruction of the grounds of her separateness is implicit in the heavily metaphorical weight which dress, and therefore disrobement, carry in the novel. Generally in Richardson dress is associated with those social forms which, in compelling " consciousness " and " distance " (C, II, 341), protect the privacy of the self. Pamela's care in choosing her clothes when she thinks she will return to her parents illustrates how strongly the association of dress with the distance between classes is present here.

More specifically, however, Pamela's dress is the constant hiding place of those letters which contain her "heart" (P, 240) and "private thoughts" (P, 236). It is no accident, then, that Pamela's bosom is both the most frequent hiding-place of her papers and the locus of most of B's advances toward her. This association implies both that her modesty functions to protect a psychological rather than a purely physical integrity, and that B's desire for Pamela is a desire to force access to her self rather than the expression of a physical need.

If violence could destroy Pamela's reserve and force her to reveal herself to B, then perhaps the promise of love could be fulfilled. Each would then have an immediate access to the other and there would exist, in the words of Richardson to Lady Bradshaigh, a "communication so equal, and so just" (L, IV, 340). In this relationship, each would know as he is known. Each would find the ground of his self in the other and their relationship would be one of mutual openness.

The instances of B's aggressiveness toward Pamela, however, record not only his attempt to achieve openness in this manner but the failure of this attempt as well. Those moments when B seems on the point of actually forcing the barrier of Pamela's reserve are precisely the moments when her consciousness disappears. Pamela's fainting spells, which are in each case caused by B's disarrangement of her clothing, are neither instances of feminine hypocrisy nor simply dramatic effects. Instead they reflect the extent to which, for Richardson, the self is initially something ephemeral. This interior consciousness is, it seems, so sensitive and so insubstantial that it cannot willingly stand the direct light of another's gaze. When Lady Bradshaigh writes to Richardson that while she is not precisely "afraid to his face ... it is something that reigns in my freedom of speech" (L, VI, 9), she is reading the mind of her correspondent perfectly, for there is always a sense in his work that a direct confrontation with an other brings a kind of paralysis and fear which prevents "communication" (L, IV, 340) from developing. Since this is true, the attempt to open another's self by a forceful intrusion into his privacy will fail as the inevitable consequence of its success.

B himself recognizes this when, immediately after his attempted rape, he remarks, "I have begun wrong: for I see terror does but add to her frost; but she is a charming girl, and may be thawed by kindness; and I should have melted her by love, instead of freezing her by fear" (P, 218). B's comment is, however, misleading, for he seems to forget that he has, in fact, tried to thaw Pamela by kindness. Even during the rape itself when he tells Pamela, "You see now you are in my power!—You cannot get away from me, nor help yourself: Yet I have not offered any thing amiss to you" (P, 213), he seems more interested in persuading Pamela freely to reveal herself than he is in forcing her revelation. This is particularly true in the scene early in the novel when B confesses to Pamela that he loves her. Here he adopts a milder, more temperate course. When, in this meeting, he forces himself to " stoop " and " beg " Pamela to " behave yourself with kindness to me " (P, 82) and limits himself to holding her hand B seems to be trying not to negate totally the distance between them but simply to lessen it.

B's restraint here suggests another strategy. Like the way of aggression, this strategy is aimed at affecting some kind of direct access to Pamela, but it hopes to accomplish this through a gradual process. If B could contain his own fear of Pamela, if he could control the initial impulse to violate the other which comes from being exposed, then perhaps Pamela's reaction to him would be less extreme and she could be coaxed rather than forced from her reserve.

No such gradual process takes place, however. B attempts at certain crucial times to restrain himself and to quiet her fears with gentleness, but these attempts always end in frustration. The failure of B's various strategies, but, more particularly, of these more tempered advances, marks the real extent of the self's mistrust of others in Richardson's fiction. This distrust is, it appears, so fundamental that any direct approach to another, no matter how circumspect, appears as a threat. It is this fear which prevents Pamela alone in the novel from recognizing the true nature of B's feelings for her. It prevents her from seeing B as anything but an encroacher on her privacy, and it inhibits Pamela's love for B, a love which has always been there potentially, from actualizing itself.

v

If these were the only alternatives open to B and, consequently, this fear of the other were the determining factor in the novel, then B would be forced to live continuously at the center of the tension between distance and presence, and *Pamela* would be a tragedy. This is not the case, however, for there is one more course open to B, one final way to resolve the conflict in which they find themselves. This way returns us once more to our starting-point: the nature of the letter.

As we have seen, the familiar letter incorporates two paradoxical movements in the mind of the writer. It is the result of an act of retirement from the " needful avocations " (L, III, 247) of the social life. Yet its function is to present the self to another in a particularly naked way. We remember that the language of correspondence is, for Richardson, perfectly transparent. It is " indicative, generally beyond the power of disguise, of the mind of the writer " (L, III, 244) and shows " soul " (L, III, 252) as well as meaning. Because of this transparency, the access to the writer's self which the letter allows the correspondent is not the removed and mediated relationship established by social usages, but instead the same kind of direct and intimate openness which love gives to the beloved.

The letter is, in this way, not only a statement of the tension between love and distance in Richardson. It is also the instrument which resolves this tension. Because it shows " soul " (L, III, 252) it enables the correspondent to achieve that intimacy with the writer which is signified by Richardson's phrase " hearts united " (L, III, 245). At the same time, because the writer is protected by that " absence " which " becomes the soul " (L, III, 246), this intimacy is established without any destructive intrusion into the privacy of the writer. For Richardson, letters do make " distance, presence " (L, III, 246), and it is the ability of correspondence to effect this reconciliation that allows us to understand the role her journal plays in the marriage of B and Pamela.

Composed largely in the " refuge " (P, 367) of her closet, Pamela's journal is associated with the withdrawal of the writer. It records all her " private thoughts " (P, 236) and, like the letter, records them in a transparent style. "I don't remember what I wrote," Pamela remarks after Mrs. Jewkes finds her papers, " yet I know I wrote my heart " (P, 240). Pamela's journal, moreover, not only embodies her heart, but, with the intentionality implicit in the letter form, reveals it as well. Like Richardson's own letters, Pamela's writings are characterized by their essential reference to a correspondent. Even when she is most isolated, immediately after her kidnapping, she begins her account, "O My Dearest Father and Mother!" although she continues, "I have no hope now what I write can be conveyed to your hands" (P, 98). This epistolary quality of her journal is recognized by both her and B. When B confronts her with the papers his first question is "To whom ... are they written" and she replies, "To my father, sir" (P, 238).

The referential quality of the journal is apparent not only in these characters' reactions to it. More importantly, this quality is inherent too in its content. Like Richardson's own letters, Pamela's journal is not a record of the mind meditating on itself alone. It records no moment in which Pamela, isolated, finds in her interiority the principle of her own existence. As we have seen, even when she is farthest from others she still addresses her writings to them, and this reference is important because it suggests how, for Richardson, the self exists only in its relation to others. Pamela's journal is significantly different in this respect from, for example, Robinson Crusoe's. Both are records of a conversion; that is, they record the birth of a new self. In Crusoe's case this new self can be described in Christian terms as the birth of the new man from the old, or, in secular terms, as the birth of a form of reflexive consciousness.[5] In either case, however, it is primarily a change in the relation of consciousness to itself.

In Pamela's case, however, the conversion is signified primarily by a change in her relation to the other who defines her. Her journal begins by being addressed to her father. Its initial reference is to a relationship which defines her by her place in society. But its content is the growth of her love for B. It contains Pamela's "private thoughts" but these are only "private thoughts of him" (P, 236). The journal records the development of a new self which forms around this love and which will be confirmed only when the journal is delivered to B and read by him.

It is, finally, the ability of the journal to perform this mediation between B and Pamela, to make distance presence, which most fully confirms its epistolary nature. Since Pamela's papers do embody her "heart" (P, 240), in the transparent style of correspondence, they allow B an access to her equivalent to that

[5] For readings of *Robinson Crusoe* in the tradition of Puritan spiritual autobiography see G. A. Starr, *Defoe and Spiritual Autobiography* (Princeton, 1965), pp. 74-125, and J. Paul Hunter, *The Reluctant Pilgrim* (Baltimore, 1966).

which B's love gives to her. The access provided by her writings has always been a mitigating factor between them. Even when B's view of Pamela was limited to the glimpse afforded by her early letters to her parents which B received through John, the "worthiness" (P, 82) which he discovers in her "charming manner of writing" (P, 83) momentarily allays his more paranoid fears of her and allows him to "stoop to beg" (P, 82) her compliance. It is, moreover, the full view of Pamela provided by her journal which stills these fears completely. Here he finds nothing which is not "innocent, lovely, and uniformly beautiful" (P, 317), no "secret of your soul" (P, 227) or "hidden regard for Williams" (P, 227) which would give substance to his feelings that she seeks to manipulate him. And it is because her writings expose Pamela in the same way that his love exposes him, because it establishes a "communication, so equal, and so just" (L, IV, 340) that he turns his thoughts toward marriage. "If my mind hold," he tells her, "and I can see those former papers of yours, and that these in my pocket give me no cause to alter my opinion, I will endeavour to defy the world and the world's censures, and make my Pamela amends . . ." (P, 253).

It is important to understand, however, that Pamela's writings allow B this access in a way which preserves the distance between them. It involves neither the face-to-face confrontation which, Lady B reminds us, "hinders conversation" (L, VI, 9) nor the even more destructive intrusion figured in B's attempted rape. Although they do talk about them together, B never reads her papers in Pamela's immediate presence. Even in the scene where B reads her account of her attempted escape while they are together in the garden, Pamela insists on partially withdrawing. "Let me walk about, at a little distance," she tells him, "for I cannot bear the thought" (P, 251).

Pamela herself implicitly acknowledges the double function of her journal in the first stanza of the song she sings for Sir Simon.

> Go, happy paper, gently steal,
> And underneath her pillow lie;
> There, in soft dreams, my love reveal,
> That love which I must still conceal,
> And, wrapt in awful silence die. (P, 303)

Like the happy papers of Pamela's song, her letters do reveal as they conceal, allowing her to withdraw to a safe remove at the moment of their greatest intimacy. It is appropriate, then, that the final reconciliation of B and Pamela should come through B's letter to Pamela. Motivated by the " affection which they (Pamela's papers) have rivetted upon me " (P, 259) B's letter is in every sense a response to her writings. It is composed at that moment when Pamela, returning home, is furthest from him. Yet it is just this distance which frees B to express most clearly his love for Pamela, and to compose that letter which allows her to discover in him " so much openness, so much affection, so much honour, too, (which was all I had before doubted, and kept me on the reserve) " (P, 260).

VI

The removal of this last " reserve " leads Pamela to her first full confession of her love for B. After this point, their relation is never in doubt, and the meaning of this is clear. In Richardson's world, it seems, men and women must first become correspondents before they can become man and wife. The marriage of Pamela and B appears in this context as a natural development of the knowledge of the other which each has gained through their exchange of letters. Secure in this knowledge, each can accept the power over themselves which love has given the other. " Kind, lovely charmer! " B tells Pamela, " now do I see you are to be trusted with power, from the generous use you make of it! " (P, 352). Because he trusts her in this way he consents to be her " prisoner " and put on " the most agreeable fetters that ever man wore " (P, 307). In an equivalent way Pamela now is able to place a " generous confidence " (P, 264) in B and rest calmly in the assurance that she will be " generously used " (P, 264).

Pamela's and B's marriage seems in this way an embodiment of that just and equal communication which Richardson longed for in his early letters to Lady Bradshaigh, a communication which would mark the harmonious resolution of distance and presence. There are elements in the novel, however, which suggest that this resolution is only a superficial one. Pamela's and B's explicit discussions of the form of their marriage in the last half of the novel imply that this marriage involves a modulation of these principles more than a true resolution of them. In these discussions, for example, they formulate a daily schedule in which the duties of each toward the other are defined. Pamela promises never to "intrude" (P, 461) on B when he is angry and he in turn promises to ask "nothing of her, that was not significant, reasonable and just" (P, 473) so that he "should not destroy her own free agency" (P, 473).

These statements imply that each accepts in the other a limited area of privacy which exists beyond the bounds of their intimacy. Like Millimant and Mirabell in *The Way of the World,* they accept marriage as a form which mediates between essentially separate selves, and this acceptance is in strange contrast to what we have understood of the nature of love in Richardson. When Lovelace asks Clarissa to "take me, take me to yourself; mould me as you please . . . give me your own impression" (C, II, 80) he is invoking a love which transcends the idea of separateness. This same desire lies behind the intensity of B's need to know Pamela, to negate the distance between them. When B tells Pamela that "love, *true* love, is the *only* motive by which *I* am induced" (P, 284) and Pamela remarks to herself that "this heart is Pamela" (P, 264), they accept their relationship to one another as their definition; and the real form of this relationship is, as we have seen, determined by the nature of a correspondence whose ideal is embodied in the phrase "hearts united" (L, III, 245).

Something of this tension between the form of their marriage and the nature of the intimacy established by their correspondence appears in B's wish that Pamela continue her writing even after they are married, for this implies that he needs some more intimate access to her other than that provided by their formalized relationship. Such a tension existing at the center of an apparent resolution of principles points to an important difference between the distance created by the writer's withdrawal and the distance created by social usages such as dress, manners and class distinctions. Although both forms of distance testify to the self's nervousness in the face of the other, in the case of the correspondent this distance exists so that it may be transcended, so that he can establish a relation "more pure, yet more ardent, and less broken in upon, than personal conversation can ever be" (L, III, 245). On the other hand, the primary function of social usages in Richardson, as we have seen, is much more to enforce separation—we remember Lovelace's statement that dress "compels distance" (C, II, 341)—than to effect a positive mediation.

If it is true that society is inevitably such a world of enforced separation, then the withdrawal of the writer takes on an additional tonality. Rather than being simply a protective strategy, it appears as an act which is necessary in order to escape this separation. He must withdraw from the distances of the social world to a solitude in which, paradoxically, relations can be established without regard to this distance. The withdrawal of the writer is reflected in the retreat of B and Pamela to Lincolnshire, to a place where, literally, they become correspondents. In the case of B this retreat defines the "chasms" which his love for Pamela have made in "my affairs, and my own family" (P, 259). In the case of Pamela, her movement is explicitly to a place where she is outside the law and has no socially accepted role. Yet it is only in this area, it seems, that Pamela and B can escape "the distance that fortune made between us" (P, 17) and unite their hearts.

To recognize that a tension exists between the union of their hearts and the mediated relation of their marriage is to place *Pamela* in a more radical light. As several critics have noted, *Pamela* is concerned with the development of identity in a social context. The pattern of the Fortunate Fall, a pattern which traditionally expresses the movement of man toward God, here describes Pamela's movement from her role as servant through her period of captivity to her new role as B's wife.[6] But if the novel on one level assumes the priority of role, it clearly does not do so in an uncritical way. It is necessary, in this context, to see the book not only from Pamela's but also from B's point of view. Unlike Pamela, whose position is made ambiguous by the death of her mistress, B himself exists at the beginning of the novel in a well-defined social position. The intensity of B's desire for

[6] Richardson's comments at the close of *Pamela* are obviously intended to focus the reader's attention on this level of the narrative and to lead him to see the ending as the result of a providential ordering of events. Yet it is just as clear that the marriage of Pamela and B is the result of their exchange of letters and these letters are, after all, their own creations. I have tried to deal with some of the implications of the letter as a creation of the self in the latter part of this essay, implications which conflict with Pamela's realization that she is "a poor instrument" (P, 326) of God. And of course I have been concerned throughout more with an explication of the psychological dynamics of the novel than with placing it in the tradition of spiritual autobiography. I hope that in doing so I have not implied that this religious level is somehow less present or less important. The particular complexity of Richardson's work derives from the tension between secular and religious patterns and it is this complexity which has led me to read and write about *Pamela*.

Pamela and his inability to abandon her cannot grow out of the insecurity of a similarly ambiguous social position. It would seem, instead, that his love reflects a sense of an insufficiency at the center of the self which is defined by his role.

There may be many ways of explaining this sense of insufficiency. Perhaps it is enough to say again that roles, because they function in Richardson's world to distance the self from others, do not provide the self with a truly positive ground. Why Richardson experiences roles in this way is another and more difficult question. The most obvious answer is that because he is himself a private person, he naturally understands and uses roles in this way. It may be that just as the eighteenth century gradually lost the sense of the immediate presence of the divine in the structure of the natural world, so it lost a sense of its presence in the structure of the social world. The negative experience of distance would express, then, the way in which the social world, like the Newtonian universe, has become something mechanical and lifeless.[7] In any case, it is the need to escape the sense of ephemerality and isolation, to find an immediate union with someone who will grant a more positive sense of self, which is the source of love in Richardson.

If the birth of love is a result of the inadequacy of social usages to confirm the self, then the failure of Pamela and B to incarnate the union of their love in the form of their marriage implies that this inadequacy is not simply a starting-point or a temporary condition. Since their marriage involves an inevitable separation, since society is inevitably a world of distinctions and differences, there will always be some degree of emptiness surrounding the self as it exists in society. In this sense, *Pamela* reveals a profound

---

[7] My argument obviously suggests that there is a correspondence between the loss of a sense of Divine immanence in the structure of the natural world and the loss of a similar sense of immanence in the structure of the social world. There is, again, something of this in *Robinson Crusoe*. The speech of Crusoe's father in the opening pages of the novel is obviously patterned on Raphael's speech to Adam in *Paradise Lost*. Both Crusoe and Adam are offered secure lives in the middle state, but they are lives which exist in a distant, mediated relation to God. Crusoe can escape this distance only by abandoning his position in the middle state of society and finding on the island an intimate conversation with the Divine. This movement describes, on one level, the pattern of the Fortunate Fall in the novel, and the application of this pattern to a movement from society to the isolation of Crusoe's island suggests that initially the levels of society stand between Crusoe and God in much the same way that, before the Fall, the higher levels of creation stood between Adam and God.

scepticism toward the ability of society to provide an adequate ground for the self.

This is not to say that Richardson himself accepts the scepticism wholeheartedly. Conservative by temperament, he was committed to the structure of society and obviously attempts to reconcile B's and Pamela's love with this structure. Yet it is just as clear that this reconciliation is not complete. It seems the particular nature of Richardson's genius that he saw more than he would have liked, that he intuited more than he was inclined to exploit. The conflict between love and society in the novel reflects, on this level, a tension between Richardson's intellectual commitment to a structure of society which is the product of "Wise Providence" and his felt experience of society's "parts" (P, 272), as something which distances and isolates the self. Such a tension is apparent in the contrast between "needful avocations" (L, III, 247), and "hearts united" (L, III, 245), in his definition of the letter. It is equally apparent in the tenor of his correspondences with Lady Bradshaigh and Sophia Westcomb, correspondences which in their intense sentimentality obviously fill some void in his public life.[8]

VII

The distance defined by the letter-writer's withdrawal, then, is in its most fundamental implication the sign of a revolt. Like the force of love, this withdrawal seems, on this level, a rejection of the isolation of the self in society. But the act of correspondence is not only a rejection of this self. Insofar as it is the form of love, it involves the choice of another as the ground of a new identity. Richardson's characters do not choose to love. Love comes "like a thief" (P, 260). But at crucial times both Pamela and B do choose to affirm the movement of their love toward one another. They choose to be defined by this relationship, and this choice is signaled by their exchange of letters, by Pamela surrendering her papers to B and by B sending the letter which brings her back to Lincolnshire.

For Pamela to say "this heart is Pamela" (P, 264) and to give

---

[8] For a study of the role of Richardson's correspondence in his life see Malvin R. Zirker, Jr., "Richardson's Correspondence: The Personal Letter as Private Experience" in *The Familiar Letter in the Eighteenth Century*, ed. Howard Anderson, Philip B. Dashlian, and Irvin Ehrenpreis (Lawrence, 1966), pp. 71-91.

B her journal is for her to make this choice and to define herself by it. The association of love with such a choice of identity is itself suggestive. It places their relationship in one tradition of Renaissance love poetry in general and in that of the sonnet sequences in particular. In this tradition, the lady is no longer seen as the mediator between the lover and God but becomes herself the final resting-place of desire. She takes upon herself the attributes of the Divine and provides a still center in a turning world. Thus Donne's lovers in " The Good-Morrow " find in one another a ground which seems to allow them to transcend distance and death, and Shakespeare in Sonnet 116 hopes to find in his love an " ever fixed mark " which " is not time's fool."

In an important way, *Pamela* is a domestication of the effort to find in " the marriage of true minds " a relationship which offers such transcendent stability and fulfillment. In this, it reflects certain realities of eighteenth century English society. Philippe Ariès has shown in his *Centuries of Childhood: A Social History of Family Life* that the eighteenth century was in fact a time when the family began to define itself as a special area of intimacy centered around the wife and children and, in Ariès' words, to " hold society at a distance, to push it back beyond a steadily expanding zone of private life." [9] It is a time when people are turning to a private world defined by the relationship between husband and wife and set in opposition to society.

More specifically, perhaps, *Pamela* looks forward to the investigation of this attempt in the English novel. The marriage of B and Pamela in the isolation of Lincolnshire prefaces the retreat of Booth and Amelia at the end of *Amelia*, the relation of Catherine and Heathcliff in *Wuthering Heights* and the love of Pip and Estella at the end of *Great Expectations*. Each of these novels is centered around a recognition of the inability of society to provide the ground of authentic identity: the image of society as a prison in *Amelia*, the effeteness of Lockwood in *Wuthering Heights*, the hollowness of Pip's great expectations. Each, in turn, investigates the ability of the self to find in its love for another a more substantial sense of self.

From this point of view, *Pamela* is an important document in the history of desire. Such a history, detailing the loss by love of

---

[9] *Centuries of Childhood: A Social History of Family Life* (New York, 1967), p. 398.

a transcendent object and the effects of its subsequent confinement to the temporal world, would be necessary to any complete understanding not only of *Pamela* but of the development of the English novel. This investigation is, of course, far beyond the scope of an essay, and I am concerned here simply with the idea of the letter as the sign of a choice.

Again, this is a focus which emphasizes radical elements in the novel, elements which Richardson clearly wanted in some sense to avoid. He has gone to great lengths to cleanse Pamela of any trace of ambition, to make her passive in her elevation to the status of B's wife. But with that ambivalence which characterizes his work, the very structure of *Pamela* frustrates his attempt. Like *Pamela*, *Tom Jones* is organized around the motif of the Fortunate Fall. The difference in the way the pattern exists in the two novels is, however, significant. When Tom, having left an orphan, returns to Paradise Hall as its future owner, his new status is not, fundamentally, the result of anything he has done during his wanderings. It is rather the result of a pre-existing relationship to Allworthy. His adventures lead him only to discover his true nature, a nature defined by his past, by his parentage. Pamela, on the other hand, has no such pre-existing relationship to B. Their marriage is the result of the love which develops between them in the course of the novel. For this reason, *Pamela* is a story of the creation rather than the discovery of the self.

It is because *Pamela* is concerned with such a creation that writing has the status it does in the novel. Pamela's manuscript is not simply the record of her and B's love. The manuscript is also its cause, the central factor in their marriage. Consequently their marriage and the self which it defines for her inevitably appear as the product of her act of writing. Writing in this way becomes associated with the freedom to choose an identity by choosing a new relation to another, and this new identity, because it is the product of writing, comes in turn to be associated with fiction. It becomes something which has been literally written into existence.

The sense that Pamela's story is fictional is not simply implicit in the logic of the book. It is suggested, too, by the reactions of the other characters to Pamela's manuscript. What is significant about these reactions is how often they are reactions appropriate to a literary object. When B reads Pamela's version of the 137th psalm for Lady Jones and the two Miss Darnfords, they react primarily to her skill as a versifier and her ability to turn a line. When Lady Davers asks to read Pamela's journal, one of her motives is that she "should take great pleasure to read all his stratagems . . . on one hand, and all your pretty counter-plottings . . . for it must be a rare and uncommon story; and will . . . give me great pleasure in reading" (P, 482). And when Lady Davers returns to London, she hopes to use this manuscript to "entertain Lady Betty with, and another lady or two" (P, 486).

The tenor of these reactions characterizes many of B's comments as well. When, after their engagement, he asks Pamela to give him the rest of her journal, his motive is, "the pleasure I take in reading what you write" (P, 291), and he later relates this pleasure to her "easy and happy manner of narration" (P, 316). B's reactions in the important scene when he confesses the full effects of Pamela's journal on him, however, go further. They make explicit the associations between the status of writing and the status of the self which flows from this writing. In this scene B first acknowledges that part of the fascination of the journal derives from its literary effect. "I long to see the particulars of your plot," he tells her, "and your disappointment, where your papers leave off: for you have so beautiful a manner, that it is partly that, and partly my love for you, that has made me desirous of reading all you write" (P, 242). But more than this he sees their marriage not simply as something which results from these qualities. He sees it as something which completes them and shares their nature. "Besides," he continues, "there is such a pretty air of romance, as you relate them, in *your* plots and *my* plots, that I shall be better directed in what manner to wind up the catastrophe of the pretty novel" (P, 242).

B is not only Pamela's lover. He is also her most acute critic, and the explanation for this is clear. *Pamela* is concerned not only with the development of Pamela's self but of B's as well. Its subject is the process of mutual definition which occurs between them. Just as the growth of Pamela's relation to B is associated with a kind of fictionalizing, so is B's relation to her. Lady Davers points to this when, after she discovers that Pamela and B are wed, she asks Pamela to "walk before me . . . that I may see how finely thou can'st act the theatrical part given thee" (P, 409). Her comment is, however, only a gloss on B's own statement above that Pamela's journal is a "romance" (P, 242). The reference here is not to

Pamela's reading but to his own comment to Pamela, early in the novel, that "you are well read, I see, and we shall make out between us, before we are done, a pretty story in romance" (P, 26). This reminds us that *Pamela* contains not only Pamela's letters but also B's. Like the identities which it defines, it is a story which they have composed together, which is made up, as B understands, of "*your* plots and *my* plots" (P, 242).

VIII

When Pamela remarks that "my story surely would furnish out a surprising kind of novel" (P, 258) or B calls her papers "the pretty novel" (P, 242) they remind us that these letters are the novel *Pamela* and, in doing so, allow us to see *Pamela* as Richardson's definition of the genre. It is no accident that Richardson thinks of the letter and the novel as fundamentally related forms. Since he conceives of human identity as an intersubjective relationship, he is led naturally to the letter as the most appropriate medium to express it. More than this, the letter describes for him not only the general but also the specific conditions which govern this identity. Generated from the emptiness which initially surrounds his characters from the distances imposed on them by social usages, the letter incarnates the movement of love and defines, in this way, the choices open to his characters.

In *Pamela*, moreover, Richardson attempts to make the letter serve as the resolution of this tension, the agency which reconciles distance and presence, the self defined by society and the self defined by love. As I have tried to show, it is a resolution which is qualified even in *Pamela*. Certainly viewed in the abstract this opposition is too complex and too intense to be bridged by any concept of correspondence, and certainly Richardson realized this by the time he began *Clarissa*. It is not in such a reconciliation, however, that Richardson's concept of the letter is most fundamentally a definition of the novel, but in the fact that the letter does describe a choice and is, therefore, the sign of the freedom which his characters have to write their own selves into being. It is this freedom which, although it appears in different forms, most clearly characterizes the protagonists of novels. Sometimes, as in the cases of Don Quixote or Robinson Crusoe or Lord Jim, they reject the self which is offered to them and choose freedom. Sometimes, as in the cases of Oliver Twist or Pip in *Great Expectations*, they are orphans who, offered no initial identity, find this freedom thrust upon them.

Pamela, with the particular ambivalence Richardson has given his novel, falls into both categories. She is forced to embrace her freedom both by the death of B's mother, which robs her of her defined place in the household, and by the distance which separates her from her parents. But she also chooses it by her reluctance to return to her parents and the place they provide. Like Quixote she sees her life not as something given to her by a higher source but as a story she must tell. It is a story which, because it must be told to others—must be, in fact, woven into the threads of their stories—is in reality a letter.

State University of New York
Buffalo

NATURE SPIRITUALIZED: ASPECTS OF ANTI-NEWTONIANISM

BY A. J. KUHN

In 1763 Bishop Warburton, whose notoriety had been achieved in large part at the expense of religious enthusiasm and freethinking, published a book asserting the orthodox doctrine of grace. The work was mainly an attack upon John Wesley and the Methodists, with some slashes at mysticism and William Law. These " new enthusiasts " preached the necessity of grace inspired directly by the spirit of God, and a faith in general which stressed the fallen and sinful nature of man and redemption through the love of Christ working within the soul. The surest proof of the existence and power of God lay in the human heart rather than in external evidence of any sort, and certainly not in human reason which, as the faculty of doubt and dissension, was itself primary evidence of man's weak and divided nature. This, examined in the contexts of Methodist and mystical testimony, Warburton deplored as horrid modern fanaticism. Wesley he sought to expose by ridiculing Methodists who had experienced miraculous powers of healing or the gift of tongues. Law he condemned as an infatuated man who had spent a lifetime hunting after " and with incredible appetite devouring the trash dropt from every species of Mysticism," an obsession that reminded him of " certain Eastern fanatics who solemnly vowed never to taste any food but what passed through the entrails of some impure or savage animal."[1]

Warburton's own faith in reason to determine the grounds of Christian belief was shown sensationally for the age in an immensely learned treatise—with dissertations on the meaning of Egyptian hieroglyphics and the Eleusinian mysteries among other matters—arguing that though the historical religion of the Jews taught no idea of a future state of rewards and punishment, it was a divine dispensation nevertheless and thereby certified, against

[1] *The Doctrine of Grace* (London, 1763), II, 306.

deists, doubters, and disbelievers, the divine authority of the Christian religion. This paradox pursued through several thick volumes, which went through several enlarged editions, it is evident why *The Divine Legation of Moses* was one of the most controversial efforts to prove Christian faith in the period. All this, remarked the crusty Dr. Bentley, in returning an insult he had once received from Warburton, showed " enormous appetite but a very poor digestion." Published in progressive parts—and in fact never finished—Warburton calculated thus, somewhat after the example of *The Dunciad*, to stimulate and then demolish criticism as it appeared. " Who has not signalized himself against the *Divine Legation?* " he complained in the preface to the second part of the book. " Bigots, Hutchinsonians, Methodists, Answerers, and Fanatics have in their turns been all up in arms against it. The scene was opened by a false zealot [Dr. William Webster], and at present seems likely to be closed by a Behmenist [William Law]. A natural and easy progress, from folly to madness." [2]

Law and Wesley had their learned answerers as well, among whom John Byrom was one of the most engaging. Byrom had met Law in 1729, but his disposition toward a religion of the heart had been set before that time. With charm and good humor he tells in his *Journal* of conversations with Bishop Joseph Butler, one of the most impressive rationalists of the day, recalling how he argued passionately for the doctrine of " credo quia impossibile est " and against reason as the guide to faith, but the Bishop won " almost every argument." [3] Like Law, who had refused to take the oath of allegiance to the Hanoverian succession, Byrom had strong Stuart sympathies, and during the uprising of 1745 had discreetly to absent himself from public notice for a time. A fellow of Trinity College during the stormy days of Dr. Bentley's mastership, Byrom was a familiar figure in the circles of the Royal Society, having attended meetings when Newton presided as President, and he was a friend of William Stukeley, Martin Folkes, William Derham, J. T. Desaguliers, and Sir Hans Sloane, among others. He was insatiably curious about philosophical and theological

---

[2] *The Divine Legation of Moses Demonstrated* (London, 1846), III, 134. In this work, as well as in his edition of *The Dunciad*, footnotes served, in Bishop Lowth's phrase, as Warburton's " ordinary places for literary executions."

[3] *The Private Journal and Literary Remains of John Byrom*, ed. Richard Parkinson, XXXIV (Chetham Society, 1855), II, 96.

problems, including such current fascinations as the effort to square the circle, to discover a sure method for finding the longitude at sea, and the cause of gravity. In his search for a solution to this latter problem, he inquired into Newtonian and anti-Newtonian efforts, considering the " Greenian " philosophy of expansive and contractive forces and the Hutchinsonian system, before resting securely in the metaphysics of Boehme and Law.

But Byrom was best known in his own day for the method of shorthand he invented, for which he received a patent presented by the king personally and which he taught to, among other notables, John and Charles Wesley. The facility Byrom had for shorthand or speedwriting was also expressed in fluent verse. At a time when much of the striving for the Sublime, especially on sacred subjects, resulted in pompous verbiage, Byrom's verse frequently achieved verve, ease, conciseness, and wit. His good-humored satire of Warburton's thesis in *The Divine Legation* is characteristic, comparing it to the fanciful centaur of fable:

> And talks away, as if he had portray'd
> A *real* creature, mixt of mare and maid:
> And who deny th' existence of the pad,
> He *centaurizes* into *Fool* and *Mad*.
> Solving, with like centauriformal ease,
> *Law, Prophets, Gospel,* quoted as you please.

Byrom's defense of Christian grace working through a love of Christ within the soul is contained in " Enthusiasm: A Poetical Essay," written in 1751. It is based on one of Law's most important books, *An Appeal to All That Doubt The Gospel* (1740), which argued fervently to divest the term *enthusiasm* of its connotations of fanatical dissent and indeed to show that it was the necessary human ground of faith. Law had written several works against the abuses of reason in matters of religion: against the deist Matthew Tindal in 1731; against the latitudinarian Bishop Hoadly in the Bangorian controversy in 1737; and against Dr. Trapp on enthusiasm.

But *An Appeal* was Law's first sustained effort to plead the necessity of committing one's self to the guidance of the holy spirit to achieve true faith and to elaborate this conviction in terms of Jacob Boehme's theosophy. The redemption of man's fallen nature was through his active will to live in God's light and to be guided by it always. This active will, an enkindled spirit of life or " enthusiasm," all men had in common and it motivated their lives toward spiritual goals. Enthusiasm rightly directed (in Byrom's precis of Law) was as desirable as the example of the saints, for it sought no more than to cast off the old Adam for the new, the natural for the spiritual man, and to live in God's light and love.

>Blame not Enthusiasm, if rightly bent;
>Or blame of Saints the holiest intent;
>The strong persuasion, the confirm'd belief,
>Of all the comforts of a soul the chief;
>That God's continual will, and work to save,
>Teach, and inspire, attend us to the grave:
>That they, who in his Faith and Love abide,
>Find in his Spirit an immediate Guide:
>This is no more a *fancy,* or a *whim,*
>Than that we *live,* and *move, and are in him.*[4]

In alluding here to Saint Paul, Byrom states the central tenet of Law's thought. The writings of mystics different in time and temper as Dionysius the Areopagite, St. John of the Cross, Thomas à Kempis, Archbishop Fénélon, and Madame Guyon had been formative influences on Law in their experiences of how, in the phrase of Malebranche, " omnia videmus in deo." But the enriching source of Law's theology was the great Apostle Paul and the humble shoemaker theosopher Boehme, both of whom had witnessed through divine inspiration " the deep and true grounds of all things," and from whom he developed both a metaphysics and a physics of Christian faith.

The metaphysics of true faith, Law wrote repeatedly, rested on the plain and simple grounds of a fall and the need for redemption. Decades of the dust of theological debate had proved nothing for Christians save that human reason itself was pitiable evidence of man's fallen nature and that thereby the very " demonstrators of the truth and reasonableness of Christianity " had betrayed their own cause. The truth of Christianity lay not in councils, doctrines, and demonstrations but within each human soul, in the sensibility or active will or spirit seeking a new birth. The two pillars of Christian faith were the fact of man's fall from an angelic life into a creaturely one and the possibility of his redemption through the working of Christ within the soul. " God is a spirit in whom you live and move and have your Being; and he stays not till you are

[4] *Miscellaneous Poems* (Manchester, 1773), II, 38.

a great Scholar, but till you turn from Evil, and love Goodness, to manifest his holy Presence, Power, and Life within you."[5] True religion was that simple.

This plain truth of religion however was in fact a mystery, and Law devoted his life to interpreting and adapting for his age the theosophy of Boehme in order to make the mystery manifest. In Boehme was to be found a comprehensive physico-theology, the mystery of the relation of eternal to temporal nature, of heaven to earth and matter to spirit, revealed in their ultimate and efficient causes and effects. Indeed, the inspiration and spiritual model for the Newtonian system itself was derived from Boehme's light, Law was convinced: "The illustrious Sir Isaac Newton, when he wrote his *Principia*, and published to the world his great Doctrine of Attraction, and those Laws of Nature by which the Planets began, and continue to move in their Orbits, could have told the World, that the true and infallible ground of what he there advanced, was to be found in the Teutonic Theosopher, in his three first properties of Eternal Nature: he could have told them, that he had been a diligent Reader of that wonderful Author. . . ."[6]

Putting aside the problem of Law's sources for this claim, it is worth trying briefly to understand Law's conviction of the precedence of mysticism over physico-mathematics in the eternal truth of things. Dr. George Cheyne was naturally curious about Law's evidence because he too had sought by means of philosophical analogy to reconcile the physical mechanism of the world with the spiritual one. Thus he had argued that the principle of attraction, or gravitation, had its spiritual analogy in the human and divine principle of reunion, or desire. "This principle of reunion in intelligent beings," he found, "wonderfully analogizes with that of attraction in the material world. As to the supreme infinite, it may very properly be called his gravitation to them, and as to them, their central tendency or gravitation (so to speak) towards him; and this principle of reunion, if attended to duly, cultivated and expanded, would as certainly bring about the temporal and eternal happiness of all intelligent beings in this spiritual world; as that of attraction brings about the comely and harmonious motions of

[5] *The Way to Divine Knowledge* (London 1752), in the *Works of William Law* (Privately Reprinted for G. Moreton, 1893), VII, 194.
[6] *Works*, VI, 201.

the great bodies of the material world."[7] It is likely indeed that Law was led to his belief of Newton's dependence on Boehme not from the *Principia* itself or Newtonians like Roger Cotes and Henry Pemberton but from such treatises as Cheyne's; for of course " desire " is the key spiritual and mechanical principle in the union of nature and grace in Boehme's theosophy.

Directly contrary to the rationalistic mode of thought, whether in deistic religion or mathematical science, the mystics argued from spirit to matter, from God to creature and creation. The methodology of natural philosophy of course, Newton had declared and determined, was to argue from phenomena without feigning hypotheses and to deduce causes from effects until one came to the very First Cause, a method of knowledge Pope had expressed as,

> Say first, of God above, or Man below,
> What can we reason, but from what we know?
> Of Man what see we, but his station here,
> From which to reason, or to which refer?
> Thro' worlds unnumber'd tho' the God be known,
> 'Tis ours to trace him only in our own.

The mystical analogy rested primarily on the authority of St. Paul. The outward world was an emanation or outbirth of the inner world: the material world is the analogy of the spiritual, and therefore, in St. Paul's words, the things of God are clearly seen by the things which He has made. Nature and the Gospel had a pervasive spiritual sense which Christ had taught archetypically in " I am the vine, ye are branches " and in his parables generally. Among Church Fathers Origen was a rich source of the mystical analogy, but closer to Law and influential in his thought were the Cambridge Platonists. Thus John Smith remarks upon the " two-fold meaning in every creature, a literal and a mystical, and the one is but the ground of the other." [8]

But for Law the deep, eternal ground of the mystical analogy of nature and grace had been revealed by Boehme. All creation, Boehme premised, is the emanation of the ineffable Godhead. The earth thus and man are only an alteration of something that was in

---

[7] George Cheyne, *Philosophical Principles of Natural Religion*, 3rd ed. (London, 1725), I, 90.

[8] From Stephen Hobhouse, *Selected Mystical Writings of William Law* (London, 1948), pp. 397ff.

heaven and heaven itself is nothing else but the first glorious outbirth of the one God in trinity. But the outbirth of creation and man is a fall and separation. They hunger, yearn, and desire redemption and reunion with the higher world. Traces of man's first perfection remain in this divine desire or attraction to God, from which astringency or desire, which is one and the same quality in every individual thing and is the first form of being and life, the very ground of every creature, from the highest angel to the lowest vegetable, man is led by an unerring thread to the first Desire, or that desire which is in the divine nature. For as this attraction or astringent desire is in all spiritual and corporeal things, one and the same quality, working in the same manner, " so it is one and the same quality with that first, unbeginning Desire, which is the Divine Nature." Believing thus in a bond between deity and man, it is clear why the orthodox doctrine of creation *ex nihilo* was repugnant to Law and his followers, for it divided God from man and nature, leaving him to worship his Maker either in his own or nature's image, both of which were deistic idolatry.[9]

Desire, or attraction, then, was the eternal ground of all things, itself a manifestation of that mysterious inwardness of deity Boehme called *Ungrund*. Desire was, in Law's understanding, the eternal *cause* of those properties in temporal nature which Newton had formulated in the first three laws of motion. These properties —attraction, equal resistance, and the orbicular motion of the planets as the effect of them—Newton had treated as facts and appearances only. " But in our Behmen, the illuminated Instrument of God, their Birth and Power in Eternity are opened; their eternal Beginning is shown, and how and why all Worlds and every creature, whether it be heavenly, earthly, or hellish, must be in them, and from them, and can have no Nature, either spiritual or material, no kind of Happiness or Misery, but according to the working Power and State of these Properties."

Desire, in Boehme's conception, had three properties: the first a compressing, inclosing, shutting up force or motion, which brings forth a contrary property, a resisting or expanding motion, the two of which in contrariety generate a third property, a " whirling anguish " or orbital motion. In these three properties, or forms, or " working powers " of nature, lay the true ground of all life, of man

[9] *The Way to Divine Knowledge, Works*, VII, 238ff.

and nature, of every created thing. "Matter, motion, darkness, fire, and every natural power or quality of anything has its beginning from them." Whence, Law reiterates, "you see the Ground and Reason of the *three* great Laws of Matter and Motion lately discovered, and so much celebrated; and need no more to be told, that the illustrious Sir Isaac ploughed with Behmen's Heifer when he brought forth the discovery of them."[10]

Law writes many pages explaining the cosmology and divine anthropology of these three working powers of desire, but it will suffice to note merely a few aspects of what he called this " Band or knot of life." Eternal nature in its original was a beautiful state of meekness, transparency, and spiritual fluidity, but the fall of the angels brought about the outbirth of hard, compacted material creation. Their fall was through a willful self-hood, as was man's afterward. Byrom versifies this important principle of Law's thought thus:

> Explain religions by a thousand schemes,
> Still God and Self will be the two extremes;
> In Him the one true Good of it is found,
> In Self, of all Idolatry, the Ground:
> False worship, paid at all its various Shrines,
> One same Departure from his Love defines.

The hardened heart of man, the abyssal, alienated wrathful Self, was the veritable hell of life, and the kingdom of nature he inhabited, in the grossness and materiality of its earth and stones, was an outward sign or type of his fallen nature. But because man and nature were an outbirth of spirit, they retained in their working powers elements of their divine origin, so that in them the contraries of heaven and hell, meekness and wrath, hardness and fluidity, good and evil, strive for dominion. Unlike the *concordia discors* resulting from the creative strife in the Newtonian system, or from fancy and judgment, or from self-love and social love in Augustan thought, the "Whirling anguish" in Law's conception of man and nature requires the redeeming love of the triune God. Certainly reason was ineffectual; to use it to quench the flames of those raging properties of life " would be acting as wisely as he, whose house is on fire, would seek to extinguish the fire by reading it a lecture on the nature of water."

[10] *The Spirit of Love, Works,* VIII, 19.

Man was redeemed through the working of Christ within him. His power transformed the raging anguish of the three properties of desire into their spiritual equivalents, light, love, and eternal fire. All creation in reality was a type or manifestation of the Holy Creative Trinity and therefore temporal nature was a volume of instruction opened to us by the spirit of God. Thus, in addition to the three working powers in man and in nature, Law believed with the Hutchinsonians and others that fire, light, and air, which were the triune form of the *materia prima* of the universe, were " but the Trinity itself in its most outward, lowest, kind of existence or manifestation; for there could be no fire, fire could not generate light, air could not proceed from both, these three could not be thus united, and thus divided, but because they have their root and original in the triunity of Deity." By making the external internal, which was to live in Christ's heavenly life, light, and love, the soul's desire was appeased and reunited with God. This was the ground and philosophy of all nature, the mystery of which Boehme had revealed and spoken of as " with a Trumpet; and chiefly to awaken Man out of the Dream and Death of rational, notional, and hearsay Knowledge; and to show him, that his own inward Hunger and Thirst after God, is that alone which can open the Fountain of Light and Divine Knowledge in him." [11]

The mystical and mechanical properties of fire which figure thus in the theosophy of Law were the subject of much enthusiastic inquiry toward the middle of the eighteenth century, and especially after the experiments with electricity made by Franklin and others. The mysterious " electrical fluid fire " seemed to answer all the requisites for the primary agent which reconciled spiritual causes and mechanical effects acting immediately under the First Cause. Learned speculation on fire as the element of elements, from Zoroaster and Plato among the ancients to Kepler's *effluvium magneticum*, Descartes' *materia prima*, and Newton's " subtle aetherial medium " and Bishop Berkeley's " ether or pure invisible fire " among the moderns, together with the tradition of mystical and alchemistical fire, converged to support all sorts of hypotheses on the " first " philosophy.

Fire philosophers of various sectarian convictions elaborated their theories on the origin, preservation, and final conflagration of the universe. The millenarian Benjamin Parker, disclaiming any

[11] *The Way to Divine Knowledge, Works*, VII, 252.

influence of Law's mystical divinity, declared the sun the center and soul of the material world which by its spiritual light sustained and preserved all things, and he looked forward to that final fire which would purify fallen man and nature. John Freke had corresponded with Law, consulted Berkeley and Boerhaave among others, and wrote treatises showing that electricity, or " vivacity," as he called it, was the first principle of nature and how the sun's fire was responsible for the mechanism of the world: " Fire is the cause, under God, not only of magnetism, but of all the phenomena in the universe." [12] One R. Lovett, a lay clerk of the Cathedral at Worcester, was pleased to call himself " the Electrical philosopher," asserting that he " was perhaps the first, that ever maintained that the Electrical fluid and the Newtonian aether were one and the same...." [13] And, in *Jubilate Agno*, Smart expounded the virtues—and possible malignancy—of a universal fire:

> For all spirits are of fire and the air is a very benign one.
> For the MAN in VACUO is a flat conceit of preposterous folly.
> For the breath of our nostrils is an electrical spirit.
> For an electrical spirit may be exasperated into a malignant fire.
> (B1, 263-66)

The fire-light-air plenum of the Hutchinsonians was central both to their anti-Newtonian mechanics and Trinitarian theology.[14] Of the fire philosophies of the age it had the most confident followers, in large part, because it explained so much. Moreover, and most important for its followers, this philosophy " confirmed " Christian revelation. The divine analogy between the ministry of fire-light-air in nature and Christ's ministry in affairs of the spirit was a surety of man's redemption. Scripture showed the way to grace and salvation through the words of God; nature manifested God's grace to man in images, in divine analogies, all about him. External nature thereby confirmed Christian mystery and revelation, not inferentially as the physico-theologians generally did by arguing the deity's attributes from design in nature but by bringing, in the words of Jones of Nayland, " the volume of Nature in aid of the volume of Scripture." Such analogy was neither forced nor feigned. It was real, it was a constant revelation

---

[12] *A Treatise on the Nature and Property of Fire* (London, 1752), p. 65.
[13] *The Electrical Philosopher* (Worcester, 1774). Also, *The Subtil Medium Prov'd* (London, 1756) and *Philosophical Essays* (Worcester, 1766).
[14] " Hutchinson vs. Newton," *JHI*, 22 (1961), 303-22.

of the spirituality of common nature, and to live by the rule of divine analogy in turning all objects to a spiritual use was, Jones declared, "the next thing to living in a spiritual world." [15]

To the Hutchinsonian system of nature, mechanical and spiritual, John Wesley was also attracted. As his letters and journals show, throughout his life he was interested in the physico-theological modes of reconciling nature and grace. His own *Survey of the Wisdom of God in Creation* (1763) sought to do that of course. Like Hutchinson, and like his erstwhile master Law, Wesley was anti-Newtonian and for the same reason, that it was the source and solace of natural religion and of irreligion so far as Christian mysteries were concerned. And both Law and Wesley prescribed a "plain Bible divinity" as the antidote to irreligion.

But they clashed irreconcilably on what was plain and fundamental to faith. On the shoals of mysticism, Wesley told Law, his own faith was nearly shipwrecked, and he was vehement against Boehme's "high-flown bombast" and "sublime nonsense." Law had once spoken against philosophical religion, Wesley reminded him. Had he forgotten that injunction? As for Law's claim that in the three first properties of nature Newton "had ploughed with Behmen's heifer," Wesley scoffed, "as Milton ploughed with Francis Quarles's heifer!" "Bad philosophy has by insensible degrees paved the way for bad divinity; in consequence of this miserable hypothesis, you advance many things in religion also, some of which are unsupported by Scripture, some even repugnant to it." [16]

But even as he was dismissing the mystical analogy of Boehme and Law, he was considering the divine analogy of the Hutchinsonians, and sporadically for the next thirty years or so he continued to be fascinated by it. At one time or another he had read in most of the Hutchinsonian treatises, and he read Robert Spearman's abridgement of Hutchinson's own works several times. Hutchinson he described as a "man of strong understanding, but greatly obscured by pride and sourness of temper. He was the twin soul of Dr. Bentley. Many of his remarks I exceedingly approve of." [17]

[15] *Works* (London, 1801), VII, 48.
[16] *The Letters of John Wesley* (London, 1931), III, 334.
[17] *The Journal of John Wesley* (London, 1938), VII, 367. For references to the Hutchinsonians see also III, 207; IV, 191, 261, 280; VII, 251.

What he approved was the Hutchinsonian effort to give " divine " or ontological relationship to image and idea, word and thing. The word " idea " was to be confined to images we have of sensible objects and the various alterations of them by the understanding, and though it was true we could have no knowledge without ideas yet it was absurd to infer from thence that we could have no knowledge beyond our ideas. Man's limitation to knowledge of concrete images was in reality a boon, for accordingly, Wesley declared, " we are not obliged to believe any doctrine which is not plain and intelligible." The images of natural creation were plain and intelligible: " In short, the world around us is the mighty volume wherein God hath declared himself. Human languages and characters are different in different nations. But the book of nature is written in an universal character, which every man may read in his own language. It consists not of words, but things which picture out the Divine Perfections." [18]

Such a reading of nature confirmed that in the divine presence man lived and moved and had his being. Our world of nature, in the enormously popular evangelical analogies of James Hervey, was a book whose every page " was rich with sacred hints." The sublimest truths of the gospel were taught in Christ's parables by spiritualizing the commonest occurrences, and this Hervey sought to make his mode. In the efficacy of the sun, for instance, is confirmed that " He is the ' resurrection and the life ': the over-flowing fountain of the one, and the all-powerful cause of the other. The second Adam is a quickening spirit, and all his saints live through him. He shines upon their affections; and they shoot forth into heavenly graces, and abound in the fruits of righteousness." To dwell upon the dying Christ among the silent shadows of the tombs, upon his acts and sufferings in the heliotrope, sensitive plant, and lowly violet, and his resurrection in the diurnal sun and annual seasons was truly to experience evangelical faith and intimations of immortality. " Thus, I think," Hervey affirmed, " we should always view the visible system with an evangelical telescope (if I may be allowed the expression), and with an evangelical microscope; regarding Jesus Christ as the great projector and architect who planned and executed the amazing scheme. Whatever is magnificent or valuable, tremendous or amiable, should ever be

[18] *A Survey of the Wisdom of God in Creation* (New York, 1823), p. 318.

ascribed to the Redeemer." Such was the Christian's "natural philosophy." [19]

The consequence of this faith, Hervey recognized, was an anthropocentricism which Pope and the Augustans generally had deplored. In believing that the chain of being had been created for man, rather than each link created for the totality of the whole, lay man's erring pride. Quite the contrary, Hervey and the evangelical theologians responded, for at the center of their faith was Jesus, the God-man whose reason for being and suffering was on man's behalf. A chain of being without Christ left both man and nature hopelessly fixed and fallen in time and history. As Blake was to state what Hervey sermonized, what many of the Wesley hymns express, and a chief tenet of the evangelical movement generally, "God becomes as we are, that we may be as he is." This was the divine anthroposophy which all external nature subserved. Nature conceived thus was moral, redeemed, prophetic, indeed spiritual and spiritualizing. Of course the intellectual paths to this goal were many and varied during the eighteenth century, including those impressive ones pursued by Bishop Berkeley and Jonathan Edwards, among others. But in its twists and turnings, the divine or mystical analogy was one of the more curious of these spiritual searches.[20]

The Ohio State University

---

[19] *Meditations and Contemplations* (London, 1796), I, 159.
[20] Earl Wasserman's fine and seminal study, "Nature Moralized," *ELH*, 20 (1953), states both the problem and solutions to the cleavage between fact and value, nature and grace, to which the above, as well as an essay on the Hutchinsonians, are but notes and illustrations.

SWIFT'S SATIRE: RULES OF THE GAME

BY ROBERT C. ELLIOTT

Claude Rawson says in his splendidly provocative essay " Order and Cruelty " that the discussion of character in Swift's satires leads to deserts of circularity.[1] This is true if we approach character in the usual novelistic sense, explaining specific utterances by reference to personality or cultural traits of the speaker, matching word and deed to motive within a frame of psychological consistency, and so on. On the other hand, to dismiss the question of character in Swift's works—to go along with Denis Donoghue, for example, who recommends that we think of the language of *A Tale of a Tub* as sourceless, ignoring the character of the speaker entirely—won't do, if only because that would be to dismiss the fundamental fictive postulate on which the satirist bases his work.[2] When in any work of the imagination the author creates a spokesman, tells the reader (as Swift does in the *Tale*) who the spokesman is, why he is writing, what his qualifications are, something of the kind of person he is (no matter in how mocking a way), all this has both purpose and function. As Thackeray, who was interested in such matters, says in a letter to a friend: under the mask of Mr. Pendennis " I can afford to say and think many things that I couldn't venture on in my own person."[3] A major function of Swift's impersonations—as a mad Modern, an Irish projector, as Gulliver—is that they allowed him to think himself into the heart of evil, to traffic with the impermissable; and if we are ever to understand the results of those encounters, it will have to be by way of the creatures under whose protection he ventured.

Swift's feats of impersonation operate according to rules which every reader senses but which no critic I know of has been able to specify very precisely. The game is this: Swift must express himself through a zany *alter ego*, say truth by means of a lie, speak

---

[1] Rawson, *Essays in Criticism*, 20 (1970), 24-56; reprinted in *Gulliver and the Gentle Reader* (London: Routledge and Kegan Paul, 1973), pp. 33-59.
[2] Donoghue, *Jonathan Swift* (Cambridge: Cambridge Univ. Press, 1969), pp. 5-9.
[3] *Letters*, ed. Gordon N. Ray (Cambridge, Mass.: Harvard Univ. Press, 1945), IV, 436.

sense through a madman's lips. He must manipulate a spokesman whose utterance simultaneously expresses and unwittingly condemns the folly Swift is pursuing. As for the reader, his part in the game is to follow the complex maneuvers as closely as possible, recreating them in his own mind as he is flung wildly about, from rides on broomsticks and flying islands to Bedlamite plunges. Curiosity—that "Spur in the Side, that Bridle in the Mouth, that Ring in the Nose of a lazy, impatient, and a grunting Reader"[4]— keeps him going through *A Tale of a Tub*: curiosity to know where the ideas lead, of course, but in an important sense, curiosity to know whether Swift in the crazy guise he has assumed can keep his footing in the perilously intricate dance he has set in motion. To keep footing means to follow the rules of the game.

The most important rules governing *A Tale of a Tub* as well as the other satires have to do with the functioning of Swift's fictional spokesmen, with in some sense character, for although these spokesmen are not refugees from the novel or from drama and cannot be expected to follow the conventions of those very different games, there are unmistakable "family resemblances" between them and the personages of better-understood literary forms. Perhaps these can best be seen from a negative perspective. In the novel a writer's initial commitment to a tone, a style, a mode of being for his spokesman limits drastically the possibilities for development in the ensuing work. After the opening pages of their respective novels Fielding could not have married Sophia to Blifil, Jane Austen could not have allowed Elizabeth Bennet to catch a fever and die. As the information theorists say, the early paragraphs of these novels contain a significant element of redundancy, as do most literary works. Think of the immense ranges of experience the first lines of *Paradise Lost* rule out for Milton.

The principle operates in a similar (although less exclusive) way even in a maverick work like *A Tale of a Tub*. As we have it now, the *Tale* opens with an Apology, which is extrinsic to the *Tale* proper, and with some pleasant mystifications from the bookseller; the first words spoken by the Tale-teller who is the source of all that follows are these in the Dedication to Prince Posterity:

[4] Quotations from *A Tale of a Tub* are from the Guthkelch-Smith edition; otherwise quotations from Swift's prose are from the Herbert Davis edition; those from the poetry are from the Harold Williams edition.

Sir,
I here present *Your Highness* with the Fruits of a very few leisure Hours, stollen from the short Intervals of a World of Business, and of an Employment quite alien from such Amusements as this: The poor Production of that Refuse of Time which has lain heavy upon my Hands, during a long Prorogation of Parliament, a great Dearth of Forein News, and a tedious Fit of rainy Weather.

The self-characterization in this utterance is enough to trigger an elaborate scanning process on the part of the reader—a process that, negatively, allows him to rule out many possibilities in the way the *Tale* might develop; one that, positively, gives him clues enabling him to guess at what kind of game he is entering on. From our initial impression of any work we intuit a sense of the whole, without which, as E. D. Hirsch says, any individual trait of the work would be rootless and without meaning.[5] As we read further, of course, we refine our sense of the whole, accommodating new details, adjusting our expectations, ruling out what had once seemed possibilities until, firmly involved in the hermeneutic circle, we approximate a grasp of the appropriate rules. But from the beginning our sense of the whole is grounded in our reading of the source of all our information: in *A Tale of a Tub* it is the crack-brained Modern whose genius lies, as he tells us, in devising tubs for the amusement of leviathanic wits.

Doubtless " character " is an inadequate word here: we are not speaking of a coherent personality or intellectual position. Rawson speaks of the Tale-teller as " an amorphous mass of disreputable energies." Nevertheless, because those energies are associated with a designated speaker, certain renunciations that we normally associate with " character " as understood in other genres necessarily are involved. For example, amorphous as he is, the Tale-teller cannot be wholly inconsistent; that is, he cannot at one moment espouse the cause of the Moderns, at the next that of the Ancients. A position and a point of view fairly steadily grounded are a necessary condition for the satire to operate intelligibly. (When in Book III of the *Travels* Gulliver expresses contempt for the Laputans, then immediately praises them warmly, we are confused, and not in an artistic way: I would say Swift here has momentarily lost his footing.) Again, the Tale-teller cannot (ex-

---

[5] Hirsch, *Validity in Interpretation* (New Haven, Conn.: Yale Univ. Press, 1967), pp. 71 ff.

cept in parody, which makes it a different thing) deliver Swift's sermon on the Trinity or even the one on sleeping in church; he cannot compose *A Project for the Advancement of Religion and Reformation of Morals*. These would be gross violations of the rules because of their inappropriateness in the mouth of a maker of tubs. As soon as the Tale-teller utters his effusion to Prince Posterity, a horizon of appropriate styles and meanings is established, a system of reasonable expectations, reasonable probabilities. The horizon is wide but its exclusions are fairly clear. Among them, fundamentally, is the possibility that the Tale-teller should without warning become a non-ironical Swift—a Swift who writes straight from his convictions. The rules of the genre allow the Tale-teller occasionally to speak Swift's sentiments but only after formal provision for the shift in point of view has been made. In the midst of the Digression on Madness, for example, the Tale-teller utters the purest kind of Swiftian doctrine: " For, the Brain, in its natural Position and State of Serenity, disposeth its Owner to pass his Life in the common Forms, without any Thought of subduing Multitudes to his own *Power*, his *Reasons* or his *Visions;* and the more he shapes his Understanding by the Pattern of Human Learning, the less he is inclined to form Parties after his particular Notions." The Tale-teller can legitimately speak in this way because immediately before he has made it clear that he himself is a partisan of the vapor which the world calls madness, without which we would be deprived of " those two great Blessings, *Conquests* and *Systems*," and consequently he has no love for the " common Forms." Thus the Tale-teller can utter Swift's sentiments without speaking in Swift's unmediated accents. The basic rule is that although the persona need not be a consistent character, the personation must be consistently maintained.

At a certain memorable point in the *Tale* Swift (I think) deliberately violates the rules. The Digression on Madness divides the world in two and demands that the reader choose. Unlike the knight in the Wife of Bath's tale, the reader cannot refuse choice itself but must align himself with one of two positions: either with happiness, delusion, credulity, the surface of things (as these are defined in the Digression), or with curiosity and officious reason which cuts and pierces and anatomizes in order to demonstrate the ugliness beneath the skin. The argument coils to its bitter climax:

whatever Philosopher or Projector can find out an Art to sodder and patch up the Flaws and Imperfections of Nature, will deserve much better of Mankind, and teach us a more useful Science, than that so much in present Esteem, of widening and exposing them (like him who held *Anatomy* to be the ultimate End of *Physick*.) And he, whose Fortunes and Dispositions have placed him in a convenient Station to enjoy the Fruits of this noble Art; He that can with *Epicurus* content his Ideas with the *Films* and *Images* that fly off upon his Senses from the *Superficies* of Things; Such a Man truly wise, creams off Nature, leaving the Sower and the Dregs, for Philosophy and Reason to lap up. This is the sublime and refined Point of Felicity, called *the Possession of being well deceived;* The Serene Peaceful State of being a Fool among Knaves.

The shock to the reader is traumatic as he suddenly finds himself trapped in an intolerable dilemma: if he has chosen happiness and the surface of things he is a fool; if he has chosen reason he is a knave. There is no way out. No wonder he is shaken. But beyond that I think the reader has a strong sense that he has been not only trapped but booby-trapped. It is not part of the game that the Tale-teller should be able to speak in the savagely hostile accents which end the paragraph; they violate his mode of being, amorphous as it is. Instead, Swift has momentarily tossed the Tale-teller aside, speaking out in his own voice, breaking his own rules. It is as though one's chess partner suddenly reached across the board and hit one in the head with one's queen.

In the passage in question the Tale-teller argues consistently for the value of happiness (" *a perpetual possession of being well deceived* "), of fantasy, imagination, the surface of things. " Such a man, truly wise, creams off nature...." In my view it makes no sense to say that it is the Tale-teller who in the next sentence identifies the happiness he has been praising with being " a Fool among Knaves." To be sure, throughout the *Tale* he can and does praise folly and madness—they are " good " words for him—but only in suitable contexts and with the appropriate formal insulation of meaning; here he cannot possibly be giving a favorable sense to *Fool* and *Knaves*. This would be simple incoherence, not irony; it would have the Tale-teller maintaining that true wisdom is to be a fool. There are contexts, of course, in which such a paradoxical assertion makes very good sense indeed—the wisdom of the holy fool, for example—but those contexts are not invoked here. It is as though Gulliver should say, " the Houyhnhnms are wise and just creatures and should be despised." If the " Fool among Knaves" is the Tale-teller's phrase, the customary transvaluation of terms does not work; if it is Swift's phrase, however, it enacts even as it expresses his sense of the human entrapment.

That Swift should be caught in his own trap was entirely appropriate as he doubtless knew. Assuredly no fool, he was snagged by the nether jaw of the device he had set. Swift's imagery shouts his awareness of the knavish character of his own satiric procedures. Throughout the Madness section it is Reason that cuts and mangles and pierces; it is Reason that explores weak sides and publishes infirmities, that unmasks what is hidden, that exposes the flaws of Nature, that flays women and anatomizes beaux. All this bloody work is knavery, but necessary knavery; for the exercise of reason as a scalpel, with all the moral ambiguity associated with the procedure, is precisely the satirist's function. Knavery of this anatomizing kind is Swift's métier.

Rawson thinks it a mistake to try to make schematic the relation between the Tale-teller and Swift, and certainly no neat system of invariant opposition will do. He thinks that despite the crushing finality of the " Fool among Knaves " the sense of the passage is left deliberately indistinct because we cannot be certain how Swift and his speaker relate. On the contrary, I think Swift's violation of the rules makes the schematism of the passage inexorable: the rhythms of the prose enforce it as does the sense. Swift imposes upon us choices ("happiness" vs. anatomizing) that are matched symmetrically by the two terms with which he springs the trap. The system is closed and out of its closure shattering energies erupt. Oddly, not all those energies are destructive. If, as Rawson says, the passage affirms an ancient proverb: "Knaves and fools divide the world," its brilliance is such as to assert its own kind of order in defiance of its literal message. Just as a physicist interferes with the "state of the system" when he undertakes a quantum description of a light beam, so Swift (or Pope in *The Dunciad*) alters the system of folly he is examining by giving form to his conception of it. "The wit gives pleasure in itself," says Rawson, "and playfully suggests the survival of linguistic order within a certain mental anarchy."

The issue of character arises again in a work like *A Modest Proposal*. No one would claim that the figure Swift creates to put forward the proposal is a consistent or complex or interesting person in his own fictional right. In a way the whole notion of character as applied to him seems irrelevant. In another sense, however, it is precisely our *idea* of character, and how that idea functions with respect to the projector, that controls our response to the work. Consider:

It is a melancholly Object to those, who walk through this great Town, or travel in the Country; when they see the *Streets,* the *Roads,* and *Cabbin-doors* crowded with *Beggars* of the Female Sex, followed by three, four, or six Children, *all in Rags,* and importuning every Passenger for an Alms. These *Mothers,* instead of being able to work for their honest Livelyhood, are forced to employ all their Time in stroling to beg Sustenance for their *helpless Infants;* who, as they grow up, either turn *Thieves* for want of Work; or leave their *dear Native Country, to fight for the Pretender in* Spain, or sell themselves to the *Barbadoes.*

Swift plays upon what he knows will be the reader's assumptions about the kind of man who can speak so sympathetically of the Irish condition. Given the conventions of character depiction, only that slight intimation is necessary to establish in the reader's mind a formidable set of expectations about what can and cannot follow from such an introduction. These are the expectations that Swift manipulates with such extraordinary results.

Although a tool of the satiric fiction, the spokesman of *A Modest Proposal* is bound by the same minimal generic rules that govern the spokesman of *A Tale of a Tub;* that is, he cannot contradict himself haphazardly, he cannot speak in Swift's unmediated voice. Nevertheless, that voice comes through once or twice in defiance of the rules. One advantage the projector sees in his cannibalistic proposal is that it will not disoblige England: " For, this Kind of Commodity will not bear Exportation; the Flesh being of too tender a Consistence, to admit a long Continuance in Salt; *although, perhaps, I could name a Country, which would be glad to eat up our whole Nation without it.*" The last part of the sentence is unmistakably not the projector but Swift himself. Whereas in *A Tale of a Tub* Swift's intervention produces a shattering experience for the reader, here the unsignalled shift in tone disturbs him momentarily if at all. An English reader in Swift's day would doubtless have responded to the intrusion much more intensely. It all depends on who the victim is.

The identification of victims of Swift's satire is no longer as simple as once it was, the catalogue having been expanded by recent criticism far beyond obvious targets to include the reader—

all readers—and, most interestingly, Swift himself. On the face of it, such identifications are startling, for they radically violate received notions about satire's aims and function, matters on which Swift's official ideas, at least, are as conventional as his ideas on religion. " There are two Ends that Men propose in writing Satyr; one of them less noble than the other, as regarding nothing further than the private Satisfaction, and Pleasure of the Writer; but without any View towards *personal Malice:* The other is a *publick Spirit,* prompting Men of *Genius* and Virtue, to mend the World as far as they are able." [6] The satirist effects this noble end by laughing men out of their follies and vices. It is one of the pattest formulas of self-justification in the lexicon and one of the least examined. Swift puts the formula under some pressure, as we shall see, but never, I think, to the point where his own role as satirist is seriously in question. His aligning himself in the passage above with men of " *Genius* and Virtue " hardly shows him as a conscious victim of his own ridicule. As for the generality of readers as victims, the discussion of the range and effect of satire in the Preface to the *Tale of a Tub* shows Swift acutely aware of the weakness in indiscriminate attack: " Satyr being levelled at all, is never resented for an offence by any, since every individual Person makes bold to understand it of others, and very wisely removes his particular Part of the Burthen upon the shoulders of the World, which are broad enough, and able to bear it." The argument for individual, local satire, as opposed to that which inveighs against mankind, is explicit and pointed: the satirist's proper target is " *such a one* [who] starved half the Fleet," not " People in general." Obviously, Swift does not stick to his own prescription: he attacks individuals, professions, institutions, creeds—in the Digression on Madness he involves the world. Our question is whether (except in the last instance and perhaps one or two others) the reader, however remote he may be from the obvious targets, is himself victimized by the satire, whether, as Rawson puts it, his escape routes are closed. And then, to what degree is Swift himself involved.

Satire is purportedly written to two audiences: in one are the guilty and those most likely to be infected by the guilty, in the other " all right-thinking men," or, as Swift says, " *a great majority*

[6] *Prose Works,* XII, 34.

among the Men of Tast," who share the author's view and values. This latter group, although sometimes in danger of ricochets, is unlikely to be brought under direct fire, most obviously because it forms a friendly camp and is presumably untainted by the vice or folly under examination. The satirist normally arranges things so that the object of his attack is definable against a background of what that object is not: Wotton is defined by contrast with Sir William Temple (clearly a Man of Tast), dissenting Jack by contrast with Martin, who, we are told, represents the "*most perfect*" of all churches in "*Discipline and Doctrine.*" *A Tale of a Tub* provides a surprising number of such positives for the reader to cling to: the coats, of course (i.e., "*the Doctrine and Faith of Christianity by the Wisdom of the Divine Founder fitted to all Times, Places and Circumstances*") and Martin, but positives also in the Digressions. Those of us who write on Swift doubtless take heart from the knowledge that at one happy time in the world's history there were critics other than that formidable race descended from the union of Momus and Hybris, who begat Zoilus. One group of critics used to restore ancient learning from the ravages of time and neglect; another group "invented or drew up Rules for themselves and the World, by observing which, a careful Reader might be able to pronounce upon the productions of the *Learned,* form his Taste to a true Relish of the *Sublime* and the *Admirable,* and divide every Beauty of Matter or Style from the Corruption that Apes it." Although these critics have long been extinct, we are told, each of us must feel that somehow we are the true heirs. How else could we write?

Even in fiercer passages of the satires—those that seem to be torn from the nightmares that tormented Swift—there is likely to be formal provision for a way out. One of his worst fears was certainly, as Empson says, that religion may be no more than a perversion of sexuality, a thesis propounded in great detail by Swift's spokesman in the *Mechanical Operation of the Spirit.* So brilliant and so shocking is this exposition that one forgets the ways to transcendance, other than the mechanical way, mentioned in the text: inspiration from God, possession by the devil, natural causes such as imagination, grief, pain. Swift has no more interest in discussing these legitimate ways of transporting the soul beyond matter than, as a clergyman, he has in discussing the doctrine of the Trinity [7]; but their presence in his text is a necessary element freeing his subversive imagination to show how the spirit may be improved by belching or by prudent management of syphilitic infection, giving him and us, at least in formal terms, a way out.

This is a characteristic mark of Swift; it is his way of exercising what Murray Krieger calls the classic vision.[8] Swift entertains the possibility that the structures which order reality, whether those of reason or religion, may be mere projections of our minds, desperate but factitious attempts to impose order on what is ineluctably chaos. He fantasizes himself into the skins of those who represent horror to him most fully—a Lord Wharton, a madman—or of those who must face head-on what he fears—a Gulliver. Through their eyes and in their voices he confronts the extreme: confronts but does not embrace. The extreme is there, invoked by the violence of thought and metaphor, but rejected at the same time by the formal ordering of his work, by the paths he leaves open.

Many readers, to be sure, find that *Gulliver's Travels* blocks all escape routes; and, clearly, if Gulliver's "All men are yahoos" is Swift's last word, then the closure of the system is complete. To read the *Travels* this way, however, is to conclude that in Swift's view no moral distinction can be made between Dr. Arbuthnot and Lord Wharton, between Sir Thomas More and Henry VIII, between Stella and Mrs. Manley. All are equally loathsome brutes, and Swift is brutish among them. I find the reading incredible, ignoring as it does the possibilities of a reasonable society adumbrated in Brobdingnag, of a decent life shown in Don Pedro. In literature Don Pedro serves Swift as an escape from Yahoodom, just as in life John, Peter, Thomas, and Councillor Such—a—One (whom Swift told Pope he dearly loved) served as an escape from total misanthropy.[9] Don Pedro provides a way out.

Thus I think it a mistake to read Swift's satire as though it were all one vast "Fool among Knaves" trap into which reader and author fall together. It is glib to say that we are all involved in all the vices that satire attacks—that we are all Lord Whartons or John Duntons or whatever, and it is a flaccid morality that refuses

---

[7] See his sermon on the Trinity, *Prose Works*, IX, 159-68.

[8] Krieger, *The Classic Vision* (Baltimore, Md.: Johns Hopkins Univ. Press, 1971), pp. 255-69.

[9] *Correspondence*, ed. Herbert Williams, III, 103.

to discriminate. On the other hand, the escape routes which make discrimination possible are ill-marked in Swift's work, obscure and easy to overlook altogether—a very different situation from that in Pope who emphatically draws the distinction between the righteous and the wicked. Swift's assaults generate such an overplus of energy, they come from so many directions with such unexpected vehemence and wit that ways out are likely to be forgotten as the reader is enveloped by the storm. Rawson is splendid on this. He speaks of how the sudden intensity of a sentence like "Last Week I saw a Woman *flay'd*, and you will hardly believe, how much it altered her Person for the worse," not only serves the argument it illustrates but spills over the surrounding context: the energies of the sentence are in excess of the demands of the logic. This spill-over phenomenon, Rawson says, is characteristic of Swift's style; it contributes to the reader's sense of impasse, of unease, to the feeling that he is somehow catching the hostility meant for someone else.

This seems to me an important insight into the way Swift's prose works. At one point or another in his satire we all recognize aspects of ourselves in the object of ridicule; if we don't we are either hypocrites or poor readers. On the other hand, we are also conscious of being battered even when free of guilt; attacks on abuses in which we as individuals can have no conceivable part hurt, not because of our complicity, but simply as a result of the overplus of hostility in the air. Normal identification with the satirist and its attendant invulnerability, although possible at a formal, rational level, is hopelessly disturbed by the dangerous charges of animus flying about. My impression is, however, that in these instances the reader feels attacked—as though someone has hit him from a dark corner—rather than made to feel guilty. Rawson writes: "Where the aggression turns indistinct, and overspills the area of specifiable moral guilt, no opportunity is given for complacent self-exculpation on a specific front, and the reader becomes implicated. Instead of permitting the individual to shift his load onto the world's shoulders, Swift forces the reader to carry the world's load on *his*." But I doubt that it is *guilt* the reader feels about the woman flayed; he is not in fact guilty of the flaying, nor is he likely to feel the same equanimity before the image of horror that Swift's spokesman exhibits—surely a matter for guilt. If the reader recognizes that, like the Tale-teller, he sometimes treats people as things, or that he lives complacently in a society that endorses unspeakable cruelties, the vaguely guilty twinges accompanying these reflections are low-order responses compared to the shock he gets from the sentence, the battering he undergoes from the spill-over of negative emotion. At the same time, as Irvin Ehrenpreis points out, the reader may experience an illicit joy (for which he feels guilt) that a man could write such a " beautiful " sentence.[10]

In analyzing the overspill phenomenon, Rawson is pointing to real effects in Swift's satire that run counter to the formal ordering of things. These are subjective matters, impossible to specify precisely or measure accurately; but I think the analysis goes a long way toward accounting for the feelings of unjustified victimization likely to result from a bout with Swift. The danger of concentrating too exclusively on these effects is that we may be led to read all Swift's satire as though it were the climactic passage of the Digression on Madness. Not even Swift's work can live consistently at that heat.

In another essay I have tried to define my sense of the degree to which Swift expresses his own complicity in the madness and the badness that he exposes;[11] here I want to explore self-reflexive implications of Swift's frequently-expressed distrust of his own medium. In the Apology to *A Tale of a Tub* Swift affirms and reaffirms the traditional justifications of satire: gross corruptions in religion and learning can best be eliminated by satire's cleansing action. On the other hand, in the Preface to the same work, he (or, as I prefer, his spokesman) launches a brilliantly destructive foray—a satirical foray—against the practice of satire itself. Satirists lash vices, says the Tale-teller, but with pathetic futility; for " there is not, through all Nature, another so callous and insensible a Member as the *World's Posteriors*." Satirists' attacks on avarice and hypocrisy are meaningless: " 'Tis but a *Ball* bandied to and fro, and every Man carries a *Racket* about Him to strike it from himself among the rest of the Company." If satirists dare to expose the villainy of individual persons, they only invite persecution. The attack on satire is managed with a great flurry of denigratory imagery, in one paragraph satirists

[10] See Ehrenpreis, "Swift and the Comedy of Evil," in *The World of Jonathan Swift*, ed. Brian Vickers (Oxford: Oxford Univ. Press, 1968), pp. 213-19.
[11] "Swift's 'I,'" *Yale Review* (Spring, 1973), pp. 372-91.

being compared with flogging pedants, nettles, weeds, thistles, their wit with dull razors and rotten teeth. The "Satyrical Itch" is a disease.

In an interesting analysis of these matters, Gardner Stout, Jr. reads the relevant passages of *A Tale of a Tub* as Swift's own admission that satire serves no useful purpose. " Though he finds Alecto's whip a congenial instrument for scourging fools, he recognizes that, in lashing the world with wit and humor to mend it, his satire is impotent, partly because those it strikes are temperamentally disqualified from feeling it by the very vices for which they are satirized."[12] Stout finds Swift condemning his own motives and procedures: like the True Critic, the Satirist—Swift included—is a collector of mankind's faults, which become distilled into his own person. The satirist messes about in the ordure of human nature, as much a part of the Bedlamite world he describes as any committed lunatic. According to this reading, Swift sees himself as implicated in all that he attacks even as he recognizes that the attack itself is impotent. Here indeed is the satirist satirized.

But is it so? The expressed distrust of satire is unmistakable, the only question being whether Swift's own satire comes within the orbit of critique. The whole passage in the Preface is framed by an elaborate disclaimer from the Tale-teller: " 'Tis a great Ease to my Conscience that I have writ so elaborate and useful a Discourse without one grain of Satyr intermixt; which is the sole point wherein I have taken leave to dissent from the famous Originals of our Age and Country." If the Tale-teller dissents from the Originals, then Swift, following the rules of the rhetorical game, can legitimately attack them through the mouth of his spokesman; hence the denigratory images. The sentence about the world's posteriors sounds like Swift, but the sentiments are those of a hundred earlier satirists, who have rarely had many illusions about their real power to effect reform. Besides, Swift's target here is the spate of satire in the 1690's which so offended Sir William Temple, the satire to which Aesop refers when, speaking with Swift's authority in the *Battle of the Books*, he asserts that the only genuine production of the Moderns is " *a large Vein of Wrangling and Satyr, much of a Nature and Substance with the* Spider's *Poison.*"

[12] Stout, "Speaker and Satiric Vision in Swift's *Tale of a Tub*," *Eighteenth-Century Studies*, 3 (1969), 186.

To attack *that* satire is by no means the same as attacking satire itself.

Furthermore, an odd paradox obtains whereby to admit that satire has little or no effect on a guilty audience is to reinforce the satirical attack. Yeats once thought that Wyndham Lewis' *Apes of God* would shake up London literary society. But Lewis disagreed: "Nothing could change the kind of people of whom I wrote—they had not the necessary vitality for that."[13] The confession of futility turns into the ultimate put down. Whether that, in turn, has effect is, of course, open to the same doubt as before. Swift's best-known statement questioning the efficacy of satire is in the Preface to the *Battle of the Books*. Here he speaks in his own person, as the author, not in the guise of a muddle-headed modern: "*Satyr is a sort of Glass, wherein Beholders do generally discover every body's Face but their Own; which is the chief Reason for that kind Reception it meets in the World and that so very few are offended with it.*" Although this wryly admits that most satire does not get home to those for whom it is intended, that fact itself condemns those who look in the glass: they wilfully refuse to see their own images and either stupidly or hypocritically welcome what exposes their folly. An admission of satiric futility here is overborn by the attack, which in the following sentences escalates into a most unpleasant threat that the wit of the satirist's opponent will end up as something fit only to be thrown to the hogs. The truculence of this satirist has nothing to do with impotence: these teeth can bite.

Interesting logical issues arise when, as in the Preface to *A Tale of a Tub*, a satirist satirizes satire. Wyndham Lewis involves himself in this situation in a very Swiftian way in his novel *Apes of God*. Horace Zagreus, who speaks for Lewis, uses Swift's imagery: "'How is it that no one ever sees *himself* in the public mirror?'" The world, he concludes, is hopelessly past mending:

"'People feel themselves under the special protection of the author when they read a satire on their circle—am I right! It is always the *other fellows* (never them) that their accredited romancer is depicting, for their sport... At all events nothing happens. It would seem that it is impossible to devise anything sufficiently cruel for the rhinoceros hides grown by a civilized man and a civilized woman.... It is almost as if, when they saw him approaching, they exclaimed: "*Here comes a*

[13] Lewis, *Rude Assignment* (London: Hutchinson, 1950), p. 201.

good satirist! We'll give him some sport. We are just the sort of animals he loves." Then the official satirist fills his pages with monsters and a sprinkling of rather sentimental " personnages sympathiques," and everybody is perfectly happy. The satirist is, of course, quite as insensitive as his subjects, as a rule. Nothing really disgusts him.' " [14]

This satirical denigration of both the function of satire and the character of the satirist comes in the midst of one of the fiercest satirical novels ever written. Is Lewis victimized by his own attack? Only in the most remote way, I should think. Satire about satire is like thinking about thought, or communication about communication: as Bertrand Russell made clear, in his theory of logical types, different logical orders are involved and should not be confused. The satirical attacks on satire of both Lewis and Swift are launched from levels higher than their object. This is metasatire, and according to the rules of this game the position of the authors is privileged. Except for non-logical effects of the kind Rawson discusses, they escape their own critique.

On January 11, 1710-11, Swift recorded in the *Journal to Stella* that he was setting up his protégé, " little " Harrison, as the new Tatler, Richard Steele having given up the journal. On March 14 he writes: " little Harrison the Tatler came to me, and begged me to dictate a paper to him, which I was forced in charity to do." Next day the *Tatler* appeared, lauding old times when men of wit had power: " The hopes of being celebrated, or the Dread of being stigmatized, procured an universal Respect and Awe " for the poets. Swift's bias is revealed when he cites Aretino as the great example: all the princes of Europe trembled lest they be pilloried in his satire.[15] A week later another paper (also attributed to Swift) playfully identifies Isaac Bickerstaff as one who, in accordance with Pythagorean doctrine, was born centuries ago and has lived through many incarnations. At one time, Bickerstaff says, he was the leading wit of France, at another time had a statue erected to him in Italy; and when he came to England at the end of the seventeenth century he entered the body of the most talented man of letters there—a man easily identified as Jonathan Swift. The common element in Isaac Bickerstaff's incarnations, he tells us, is that " I have in every one of them opposed my self with the utmost Resolution to the Follies and Vices of the

[14] Lewis, *Apes of God* (New York: Robert McBride, 1932), pp. 255-56.
[15] *Prose Works,* II, 257-63.

several Ages I have been acquainted with, that I have often rallied the World into good Manners, and kept the greatest Princes in Awe of my Satyr."

The battered reader of his work finds it pleasant to see Swift relaxing into fantasy, playing the role of satirist-hero: slaying dragons, rescuing princesses, laughing the world into civility. It is one of many images of the satirist in his work, from the rotten-toothed mumbler of the *Tale,* through the anatomist and the culture-hero to the derisive Jove of the poem " The Day of Judgment." In that nightmare vision Jove lays bare hypocrisy, exposes secret pride and mean motives—acts, in short, as a satirist; acts, as Lord Chesterfield said, like Voltaire:

> I to such Blockheads set my Wit!
> I damn such Fools! Go, go, you're bit.[16]

As part of the " Offending Race of Human Kind " Swift is damned with the rest, but his major identification is clearly with the satirist-god of the vision. In public apologiae Swift asserted the conventional moral justification of the satirist; in private he battled the doubts that assailed him; but in the compensatory mode of fantasy he laid claim to mythical powers.

" My Lord," wrote Swift in *A Letter Concerning the Weavers,* " I freely own it a wild Imagination that any words will cure the sottishness of men or the vanity of women. . . . ," but the confession of futility becomes the springboard of attack as he pushes forward his argument with a caustic jibe. Whatever doubts Swift entertained about satire, he never allowed them to interfere with his métier. That he explored to the limit.

University of California
San Diego

[16] *Poems,* II, 576-79.

CHRISTOPHER SMART'S *MAGNIFICAT:* TOWARD A THEORY OF REPRESENTATION

BY GEOFFREY H. HARTMAN

> What is the consummation of perfect freedom? Not to be ashamed of one's self. *Nietzsche*
>
> For when men get their horns again, they will delight to go uncovered. *C. Smart*

I

Theory as Prologue. When we present one person to another, a feeling of formality persists. It may be a residual awe, relating to exceptional presentations (of the child to elders in early or ritual circumstances) or it may be a more general sense of the distance between persons. The latter feeling would still have a psychological component, for the distance between persons is like that between self and other.

What if someone cannot be presented? The sense of distance has been thrown out of balance: either the self feels defective vis-a-vis the other, or the other appears magnified, unapproachable. The someone can be a something: certain subjects may not be introduced into discourse, certain taboos restrict or delimit the kinds of words used.

I introduce the example of words early, because words commonly help to present us.[1] Should we feel that words are defective, or else that we are defective vis-a-vis them (words becoming the other, as is not unusual in poets who have a magnified regard for a great precursor or tradition), then a complex psychic situation

[1] In this discussion I occasionally rely on a previous essay, "The Dream of Communication" in *I. A. Richards: Essays in his Honor,* eds. R. Brower, H. Vendler and J. Hollander (New York, 1973), pp. 169-77. On self-presence, see also E. Goffman, *The Presentation of the Self in Everyday Life* (New York, 1959); on shame (and embarrassment) O. F. Bollnow, *Die Ehrfurcht* (Frankfurt a/M., 1947); and H. M. Lynd, *On Shame and the Search for Identity* (New York, 1958); and on the relation of theatricality to presence of self, the studies of Jonas A. Barish on "Antitheatrical Prejudice," *Critical Quarterly,* 8 (1966), 329-48, and *ELH,* 36 (1969), 1-29, as well as Lionel Trilling, *Sincerity and Authenticity* (New York, 1972), *passim.*

arises. It is fair to assume, however, that the distance between self and other is always disturbed, or being disturbed; that there is always some difficulty of self-presentation in us; and that, therefore, we are obliged to fall back on a form of "representation."

Representation implies that the subject cannot be adequately "present" in his own person or substance, so that advocacy is called for. The reason for this "absence," compensated for by "representation," can be various. In legal or ritual matters, the subject may not be of age or not competent. But even when he is competent, of age, fully presentable, situations arise which produce a fiction of his having to be "seconded": in presentation at court (and sometimes in courts of law) he does not appear by himself but needs the support of someone already admitted into the superior presence.

The self does not, of course, disappear into its representative, for then the means would defeat the end, which remains self-presentation. Even in visionary poetry which so clearly sublimes the self into the other, or exalts the other into quasi-supernatural otherness, the self persists in selfhood. Though Charles Lamb is right in remarking that Coleridge's Ancient Mariner "undergoes such trials as overwhelm and bury all individuality or memory of what he was—like the state of a man in a bad dream, one terrible peculiarity of which is that all consciousness of personality is gone," the spectral happenings in the poem actually *doom* the Mariner to survival. He is unable to die, or find release from his experience except in the "punctual agony" of story-telling.

Whether or not this doom of deathlessness is preferable to nothingness—"Who would lose," says Milton's Belial, "Though full of pain, this intellectual being, / Those thoughts that wander through Eternity, / To perish rather, swallow'd up and lost / In the wide womb of uncreated night . . ."—the self can never be so sublimated, or so objectified, that only its representative is left. Even granted that self desires an absolute escape from self, what would be satisfied by that escape: indeed would anything of self be left to register the satisfaction? To urge questions of this kind is to approach psychoanalysis, but at the same time to link it up with speculations on the sublime going back at least to Edmund Burke. These speculations ponder the vertiginous relation between self-loss and self-aggrandizement.

140   Christopher Smart's *Magnificat*

Let me return briefly to Coleridge's poem. Why does the Mariner kill the albatross? A fascinating question; but even the simplest answer, that it was willfulness, implies a drive on the Mariner's part for self-presence. The killing is a shadow of the Mariner's own casting.[2] What follows his self-determining, self-inaugural act is, paradoxically, the presence of otherness. In seeking to "emerge," the self experiences separation-anxieties; and these express themselves in emotions akin to the defense mechanism of "beautiful indifference" (noted by Charcot in patients suffering from hysteria) as well as to the terror which may accompany isolation.

At the same time, there is a movement toward atonement (at-one-ment, reconciliation) in Coleridge's poem. "Representation" cannot be divorced from advocacy. You justify either the self or that which stands greatly against it: perhaps both at once. The situation could be likened to a trial, though not to one resulting in a definite verdict. The trouble with this line of inquiry is that too many metaphors come into play until one begins to move within art's own richness of thematic variation. Yet such metaphors as trial, court, theater, debut and so on, converge on the idea of a place of heightened demand and intensified consciousness. "The daemon," says Yeats, ". . . brings man again and again to the place of choice, heightening temptation that the choice may be as final as possible. . . ." Let us consider the nature of this "place," imagined or real.

When Christopher Smart writes in *Jubilate Agno*, "For I pray the Lord Jesus to translate my MAGNIFICAT into verse and represent it,"[3] the pun (magnifi-cat) alluding to the "magnification" of the cat Jeoffrey and of the animal kingdom generally, corroborates what Freud says about wit both submitting to and escaping the censor. To compare a hymn (the Magnificat) associated with the Virgin Mary to the gambols of Jeoffrey is blasphemous—except that the pun remains unexplicit and the poet, in

---

[2] See Coleridge, "On Original Sin" in *Aids to Reflection* (London, 1831): "Where there is no discontinuity there can be no origination, and every appearance of origination in nature is but a shadow of our own casting. It is a reflection from our own will or spirit. Herein, indeed, the will consists. This is the essential character by which Will is opposed to Nature, as spirit, and raised above Nature as self-determining spirit. . . ."

[3] Fragment B 1, 43. My references throughout are to W. H. Bond's edition of the *Jubilate Agno* (London, 1954).

any case, "gives the glory" to God by asking Christ to make his verses acceptable. Yet the anxiety, I believe, or the pressure resulting in this kind of wit, goes deeper. It is not one outrageously smart comparison which is at stake, but the legitimacy of artistic representation as a whole. The magnifi-cat theme expresses, in its marvelous mixture of humility and daring, the artist's sense that he is disturbing the "holy Sabbath" of creation by his recreation; that he is trespassing on sacred property or stealing an image of it or even exalting himself as a maker—in short, that he is magnifying mankind instead of "giving the glory" to God. Smart therefore atones the exposed, self-conscious self by at-one-ing it with the creature. He shows mankind "presenting" before God the animal creation it has exploited. And, in return, he asks that his verse-representation be "represented" before God by a mediator who enters the first line of his poem as "Lord, and Lamb." The opening of *Jubilate Agno* sets the pattern by compounding man and animal into ritual pairs:

> Let man and beast appear before him, and magnify his name together.
> Let Noah and his company approach the throne of Grace, and do homage to the Ark of their Salvation.
> Let Abraham present a Ram, and worship the God of his Redemption.
> Let Isaac, the Bridegroom, kneel with his Camels, and bless the hope of his pilgrimage.
> (A, 3-6)

Inspired by *Revelations,* Smart begins with a judgment scene: it envisages an ark that might survive a second flood. We find ourselves in a place of demand where everything must be "presented." The precise nature of the demand is not absolutely clear, and need not be the same in all works of art: perhaps it varies with historical circumstances, and perhaps it is the interpreter's task to make the relation between demand and response (demand and inner capability) perfectly clear. But artistic representation does seem to mediate a demand of this kind: one, moreover, not to be thought of as coming from outside, but rather, or also, from within. Again, whether "within" means the unconscious, or refers to a self-realizing instinct, may not be possible to determine generally but only in each case.

There is no way of being precise about this without engaging in considered acts of textual interpretation. We have to identify the nature of the challenge met by Smart and the "place" or "situation" he is in. It would be inadequate, for instance, to say of his "representation" of the animal creation that it springs from the same anxiety for the survival of the physical species that, according to Gertrude Levy's *The Gate of Horn* (1948), inspired the Cro-Magnon cave paintings at Lascaux. They may have had an apotropaic function, for they gather the essential traits of the hunted species into totemic sketches that intend to placate the Spirit of the hunted creature and so assure its fertile continuance. The creature is graphically "represented" by man to a Spirit in order for both human kind and the creature to survive.

Such recreative or reparative magic *is* relevant to Smart's poem; the analogy is too strong, and the theme of generation haunts too many of his verses. Yet it is only a beginning to specific interpretation. For we must add that in Smart the very *medium* of representation—visionary language itself—has become questionable, or subject to a demand which it cannot meet except by being renewed. His recreation of visionary categories is literally a recreation: the source of vision is not exhausted but still operative through him. That, at least, is the claim he seems to make, or the test he puts himself to. The anxiety for survival has associated itself with an anxiety for language-source, liturgy, and the entire process of representation.

II

Enthusiasm and Entropy. The fear that visionary language has lost its effectiveness may not be very different from the fear that nature grows old. Such "depletion anxieties" are linked to the not unrational feeling in us that our appetites—including that for presence—put a demand on the order of things which that order may not be able to satisfy: which, indeed, it may resent and reject.[4] The "economy" of language-use arising from depletion anxiety ranges from such devices of conservation as double-entendre, hermeticism and classical restraint, to the complementary if opposite ones of revivalist forgery, radical innovation and

[4] Cf. "The Dream of Communication," pp. 175-76. Since the first demands of the child focus on the mother, there may be a tendency later on to imagine a less used up, that is, *male*, source of comfort.

homeopathic promiscuity. You can write as sparse a hymn as Addison's famous "The spatious firmament on high" (1712), which, in spite of its source in Psalm 19, reflects Pascal's fright at the silence of the starry spaces; or you can fill the vacuum with the clang expressions of *Jubilate Agno,* till " barrenness becomes a thousand things " (Wallace Stevens).

Smart's aberrant verses would have been classified in their time as a product of " enthusiasm "; and this widespread and loosely knit religious movement was also a kind of counter-entropy. Affecting principally Puritans and Dissenters, it claimed to have uncovered a new source of truth, that of the individual in his privacy, who would know from " internal " grounds what revelation there was; but if that was all there was, then we were abandoned to individuality, and prone to the hell of unrelieved, sterile selfhood. The blessing proved to be the curse; the precious was also the accursed object. " My selfhood, Satan, arm'd in Gold " (Blake). The danger in enthusiasm, moreover, was its inevitable closeness to fanaticism, for the enthusiast found it difficult not to impose his " internal " evidences on others, not to exhibit his " antitheatrical " truth. He sought out or compelled a like-minded community.[5]

Enthusiasm in literature took many forms: it attacked, for example, the scientific " Religion of Nature " which affirmed the stability of the cosmos (nature would *not* grow old) at the cost of dehumanizing it and "untenanting Creation of its God" (Coleridge); and it overrode the pessimism of the neoclassic artist who felt he had come too late in history. The Visionary or even the Poet was felt to be superfluous in an Age of Reason; while the wish for originality, which enthusiasm abetted, increased in direct proportion to one's distance from the possibility. Yet the dilemma, even for the enthusiasts, was that originality and Original Sin were hard to tell apart.

Smart had to find, therefore, not only a well of visionary English but also an undefiled well. Every attempt to replenish, or imitate directly, the great source-books of secular and religious culture was open to the charge of false testimony—of giving glory to God as a cover for " representing " one's own passions. Today we have no problem with the first person singular, and fiction is

[5] Coleridge, a century after Swift, is still deeply worried by enthusiasm, and makes this analysis in the " Conclusion " to *Aids to Reflection.*

inconceivable without a semblance of self-exposure. Enthusiasm in art has gone public and taken the name of confessionalism. Consequently, it is hard for us to appreciate Pascal's notorious maxim, " Le moi est haïssable," and the fact that he was so sensitive to the liaison between egotism and enthusiasm that he condemned even Montaigne:

> The stupid plan he has to depict himself, and this not incidentally and against his better judgment as it may happen to all us mortals, but by design and as a matter of principle. For to say foolish things by chance or weakness is an ordinary fault; but to say them intentionally, that is not tolerable, and moreover his kind of stuff.[6]

Yet Pascal is protesting too much, for the lines of confession (his *Mémorial*) found hemmed in his garments at his death showed how close he was to what his time, and the next century, castigated as enthusiasm:

> The year of grace 1654. Monday 23rd November. Feast of St. Clement, Pope and Martyr, and of others in the martyrology. Eve of Chrysogonous. Martyr and others. From about half past 10 in the evening until half past midnight. Fire. God of Abraham, God of Isaac, God of Jacob, not of philosophers and scholars. Certainty, certainty, heart-felt, joy, peace. God of Jesus Christ. God of Jesus Christ. *My God and your God.* Thy God shall be my God. The world forgotten and everything except God . . . Joy, joy, joy, tears of joy.[7]

Apocalyptic Visions, trances, egomania, or what Dr. Johnson will call, memorably, the " hunger " and " dangerous prevalence " of imagination, were the diseases of enthusiasm against which Pascal and others erected their ideal of the " honnête homme," with his good sense, moderation, reasonable language. England, after the Puritan Revolution, imported this neoclassical ideal of correcting and improving not only the understanding but also speech itself, since an erroneous or corrupt language encourages intellectual and religious error. Swift's *Proposal for Correcting, Improving and Ascertaining the English Tongue* (1712) de-

---

[6] " Le sot projet qu'il à de se peindre et cela non pas en passant et contre ses maximes, comme il arrive à tout le monde de faillir, mais par ses propres maximes et par un dessein premier et principal. Car de dire des sottises par hasard et par faiblesse, c'est un mal ordinaire; mais d'en dire par dessein, c'est ce qui n'est pas supportable, et d'en dire de telles que celle-ci " (Blaise Pascal, *L'Apologie de la Religion Chrétienne* in *Oeuvres Complètes,* III, ed. Fortunat Strowski [Paris, 1931]).

[7] I have considerably abridged Pascal's *Mémorial* as found in his *Pensées.* trans. A. J. Krailsheimer (Baltimore, 1964), pp. 309-10.

nounced the "Enthusiastick Jargon" of "Fanatick Times" (the Puritan Revolution and its epigones); and as Professor Wimsatt has noted in a remarkable essay on the "laughter" of the Augustans, behind all these calls for decorum there lurked a heightened sense of unreality, which was not dissimilar, perhaps, to experiences of spiritual vastation.[8] The nearness of *flatus* and *afflatus*, of wind and inspiration, the manic-depressive cycle which all these doctors were seeking to cure, kept reasserting itself in epidemics of wit and far-fetched conceits, in the incurable prevalence of the mock-heroic mode, in the hysterical style of the sublime ode, and the laughing, biting speech that joins Swift to a late Augustan poet called William Blake.

The wars of religion against enthusiasm are an old story. But why should so irreligious a poet as Keats complain of Wordsworth's *egotistical sublime?* Why is he so defensive with Moneta, denouncing to her "all mock lyrists, large self-worshipers, / And careless Hectorers in proud bad verse" (*The Fall of Hyperion*, I, 207-08)? The reason is that he could not give up the sublime. He feared that poetry without enthusiasm was no longer poetry; and he was all the more sensitive to the charge of self-inflation because he knew that to create a sublime mode not based on personal experience was to revert to a vacuous archaism, to that impersonation of impersonality which MacPherson and Chatterton succumbed to. The sublime had to be associated with personal experience: there was no other way. Something drives fiction to that recognition in the two hundred years which comprise *Paradise Lost*, the neoclassical reaction, the emergence of Romanticism, and that renewed valediction to the Sublime which fails so gloriously in Browning's "Childe Roland" and Tennyson's "Morte D'Arthur."

Let me add, before returning to Smart, that Freud also treats enthusiasm. He is our latest Doctor of the Sublime, the Twentieth Century facing the gods, or the pathology of ecstasy. A modern Analytics of the Sublime must begin with Boileau's remarks on Longinus, study Vico on the way to Burke, Kant and Schopenhauer, and then admit that Freud is the inheritor of all these in his canny knowledge of the fortress against enthusiasm which polite society, or the soul itself, builds in the soul. Defense

---

[8] W. K. Wimsatt, Jr., "The Augustan Mode in English Poetry" in *Hateful Contraries* (Lexington, 1966), pp. 158-62.

mechanisms cannot blossom when there is nothing—no fire or flood—to defend against.

Smart's poetic career is emblematic of the fate of enthusiasm. It divides neatly into two parts. Before 1756 he was "the ingenious Mr. Smart," a facile and brilliant practitioner of neoclassic modes of verse. But recovering from a serious fever he began "confessing God openly" by praying aloud whenever the impulse came. "I blessed God in St James's Park till I routed all the company" (B 1, 89). He was confined for insanity in 1757-58 and again from 1759-63. During his "illness" he produced two long poems as daring and personal as any the Romantics were to write. The *Song to David* (1763) was dismissed in its time as a "fine piece of ruins," while the *Jubilate Agno* was not published till 1939. Smart's contemporaries saw him as an excellent versifier misled by religious mania, and though he reverted to such modest tasks as translating Horace and composing hymns for children, he never reestablished himself in their eyes.

What is one to do, even today, with verses like "Let Lapidoth with Percnos the Lord is the builder of the wall of CHINA—REJOICE" (B 1, 97)? The marvelous thing here is not, despite appearance, "Enthusiasm, Spiritual Operations, and pretences to the Gifts of the Spirit, with the whole train of New Lights, Raptures, Experiences, and the like."[9] It is the poet's total, consistent, critical rather than crazy, attack on the attenuated religious language of his day. "Percnos" is a bird of prey, like the Persian "Roc," punningly associated with the "Rock of Israel" in a previous line (B 1, 94), while "Lapidoth" (Judges 4:4) is linked to "Percnos-Roc" by an etymological pun which gives the Hebrew name a Latin root, meaning "stone" *(lapis, lapidis)*. Add the "Wall of China" as the greatest stone-work in the world, and the line as a whole is seen to "give the glory" to the Lord. It says, in effect, "Let Rock with Rock, the Lord is the Rock of Rocks, rejoice."

"In this plenty," to quote Stevens once more, "the poem makes meanings of the rock." Visionary language knows itself as superfluous, redundant; yet its very breaking against the rock reveals a more than gratuitous splendor. The disparity between the sustained base (the unvarying ROCK or REJOICE) and Smart's

---

[9] Part of Coleridge's attack on Enthusiasm in *Aids to Reflection*.

ever-shifting, eclectic play of fancy, discloses a twofold problem of representation: the traditional one of ineffability, related to the belief that God is " dark with excessive bright," or not attainable through mortal speech; and the somewhat rarer view, that the fault lies with language, which has lost yet may regain its representational power. To the crisis which stresses the inattainability of the signified, Smart adds the impressively important splendor of the signifier.

This is too cold a description, however, of the agony of the signifier. The question is less whether language can *represent* than whether by doing so it *seconds* or *comforts* the creature. Representation, I have argued, contains the idea of advocacy; and in Christian theology it is Christ who preeminently acts as comforter and advocate. To rejoice in the " Lord, and the Lamb " is to rejoice in the hope that the Judge (Lord) will turn out to be the Comforter (Lamb).

Yet the premise of that comfort, hidden way for the most part in the " Songs of Innocence " of Smart's time—in children's poetry or catechistical emblem books—was that the creation (*res creatae*, Romans 1:20 and 8:19) would help the tormented or doubting spirit to be instructed. By a proliferation of types, emblems, analogies, and the like, the Christian was encouraged to " suck Divinity from the flowers of Nature," in Sir Thomas Browne's words. As long as instruction could be drawn from flower or beast, then " Man and Earth suffer together " (C, 155) while waiting to be redeemed. Smart's poetry serves to strengthen their bond, even if it is one of suffering. But in doing so, in seeking to " represent " the creature, the poet discovers that language too is a creature in need of reparation.

For Smart's *animated* diction is the other side of his feeling for the lost animal spirits of a language " amerced " of its " horn " (C, 118-62). His poem, therefore, blends theriomorphic and theomorphic as the animals named by Adam in the first act of divinely instituted speech are now named again, restitutively. Language is the rib taken from Adam's tongue to " helpmate " his solitude before Eve. And it is interesting that in *Jubilate Agno* Eve does not formally appear. Even Mary's " Magnificat," when mentioned in B 1, 43, exalts not the woman and mother but rather language in its creature-naming and creature-presenting function. So close is the bondage of language and the bondage of the creature that both are one for a poet who is their *male* comforter, their *logos*. His Magnificat consoles what originally was to console Adam, by "translating" and "representing" it.

III

Cat and Bat. By magnifying Jeoffrey, Smart is training the telescope of wit on any ordinary creature instead of on the heavens or a certifiably divine subject. The meditation on the creature (i.e. on anything created, which included the heavens) was not uncommon; and a contemporary of Smart's, James Hervey, Methodist Rector of Weston-Favell, had popularized the genre by his *Meditations Among the Tombs* and *Contemplations of the Starry Heavens* etc. (1746-47). Hervey provides his readers with a flattering humiliation of the spirit, a Urizenic (so Blake will call it) calculus of apparent human power and actual limitation. Hervey, in short, is second-rate Sir Thomas Browne and third-rate Book of Job. "I have often been charmed and awed," he writes,

at the sight of the nocturnal Heavens; even before I knew how to consider them in their proper circumstances of majesty and beauty. Something like magic, has struck my mind, on a transient and unthinking survey of the aethereal vault, tinged throughout with the purest azure, and decorated with innumerable starry lamps. I have felt, I know not what powerful and aggrandizing impulse; which seemed to snatch me from the low entanglements of vanity, and prompted an ardent sigh for sublimer objects. Methought I heard, even from the silent spheres, a commanding call, to spurn the abject earth, and pant after unseen delights.—Henceforward, I hope to imbibe more copiously this moral emanation of the skies, when, in some such manner as the preceding, they are rationally seen, and the sight is duly improved. The stars, I trust, will teach me as well as shine; and help to dispel, both Nature's gloom, and my intellectual darkness. . . .

I gaze, I ponder. I ponder, I gaze; and think ineffable things.—I roll an eye of awe and admiration. Again and again I repeat my ravished views, and can never satiate my immense field, till even Fancy tires upon her wing. I find wonders ever new; wonders more and more amazing.—Yet, after all my present inquiries, what a mere nothing do I know; by all my future searches, how little shall I be able to learn, of those vastly distant suns, and their circling retinue of worlds! Could I pry with Newton's piercing sagacity, or launch into his extensive surveys; even then my apprehensions would be little better, than those dim and scanty images, which the mole, just emerged from her cavern, receives on her feeble optic. . . . To fathom the depths of the Divine Essence, or to scan universal Nature with a critical exactness, is an attempt with sets the acutest philosopher very nearly on a level with the ideot....[10]

This is also the period of Robert Blair's *The Grave* (1743) and Edward Young's *Night Thoughts* (1742-45). Smart's meditation on Jeoffrey is surely a criticism of such effusions. It replaces their self-regarding, didactic gloom with real observation, empathy, and a spirit as playful as that of the creature portrayed. The cat is the style; and the style, as a sustained song of Innocence, is totally unchary. It leaps; it is prankish; not only in its "mixture of gravity and waggery," as when Smart avers "For the Lord commanded Moses concerning the cats at the departure of the Children of Israel from Egypt," but also in its semblance of plot.

The opening of the passage shows Jeoffrey at his "exercises." These ordinary gambols turn into a ritual calisthenics curiously like the "Spiritual Exercises" of Ignatius of Loyola. When the poet "considers" his cat, the word "considers," which seems to have the Latin root for "star" in it, is a technical term from the tradition of the Spiritual Exercises (cf. "I have often been charmed and awed at the sight of the nocturnal Heavens; even before I knew how to consider them in their proper circumstances," etc.). Here the term is applied *à rebours* to an uncelestial object; yet Jeoffrey *is* a solar creature, worshipping at "the first glance of the glory of God in the East" and counteracting the powers of darkness "by his electrical skin and glaring eyes." The poet's consideration of Jeoffrey is reenforced when Jeoffrey "begins to consider himself" (B 2, 703) "in ten degrees"—"degrees" are also a term common to the genre of the Spiritual Exercises. In the argument prefaced to Smart's *A Song to David,* stanzas 65-71 constitute "An exercise upon the senses, and how to subdue them.... [with] An amplification in five degrees."

It is not my intent to turn Jeoffrey the cat into a Christian Soldier marching with Loyola. What the poem conveys is a spreading *consideration* from which nothing will eventually be excluded: Smart opens the covenant so that every creature— "The cat does not appear in the Bible," W. F. Stead, Smart's editor, notes drily—or at least the *names* of all created things may enter. "Let the Levites of the Lord take the Beavers of ye Brook alive into the Ark of the Testimony" (A, 16): the Beavers

[10] From Hervey's "Contemplations on the Starry Heavens."

do not appear in the Bible either, but here they enter alive into an Ark which could have proved as deadly as in Exodus 25: 9.

At this moment in time the covenant is merely the rainbow language before us, revived by Smart. But perhaps language is the only covenant. Smart renews the responsive prayer of the Psalms and of the Liturgy as if to provide the Church with a Book of Common Prayer genuinely "common." More and more of creation enters the Ark of Testimony as not only the verses pair ("Yet . . . For") but also different orders of creation; and it becomes vain to distinguish in Smart responsive poetry and resurrected wit. Both deal with strange conjunctions, hidden echoes, powerful yokings together, the "grappling of the words upon one another" (B 2, 632). This principle of "clapperclaw," with its residual sexuality, sometimes extends itself into the phonation of single verses, which then seem built, like "clapperclaw" itself, out of the competing responsiveness of mutual parts.[11] "Let Ross, house of Ross rejoice with the Great Flabber Dabber Flat Clapping Fish with hands" (D, 11).

Imagine the House of Ahab rejoicing with Moby Dick. . . . We hear the voice of the hands, in this applause; indeed the animal body itself grows to be all voice and enters the language. "For the power of some animal is predominant in every language" (B 2, 627), writes Smart; and he exemplifies this by an outrageous onomatopoeic punning. "For the pleasantry of a cat at pranks is in the language ten thousand times over. / For JACK UPON PRANCK is in the performance of *peri* together or separate" (B 2, 630-31). (Read *purr* for *pr* or *per*.) This convenant-language is quite literally the Ark where man and animal pair in amity, and the "Cherub Cat is a term of the Angel Tiger" (B 2, 725).

---

[11] "'Clapperclaw' is an archaic verb, meaning to scratch and claw, to attack with tooth and nail. Smart seems to be implying that the words in a poem should be associated as violently and powerfully as cats in a fight claw and bite one another" (Moira Dearnley, *The Poetry of Christopher Smart* [London, 1969], pp. 163-64). But "clapperclaw" was also theater-slang for applause (a topic dear to Smart) so that an ambivalent and complex relation is suggested between various drives: the sexual-aggressive, the verbal-expressive, the applause-seeking (theatrical and exhibitionist) and the applause-seeking (antiphonal and divine). For the slang term, see the printer's address to the reader in the first quarto of Shakespeare's *Troilus and Cressida*: "*A never writer to an ever reader. News.* Eternal reader, you have here a new play, never staled with the stage, never clapper-clawed with the palms of the vulgar, and yet passing full of the palm comical," etc.

All creatures in Smart become flaming creatures, and the Great Chain of Being a Great Chain of Language. To characterize Smart as a late or parodic meditationist is not adequate, therefore. It does not clarify the nature of the demand on him or the burden of his response. " Gird up thy loins now, like a man, I will demand of thee and answer thou me," God thunders at Job. And Job is finally persuaded to put his finger on his mouth. James Hervey, and other pseudo-enthusiast worshippers of the whirlwind, put their deflating finger of inflated moralistic prose on our mouths. They make us kiss the rod. But Smart is not put out by Newton, Nature, or Nature's God. He escapes the stupor induced by Natural Religion—by the contemplation of Leviathan, Tiger, or the System of the World. And he does so by answering its " cunning alphabet " with his own force of language. I will demand of thee and answer thou me, means, for Smart, girding up the loins of language and meeting the challenge of a divine text. The Bible is less a proof text than a shame text; and to escape this shame which affects, preeminently, the tongue, he must become David again and restore the Chain of Inspiration. " Rejoice in God, O ye Tongues. . . ." The Great Chain of Being is simply the Chain of Inspiration: it is honored not on account of order and hierarchy but only as it continues to electrify the tongue and represent the creature. In Smart's " consideration " everything stars; and the elation, or jubilation, of speech seems to sustain a demand put on it by the Book of God or the " cunning alphabet " of the Book of Nature.

Yet Bethlehem is not far from Bedlam. The madhouses of Smart's time had more than one King David in them, not to mention King Solomons and Queens of Sheba. The pressure on Smart of the divine text or of the need to respond to it by the creation of a New Song, that is, by a Language Covenant embracing the creature which had fallen with and away from man, heaps this Christopher as thoroughly as Melville's White Whale " heaped " Ahab. When we read Smart's boast, " I am the Reviver of Adoration amongst English Men," we do not feel the tension of a pun that mounts up in stanzas 50ff. of the *Song of David:*

> Praise above all—for praise prevails,
> Heap up the measure, load the scales. . . .

This is followed by twenty stanzas centering on the repeated word ADORATION. The method is indeed accumulative, additive rather than calculating and accounting. Double the "d" in "Adoration" and the pun becomes visible.

A "Song to David" means dedicated to, or spoken toward, David, but also *add*ing itself by *ad*oration until measure and scale break and the account is closed. Smart's ad libitum at once acknowledges and destroys the Johnsonian morality of style; the Doctor's reservation, for instance, that "Sublimity is by aggregation" yet that it is impossible to add to the divine glory:

> The ideas of Christian theology are too simple for eloquence, too sacred for fiction, and too majestick for ornament. To recommend them by tropes and figures is to magnify by a concave mirror the sidereal universe.
>
> Omnipotence cannot be exalted; infinity cannot be amplified; perfection cannot be improved.[12]

Smart might have enjoyed William Blake's joshing of Dr. Johnson in *An Island in the Moon:*

> I say this evening we'll all get drunk. I say
> dash, an Anthem, an Anthem, said Suction
> Lo the Bat with Leathern Wing
> Winking & blinking
> Winking & blinking
> Winking & blinking
> Like Doctor Johnson....

I quote only the more decent part. Compare cat and bat.

IV

A Speckled Language. Our delight in Smart is not a constant thing. Even in controlled sequences, like that on Jeoffrey, where the catalogue (no pun intended) is less chaotic than usual, the poet's exuberance may fall into a near-infantile strain:

> For he rolls upon prank to work it in.
> For having done duty and received blessing he
>   begins to consider himself.
>   (B 2, 702-03)

"Having done duty" may refer to Jeoffrey's sunrise worship, but it could also be a euphemism, especially when followed by a lengthy description of a cat cleaning itself.

---

[12] See his "Life of Milton" and "Life of Waller" in *The Lives of the English Poets* (London, 1779-81).

> For first he looks upon his fore-paws to see if
>   they are clean.
> For secondly he kicks up behind to clear away
>   there.
> For thirdly he works it upon stretch with the
>   fore paws extended.
>
> (B 2, 705-07)

As every child knows, cleanliness is next to godliness, and Jeoffrey provides an emblematic and charming illustration. Yet since Smart seems more wary of mentioning excrement than of mentioning the devil (B 2, 720ff.), and Jeoffrey's ritual exorcism of dirt is continuous with his "dutiful" worship of God, the thought may arise as to what is being euphemistically "pranked" or "worked in" at the higher level of godliness, benevolence, or jubilant verse-making.

One could try to find that "foundation on slander" (or "on the devil") which Smart mentions in B 1, 170. "The furnace itself shall come up at the last" (B 1, 293) he also writes, alluding to Abraham's fearful vision. Whether at the bottom of it all is a lie or evil or detritus, a redemptive poet like Smart has to extend the *contrafactura* method to cover even the excrementitious. The "soil" needed to fertilize the soil works on language too. Yet Smart's consciousness that when the deep opens, or the foundation rises up, it is the "Adversary" who may appear—indeed the shadow-thought, perhaps there from the beginning, that the Tongues invoked in the very first line of the poem might be used for the opposite of glorification—for slander or blasphemy or accusation—could help explain the *Jubilate*'s ritual or litany-like character, that apotropaic iteration which limits an otherwise emancipated verse-line. Smart's verses are, as he implies, a "conjecture" (B 1, 173) a "cast" of the line or tongue whose outcome is uncertain enough to be the object of a wager like that between God and the Accuser (Satan) in the Book of Job.

The nature of Smart's anxiety about "slander" may never be clear to us. It may not have been clear to himself. It is an anxiety about the foundation, about origins, about genealogy;[13] and so about the truth issuing from his own tongue:

---

[13] Consider how many aspects of this poetry reflect a concern with generation: the Biblical genealogies, from which Smart borrows many names; the generic emphasis of the names themselves; the personal allusions to family; and puns that range from the simple and innocuous to the complex and atrocious. Of the first kind is "Let Gibeon

> Let Ziba rejoice with Glottis whose tongue is
> wreathed in his throat.
> For I am the seed of the WELCH WOMAN and speak
> the truth from my heart.
> Let Micah rejoice with the spotted Spider, who
> counterfeits death to effect his purposes.
> For they lay wagers touching my life.—God be
> gracious to the winners.
>
> (B 1, 91-92)

Yet Smart's anxiety about "tongues" may have produced too good a poetic defense mechanism. It is not immediately obvious that the animals here are cited for *their* defense mechanisms. "Let Abiezer, the Anethothite, rejoice with Phrynos who is the scaled frog. For I am like a frog in the brambles, but the Lord hath put his whole armour upon me" (B 1, 95). Euphemism and benediction feed the perpetual motion machine of Smart's poetry. "Let" and "For," and such punnable morphemes as "at" and "ble" (bull), are linguistic *simples,* easily combined into phrases and sentences. They support the poet's run-on, combinatory technique, his compulsion to perpetual benevolence.

This may turn, also, by a momentum of its own, into a cat-and-mouse game with language, to see how much life can be eked out before the spirit fails and an adversary consciousness, or melancholia,[14] penetrates:

> For the power of some animal is predominant in
> every language.
> For the power and spirit of a CAT is in the Greek.
> For the sound of a cat is in the most useful
> preposition κατ' ευχην.
> For the pleasantry of a cat at pranks is in the
> language ten thousand times over.
> For JACK UPON PRANCK is in the performance of περι
> together or separate.
> For Clapperclaw is in the grappling of the words
> upon one another in all the modes of versification.

rejoice with the Puttock, who will shift for himself to the last extremity" (B 1, 81), and of the second, perhaps, "For the power of the Shears is direct as the life" (B 1, 179). Stead and Bond give a tenuous explanation of this line by referring to ancient methods of divination and so on, but a cruder and more powerful one emerges of "Shears" is read as "She-ars."

[14] One reason David fascinated Smart was that this "cunning player on an harp" drove away "the evil spirit" from Saul (1 Samuel 16:14-23).

> For the sleekness of a Cat is in his αγλαιηφι.
> For the Greek is thrown from heaven and falls
> upon its feet.
> For the Greek when distracted from the line is
> sooner restored to rank & rallied into some
> form than any other.
> For the purring of a Cat is his own τρυζει.
> For his cry is in οναι, which I am sorry for.
> For the Mouse (Mus) prevails in the Latin.
> For Edi-mus, bibi-mus, vivi-mus — ore-mus.
> (B 2, 627-39)

In brief, the overdetermination of simples like " cat " or "mus " keeps us within a sphere of childlike instruction. Smart's poem, at these points, is not so much a renovated liturgy as a marvelously inflated hornbook: a Spiritual Grammar Rock (" Conjunction Junction, What's your function? ") which averts discontinuity or catastrophic thoughts. However serious the content, the form remains propadeutic; however dangerous Smart's insight, the verse recovers into business (" benevolence ") as usual.

Despite Smart's delightful and outrageous word-play, then, his resourcefulness may be a testing of the source, and his witty, promiscuous conjunctions may point to the fear of being cut off—by his family, or eternally by Satanic accusation. How else are we to understand that long fragment which is but a variation of " Let X, house of X, rejoice with creature Y "?

> Let Westbrooke, house of Westbrooke rejoice with
> the Quail of Bengal. God be gracious to the
> people of Maidstone.
> Let Allcock, house of Allcock rejoice with The
> King of the Wavows a strange fowl. I pray
> for the whole University of Cambridge espe-
> cially Jesus College this blessed day.
> Let Audley, house of Audley rejoice with The Green
> Crown Bird. The Lord help on with the hymns.
> Let Bloom, house of Bloom rejoice with Hecatompus
> a fish with an hundred feet.
> Let Beacon, house of Beacon rejoice with Amadavad
> a fine bird in the East Indies.
> Let Blomer, house of Blomer rejoice with Halimus
> a Shrub to hedge with. Lord have mercy upon
> poor labourers this bitter frost Dec. 29 N.S.
> 1762.
> (D, 197-202)

Here the themes of house, foundation, fertility and rejoicing are interlaced with cries for help and mercy. The contiguity of "Maidstone" and "Allcock" is a parallel puzzle. "Without contraries," Blake wrote, "no progression"—but what is progressive here except a verse that somehow keeps renewing itself?

I want to explore further the "wreathed" way in which Smart builds his verse. Take his basic words "Let" and "For." Though they "generate" sentences, they are really a *stutterance*: a verbal compromise-formation which at once "lets" (hinders) and forwards his song ("Let Forward, house of Forward rejoice with Immussulus a kind of bird the Lord forward my translation of the psalms this year" D, 220). "Let" is close to being a primal word with antithetical meanings; and the tension between these meanings—whether identified as control and permissiveness or contraction and expansiveness or chastity and promiscuity—can give an extraordinary twist effect to the verse. Sometimes the contraries are almost too close to be spotted ("*Let Forward . . .*"); sometimes they seem apposites rather than opposites because of their position in the paired pattern of the verse ("Let. . . . For. . . ."); and sometimes they form a criss-cross pattern varying in distance (how far is it from "Maidstone" to "Allcock"?).

Smart has left us hints of a poetics of pairing, opposition and distancing:

> For the relations of words are in pairs first.
> For the relations of words are sometimes in
>   oppositions.
> For the relations of words are according to their
>   distances from the pair.
>   (B, 2, 600-02)

It could roughly summarize the actual unfolding of verse sentences in Smart: words are in pairs first, "Let Jubal rejoice with Caecilia"; this pairing may also introduce a contrast, "the woman and the slow-worm" (B 1, 43). The contrast may be more pathetic as when "Let Jorim rejoice with the Roach" is followed by "God bless my throat & keep me from things stranggled" (B 1, 179). The oppositions Smart mentions can also be that of the "Let" verse and the "For" response. Relations of distance, finally, are clearest in a group of iterative or antiphonal verses. In

> Let Jubal rejoice with Caecilia, the woman and
>   the slow-worm praise the name of the Lord.

> For I pray the Lord Jesus to translate my
> MAGNIFICAT into verse and represent it.
> (B 1, 43)

the first, relatively easy relation of words (Jubal and Caecilia being well-known patrons of music) becomes progressively more allusive and distant. Caecilia and the worm are linked by an etymological play on the Latin for the slow- or blind-worm (Caecilian, from *caecus*), but it needs more than curious learning to connect woman and worm with Mary's Magnificat through 1. the identification of Jesus as the seed of the woman who bruised the serpent's head (slowworm/Caecilia: serpent/Eve); 2. the idea of "translation," i.e. transformation, as from low to high, or from one species to another; and 3. the pun on Magnificat which turns the word into a compound (Magnifi-cat) and so establishes fully the relation between the "Let" and "For" verses through the paired opposition of lowly worm and magnified creature.[15]

To refine this kind of analysis is to come ultimately on the *hendiadys* in covert or open form. Puns are condensed or covert two-in-one structures, while Smart's synthetic "compounding" of nouns or noun-like words provides a more open form of the hendiadys. Allcock and Maidstone, when interpreted as twofolds, are simple hendiadys; Magnificat is a somewhat more complex instance; Jorim seems atomic until we notice its Hebrew plural ending (creating, once again, uncertainty as to whether a creature is to be thought of as one or more than one); and "the woman and the slow-worm," as it emerges from the name "Caecilia," is an especially characteristic hendiadys. One begins to suspect every name, in this name-freighted poetry, of being potentially emanative: other parts of speech too seem often like the attributes or derived sounds of some magical noun. Smart composes as if he had a choice between analytic and synthetic language formation, as if he were writing a Hebrew-English or Hebrew-Greek-Latin-English. Something of this is certainly in his mind, since he shares in the pentecostal aim to reconcile Babel into a universal code of worship. But whatever it is he wishes to achieve,

---

[15] Cf. W. M. Merchant, "Patterns of Reference in Smart's *Jubilate Agno*," *Harvard Library Bulletin*, 14 (1960), 23; and Moira Dearnley, *The Poetry of Christopher Smart*, pp. 156-59.

the hendiadys is indispensable. There are remarkable moments in which his verses "reproduce" or "replicate" by drawing two or even three words out of one, yet remain one-ly:

> Let Jorim rejoice with the Roach—God bless
> my throat & keep me from things stranggled.
> Let Addi rejoice with the Dace—It is good
> to angle with meditation.
> Let Luke rejoice with the Trout—Blessed be
> Jesus in Aa, in Dee and in Isis.
> (B 1, 179-81)

In the first verse above, Roach, a monosyllable, if read on the analogy of Jorim, becomes dysyllabic, with an aspirated ending (Ro-ach), so that the "stranggled" is not only thematically sustained by the image of the caught fish but equally by the throaty sound.[16] In the following verses we see a proper noun, Addi, breaking up into three components that are sounds or rivers or both: Aa, Dee, Isis (A-D-I). Strictly speaking, we need only the "i" of Isis to complete Addi (itself a pun on the additive process?). But even the -sis may be accounted for if we read Isis as I-c's, and by a bit of scrabbling involve the second proper noun, Dace, also composed of the letter-sounds, A, D, and—this time—C. One name is A, D, plus I; the other A, D, plus C; so that Jesus (that famous fish, almost riming here with Isis, considering the closeness of I and J) comprehends both names, being blessed in A, in D, and in I, C's.

It is almost impossible to summarize Smart's poetic method. It is not, or not only, a "mad, philological vision of realty."[17] It does not, or not merely, subvert the referential aspect of words like Isis by deconstructing them as acoustic images or magical sounds. It is best seen as a sacred poetics driving to astonishing extremes the principle of antiphony or "parallelism of members" (Is-is!) discovered by Bishop Lowth in the Psalms. So, Jorim goes with the Roach and is paralleled by Addi with the Dace, and even by angle "with" meditation; while Addi and Dace and Isis can be shown to be "members" of Jesus. But how do you fit in

---

[16] "Ro-ach," in fact, moves close to "Ru-ach," Hebrew for breath or spirit. Cf. *Jubilate Agno*, B2, 626, and also the play on "peri" (Greek) in B2, 631, which is understood as "purry" and, perhaps, "pair-y" ("the relations of words are in pairs," etc.).

[17] Moira Dearnley, p. 164.

Hecatompus with an hundred feet? "Why, then, I'le fit you!" And, indeed, there is a mad attempt to speak with tongues and write with all those feet, to re-member or re-present every last creature by a " pairing " that will exclude nothing from the " Ark " of testimony.

In society the simplest form of representation (in the sense of a normative presentation of the self) is by one's personal name. Names are a compromise, of course; for no name is unique; and Smart's use of single names (Abraham, Jorim, Dace, Hecatompus) makes them ambiguously individual and generic.[18] Names, moreover, like all proper nouns, are curiously split in their semantic character. They tend to be both subsemantic (so conventional as to be meaningless, semantically neutral) and supersemantic (they can be analyzed or pseudoanalyzed into richly meaningful parts). The idea of naming, therefore, recapitulates the drama played out in Smart's verse. Names individualize and socialize: they are always a kind of two-in-one. " Christopher Smart " names a single person whose Christ-bearing (Christopher) wit and wound (Smart) are one like the " Lord, and the Lamb " (A, 1) are one.

Every individual is impair. He sticks out or should stick out. Yet selfhood is both a demand to be met and subject to accusation. Analysis could go from here in many directions: religious, sociological, or what I have called psychoesthetic. Smart invariably connects representability of the self (*by* language, *with* the creature, and *to* God) and the treatment of the impair (also the impaired). He first reduces the impair to an infantile charm or a linguistic simple (cat, mus, the opaque proper noun, etc.). By this method he both acknowledges and comforts the isolation of each creature. The linguistic simple, at the same time, is given the chance to multiply or replicate, but the match that results also escapes divine assessment. It cannot be *judged*. Will you frown at " Rehob " because he " rejoices with Caucalis Bastard Parsley "? Or at the Wild Cucumber with which " Nebai " is asked to rejoice (C, 152, 160) ? Such matchmakings are beyond good and evil.

It may be useful to summarize the ways of Smart with language

---

[18] Even representation by the personal name is not so simple a matter, then: Smart's enumerative evocation of names (taken from obituaries as well as genealogies) is analogous to invoking saints or intermediaries. Yet he so expands the roster that representation, while verging on mediation, insists on the *proprium* of each proper noun.

because his comforting of creatureliness extends to language—to sounds and words, large and small. He delights in 1. morphemes which can be individualized as words (cat, Dee); 2. words that are reduplicative in structure and remain simples because quasi-reversible (Aa, David, Amadavad, Wavow, Immussulus); 3. self-replicating or redundant phrases which can expand into a whole verse, as in the following (D, 175) inspired by the very idea of " re ": "Let Ready, house of Ready" (redundancy) " rejoice " (Re . . . Re . . . re . . .) " with Junco The Reed Sparrow " (Ready . . . Reed); 4. the categorical hendiadys, which brings together, not as in the story of Noah, pairs of the same species but unmatable *res creatae*.

If the ark into which these pairs enter cannot be that of generation, it must be that of regeneration. But does regeneration involve or exclude generation? The new order here invoked, at once linguistic and ontic, coexists ambivalently with an older order which it neither subsumes nor yet suppresses. Smart's poetics of *relation* never quite turn into a poetics of *translation*. The name " Jesus " embraces the name " Isis" and the result is a speckled language. In the opening scene of the *Jubilate,* when Abraham presents a ram and Jacob his speckled drove, we cannot tell whether sexual generation is being sacrificed or consecrated.

V

> A swallow is an emancipated owl,
> and a glorified bat . . . an owl
> that has been trained by the
> Graces . . . a bat that loves the
> morning light.
> J. Ruskin, *Love's Meinie*

Theory as Epilogue. The newest movement in philosophy, which extends into literary studies, questions the idea of presence. It is said to be an illusion fostered by our tendency to privilege voice over the written word. Voice, for Jacques Derrida, is the egotistical sublime; and our desire for the proper name (" mot propre," " nom unique ") a metaphysical comfort. The best voice can do is to become literature: that is, to subvert its referential or representational function by bruising itself on the limits of language.

Derrida moves within a philosophical context of his own, and it is confusing to juxtapose his theory and Smart's poetics. I apologize for this "perspective by incongruity," as Kenneth Burke would call it, but I see no better way of suggesting how complex yet empty the concept of representation may become. Even if one acknowledges that Derrida's very aim is to empty this concept, at least of its psychologistic and metaphysical pathos, the "nature" of representation remains a puzzle.[19]

I have argued that representation supports the ideal of self-presence in its psychic and social aspects. "Vilest things become themselves in her," Shakespeare's Enobarbus says of Cleopatra. She is "beautiful in corruption," like Smart's "Eyed Moth" (B 1, 93); and Enobarbus may indeed be playing on the idea of life engendered by Nilotic slime. Yet toward this "becoming," this triumph over the shame of creaturely origin, artistic representation also aspires. It may turn out, of course, that representation is all there is; and that we will never experience a self-presence in which we see—and are seen—not as in a glass darkly but face to face. Yet who can decide how ultimate the category of substitution is, and in particular the substitution of representation for presence?

The tropes of literature, or similar kinds of imaginative substitution, could as easily be said to pursue that "presence," which "identifies" all creatures, as to defer it. Perhaps it does not matter which, since both pursuit and deferment are endless. That the identifying moment, like a snapshot, is too deathlike or ecstatic; that movement or troping must begin again; that the acute self-consciousness must be transcended by an act of what is commonly called imagination—all this is part of the psychopathology of ordinary life, or of that principle of "clapperclaw" which "joyces" language in Shakespeare, Smart, and even in Derrida.

It may be that the theory of representation finds a less problematic exponent in an intermediate figure, more congruous with Smart, and exerting through Proust some influence on French thought. Let me conclude, then, with a note on John

[19] I do not know how Derrida would interpret Smart's use of names and proper nouns. Or his ritually insistent, repetitive, affirmations. Would he compare all this with Nietzsche's "affirmation en jeu" or Heidegger's risky "espérance"? See his crucial essay on "La différance" in *Marges de la Philosophie* (Paris, 1972), especially pp. 25-29.

Ruskin. His prose may be the best nature-poetry in the language. Ruskin also " represents " the creature, though to his fellow-man rather than God. How sane he appears when placed beside Smart, even if touched by a madness and childishness similar to Smart's. There is probably no better antidote to the *Jubilate Agno* than Ruskin's celebration of robin and swallow in *Love's Meinie*.[20]

These lectures, given by him as Slade Professor of Fine Art before the University of Oxford, are clearly acts of reparation toward robin and swallow and, indeed, all " lower classes " exploited by the Victorian combination of Wealth and Science. " That, then, is the utmost which the lords of land, and masters of science, do for us in their watch upon our feathered suppliants. One kills them, the other writes classifying epitaphs." The painters and monks, lumped together by Ruskin, do us no good either. " They have plucked the wings from birds, to make angels of men, and the claws from birds, to make devils of men." The emphasis on genetic development in Darwinian science seems equally pernicious to Ruskin, who fears that all such speculation on origins will distract us from the present, from the endangered beauty and aptness of the *living* creature.

But it is not the common creatures alone, the swallows, fissirostres, or split-beaks, which must be saved. The common words too must be " represented ": English names in their vernacular being, winged expressions which lead Ruskin to reflect on the troubadours, Chaucer and the *Roman de la Rose*. The habitat of the creature is in literature and art as well as in wood and field. Nature and art are both endangered by the deadly Latin of modern anatomical analysis. We should not see the things of this world under the species of a false objectivity, or by its killing nomenclature, but through the medium of their own natures and

[20] Much of Ruskin's work in the 1860s and early 1870s was secretly aimed at weaning young Rose La Touche from a religious enthusiasm (not unlike Smart's, though morbid and distinctly Evangelical in origin) which was to end in her mental derangement, symptoms of which Ruskin also carried within himself. *Love's Meinie* (Parts I and II on robin and swallow were published in 1873; Part III on the chough in 1881) ministers to a mind diseased by giving glory back to life. It has its private as well as public dimension: Ruskin weaves, for example, the *Roman de la Rose* into his book because it must have seemed an equally troubled yet saner version of the " Romance " he was experiencing in his own courtship of Rose; and he constructs, toward this, sensitive if fanciful connections between " oiseau," " oisel," " demoiselle " and " oiseau," " avis," " advice " (see his substitution of a prefatory " Advice " for the more usual " Advertisement ").

the *lingua franca et jocundissima* of vernacular perception. Reading *Love's Meinie* I repent me for not being able to "translate" such words as "representation." "All of you who care for life as well as literature," Ruskin advises, "and for spirit,—even the poor souls of birds,—as well as lettering of their classes in books,— you, with all care, should cherish the old Saxon, English and Norman-French names of birds, and ascertan them with the most affectionate research."

Yale University

NARRATIVE AND HISTORY

BY J. HILLIS MILLER

Hegel says: " That at the bottom of history, and particularly of world history, there is a final aim, and that this has actually been realized in it and is being realized—the plan of Providence—that there is *reason* in history: that is to be shown philosophically and thus as altogether necessary." And: "A history without such an aim and without such a point of view would be merely a feeble-minded pastime of the imagination, not even a children's fairy tale, for even children demand some interest in stories, i.e., some aim one can at least feel, and the relation of the occurrences and actions to it." Conclusion: Every story must have an aim, hence also the history of a people and the history of the world. That means: because there is " world history " there must also be some aim in the world process. That means: we demand stories only with aims. But we do not at all *demand* stories about the world process, for we consider it a swindle to talk about it. That my life has no aim is evident even from the accidental nature of its origin; that *I can posit an aim for myself* is another matter. But a state has no aim; we alone give it this aim or that. (Friedrich Nietzsche, notes of 1873)[1]

[1] Trans. Walter Kaufmann, *The Portable Nietzsche* (New York: The Viking Press, 1954), pp. 39-40. For the German see F. Nietzsche, *Werke,* Musarionausgabe, VI (Munich: Musarion Verlag, 1920-49), 336: " Hegel: ' Dass der Geschichte, und zwar wesentlich der Weltgeschichte ein Endzweck an und für sich zum Grunde liege und derselbe wirklich in ihr realisirt worden sei und werde—der Plan der Vorsehung—dass überhaupt *Vernunft* in der Geschichte sei, muss für sich selbst philosophisch und damit als an und für sich nothwendig ausgemacht werden.' ' Eine Geschichte ohne solchen Zweck und ohne solche Beurtheilung wäre nur ein schwachsinniges Ergehen des Vorstellens, nicht einmal ein Kindermärchen, denn selbst die Kinder fordern in den Erzählungen ein interesse, das ist: einen wenigstens zu ahnden gegebenen Zweck und die Beziehung der Begebenheiten und Handlungen auf denselben.' Schluss: jede Erzählung muss einen Zweck haben, also auch die Geschichte eines Volkes, die Geschichte der Welt. Das heisst: weil es ' Weltgeschichte ' giebt, muss auch im Weltprocess ein Zweck sein; das heisst: wir fordern Erzählungen nur mit Zwecken. Aber wir *fordern* gar keine Erzählungen vom Weltprocess, weil wir es für Schwindel halten, davon zu reden. Dass mein Leben keinen Zweck hat, ist schon aus der Zufälligkeit seines Entstehens klar: *dass ich einen Zweck mir setzen kann,* ist etwas andres. Aber ein Staat hat keinen Zweck: sondern nur wir geben ihm diesen oder jenen." The quotations from Hegel are from " Die Weltgeschichte," *Enzyklopädie der philosophischen Wissenschaften im Grundrisse* (1830), para. 549, Zusatz, pp. 426, 428 of the ed. of F. Nicolin and D. Poggeler (Hamburg: F. Meiner, 1969).

The nourishing fruit of the historically understood contains time as a precious but tasteless seed. (Walter Benjamin, "Theses on the Philosophy of History," 1940)[2]

A novel is in various ways a chain of displacements—displacement of its author into the invented role of the narrator, further displacement of the narrator into the lives of imaginary characters whose thoughts and feelings are presented in that odd kind of ventriloquism called " indirect discourse,"[3] displacement of the " origin " of the story (in historical events or in the life experience of the author) into the fictitious events of the narrative. One of the ways in which this sideways movement into the void of fiction is effaced and at the same time surreptitiously revealed is the curious tradition, present in the modern middle-class novel from its sixteenth-century beginnings on, whereby a work of fiction is conventionally presented not as a work of fiction but as some other form of language. This is almost always some " representational " form rooted in history and in the direct report of " real " human experience. It seems as if works of fiction are ashamed to present themselves as what they are but must always present themselves as what they are not, as some non-fictional form of language. A novel must pretend to be some kind of language validated by its one-to-one correspondence to psychological or historical reality.

This reversal or suppression of the displacement involved in writing a work of fiction takes several forms. A novel may present itself as a collection of letters (*Clarissa, Les Liaisons dangereuses*), as memoirs or edited documents (*The Posthumous Papers of the Pickwick Club*), as an old manuscript found in a trunk or bottle (Poe's " Manuscript Found in a Bottle "), as an autobiography (*Robinson Crusoe, David Copperfield, Henry Esmond*), as a legal deposition (as in the last section of Melville's *Benito Cereno*), as journalism (Dickens's *Sketches by Boz*), as a travel book (*Typee*),

[2] *Illuminations,* trans. H. Zohn (New York: Schocken, 1969), p. 263; *Illuminationen* (Frankfurt am Main: Suhrkamp Verlag, 1961), p. 278: " Die nahrhafte Frucht des historisch Begriffenen hat die Zeit als den kostbaren, aber des Geschmacks entratener Samen in ihrem Innern."

[3] Odd because rather than speaking directly as the character, as Edgar Bergen speaks as Charlie McCarthy, or as Joyce speaks as Molly Bloom in the interior monologue of her soliloquy, the author in indirect discourse pretends to be a narrator who speaks for the character, lending him words in a form of language which always involves some degree of ironical distance or difference. The displacement involved is present in the linguistic strategy employed.

or even as a realistic painting (as the subtitle of Thomas Hardy's *Under the Greenwood Tree or The Mellstock Quire* is " A Rural Painting of the Dutch School " or as the subtitle of *Middlemarch* is " A Study of Provincial Life," though the word " study " here may refer as much to a sociological or scientific treatise as to a form of painting, which would add another form of displacement to my list).

Perhaps the most important form of this masking is the presentation of a novel as a form of history. In fact the term history tends to contaminate other forms of displacement and to displace even them, as the full title of *Henry Esmond*, a fictional autobiography in form, is *The History of Henry Esmond, Esq., A Colonel in the Service of Her Majesty Q. Anne, Written by Himself*, or as the full title of Dickens's novel is *The Personal History of David Copperfield*. Perhaps the most famous example of the use of the term " history " in the title of a novel is *The History of Tom Jones, A Foundling*. Abundant examples may be found, however, from one end of the modern tradition of the novel to the other. The final Barset novel is called *The Last Chronicle of Barset* (though the distinction between a " chronicle " and a " history " is important), and H. G. Wells published in 1910 *The History of Mr. Polly*.

The reasons for the predominance of this particular form of counter-displacement are evident. By calling a novel a history its author at one stroke covers over all the implications of gratuitousness, of baseless creativity and lie, involved in the word " fiction." At the same time he affirms for his novel that verisimilitude, that solid basis in pre-existing fact, which is associated with the idea of history. A particularly striking example of this anxiety to hide the fact that the work of fiction is a work of fiction, along with an eagerness to enroll it under the banner of history, is a passage in Henry James's essay on Trollope (1888). It seems as if the fictional imagination, for James at least, can only be liberated as long as it hides from itself what it actually is. It seems as if a novel, in James's sense of it, can only be taken seriously by its readers if it pretends to be what it is not. In the essay James deplores Trollope's " wanton " " violation " of " that illusion dear to the intending novelist." (He much exaggerates, by the way, the degree to which Trollope commits this " pernicious trick." It occurs much less frequently in Trollope's later fiction than in his earlier novels.

Moreover, a present-day critic would find these examples of the "anti-novel" in Trollope much more defensible and significant, much more, in fact, part of the traditional technique of the novel from *Don Quixote* on, than does James.) Trollope, says James, "took a suicidal satisfaction in reminding the reader that the story he was telling was only, after all, a make-believe. He habitually referred to the work in hand (in the course of that work) as a novel, and to himself as a novelist, and was fond of letting the reader know that this novelist could direct the course of events according to his pleasure." Against this James affirms his strong commitment to the idea that a work of fiction depends for its very existence on claiming that it is history:

It is impossible to imagine what a novelist takes himself to be unless he regards himself as an historian and his narrative as history. It is only as an historian that he has the smallest *locus standi*. As a narrator of fictitious events he is nowhere; to insert into his attempt a back-bone of logic, he must relate events that are assumed to be real. This assumption permeates, animates all the work of the most solid story-tellers; we need only mention (to select a single instance) the magnificent historical tone of Balzac, who would as soon have thought of admitting to the reader that he was deceiving him, as Garrick or John Kemble would have thought of pulling off his disguise in front of the foot-lights. Therefore, when Trollope suddenly winks at us and reminds us that he is telling us an arbitrary thing, we are startled and shocked in quite the same way as if Macaulay or Motley were to drop the historic mask and intimate that William of Orange was a myth or the Duke of Alva an invention.[4]

An admirably suggestive passage! Here the rationale of the tradition of calling a novel a history is brought to the surface, not least in the metaphors James uses, in the hyperbolic "heat" (his term) of his tone, and in his oblique confession that it is just because a work of fiction is not history that it must maintain so

---

[4] *The Art of Fiction and Other Essays* (New York: Oxford University Press, 1948), pp. 59-60. The same polemic appears in "The Art of Fiction" (1888), *ibid.*, pp. 5-6: "Such a betrayal of a sacred office seems to me, I confess, a terrible crime; it is what I mean by the attitude of apology, and it shocks me every whit as much in Trollope as it would have shocked me in Gibbon or Macaulay. It implies that the novelist is less occupied in looking for the truth (the truth, of course I mean, that he assumes, the premises that we must grant him, whatever they may be) than the historian, and in doing so it deprives him at a stroke of all his standing-room. To represent and illustrate the past, the actions of men, is the task of either writer, and the only difference that I can see is, in proportion as he succeeds, to the honour of the novelist, consisting as it does in his having more difficulty in collecting his evidence. . . ."

carefully the fiction that it is. Though William of Orange and the Duke of Alva were real persons and the characters of Balzac unreal, as much a lie as the play-acting of Garrick or Kemble, the novelist must maintain the fiction that his characters have historical reality or else he is " nowhere." This means, I take it, that a fiction confessing itself to be a fiction vanishes into airy vapor or falls into a fathomless abyss, like a man who loses his footing, the ground he stands on, his *locus standi*. The substantiality of " the most solid story-tellers " depends on having a " somewhere," an assumed historical reality as a background or scene. Such a context, by that species of metonymic transfer which is the basis of all narrative, will give solidity to the story narrated within the *locus* and to the interpretation of the story performed by its narrator.

The assumption that his narrative is history gives more, however, than simply a foundation to the novelist's work. It also " insert[s] into his attempt a back-bone of logic." Without the assumption of an historical basis a work of fiction would, it seems, disintegrate into unconnected fragments, or become a " large loose baggy monster," in James's famous phrase, an invertebrate, a jellyfish or Medusa. Only if it is assumed to be history will a novel have a beginning, middle, and end, so forming a coherent whole, with a single meaning or individuality, like a vertebrated animal. In his use of the word " logic," with its accompanying metaphors of " *locus* " and " backbone " James exposes the connection between the notion of organic form in the novel and the system of assumptions which is associated with the idea of history in Western culture. The traditional notions of form in fiction, James implicitly recognizes, are displaced versions of ideas about history. The entire fabric of assumptions about form and meaning in the novel, whose master expression is James's own admirable prefaces to his works, stands or falls with the metaphor defining a work of fiction as a species of history.

The assumptions about history which have been transferred to the traditional conception of the form of fiction may be identified. They include the notions of origin and end (" archeology " and " teleology ") ; of unity and totality or " totalization "; of underlying " reason " or " ground "; of selfhood, consciousness, or " human nature "; of the homogeneity, linearity, and continuity of time; of necessary progress; of " fate," "destiny," or " Providence " ; of causality; of gradually emerging " meaning " ; of representation and truth—in short, all those assumptions made about world history in the citations from Hegel by Nietzsche in my initial epigraph. Certain metaphors, like those of flowing water, woven cloth, or a living organism, tend to recur in expressions of this system of assumptions, or rather the regular and inevitable appearance of these overt metaphors whenever the system is being expressed reveals the fact that the system is itself a metaphor, a figure whose originally metaphorical or fictive character has been effaced. As Hegel says, using in reverse the metaphorical equation I am exploring, " even children demand some interest in stories, i.e., some aim one can at least feel, and the relation of the occurrences and actions to it." A story without such an aim and the subservience of all its parts to that aim would " be merely a feeble-minded pastime of the imagination."

The set of assumptions common to both Western ideas of history and Western ideas of fiction are not—it is a point of importance— a collection of diverse attributes, the distinctive features which happen to be there. They are on the contrary a true system, in the sense that each implies all the others. No one of them may be shaken or solicited, without a simultaneous putting in question of all the others. Jacques Derrida expresses admirably the mutual inherence of all these aspects in one another:

[L]e concept *métaphysique* d'histoire . . . est le concept de l'histoire comme histoire du sens, . . . histoire du sens se produisant, se développant, s'accomplissant. Linéairement, . . . en ligne droite ou circulaire. . . . Le charactère métaphysique du concept d'histoire n'est pas seulement lié à la linéarité mais à tout un *système* d'implications (télélogie, eschatologie, accumulation relevante et intériorisante du sens, un certain type de traditionnalité, un certain concept de continuité, de vérité, etc.). Ce [la linéarité] n'est donc pas un prédicat accidentel dont on pourrait se défaire par une ablation locale, en quelque sorte, sans un déplacement général de l'organisation, sans faire travailler le système lui-même.[5]

All the elements of this system of ideas about history may be transferred without distortion to the customary notion of the form of fiction. The formal structure of a novel is usually conceived of as the gradual emergence of its meaning. This coincides with its end, the fulfillment of the teleology of the work. The end is the retrospective revelation of the unity of the whole, its " organic

[5] *Positions* (Paris: Les Éditions de Minuit, 1972), p. 77.

unity." The last page is the goal toward which it has been moving, inhabited as it has been throughout by "the sense of an ending." This sense articulates all the parts as the backbone of the narrative. At the same time the image of a progressive revelation of meaning is to be applied to the idea of the "destinies" of the characters. Their lives make "sense" as the gradual revelation of a whole, the "meaning of their lives." The end of the novel is the final exposing of the fates of the characters as well as of the formal unity of the text. The notions of narrative, of character, and of formal unity in fiction are all congruent with the system of concepts making up the Western idea of history.

No doubt historians have not needed to wait for writers of fiction to perform that act of interrogation which would make this system of assumptions tremble or perhaps vanish like a spider-web blown away by the wind. Nor has the putting in question of this system had to wait for the deconstructive rigor of a Derrida or a Roland Barthes.[6] As Leo Braudy in *Narrative Form in History and Fiction: Hume, Fielding, and Gibbon* and Hayden White in *Metahistory*[7] have shown, the writing of history was already a problematic enterprise for eighteenth and nineteenth-century historians, or indeed for modern historians since Vico. No doubt it seemed problematic to Thucydides and Plutarch, or even to Herodotus. As James's revealing final metaphor indicates, all historians have consciously worn "the historic mask," much as an actor wears his costume and makeup. This is true not in the sense that historians have believed that William of Orange was a myth or the Duke of Alva an invention, but in the sense that they have been aware that the narrating of an historical sequence in one way or another involves a constructive, interpretative, fictive act. Historians have always known that history and the narrative of history never wholly coincide. Nevertheless, the system of assumptions about history which I have briefly described has had great coercive power to bewitch not only historians and philosophers of history but also writers of fiction who model their enterprise on that of the narrative historian. The system tends magically to weave itself in a new form even when it has been deliberately abolished, like a

---

[6] For an essay on this topic by Barthes, see "Le discours de l'histoire," *Information sur les sciences sociales* (août 1967), trans. in *Introduction to Structuralism*, ed. M. Lane (New York: Basic Books, 1970), pp. 145-55.

[7] (Princeton: Princeton University Press, 1970) and (Baltimore: The Johns Hopkins Press, 1973).

spider-web spun again out of the entrails of our Western languages, or like Penelope's web spun anew each morning after its nightly destruction.

One of the most persistent forms of this endlessly renewed, endlessly defeated, unweaving has in fact been performed by works of fiction. Insofar as a putting in question of its own enterprise has been an intrinsic part of the practice of prose fiction in its modern form from *Don Quixote* on through *Tristram Shandy* to John Barth and J. L. Borges, this unravelling has also been a dismantling of the basic metaphor by means of which prose fiction has defined itself, that is, a certain idea of history. Insofar as a novel raises questions about the key assumptions of story-telling, for example about the notions of origin and end, about consciousness or selfhood, about causality, or about gradually emerging unified meaning, then this putting in question of narrative form becomes also obliquely a putting in question of history or of the writing of history. What seemed to be the *locus standi* by analogy with which the novel was written turns out to be itself undermined by the activity of story-telling. Insofar as a novel " deconstructs " the assumptions of " realism " in fiction, it also turns out to " deconstruct " naive notions about history or about the writing of history. To call attention to this self-defeating turning back of the novel to undermine its own ground is the chief point of this paper.

I choose as one example of this George Eliot's *Middlemarch* (1871-72). The example is perhaps a good one because *Middlemarch* is not in any obvious way part of that tradition of the anti-novel to which I alluded above in invoking the names of Cervantes, Sterne, and Borges. *Middlemarch* is solidly within the tradition of realistic fiction and in fact might be taken as the English masterpiece of the genre. *Middlemarch* places its events carefully in a particular historical time and place, English provincial life in the period just before the first reform bill. It builds up carefully the historical background of this time and place. In that sense it is an " historical novel." It presents its narrator explicitly as an " historian " and is overtly based on certain historical assumptions. These include the assumption that each historical period is unique and the assumption that " historical forces " determine the kind of life that can be lived at a certain time. Dorothea Brooke's life, for example, is disabled by the lack of any " coherent social faith and order which could perform the function of knowledge for the ardently willing soul."[8] The "determining acts of her life" are "the mixed result of young and noble impulse struggling amidst the conditions of an imperfect social state," for, as George Eliot says, "there is no creature whose inward being is so strong that it is not greatly determined by what lies outside it" (III, "Finale," 464). In fact the word "history" is the key term in the opening phrase of *Middlemarch*, where Dorothea, in a famous analogy, is presented as the repetition with a difference of St. Theresa, a St. Theresa born out of her time: "Who that cares much to know the history of man, and how the mysterious mixture behaves under the varying experiments of Time, has not dwelt, at least briefly, on the life of Saint Theresa . . ." (I, "Prelude," 1). In *Middlemarch*, moreover, history is a theme within the story itself, in the historical researches of Casaubon, and in the relation of art and history as it is put in question in the discussions between Will Ladislaw and his German friend Naumann. History is also constantly kept before the reader as the basic analogy for the narrator's own enterprise.

There is not space in this brief paper to interpret fully the chief passages where the notion of history is an overt issue in *Middlemarch*. One example is an admirable passage in Chapter XI describing the "shifting . . . boundaries," the "subtle movement" of "old provincial society."[9] Here George Eliot's presentation of a model of social "interdependence" and gradual change in *Middlemarch* is put explicitly under the aegis of the similar enterprise of Herodotus: "In fact, much the same sort of movement and mixture went on in old England as we find in older Herodotus, who also, in telling what had been, thought it well to take a woman's lot for his starting-point" (I, xi, 143). Another example is the splendid passage in Chapter XX describing Dorothea's response to the "stupendous fragmentariness," the "unintelligible" "weight," of Rome:

[8] *Middlemarch*, Cabinet Edition, I, "Prelude" (Edinburgh and London: William Blackwood and Sons: n. d.), 2. Further quotations from *Middlemarch* will be identified by volume, chapter, and page in this edition.

[9] "Some slipped a little downward, some got higher footing: people denied aspirates, gained wealth, and fastidious gentlemen stood for boroughs; some were caught in political currents, some in ecclesiastical, and perhaps found themselves surprisingly grouped in consequence; while a few personages or families that stood with rocky firmness amid all this fluctuation, were slowly presenting new aspects in spite of solidity, and altering with the double change of self and beholder" (I, xi, 142).

> To those who have looked at Rome with the quickening power of a knowledge which breathes a growing soul into all historic shapes, and traces out the suppressed transitions which unite all contrasts, Rome may still be the spiritual centre and interpreter of the world. But let them conceive one more historical contrast: the gigantic broken revelations of that Imperial and Papal city thrust abruptly on the notions of a girl who had been brought up in English and Swiss Puritanism, fed on meagre Protestant histories and on art chiefly of the hand-screen sort; a girl whose ardent nature turned all her small allowance of knowledge into principles, fusing her actions into their mould, and whose quick emotions gave the most abstract things the quality of a pleasure or a pain.... (I, xx, 295)

A final example is the opening of Chapter XV in which George Eliot explicitly defines her strategy as a novelist in contrast to that of " a great historian, as he insisted on calling himself," Henry Fielding:

> But Fielding lived when the days were longer (for time, like money, is measured by our needs), when summer afternoons were spacious, and the clock ticked slowly in the winter evenings. We belated historians must not linger after his example; and if we did so, it is probable that our chat would be thin and eager, as if delivered from a camp-stool in a parrot-house. I at least have so much to do in unravelling certain human lots, and seeing how they were woven and interwoven, that all the light I can command must be concentrated on this particular web, and not dispersed over that tempting range of relevancies called the universe. (I, xv, 213-14) [10]

History takes its place in *Middlemarch,* then, as one theme parallel to a chain of other themes. Among these themes are religion (dramatized in Bulstrode's story), love (in the three love stories), science (Lydgate), art (Naumann and Ladislaw) and superstition (Fred Vincy). The treatment of each of these themes falls into the same pattern. In each case the character is shown to be mystified by a belief that all the details he confronts make a whole governed by a single center, origin, or end. In each case the narrator demystifies the illusion and shows it to be based on an error, the fundamental linguistic error of taking a figure of speech literally, of assuming that because two things are similar they are equivalent, sprung from the same source, or bound for the same end, explicable by the same principle. As the narrator says, in what might be taken as a diagnosis of the mental illness

[10] See also I, vii, 96-97, and II, xxxv, 102-03.

from which all of the characters in *Middlemarch* suffer, " we all of us, grave or light, get our thoughts entangled in metaphors, and act fatally on the strength of them " (I, x, 127). Casaubon is beguiled into wandering endlessly and fruitlessly in the labyrinthine complexity of ancient myth by his false assumption that there is a " Key to All Mythologies," his belief " that all the mythical systems or erratic mythical fragments in the world were corruptions of a tradition originally revealed " (I, iii, 33). Lydgate searches for the " primitive tissue " of which all the bodily organs will be differentiations: ". . . have not these structures some common basis from which they have all started, as your sarsnet, gauze, net, satin and velvet from the raw cocoon? " (I, xv, 224). Bulstrode thinks Providence justifies his deceptions and that his worldly success is proof that God is guiding his life toward his salvation. Poor Fred Vincy believes that because he is a good fellow luck will be on his side, " keeping up a joyously imaginative activity which fashions events according to desire " (I, xxiii, 358) : " What can the fitness of things mean, if not their fitness to a man's expectations? Failing this, absurdity and atheism gape behind him " (I, xiv, 203). Rosamond's spinning of the " gossamer web " of love (I, xxxvi, 304) in her courtship by Lydgate falls into the same paradigm. It too is the construction of a fiction governed by an illusory beginning and end. In her case the model is literary. Like Emma Bovary she has read too many bad novels. " Rosamond," says the narrator, " had registered every look and word, and estimated them as the opening incidents of a preconceived romance—incidents which gather value from the foreseen development and climax " (I, xvi, 251). Though the " basis for her structure had the usual airy lightness " and is, so to speak, a groundless ground, nevertheless she " was of remarkably detailed and realistic imagination when the foundation had been once presupposed " (I, xii, 177).

Dorothea's nearly fatal mistake in marrying Casaubon is only the most elaborately described version of this universal error. She is both " ardent " and "theoretic." Her ardor takes the form of seeking some guide who will transfigure the details of her everyday life by justifying them in terms of some ideal end. Her error is generated by her " exalted enthusiasm about the ends of life, an enthusiasm which was lit chiefly by its own fire " (I, iii, 38). It is an error of interpretation, once again the error of taking a figurative similarity as an identity. She thinks that because Casaubon reminds her of St. Augustine, of Pascal, of Bossuet, of Oberlin, of his seventeenth-century namesake, of Milton and "the judicious Hooker," he must be the equivalent of those spiritual geniuses, " a guide who would take her along the grandest path " (I, i, 12; iii, 40).[11] " The really delightful marriage must be that where your husband was a sort of father " (I, i, 12). Casaubon is a text, a collection of signs which Dorothea misreads, according to that universal propensity for misinterpretation which infects all the characters in *Middlemarch*. " The text, whether of prophet or of poet," says the narrator apropos of Dorothea's " reading " of Casaubon, " expands for whatever we can put into it, and even his bad grammar is sublime " (I, v, 72), and, in another place, " signs are small measurable things, but interpretations are illimitable, and in girls of sweet, ardent nature, every sign is apt to conjure up wonder, hope, belief, vast as a sky, and coloured by a diffused thimbleful of matter in the shape of knowledge " (I, iii, 34).

Exactly parallel to all these forms of mystification is the belief that history is progressive, teleological. This illusion is deconstructed along with the rest, perhaps even more explicitly, and in ways which are for my purposes especially apt, since the example George Eliot gives is the Hegelian theory that art cooperates in the world process and assists in the self-development of the world spirit. Will Ladislaw is the spokesman for George Eliot's demolition of this particular version of the association between history and narrative. Unlike all the other characters, he has no desire to find out origins. Casaubon acidly reports him to have " said he should prefer not to know the sources of the Nile, and that there should be some unknown regions preserved as hunting-grounds for the poetic imagination " (I, ix, 120). He makes fun of Naumann's Hegelian or " Nazarene " theory of art: " the divinity passing into higher completeness and all but exhausted in the act of covering your bit of canvas. I am amateurish if you like: I do *not* think that all the universe is straining towards the obscure significance of your pictures " (I, xix, 290), and he presents Dorothea with a mocking

[11] It is worth noting that Dorothea also makes the mistake of believing in the explanatory power of origins: "Perhaps even Hebrew might be necessary—at least the alphabet and a few roots—in order to arrive at the core of things . . ." (I, vii, 93). For the search for origins of Casaubon and Lydgate see W. J. Harvey, " The Intellectual Background of the Novel," *Middlemarch: Critical Approaches to the Novel*, ed. B. Hardy (London: University of London, The Athlone Press, 1967), pp. 25-37.

parody of Naumann's theory in his description of his own painting: " I take Tamburlaine in his chariot for the tremendous course of the world's physical history lashing on the harnessed dynasties. In my opinion, that is a good mythical interpretation." Dorothea asks, " Do you intend Tamburlaine to represent earthquakes and volcanoes? " To which Will answers, " O yes, . . . and migrations of races and clearings of forests—and America and the steam-engine. Everything you can imagine! " "What a difficult kind of shorthand! " says Dorothea (I, xxii, 326-27).

The effort of demythologizing in *Middlemarch*, then, can be defined as a dismantling of various versions of the metaphysical system on which the traditional idea of history depends. In spite of its recourse to the conventional *locus standi* of defining itself as a displaced form of history, the novel, so to speak, pulls the rug out from under itself and deprives itself of that solid ground without which, if Henry James is right, it is " nowhere." Her fiction deprives itself of its ground in history by demonstrating that ground to be a fiction too, a figure, a myth, a lie, like Dorothea's interpretation of Casaubon or Bulstrode's reading of his religious destiny.

George Eliot's effort in *Middlemarch* is not, however, wholly negative. The metaphysical notions of history, of story-telling, and of individual human lives are replaced by different notions. The concepts of origin, end, and continuity are replaced by the categories of repetition, of difference, of discontinuity, of openness, and of the free and contradictory struggle of individual human energies, each seen as a center of interpretation, which means misinterpretation, of the whole. History, for George Eliot, is not chaos, but it is governed by no ordering principle or aim. It is a set of acts, not a passive, inevitable process. It is the result of the unordered energies of those who have made it, as well as of the interpretations these energies have imposed on history. History, for her, is stratified, always in movement, always in the middle of a march, always open to the reordering of those who come later. Rome is the " spiritual center " not because it is an occult origin but because it is " the interpreter of the world." Rome is the place where over the centuries has congregated the most intense activity of interpretation. As the narrator says in another place, " souls live on in perpetual echoes, and to all fine expression there goes somewhere an originating activity if it be only that of an interpreter "

(I, xvi, 243). The only origin is an act of interpretation, that is, an act of the will to power imposed on a prior " text," which may be the world itself seen as a text, a set of signs. Such signs are not inert. They are nothing but matter, like the " stupendous fragmentariness " of Rome. At the same time, however, they are always already heavy with a weight of previous interpretations. So Dorothea's response to Rome adds itself to the layer upon layer of interpretations of it which have been made before, " the gigantic broken revelations of that Imperial and Papal city thrust abruptly on the notions of a girl who had been brought up in English and Swiss Puritanism " forming " one more historical contrast " and taking a new meaning in her response to it. Though Dorothea's life does not have a given aim any more than it has an other than accidental origin, nevertheless she may give it an aim, as she ultimately does in her decision to marry Ladislaw. In the same way, though the past does not have a fixed " meaning " I may give it meaning in the way I appropriate it for the present, just as the narrator gives Dorothea's life a meaning by repeating it in her story, and just as the reader in his turn adds himself to the chain when he interprets the novel.

Against the notion of a work of art which is an organic unity and against the notion that a human life gradually reveals its destined meaning, George Eliot opposes the concepts of a text made of differences and of human lives which have no unitary meaning, for whom " every limit is a beginning as well as an ending " (III, " Finale," 455). Such lives have meaning not in themselves but in terms of their influence on other people, that is to say, in the interpretation which other people make of them. In place of those errors which cause the characters in *Middlemarch* to suffer so, George Eliot presents each life in the novel as justifiable by no ideal origin or end. Each has such effect as it does have on those around, an influence not capable of being generalized or predicted, but " incalculably diffusive," like Dorothea's " full nature " which " had still its fine issues," though they were " like that river of which Cyrus broke the strength," so that it " spent itself in channels which had no great name on the earth " (III, " Finale," 465). And in place of the concept of elaborate organic form, centered form, form organized around certain absolute generalizable themes, George Eliot presents a view of artistic form as inorganic, acentered, and discontinuous. Such a view sees form as based on unlikeness and difference. This view is expressed in her extraordinary little essay, "Notes on Form of Art" (1868),[12] and in the actual structure of *Middlemarch* (not least in its metaphorical texture), as well as in explicit statements in the novel.

"Fundamentally," says George Eliot in "Notes on Form in Art," "form is unlikeness, ... and ... every difference is form."[13] "I protest against any absolute conclusion," she affirms in one place in *Middlemarch* (I, x, 125). In several passages in the novel she argues that all generalizations are falsifications because they derive from the almagamation of specific instances which are all different. "But this," she says of the stimulation of imagination by emotion, "which happens to us all, happens to some with a wide difference" (II, xlvii, 297). In another place she says, "all conceit is not the same conceit, but varies in correspondence with the minutiae of mental make in which one of us differs from another" (I, xv, 226). A final example is the observation that "there are many wonderful mixtures in the world which are all alike called love, and claim the privileges of a sublime rage which is an apology for everything" (II, xxxi, 41). In fact, it is "this power of generalising which gives men so much the superiority in mistake over the dumb animals" (III, lviii, 90).

Middlemarch itself is an example of form arising from unlikeness and difference, a form governed by no absolute center, origin, or end. Its meaning is generated by the juxtaposition of its several plots. The three love stories, for example, are as much different from one another as they are similar. Even the styles in which they are written differ. The story of Dorothea, Casaubon, and Will employs an abstract, metaphysical vocabulary, as in the early descriptions of Dorothea as " ardent " and " theoretic," in search of the way to an " ideal end." This elevated style is supported by a carefully but somewhat covertly manipulated parallel with the myth of Ariadne and Dionysus. The rationale for this repetition of an ancient myth in modern England is doubtless George Eliot's version of the theory of myth she had learned from David Friedrich Strauss and Ludwig Feuerbach, a theory which anticipates the similar conceptions of myth latent in such " imaginary portraits " by Walter Pater as " Denys L'Auxerrois " and " Apollo in Pi-

[12] *Essays by George Eliot,* ed. Thomas Pinney (New York: Columbia University Press, 1963), pp. 432-36.
[13] *Ibid.,* pp. 432-33.

cardy." The story of Rosamond and Lydgate, on the other hand, is told in a middle style, the basic style of nineteenth-century realistic fiction. A lower, pastoral, comic, or ironic style is used for the courtship of Fred Vincy and Mary Garth. Critics have erred in expecting the novel to be in one homogeneous " realistic " style throughout. They have misunderstood and misjudged it as a consequence, for example in what they have sometimes said about Will Ladislaw.

Middlemarch itself, finally, is an example of form as difference in its effect on its readers. The novel, like Dorothea, is " incalculably diffusive." It has such effect on its readers as it does have, as they thread their ways through its labyrinth of words, making such interpretations of it as they can, none absolute, each a misreading in the sense that the text is expanded for what the reader can put into it. The reader of the novel, like Dorothea, Lydgate, or Casaubon, links similar elements and makes patterns out of diversity in an activity which is shown in the narrative as being both entirely human and also inevitably in error, the imposition of a will to mastery over the text. As Nietzsche says, unwittingly echoing George Eliot herself, " to be able to read off a text as a text without interposing an interpretation is the last-developed form of ' inner experience '—perhaps one that is hardly possible." [14]

It is no accident that *Middlemarch* has been so consistently misread as affirming the metaphysical system of history it in fact so elaborately deconstructs. That system is there, along with its subversion, there in the apparent strict parallelism of the various plots, there in the penchant for absolute generalization of the narrator (" We are all of us born in moral stupidity, taking the world as an udder to feed our supreme selves " [I, xxi, 323]), there in the apparent organization of the whole text according to certain totalizing metaphors—the metaphor of the web or that of flowing water. *Middlemarch* is an example of the inevitable reweaving of the spider-web of metaphysics even in a text so explicitly devoted to contracting it to its " pilulous smallness " [15] and so showing it as what it is.

[14] Friedrich Nietzsche, *The Will to Power*, para. 479, trans. W. Kaufmann and R. J. Hollingdale (New York: Vintage Books, 1968), p. 266; *Werke*, ed. Karl Schlecta, III (München: Carl Hanser Verlag, 1966), p. 805: " einen Text *als Text* ablesen können, ohne eine Interpretation dazwischen zu mengen, ist die späteste Form der ' inneren Erfahrung '—vielleicht eine kaum mögliche . . ."

[15] " Has any one ever pinched into its pilulous smallness the cobweb of prematrimonial acquaintanceship? " (I, ii, 30).

Nevertheless, for those who have eyes to see it, *Middlemarch* is an example of a work of fiction which not only exposes the metaphysical system of history but also proposes an alternative consonant with those of Nietzsche and Benjamin in the citations with which I began this paper. Like Benjamin, George Eliot rejects historicism with its ideas of progress and of a homogeneous time within which that progress unfolds. Like Benjamin she proposes a view of the writing of history as an act of repetition in which the present takes possession of the past and liberates it for a present purpose, thereby exploding the continuum of history.

I conclude by quoting and commentating on the passage in Benjamin's " Theses on the Philosophy of History " just prior to my initial citation from him. The text presents one model of a relation to history which would match Dorothea's relation to the history she confronts in Rome, George Eliot's relation to the story she tells, the reader's relation to the text of *Middlemarch* as he seizes it out of the past as a means of understanding one aspect of the connection between history and narrative. The difficulty of the passage lies in the fact that, like *Middlemarch* itself, it may be read as reaffirming the metaphysical system it in fact subverts, in this case in the use of Hegelian language and the language of Jewish Messianism.[16] The passage contains both metaphysics and its deconstruction, like all such attempts to win freedom from what is inescapably inscribed in the words we must use to speak at all:

Thinking involves not only the flow of thoughts, but their arrest as well. Where thinking suddenly stops in a configuration pregnant with tensions, it gives that configuration a shock, by which it crystallizes into a monad. A historical materialist approaches a historical subject only where he encounters it as a monad. In this structure he recognizes the sign of a Messianic cessation of happening, or, put differently, a revolutionary chance in the fight for the oppressed past. He takes cognizance of it in order to blast a specific era out of the homogeneous course of history—blasting a specific life out of the era or a specific work out of the lifework. As a result of this method the lifework is preserved in this work and at the same time canceled; in the lifework, the era; and in the era, the entire course of history. The nourishing fruit

---

[16] Even Martin Jay, in his authoritative history of the Frankfurt School, makes this error of interpretation, as did, apparently, Benjamin's friends in the Frankfurt Institut. See *The Dialectical Imagination* (Boston and Toronto: Little, Brown, 1973) pp. 200-201.

of the historically understood contains time as a precious but tasteless seed.[17]

The Messianic cessation of happening, as one can tell from others of the "Theses on the Philosophy of History," is not a "now" in the sense of the German word *Gegenwart*. It is not the presence of the present, and not, as the note to the English translation incorrectly asserts, in any straightforward way "the mystical *nunc stans*."[18] It is the *Jetztzeit* of time as repetition, in a perhaps peculiarly Jewish intuition of authentic human time. It is time as the emptying out of the present by way of its eternal reiteration of a past in which the Messiah had not yet come but was coming in a now in which once more he has not yet come but is coming, according to that aphorism from Karl Kraus which Benjamin quotes, whereby "Origin is the goal."[19] It is a now which is the empty repetition of a past which was never a presence, and at the same time it is the prolepsis of the future as a "something evermore about to be." "Thus," says Benjamin, in echo of Marx's *Eighteenth Brumaire*, "to Robespierre ancient Rome was a past charged with the time of the now [*Jetztzeit*] which he blasted out of the continuum of history. The French Revolution viewed itself as Rome incarnate. It evoked ancient Rome the way fashion evokes the costumes of the past."[20] The tasteless seed of time released by the fruit of history understood as repetition is time not

[17] *Illuminations*, p. 262-263; *Illuminationen*, p. 278: "Zum Denken gehört nicht nur die Bewegung der Gedanken, sondern ebenso ihre Stillstellung. Wo das Denken in einer von Spannungen gesättigten Konstellation plötzlich einhält, da erteilt es derselben einen Chok, durch den es sich als Monade kristallisiert. Der historische Materialist geht an einen geschichtlichen Gegenstand einzig und allein da heran, wo er ihm als Monade entgegentritt. In dieser Struktur erkennt er das Zeichen einer messianischen Stillstellung des Geschehens, anders gesagt, einer revolutionären Chance im Kampfe für die unterdrückte Vergangenheit. Er nimmt sie wahr, um eine bestimmte Epoche aus dem homogenen Verlauf der Geschichte heraus-zusprengen, so sprengt er ein bestimmtes Leben aus der Epoche, so ein bestimmtes Werk aus dem Lebenswerk. Der Ertrag seines Verfahrens besteht darin, dass *im* Werk das Lebenswerk, *im* Lebenswerk die Epoche und *in* der Epoche der gesamte Geschichtsverlauf aufbewahrt ist und aufgehoben. Die nahrhafte Frucht des historisch Begriffenen hat die Zeit als den kostbaren, aber des Geschmacks entratenen Samen in ihrem Innern."
[18] *Illuminations*, p. 261.
[19] *Ibid.*, p. 261; *Illuminationen*, p. 276: "Ursprung ist das Ziel."
[20] *Illuminations*, p. 261; *Illuminationen*, p. 276: "So war für Robespierre das antike Rom eine mit Jetztzeit geladene Vergangenheit, die er aus dem Kontinuum der Geschichte heraussprengte. Die Französische Revolution verstand sich als ein wiedergekehrtes Rom. Sie zitierte das alte Rom genauso, wie die Mode eine vergangene Tracht zitiert."

as homogeneous continuity, but time as the eternal absence of any *locus standi*. This tasteless seed of time is the true name for that "nowhere" of fiction Henry James so fears to confront. The discontinuity of a repetition blasts a detached monad, crystallized into immobility, out of the homogeneous course of history, in order to take possession of it in a present which is no present. It is the cessation of happening in a metaleptic assumption of the past, preserving and annulling it at the same time. This repetition disarticulates the backbone of logic and frees both history and fiction, for the moment, before the spider-web is rewoven, from the illusory continuities of origin leading to aim leading to end.

Yale University

THE CONSTANT COUPLE: FARQUHAR'S FOUR-PLAYS-IN-ONE

BY JACKSON I. COPE

George Farquhar the playwright emerged from the failure of George Farquhar the actor. He arrived in the London stage world just a few years after the great theatrical schism of 1695 had created a second war of the theaters, a war generated by the actors. One of the most prominent of these actors was Robert Wilks, and it was he, of course, who returned to Dublin from London to discover Farquhar's weakness as an actor and promise as a dramatist. He allegedly advised Farquhar

> to relinquish that Method of life [i. e., acting], and think of writing for the Stage; he told him at the same time that he would not meet with Encouragement in *Ireland*, adequate to his Merit, and therefore counselled him to go to *London*. . . . By this time Mr. *Farquhar* had prepared the *Drama* of his Comedy, call'd *Love and a Bottle*, which he shewed to Mr. *Wilks*, who approving of it, advised him to set out for *London* before the Tide was too far spent, meaning while he had any Money left to support him; he took his Counsel, and bid him adieu, and the next Day went on board a Ship bound for *West-Chester*.[1]

It has been argued convincingly that the plot which Wilks admired was a burlesque of Nathaniel Lee's heroic afflatus over much of its surface and a satire upon the conventions of Restoration comedy in its overall form.[2]

Soon, Farquhar had come to know the members of Rich's Company at Drury Lane, a group augmented by his friend Wilks' arrival for the season of 1698-99. It was around his own (and

---

[1] Daniel O'Bryan, *Authentic Memoirs . . . Of the most Celebrated Comedian, Mr. Robert Wilks* (1732), p. 13, cited in Eric Rothstein's biographical account, *George Farquhar* (New York, 1967), p. 17.

[2] Eugene Nelson James, "The Burlesque of Restoration Comedy in *Love and a Bottle*," *SEL*, 5 (1965), 469-90.

his audience's) knowledge of this group that Farquhar created his second play, *The Constant Couple, or a Trip to the Jubilee*. It was an instant success, continuing the theatrical self-awareness of *Love and a Bottle* and taking up hints from the earlier play, but creating a dizzying impact for contemporary theater-goers by complicating the allusive surfaces and deepening the exploration of their own dramatic taste and what that implied about social and ethical values. This was Farquhar's four-plays-in-one: a comedy of wit; a burlesque; a scandalous *roman-a-clef*; and a problem play focused upon the ethical paradoxes shared by the role-playing societies upon both sides of the proscenium.

Let us read *The Constant Couple* four times, then, in these four contexts, with the hope that as they evolve they will begin to interact in something approximating a recreation of the interest which earned this largely forgotten play a boasted fifty-odd London performances within a few months, and made it the most exciting dramatic event of the dawning years of the eighteenth century.

I

As a comedy of sex and wit the play opens with three young men laying a bet upon the relative merits and beauty of their mistresses, a ploy familiar in one form or another at least since its early sixteenth-century employment in *La Mandragola*. They are the niggardly hypocrite Vizard, disbanded army Colonel Standard, and the Gallicized beau Sir Harry Wildair. However, complications set in when it becomes apparent that the three are (at first) unwittingly rivals for Lady Lurewell. And the conventional expectations are soon reversed when it is discovered that the key to the outcome is held by none of the plotting males, but by the master counter-plotter Lurewell herself, "A Lady," as the *dramatis personae* indicates, " of a jilting Temper proceeding from a resentment of her Wrongs from Men."[3]

Vizard is a parody of Restoration wits of earlier vintage. Walking in the park he opens the play reading from Hobbes, and plotting love intrigues and vengeance: "May Obstinacy

[3] *The Complete Works of George Farquhar*, ed. Charles Stonehill (London, 1930), I, 91. All references to Farquhar's text will be to volume and page numbers in this edition.

guard her Beauty till Wrinkles bury it, . . . Run to Lady *Lurewell's*. . . . Her Beauty is sufficient Cure for Angelica's Scorn" (I, 93). But behind his libertine façade (itself hidden behind priggery in dealing with his rich uncle Smuggler) Vizard masks a viciousness of real consequence foreign to his models: "The Colonel my Rival too! how shall I manage? There is but one way—him and the Knight will I set a tilting, where one cuts t'other's Throat, and the Survivor's hang'd. So there will be two Rivals pretty decently disposed of. Since Honour may oblige them to play the Fool, why should not Necessity engage me to play the Knave?" (I, 110). Wildair, on the other hand, intrigues, loves and quarrels with a stoic complacency exaggerated beyond that of earlier stage wits: "His florid Constitution being never ruffled by misfortune, nor stinted in its pleasures, has render'd him entertaining to others, and easy to himself" (I, 96). The description is Vizard's, but it is true—to the point of burlesque—as, for example, in Wildair's meditation upon a thrashing and humiliation he has dealt to Smuggler when he traps the old man in a boudoir:

> How pleasant is resenting an Injury without Passion: "Tis the Beauty of Revenge. . . . .
> *I make the most of Life, no hour mispend,*
> *Pleasure's the Means, and Pleasure is my End.*
> *No Spleen, no Trouble, shall my time destroy,*
> *Life's but a Span; I'll every Inch enjoy.* (I, 116)

And he is equally at ease in love as in war: "Now why should I be angry that a Woman is a Woman? since Inconstancy and Falshood are grounded in their Natures, how can they help it?" (I, 109).

But these inheritors of tradition (along with Standard, who appears to owe a vague legacy of martial bluffness and amorous naiveté to Wycherley's Manly) do not round out Lurewell's academy of aspirants: she is pursued as well by Smuggler the merchant *senex* and by Clincher, the fop-in-waiting: her destiny is to "hate all that don't love me, and slight all that do . . . tho' a Woman swear, forswear, lie, dissemble, backbite, be proud, vain, malicious, any thing, if she secures the main Chance, she's still virtuous, That's a Maxim" (I, 101).

Vizard invents a coup in sending Wildair to his young cousin Angelica and her mother, Lady Darling, with a letter of marital proposal which Wildair believes to be an introduction to a brothel; this complication is enhanced by Lurewell's double-play with which she sets Standard and Wildair into violent competition by ambiguous gestures which leave each feeling himself to be her favorite.

There is an abortive duel; there is the almost obligatory closet scene in which a wittol trapped in Lurewell's rooms escapes at a loss by exchanging clothes with a convenient servant; there are mistaken arrests—all the familiar pieces of action which were shuffled and reshuffled in the context of the sexual wars between so many dozens of Restoration couples. And, of course, the outcome is reformation through marriage. Standard is revealed as Lurewell's first lover in her youth, and happily recognises the elective affinities which have drawn them together again. And, finally disabused of his illusion that Angelica is a whore, Wildair faces the fact that he must erase his affront to her by marriage or by a confrontation of honor with the plotting Vizard in this fashion:

> Here am I brought to a very pretty Dilemma; I must commit Murder, or commit Matrimony. . . . but dam it,—Cowards dare fight, I'll marry, that's the most daring Action of the two, so my dear Cousin Angelica, have at you. (I, 144)

Farquhar emphasizes the conventionality of character and action by enveloping his witty comedy within a network of theatrical reminders. In the first moments of the play the aptly-named Vizard, anticipating sexual conquest, gloats " That's my cue " (I, 93). Later, Smuggler unexpectedly peers under Vizard's hypocrisy to discover him " possess'd with an Evil Spirit, he talks as prophanely, as an actor possess'd with a Poet " (I, 135). Still later, revealed to and revealing his former apprentice-turned-fop, Smuggler reacts with the bourgeois citizen's fear of satire (first immortalized in *The Knight of the Burning Pestle*):

> . . . What Business has a Prentice at a Play-house, unless it be to hear his Master made a Cuckold, and his Mistress a Whore? 'Tis ten to one now, but some malicious Poet has my Character upon the Stage within this *Month*. (I, 145).

And Wildair is first introduced as a bridge between the stage of Drury Lane and the Hyde Park of both audience and actors: he is " The Joy of the Play-house, and the Life of the Park " (I, 96).

If, in this first context for reading *The Constant Couple*, these little cues boast that the most traditional stuff of social comedy is being used but transcended by the author's unusual shuffling of parts, at the next they lead into a burlesque of the rival company and its leader's most famous vehicle.

II

When Thomas Betterton in 1695 successfully led the revolt of players against the wily Drury Lane patentee Christopher Rich, he succeeded in establishing the rival company at Lincoln's Inn Fields because he was unchallenged as the premier actor in London. But it was a dominance obtained through thirty-five years on the stage: Betterton was a master, but a master in an heroic tradition now running its course. The Drury Lane troupe, soon reinforced by Wilks and Farquhar, developed a different style. And in *The Constant Couple* Farquhar not only exploited Wilks' talent, but joined in the wars of the theater to spoof Betterton's own antiquated tastes and style.

The most consistently popular play of the Restoration was Lee's *The Rival Queens, or, the Death of Alexander the Great*,[4] the popularity of which was sustained toward the end of the century by Betterton's powers alone, as Cibber remembers:

> In what Raptures have I seen an audience at the furious Fustian and turgid Rants in *Nat. Lee's Alexander the Great!* ... When these flowing Numbers came from the Mouth of a *Betterton* the Multitude no more desired Sense to them than our musical *Connoisseurs* think it essential in the celebrate Airs of an *Italian Opera*. Does not this prove that there is very near as much Enchantment in the well-govern'd Voice of an Actor as in the sweet Pipe of an Eunuch? ... And I am of opinion that to the extraordinary Success of this very Play we may impute the Corruption of so many Actors and Tragick Writers, as were immediately misled by it.[5]

Cibbers's supplementarian " Anthony, Vulgò Tony Aston " also records that, for Rich's Company, Betterton's " younger Contemporary, ... POWEL, attempted several of *Betterton's* Parts ... but lost his Credit; as, in *Alexander*, he maintain'd not the

---

[4] Introduction to *The Rival Queens*, ed. P. F. Vernon (Lincoln: Univ. of Nebraska Press, 1970), pp. xvi-xix.

Dignity of a King, but *Out-Heroded* Herod." [6] This is the George Powell who played the role of Standard in *The Constant Couple*. And it is with this orientation that we can begin to understand Farquhar's public play upon the rival theater.

It was a ploy to stimulate a shock of recognition in regular patrons which went back to the first weeks of competition. In May, 1695, Betterton's Company had advertised a production of *The Old Bachelor* to coincide with a *Hamlet* by Rich's players. Then, capitalising upon Betterton's known talents in the title role, his company proposed a rival *Hamlet* at the penultimate moment.

> *Powell*, who was vain enough to envy *Betterton* as his Rival, proposed to change Plays with them, . . . he would play the *Old Batchelor* himself, and mimick *Betterton* throughout the whole Part.[7]

This was the tradition—now for some specifics. A month before Drury Lane first produced Farquhar's *Love and a Bottle* they did a revival of *The Rival Queens*, undoubtedly featuring Powell. Six weeks later Betterton took up his old role of Alexander at Lincoln's Inn Fields as part of a wedding entertainment—a performance upon request of this sweeping tragedy in the small tennis-court theater which must have been ridiculed by more spectators than the author of *A Comparison Between the Two Stages* who said "I have seen . . . *Alexander's Exploits* . . . all epitomiz'd into a Raree-show, carry'd about on a Man's Head." [8] During the closing month of 1699 which saw the first performance of *The Constant Couple*, Betterton was leading his company in such heroic tragedies as Charles Hopkins' *Friendship Improved, or the Female Warrior* and Dennis' Euripidean adaptation, *Iphigenia*. This was the aging actor's preferred genre, but a genre principally identified for over twenty years with that most famous of Betterton's roles, Alexander trapped and dying between his

---

[5] Colly Cibber, *Apology*, ed. Robert W. Lowe (London, 1889), I, 105-07.

[6] *A Brief Supplement* included in *Apology*, II, 301.

[7] *Apology*, I, 205; cf. *The London Stage, 1660-1800* (Carbondale, Ill., 1965), I, 446. There are indications that this sort of theatrical allusion was in some part a publicity collusion. The comedian Joe Haines was indispensable, and so played in both companies during the 1697-98 season. Among other parts, he played Pamphlet in *Love and a Bottle*, then (wrote and) spoke the epilogue to that play as though he were a member of Betterton's Company complaining of Drury Lane's recent successes.

[8] *A Comparison Between the Two Stages* [1702], ed. Sterling B. Wells (Princeton, 1942). p. 22. All production details are borrowed from calendars in *The London Stage*.

rival queens, faithful Statira and treacherous Roxana. In Lee's revisionist version of history, Statira takes a vow of chastity when the absent conqueror falls into the arms of captive Roxana. Returning to Babylon, Alexander is desolated at the result of his adultery and wins Statira back only to see her murdered by a vengeful Roxana who also connives in a political plot to poison the slipping master of the world; Alexander's character in this vehicle alternates in tone between the closing days in the lives of Marlowe's Tamburlaine and Shakespeare's Antony. He boasts, he pleads, he drinks, he threatens—little wonder that Powell was tempted to out-Herod Betterton's Alexander. And it is upon this play that Farquhar builds his structure of burlesque in *The Constant Couple*.

Farquhar ignites the possibility for commentary upon an older dramatic mode almost immediately when Wildair begins to "mistrust some rivalship" with Standard (I, 98) and Standard himself tells Lurewell that "Emulation in Glory is transporting, but Rivals here [in love] intolerable" (I, 101), introducing the usual flood of references to love and honour. But the heroic rivalry is reduced to a struggle to obtain possession of Lurewell the courtesan and the supposed whore Angelica—a struggle, literally, for possession of what Colly Cibber titled in a later, lighter parody of Lee's play, *The Rival Queans*.

Lee's penchant for heroic rhetoric (and repetitiveness) is ridiculed directly with the opening scenes of Act II of *The Constant Couple* in which the foppish Clincher introduces his own and Alexander's favorite oath, "*O Jupiter Ammon*"[9] and Wildair first approaches Angelica's house hopefully quoting a glorification of sexual consummation from Lee's *Sophonisba*.[10] These reminders, along with a discussion of love and honour which sets the heroico-tragical dilemmas of *The Rival Queens* into the entire context of Restoration heroic drama, run throughout *The Constant Couple* from beginning to close. The action of the earlier play, too, is taken up, but taken up as ambivalent parody upon the sentiments of genre. *The Rival Queens* opens with a fight

---

[9] I, 104, 119, 132, 148; Wildair is infected once: I, 110. Lee mentions the temple to Jupiter Ammon in the dedication to *The Rival Queens* and Alexander identifies himself with Ammon throughout the play: see *Dramatick Works of Mr. Nathaniel Lee* (London, 1734), III, 206, 224, 237, 254, 265, 266, 282.

[10] Stonehill, I, 105.

between Prince Lysimachus and Alexander's favorite Hephestion over their love rivalry for Statira's sister. They are interrupted by Alexander's eldest and most loyal soldier who shames them into peace with the reminders of a primitivistic virtue:

> What big Ambition blows this dangerous Fire?
> A *Cupid's* Puff is it not, Woman's Breath?
> By all your Triumphs in the heat of Youth,
> When Towns were sack'd, and Beauties prostrate lay,
> When my Blood boil'd, and Nature work'd me high,
> *Clytus* ne'r bow'd his Body to such shame:
> The brave will scorn the Cobweb Arts—The Souls
> Of all that whining, smiling, coz'ning Sex.[11]

Standard challenges Wildair to a duel ("You fought in *Flanders* to my knowledge" I, 128), and is turned aside by a modern common sense which both echoes and up-dates Clytus' scorn of women:

> ... I tell you once more, Colonel, that I am a Baronet, and have eight thousand pounds a Year. I can dance, sing, ride, fence, understand the Languages. Now, I can't conceive how running you through the Body should contribute one Jot more to my Gentility. But, pray Colonel, I had forgot to to ask you: what's the Quarrel?
> *Standard.* A Woman, Sir.
> *Wildair.* Then I put up my Sword. Take her.
> *Standard.* Sir, my Honour's concern'd.
> *Wildair.* Nay, if your Honour be concern'd with a Woman, get it out of her Hands as soon as you can. An honourable Lover is the greatest Slave in Nature; some will say, the greatest Fool.

A later generation of young men has taken over the wisdom of the old: love and honour are incompatible follies. It is a situation which satirizes the posturing rhetoric of Betterton's Alexander and his legacy in lesser plays. Also, it prepares for the double parody of Angelica in Act V of *The Constant Couple*.

At this point, Wildair, still under the impression that Angelica is a whore and her mother a bawd, returns to their house to press his passion with an escalated offer of money. Because he has been introduced as a suitor in a letter from their relative Vizard, the mother assumes that Wildair is seeking marriage, and leaves him

---

[11] Lee, *Works*, III, 218.

alone with Angelica. He soon disabuses her, and Angelica, caught in his arms, pleads in stilted terms:

> I conjure you, Sir, by the sacred Name of Honour, by your dead Father's Name, and the fair Reputation of your Mothers Chastity, that you offer not the least Offense. . . . what wild Dream of loose Desire could prompt you to attempt this Baseness? View me well.— The Brightness of my Mind, methinks, should lighten outwards, and let you see your Mistake in my behaviour.

Then she suddenly breaks into loose blank verse:

> I think it shines with so much Innocence in my Face, / that it should dazzle all your vicious Thoughts: / Think not I am defenceless 'cause alone. / Your very self is Guard against your self: / I'm sure there's something generous in your Soul: / My Words shall search it out, / And Eyes shall fire it for my own defence.

Sir Harry's aside points to the tradition: " This is the first Whore in *Heroicks* that I have met." And his response points to Lee's Alexander as he mimics Angelica:

> Tall di dum, ti dum, tall ti didi, didum. / A Million to one now, but this Girl is just come flush from reading the *Rival Queens*— I gad, I'll at her in her own cant.—
> O my Statyra, O my angry dear,
> turn thy Eyes on me, behold thy Beau in Buskins (I, 140-41).

But at this point the burlesque merges into the third context of *The Constant Couple*, one in which regular London theatergoers might easily pierce the plot to find beneath it a living *roman-à-clef*, giving ironic doubleness to the social settlements being enacted upon the stage. In Lee's play the lines occur when Alexander first sees Statira after her vow of chastity and begins to persuade her to break it:

> O my *Statira!* O my angry Dear!
> Turn thine Eyes on me, I wou'd talk to them:
> What shall I say to work upon thy Soul? [12]

---

[12] *Ibid.*, III, 249. The coincidence with Wildair's citation suggests that Farquhar may be the author of the prologue to the anonymous play presented at Drury Lane in late February, 1698. It was published as a " Prologue: Spoke by Mr. Powell, in answer to a scurrilous one, spoke against him, at *Betterton's* Booth in Little-Lincolns-Inn-Fields," and includes the lines: " Oh! my Statira! Oh, my angry dear, / Lord, what a dismal sound wou'd that make here " (*The Fatal Discovery; or, Love in the Ruines* [London, 1698], sig. A4ʳ).

While no cast list exists for the Drury Lane performance of *The Rival Queens* in November, 1698, Statira was undoubtedly played by the same Jane Rogers who, as Angelica, is here being reminded—along with the audience—of her earlier role. We can safely infer this from the notoriety she received as Bellamira in the Drury Lane production of the anonymous *Triumphs of Virtue* at the beginning of 1697.

In this play, Antonio has squandered the patrimony of both himself and his sister Bellamira. Even so, Bellamira is honorably loved by wealthy young Perollo and lusted after by Duke Polycastro, new Viceroy of Naples. Perollo is persuaded after a time to jilt Bellamira because of her poverty, and the Duke takes her away into what everyone assumes is a courtesan's life. However, in private she frustrates his expected triumph in such a fashion as to make him genuinely transcend his lust in a rhetoric not much more stilted than that of Farquhar's Angelica:

> *Bellamira.* I fix the Bounds, where no transgressing Step
> Must ever dare to enter. Hear me, Duke,
> And mark the Bars I set. Touch not my chaste Bed;
> Make not one loose Demand; tempt me not with a Word
> Of unbecoming Sense; or on my Lips
> Print but a wanton Kiss; breathe not one Sigh
> That looks like begging of an amorous Pity;
> But use your Visits as a Brother to a Sister.
> *Polycastro.* This is all Cruelty.
> *Bellamira.* No, 'Tis all Mercy:
> Mercy to the whole Welfare of my Life,
> The Guard and Shield of my unspotted Soul . . .
> . . . .
> . . . . . . my Tongue and Heart
> Breathe but one Air, and Virtue is their Soul.
> *Polycastro.* Thou hast prevail'd; I yield the hard Conditions.
> . . . .
> Oh *Bellamira!* thou hast intirely vanquish'd;
> My Soul, new-moulded, stampt it with thy own
> Bright Image of Divinity, chang'd all
> My sooty Love to sacred Adoration.
> . . . .
> And now with more than common Raptures blest,
> My Love, all fragrant, as the Phoenix Nest;
> I'll meet those Eyes with all that chaste Desire,
> And warm in Virtue, at thy Vestal Fire.[13]

[13] *The Triumphs of Virtue* (London, 1697), pp. 31-32.

Bellamira's tactics of conversion are strikingly similar to those employed by Angelica in the first quarto of *The Constant Couple*: [14]

> If my Beauty has power to raise a Flame, be sure it is a vertuous one: if otherwise, 'tis owing to the Foulness of your own Thought, which throwing this mean Affront upon my Honour, has alarm'd my Soul, and fires it with a brave Disdain.
> *Wildair*. . . . Madam, whate'er my unruly Passion did at first suggest; I now must own you've turn'd my Love to Veneration, and my unmannerly Demands to a most humble Prayer.—Your surprizing Conduct has quench't the gross material Flame; but rais'd a subtil piercing Fire, which flies like lambent Lightning, through my Blood, disdaining common Fuel, preys upon the nobler Part, my Soul.[15]

Bellamira has been willing to appear a whore to convert the Duke; Angelica, mistaken for a noble Magdalene converts Wildair. But for a contemporary audience, behind both conversions looms that of Jane Rogers herself, announced in the Epilogue to *The Triumph of Virtue* addressed to the ladies of London:

> You shall reform the World, and wee'll reform the Stage.
> But Ladies, now not for the Play alone,
> I have a small Petition of my own:
> . . . .
> If I from those fair Eyes a Smile may find,
> If possible to deserve a Grace so kind;
> I'll pay this dutious Gratitude; I'll do
> That which the Play has done; I'll copy You.
> At your own Vertues Shrine my Vows I'll pay:
> Study to live the Character I play.

The actress' vow apparently became a London *cause célèbre*; Cibber, who played her brother Antonio, remembered the event and its upshot years later:

> I have formerly known an Actress carry this Theatrical Prudery to such a height, that she was very near keeping herself chaste by it: Her Fondness for Virtue on the Stage she began to think might perswade the World that it had made an Impression on her private Life; and the Appear-

---

[14] For dating of the revision see George W. Whiting, "The Date of the Second Edition of *The Constant Couple*," *MLN*, 47 (1932), 147-48.
[15] I, 361.

ances of it actually went so far that, in an Epilogue to an obscure Play, ... wherein she acted a Part of impregnable Chastity, she bespoke the Favour of the Ladies by a Protestation that in Honour of their Goodness and Virtue she would dedicate her unblemish'd Life to their Example ... But alas! how weak are the strongest Works of Art when Nature besieges it? for though this good Creature so far held out her Distaste to Mankind that they could never reduce her to marry any one of 'em; yet we must own she grew, like *Caesar*, greater by her Fall! Her first heroick Motive to a Surrender was to save the Life of a Lover who in his Despair had vow'd to destroy himself, ... The generous Lover, in return to that first tender Obligation, gave Life to her First-born.[16]

The generous lover was Wilks, who had a long and turbulent relationship with Jane Rogers. As usual, history offers scant documentation on the origins of affairs of the heart, but Farquhar's revision of the final scene between Angelica and Wildair in a play written around his friend Wilks suggests that this one had already begun in the winter of 1699—perhaps in those weeks between the first performance in November and the following January, when the second edition came out " With a New Scene added to the part of Wildair." [17] Wildair's sudden conversion in the first edition employed Rogers' stereotype as the virtuous virgin; the scene is thoroughly transformed in the revision. Wildair, instead of his inspiration by Angelica's nobility, now introduces the mocking allusions to Statira and *The Rival Queens*, then addresses this " first Whore in Heroicks " with a parody of Falstaff's catechism on honour: " Can your Vertue bespeak you a Front Row in the Boxes? No: for the players can't live upon Vertue," etc. (I, 141). Whereas in the early text Wildair is drawn into marriage by Angelica alone, in the later the couple are seen joined by Lady Darling, and the women gradually unfold Vizard's plot and Wildair's mistake in a rapid-fire catechism which balances his own catechism of seduction, until he cries out in self-defence: " Now dear *Roxana,* and you my fair *Statyra,* be not so very

[16] *Apology,* I, 135-36.
[17] Whiting, pp. 147-48. The probability that the Wilks-Rogers relationship became common knowledge early is strengthened by a jibe at the Drury Lane actresses in *A Comparison Between the Two Stages*: " *Sullen*: Well then, what think you of the *Lurewells* and *Angelicas* of t'other House? *Critic*: To my knowledge there are many *Lurewell's* among 'em, but not one *Angelica*: Many Punks, but not one honest Woman " (p. 13).

Heroick in your Styles" (I, 143). And the whole concludes with his decision for marriage which we have cited before: "Cowards may dare fight, I'll marry, that's the most daring Action of the two," a far cry from the closing dialogue after Wildair's marriage proposal in the first edition, climaxing with his response to Angelica's warning, "You must promise me, Sir *Harry*, to have a care of *Burgundy* henceforth": "Fear not, sweet Innocence; Your Presence, like a Guardian Angel, shall fright away all Vice" (I, 363).

The effect has been to evoke Jane Rogers' vow of chastity, to couple it with allusion to Statira's vow of chastity (which she also breaks), and to play off against the rhetorical "heroics" of Lee the impossibility of maintaining such sentiments in the reality of everyday London. Rogers' boast was maintained only until Wilks joined Rich's company of Drury Lane players; now, he is courting her stage avatar (mistakenly) as that mistress which she has (really) become. It was a nice, complicated in-joke for the many spectators who must have known the hubris of Jane Rogers' puritanical stance and its failure once Wilks determined to break it down. But the revisions here can also help us understand that Farquhar was, between the two versions, recognising more fully that fourth and most seriously critical area of *The Constant Couple*, its analysis of the implications behind London dramatic tastes.

III

Examining the establishment of Betterton's rebels in Lincoln's Inn Fields, Cibber says, "The first Error this new Colony of Actors fell into was their inconsiderately parting with ... Mrs. *Monfort* upon a too nice (not to say severe) Punctilio ... which before they had acted one Play occasioned [her] Return to the Service of the Patentees."[18] Cibber was right about the seriousness of the mistake because, as he elsewhere says, "Mrs. *Monfort*, whose second Marriage gave her the Name of Mrs. *Verbruggen*, was Mistress of more variety of Humour than I ever knew in any one Woman Actress.... Nothing, tho' ever so barren, if within the Bounds of Nature, could be flat in her Hands.... though I doubt it will be a vain Labour to offer you a just Likeness of

[18] *Apology*, I, 200.

Mrs. *Monfort's* Action, yet the fantastick Impression is still so strong in my Memory that I cannot help saying something, tho' fantastically, about it."[19] And this panegyric was written over thirty years after Susanna Verbruggen's death. The eccentric actor Anthony Aston did not admire her legs, but did admire her style: "She was all Art, and her Acting all acquir'd, but dress'd so nice it look'd like Nature. . . . Whatever she did was not to be call'd Acting; no, no, it was what she represented: She was neither more nor less, and was the most easy Actress in the World."[20] This account of her stylistic ability to combine art and nature is pertinent because it describes not only the actress but her role as Lurewell, a role which made Mrs. Verbruggen the third pillar, along with Wilks and Farquhar, of the dramatic London mirror world in *The Constant Couple*.

Midway in the action Captain Standard—enmeshed in her labyrinth of vengeful scheming against men—accuses Lurewell of lying, and she responds with the most important of the theatrical allusions in the play: "Hold, Sir, You have got the Play-house Cant upon your Tongue; and think that Wit may privilege your Railing: But I must tell you, Sir, that what is Satyr upon the Stage, is ill Manners here." Standard's answer cuts to the heart of Farquhar's vision: "What is feign'd upon the Stage, is here in Reality. Real Falsehood" (I, 123). It is the young, provincial author's comment upon the society into which he had come through Wilks' encouragement: a society which might watch Wildair follow so many stage beaux into risking the matrimonial noose with Angelica, all the time aware that Wilks would offer Jane Rogers only the dubious gift of "her First-born." It was the society for which Etherege spoke when, writing from Ratisbon to comfort a friend who had been unable to seduce Susanna Verbruggen, he said: "The best fortune I have had here has been a player, something handsomer, and as much a jilt, as Mrs. Barry . . . few foul their fingers with touching of a Cunt that does not belong to a Countess."[21] It was also the society into which Lurewell had entered, a young provincial who, emu-

---

[19] *Ibid.*, I, 165-68. The anonymous "Satyr on the Players" is, of course, less complimentary: see John Downes, *Roscius Anglicanus*, ed. Montague Summers (London, 1929), p. 59. Cf. John Harold Wilson, *All the King's Ladies* (Chicago, 1958), pp. 177-81.
[20] *Supplement* in *Apology*, II, 313.
[21] *Letters of Sir George Etherege*, ed. Frederick Bracher (Berkeley, 1974), p. 186.

lating the ideals of love and honour promulgated on the stage of *The Rival Queens* or *The Conquest of Granada*, had found herself reduced to the duplicity in sexual war implicit in her assumed name (in truth she is "Manly").[22]

"Love" and "honour" are words which are sprinkled wholesale in the dialogue whenever Standard appears, an effect natural to Powell, a failed Alexander in Lee's heroics and to the stage Colonel who has just been disbanded after the peace of Ryswick. They are anachronistic ideals in a world where sex presents the only battlefield, as Wildair persuades him when refusing to duel over the complications plotted by Lurewell (cf. p. 484 above). It is not a response from a fop, but from a man Standard admires for his reputation in the wars; shaken, Standard presses: "Sir, my Honour's concern'd," and Wildair forces him to confront the reality of life in modern London: "Nay, if your Honour be concern'd with a Woman, get it out of her Hands as soon as you can. An honourable Lover is the greatest Slave in Nature" (I, 129).

It is a truth for both sexes, though, as people try to survive without cynicism in the world of wits. Lurewell's maid raises the issue as she watches her mistress torment the several suitors: "Methinks, Madam, the Injuries you have suffer'd by Men must be very great, to raise such heavy Resentments against the whole sex." This elicits Lurewell's whole history of early seduction. Some anonymous students, through a prank, came to her father's country estate when she was fifteen and one seduced her: "what Wit had Innocence like mine? ... I gave him a Ring with this Motto, *Love and Honour*, then we parted." Her father dead, Lurewell became a wealthy target and a deadly man-killer, armed with money and beauty against the male: "my Love for this single Dissembler turn'd to a hatred of the whole Sex, and resolving to divert my Melancholy ... I have done some Execution: Here I will play my last scene; then retire to my Country-house, live solitary, and die a penitent" (I, 127).

[22] Farquhar adumbrated the dilemma of idealistic sentiments in high society in *Love and a Bottle*: see James, pp. 483-84. There is a slight but clear echo of Lurewell's conduct in Silvia's explanation of her disguise in *The Recruiting Officer*: "Do you think it strange, Cousin, that a Woman should change? But, I hope, you'll excuse a Change that has proceeded from Constancy; I alter'd my Outside, because I was the same within" (II, 198).

Lurewell knowingly and Angelica innocently have played the scene well: even while mocking the old principles of love and honour, Sir Harry succumbs to them. And this seems to me both the dramatic and ideational point of Farquhar's revision. In the first version, the last act encounter between Wildair and Angelica converts Wildair into a suddenly heroic Standard without Angelica embodying any of the experience which complicates Lurewell's efforts to live by heroic ideals in a comic society. Both his complacent cynicism and the mockery of Betterton's antiquated vehicle *The Rival Queens* are lost. But between the two versions Farquhar recognised that the critique of sociotheatrical posturing was the real center of his play. Lurewell and Standard emerged as more important than the first, Fletcherian conception of Wildair and Angelica, causing Farquhar to rewrite the immensely popular role of Wildair in subordination to Lurewell's dilemma of being, willy nilly, a heroine from heroic drama trapped in Wildair's witty world, one less comic in the salon than on the stage. This meant relieving Wildair of his conversion by the *ingénue* Angelica and making him sustain the role of trapped *roué* which carried over into the sequel to this immensely popular play, *Sir Harry Wildair*.[23]

Between Standard and Lurewell, Farquhar developed parallels which might be called structural imperatives. Standard's youthful treatment of the girl has occasioned the staged role of misanthropic courtesan which draws her maid's dismayed reaction: "Methinks, Madam, the Injuries you have suffer'd by Man must be very great, to raise such heavy Resentments against the whole Sex." But Wildair is no less surprised by the misogyny of Standard: "'tis unpardonable to charge the Failings of a single Woman upon the whole Sex." Oblivious to his own irony, Standard attributes this stance to the cynicism of the Lurewell he himself unwittingly created with his desertion of the young Manly heiress years before: "I have found one whose pride's above yielding to a Prince. And if Lying, Dissembling, Perjury and

[23] In this sequel both Wildair and Lurewell have surrendered to the theatrical mores mirrored as well as questioned in *The Constant Couple*. When Angelica, supposed dead, returns, Wildair apologises for his conduct: "Don't be angry, my Dear, you took me unprovided: had you but sent me Word of coming, I had got three or four Speeches out of *Oroonoko* and the *Mourning Bride* upon this occasion, that wou'd have charm'd your very Heart" (I, 208). Lurewell has already admitted to him that "I hate Love that's impudent. These Poets dress it up so in their Tragedies, that no modest Woman can bear it. Your way is much the more tolerable, I must confess" (I, 189).

Falsehood, be no Breaches in Woman's Honour, she's as innocent as Infancy " (I, 146). Only moments later, in the discovery scene, Standard confronts Lurewell herself with these charges and she accepts them as the way of the world: " dissembling to the prejudice of Men is virtue; and every Look, or Sigh, or Smile, or Tear that can deceive is Meritorious " (I, 249). Then the inscribed betrothal ring appears and Lurewell challenges him: " if you have Love and Honour in Your soul, 'tis then most justly yours," and recognising his lost love Standard tells a story of past mistakes " to discharge my self from the stain of Dishonour " (I, 150). Lurewell drops the mask of witty plotter under which she has fought the battle of the sexes: " if I can satisfie you in my past Conduct, and the reasons that engag'd me to deceive all Men, I shall expect the honourable performance of your Promise." And Standard finds that the ideal of honour is not, finally, to be sought on the battlefields of the Low Countries, or on those of Alexander or Almanzor, where the Restoration theater audience sought them: " not Fame nor Glory e'er shall part us more. My Honour can be no where more concern'd than here " (I, 150).

It is a sentimental conclusion, but an earned one, tempered in the other perspectives of the play. Farquhar would go on to write *Sir Harry Wildair*, a sequel having the same relation to *The Constant Couple* as *The Relapse* had to *Love's Last Shift*, because in London, as he soon found when tricked into a desperate marriage, duplicity *is* the way of the world, on stage, beyond, or behind it. As an astonishingly able playwright for one just past twenty, he acknowledged the fact in the teasing presentation of Wilks' conquest of Jane Rogers, in the creation of " complacent " Wildair and in the revision of Wildair's conversion. But Farquhar went beyond this to scoff the sentimental posturings of Lee's Alexander off the stage, and return the wedding of love and honour to quotidian London society in the mirror-world of Drury Lane.

University of Southern California

COOPERS HILL: THE MANIFESTO OF PARLIAMENTARY ROYALISM, 1641

BY JOHN M. WALLACE

If we could discover the very day on which Denham stood on Cooper's Hill, staring out across the Thames valley and reflecting upon the history of its landmarks, we should not only be able to read his famous poem with more exactitude, but we could see where it belonged in the exciting history of which it is a part. Professor Brendan O Hehir in his edition of the drafts of the poem has concluded on the evidence of the stag hunt that *Coopers Hill* was begun in all probability shortly after the death of Strafford; that is to say, after 12 May 1641 and before the summer was much older.[1] Yet if the stag is not a quasi-allegorical account of the Earl's execution, and I am sure it is not, then the question is open once more, and one has to start again.

The external evidence is inconclusive, although the outer limits are defined with virtual certainty by the date of the assembly of the Long Parliament in November 1640 and Thomason's record of buying the first edition on 5 August 1642. Within these boundaries, O Hehir's reasons for believing that the earliest surviving draft of the poem was completed in 1641 remain con-

---

[1] Brendan O Hehir, *Expans'd Hieroglyphicks: A Critical Edition of Sir John Denham's "Coopers Hill"* (Berkeley and Los Angeles, 1969), pp. 31-32. All quotations from *Coopers Hill* are from the first draft of the poem in this edition, hereafter cited as "O Hehir." Professor Herbert Berry kindly sent me a photostat of the Ms. of Draft I that he discovered in the P.R.O., together with his convincing argument that this Ms. should be the copy text. Since his transcript has not yet appeared, I have followed O Hehir, without whose edition and commentary this revisionist essay could hardly have been attempted. A copy of the 1642 edition in the University of Illinois at Champaign-Urbana has inked corrections in an early hand; most of them are based on the mss. traditions O Hehir has traced, but it adds "assailes" (line 290), "returnes" (line 296), "By" for "But" (line 322), "power" for "powers" (line 342), "striuing" for "stirring" (line 348), "let" for "tell" (line 351). Line numbers from O Hehir's Draft III. To the early appreciations of the poem could be added John Aubrey's quotations from the "B' text in *A Perambulation of the County of Surrey; Begun 1673. Ended 1692* (1718), I, 2; see also III, 164-66. The place of publication for all references is London unless otherwise stated.

vincing, but most readers would agree with him that the internal evidence for a more precise date is cryptic to say the least. Theoretically, however, we could expect more help from a poem as topical as *Coopers Hill*, especially in a period shaken by such momentous events that almost every month brought new developments and concerns, and new alignments among the groups involved in the struggle; it would be surprising if the text did not reflect a particular coincidence of interests that was characteristic only of a narrow span of time, and the three drafts of the " A " text do in fact show Denham making small accommodations to changing historical events. To put the matter another way: O Hehir has cleared away much earlier nonsense about Denham's political " neutrality " and has concluded that he was a " committed royalist " when he wrote the poem. With the argument that he was " royalist " in some sense I have no quarrel at all, but the word begs as many questions as it solves, because historians have become justifiably cautious about a label that underwent such radical alteration within fifteen months, and which described at different times men of such variable allegiance and ideas. Some truth yet remains in Macaulay's statement that the parties were formed on 20 October 1641 when parliament reassembled after the recess [2] (in which case " committed royalist " might imply a late date for the poem), but the history of royalism until the outbreak of civil war is a complicated narrative that ought to provide clues to the period in which Denham was writing. Contrariwise, if we could date the poem we should know a little more about the history of that cause, and of the components from which the final coalition was pieced together.

The disturbing consequence of this train of thought is that *Coopers Hill* becomes a classic example of the Catch 22 in literary criticism. An accurate interpretation of the poem requires a date, and to find the date we must offer an interpretation. The problem is compounded by the suggestion that if Denham published the poem in August 1642 on the eve of open warfare, he must have had a clear sense of its relevance to the current predicament, and we could therefore be excused if we read the final version of the " A " text as an expression of Denham's opinions at mid-year 1642.

[2] *The History of England*, ed. C. H. Firth (1913), I, 87; B. H. G. Wormald, *Clarendon* (Cambridge, England, 1951), p. 28, dates the formation of the parliamentarian " party " from the small hours of 23 November 1641.

To make that mistake is to waste a lot of time, because the last draft is not substantially different from the first, and it is wellnigh impossible that any " royalist," or parliamentarian for that matter, would have had identical feelings or would have written the same topical poem if a year or more of increasingly ugly confrontations had intervened on the historical scene. To use only O Hehir's evidence, if the stag is Strafford then Strafford was a peculiar subject about which to be writing in the summer of 1642, and the publication of the poem was something of an anomaly. The conclusion is inevitable, on the one hand, that Denham believed *Coopers Hill* still contained a topical application or relevance when he published it, but, on the other, that the main body of the poem was dictated by an earlier sequence of events and responses. Nor would the poem have been read in the same fashion in 1641 and 1642. By radically revising his work during the Interregnum, Denham continued to assert that it had a " general " meaning which was impervious to time and permanently important, while he retained the major sections which had originated in a temporal, not to say temporary, context. For the purposes of practical criticism it is necessary to distinguish not only the drafts of the poem, but between their probable implications at a given time; or, as I should prefer, between the different intentions and hopes that Denham must have entertained in composing, publishing, and rewriting his *magnum opus*.

Readers will agree at once with Alexander Pope, who emphasized the naturalness of the poem's process of reflection, in which images and places " are still tending to some hint, or leading into some reflection upon moral life or political institution, much in the same manner as the real sight of such scenes and prospects is apt to give the mind a composed turn, and incline it to thoughts and contemplations that have a relation to the object "; [3] but they must therefore also agree that Denham would have had different associations with Windsor or the Thames, and would have recalled different historical episodes, had he been writing in 1649, 1660, or 1666. This may be obvious, but then it is only slightly more contentious to argue that a similar difference could and did exist between 1641 and 1642, and that *Coopers Hill* in being the product of its own time should reflect the precise circumstances that prompted it. An intriguing puzzle remains, the solution of which

[3] Quoted by O Hehir, p.4.

lies in balancing all the features of the first draft of the poem, and all the implications which they legitimately suggest, against the numerous alternatives presented by the complexities of history. The result of this maneuver is to narrow the period of composition to the three months between the king's departure from London on 10 August 1641 and his return on 25 November, but with a very strong presumption that Denham was writing in September. It is only then that the topical meaning of *Coopers Hill* makes immediate and powerful sense, and the poem becomes an important document during a hiatus in the forward march of the revolution. However, as Denham tried so hard to raise his discourse above the fevers of political disputation, and to be topical in such an oblique way that no tempers would be aroused, we must start by considering this intention and explaining its coexistence with a specific purpose to produce effective propaganda for the king. In the poem itself they are never separable, because the more disinterested Denham could appear the more convincing was his function as a royal spokesman, but for clarity's sake it is convenient to isolate them here.

He established his impartiality by various means, and of course by necessity in his opening lines, when readers required assurance about the character of the speaker. The view from a hill afforded him the needed distance to see all the problems of the crown and the capital in perspective, just as his later recourse to history affirmed his wish to separate himself from the passions with which the men who were making history were afflicted. In the familiar language of the time, and in the phrase which the judgment in the case of ship-money sent echoing down the years of revolution, the distance enabled him to become " sole Judge both of the Danger, and when, and how the same is to be prevented." [4] King and parliament each claimed the eminence to decide the issue in all cases of necessity, and Denham's literal eminence was of the same kind.[5] Looking out towards London, " that warm region

[4] John Rushworth, *Historical Collections* (1721), III, Appendix, 250. Hereafter cited as " Rushworth." Volume and page numbers follow this edition, not Rushworth's volume numbers.

[5] " Who like a man that standing upon the beach at *Dover* will not beleeve that the Sea hath any shore towards France, untill he bee brought to the top of the Hill. It is not within their view to tell better than the Parliament whether there be danger or not. His Majestie indeed hath the most eminent place to observe what Collection of Clouds are in any quarter of Heaven, and what weather it will be, but his calculations

where thunder and lightning was made," [6] and standing above the gathering storm " Secure from danger & from feare," Denham could already discern that men's " vast desires " were the cause from which the danger sprang:

> men like Ants
> Preying on others to supply their wants
> Yet all in vaine, increasing with their Store
> Their vast desires, but make their wants the more.
> Oh happines of Sweete retyr'd content
> To be at once Secure, and Innocent.   (21-26)

" Desire," and especially "humble desire" was the invariable expression used by parliament to petition the king, and to at least some readers Denham's impartiality would have looked rather thin, although he was later to characterize two English kings as suffering from the same delusion. Yet if Denham was congratulating himself on his exemption in sweet retirement from the fears and dangers, the desires and self-deceptions that beset the city, he was also announcing what his poem was about. His theme was no less than the public safety, endangered now by the deficient understandings and infected wills of the people. Security pertained to places, and guilt and innocence to minds, and the safety of England depended on the morality of her inhabitants' actions. From his own vantage-point he could see that London was neither secure nor innocent, and in the second draft of *Coopers Hill* he was to underline his theme by suggesting that St. Paul's was "Secure, while thee the best of Poetts sings / Preserv'd from ruine by the best of Kings." Denham could not have chosen a subject that would have been more instantly recognizable, or that appealed to a wider range of persons and interests. The king had called the Long Parliament, he said, " to consider the best way both for the Safety and Security of this Kingdom." [7] and almost every page of the great historical collections of the period bears witness to the universal concern with " the publike peace, safety, and happinesse

---

(suppos'd to be made by others from a lower ground) are therefore not so well beleeved " (*A Discourse upon the Questions in Debate Between the King and Parliament* [1642], p. 15).

[6] Clarendon, *The History of the Rebellion and Civil Wars in England*, ed. W. Dunn Macray (Oxford, 1888), I, 390-91. Hereafter "Clarendon," citing volume and page numbers of this edition.

[7] Rushworth, III, 1335; also *Cobbett's Parliamentary History of England* (1807), II, 628. Hereafter cited as "*Parl. Hist.*"

of this Realme," or the "Honour, Greatnesse, and Security of this Crowne and Nation."[8] No party had a monopoly of this language, although each of them claimed the prerogative of knowing where safety was to be found. Denham was merely speaking to the hopes of all, and claiming too that his far-sighted prospect gave him the ability to diagnose and the right to speak. Five years later, at the very beginning of his *History of the Rebellion*, Clarendon was to declare that the wise had been imposed upon and the innocent had been possessed with laziness and sleep in the most visible article of danger,[9] and *Coopers Hill* was a timely warning about the consequences to the common safety if the wise and the innocent did not come to its rescue in time.

I will return later to the statement " Courts make not Kings " (line 5) that O Hehir has argued hides a " proroyal bias," but the opening section as a whole is apprehensive rather than tendentious, and initiates the dialectical and ethical theme involving safety, knowledge, and desire that will not be completed until the poem's concluding lines. The description of Windsor hill that follows (27-28) might seem, on the contrary, to be the most "royalist" passage in *Coopers Hill,* and in so far as it praises a king who needed all the favorable publicity he could get, it certainly reveals the side on which Denham's sympathies lay. Yet the entire section points to fundamentals that lie beyond controversy—to the glories of the past, to the naturalness of the English monarchy, and, above all, to the loyalty that all Englishmen bore to the king himself. Whatever the sovereign's mistakes, for which his evil counselors were solely responsible, the subjects' allegiance was to his person, not his policies, so Denham's appeal was to feelings that lay much deeper than the animosities that divided the country. Charles's private virtues were not in dispute, but Denham saw in the king's " frendlike sweetnes & ... Kinglike Awe," or his " Majesty & love," an expression of nature's law of *concordia discors*. Nature's wisdom in designing "First a brave place, & then as brave a mynde" (68) is meant to contrast with the vain activities and desires of the Londoners, but it serves also to make the historical polemic about the origin of the castle superfluous. "Nature this Mount soe fitly did advaunce / Wee

[8] Quotations chosen at random from *An Exact Collection of All Remonstrances, Declarations, Votes* [etc.] (1643), sig. B2^r.

[9] Clarendon, I, 2.

might conclude then nothinge is by Chance . . . (For none commends his iudgement that doth chuse / That which a blind man only could refuse.) " To look at Windsor was to be reminded of the basic fact that England had always been a monarchy, and that neither the lusts of kings, the sufferings of the people, nor the vagaries of subsequent history could harm the rock on which the constitution was founded. History itself, from which the poem later gives us selected incidents, is superficial by comparison, and merely demonstrates that men have always deviated from one extreme to another in their attempt to return to the balanced norm from which they started. Platitudes of such magnitude command the assent of all, and need only to be stated to be believed. Although all Denham's contemporaries would have known at once that they were reading a "royalist" declaration, they would also have recognized the accents not of a "party" poet but of a firm believer in the old balanced monarchy which parliament was fighting for, and which the revolution of 1640-41 had already almost restored.[10]

[10] In the interests of his theme Denham made Windsor castle more ancient than it was, and exaggerated the ambiguities of its origins. Froissart attributed the building to King Arthur, and William Harrison speculated that Arviragus might have founded it even earlier. Camden traced the name to a charter of Edward the Confessor and added "I have read nothing more ancient, concerning Windsore." Everyone knew, however, that the site had changed from Old to New Windsor and that Edward III "heere built new out of the ground a most strong Castle" (Camden). Stow differed only slightly, recording that Henry I built the new castle with the chapel and town of Windsor one mile from Old Windsor, and that Edward III had substantially enlarged it. William Lambarde, in the most careful investigation, dismissed Froissart and King Arthur in favor of the Saxons. The evidence did not permit him to decide whether Old or New Windsor had been the scene of Edward the Confessor's "disporting." William I enjoyed Windsor, but Henry II moved the palace from "the Bottome to the Hille," where Edward III later completely rebuilt it. The three kings buried at Windsor were Henry VI, Edward IV, and Henry VIII; and the three kings born there were Edward III, Henry VI, and Edward VI. I have found no connection between Caesar and Windsor beyond Polydore Vergil's statement that Caesar may have forded the Thames nearby. To Lambarde the castle is "renowned for Strengthe, and esteamed for Pleasure," whereas to Camden it is "lightsome" and "magnificent." The topography of Windsor was apparently a traditional example of *concordia discors.* Most writers regularly think of the Order of the Garter when they discuss Windsor, but the most likely "source" for Denham's remarks on the Order is Camden, not Heylin. Camden has all the details that Heylin mentions (who was copying him), besides a greater emphasis on the physical features of Windsor. He characteristically states, for example, "Let us returne againe from persons to places," exactly in the fashion that Denham structures his poem. I suspect that the topographical poem derives from Camden more directly than from Drayton or Ben Jonson. References: Froissart, *Chronicle,* ed. Lord Berners, Tudor Translations (1901), Book I, ch. 100; Harrison,

When Denham chose to continue his account of Windsor by recalling the history of Edward III he managed simultaneously to maintain his detachment and to move closer to his principal topical concern. The virtues and vices of Edward III were fairly well known in 1641. Raleigh in his *Prerogative of Parliaments* (reprinted in 1640) mentioned that "the three estates did [Edward] the greatest affront that ever King received or endured," but clearly implied that the king had been greedy for money and had not acted wisely himself.[11] Stow recorded Edward's concupiscence, Sir Thomas Roe noted that both Edward III and Henry VIII had debased the coinage, and William Hakewill devoted twenty pages to the history of Edward's efforts to raise money without the benefit of parliaments.[12] Sir Simonds D'Ewes, however, said more than once in the House of Commons that Edward was a "wise Prince" and "one of the most excellent princes that ever this kingdom had.[13] O Hehir has sided with D'Ewes, and points out, quite properly, that Denham praised Edward for uniting the crowns of France, Scotland, and England, for founding the Order of the Garter, and for choosing St. George as a patron saint: "the royal citadel of Windsor is then, to him who reads aright, a hieroglyphic inscription. . . . it speaks of British imperial greatness, of the superiority of peace to strife, of the divine warrant of the British monarchy. It reveals the history of English kingship to have been in sum a preamble to and prediction of the potential harmony now within reach of actualization in the Stuart reign."[14] This is very happily expressed, and the justice of its conclusion can be underlined by the observation that Denham was also perfectly aware of Edward's limitations, and hence was contrasting him with Charles, who had peacefully reunited the countries that Edward had bound by force:

"Description of England" prefixed to Holinshed's *Chronicles* (1587), p. 196; Camden, *Britain* (1637), pp. 286-93; Stow, *Annales* (1601), pp. 194, 205; Lambarde, *Dictionarium Angliae Topographicum & Historicum* (1730), pp. 414-23. See also John Leland's *Itinerary*, ed. Thomas Hearne (Oxford, 1770), IX, 103, and Robert R. Tighe and J. E. Davis, *Annals of Windsor* (1858), I, 1-23.

[11] (1640), pp. 21-22.

[12] John Stow, *Annales* (1631), p. 276, misnumbered 269; Roe, in Rushworth, III, 1219; Hakewill, *The Liberties of the Subject* (1641), pp. 51-72.

[13] D'Ewes, *Journal*, ed. Notestein (New Haven, 1923), pp. 196, 215; see also Rudyard's speech in the Short Parliament, in Rushworth, III, 1130, and George Digby's invocation of Edward III for annual parliaments, Rushworth, III, 1352.

[14] O Hehir, p. 190.

> Had thy greate destiny but given thee skill
> To know aswell as power to Act her will
> That from those Kings who then thy Captives were
> In after tymes should springe a Royall paire
> Who should possesse all that thy mighty power
> Or thy desires more mighty did devoure
> To whome thire better Fate reserves what Ere
> The victor hopes for, or the vanquisht feare,
> That blood which thou & thy greate Grandsire shead
> And all that since these Sister nations bledd
> Had beene unspilt had happie Edward knowne
> That all the blood he spilt had beene his owne
> Thou hadst extended through the Conquered East
> Thyne & the Christian name & made them blest
> To serve thee, while that losse, this gaine would bring
> Christ for their God, & Edward for their Kinge. (87-102)

Edward III, like the Londoners, and like his successor Henry VIII, was deficient in knowledge and over-endowed with desire, so that the great Christian crusade he might have waged had never been undertaken. The promise of his reign was unfulfilled, just as (later in the poem) the potential good of Magna Charta is seen to have been quickly vitiated by the " Subiects Arm'd, [who] the more theire princes gave, / But this advantage tooke the more to crave " (299-300). The moral lesson taught by Edward's example, as by the others', is no more royalist than any call to temperance and wisdom at any time, and by criticizing an English monarch so severely Denham showed that he was no believer in a divine right theory which claimed that kings could do no wrong. All the versions of Draft I, as if calling attention to Denham's high-mindedness, note in the margin that the poet interpreted Edward's Order of the Garter as a prophecy of the union of England and Scotland under James I, and Denham certainly worded his lines with extreme care, so that it is quite possible to read them as a celebration in the most general terms of the Stuarts' Anglo-Scots alliance. " Possible," one may say, but not in the least probable, because the most important fact about the poem is that Denham was writing during the aftermath of the Scots treaty in the summer of 1641.

Although the complexities of Anglo-Scots relations constitute the missing piece in the puzzle, the indispensable context for Denham's meaning and intentions, the difficulty of the section on Edward III lies not in its obscurity but in the long-sustained and pervasive importance of the subject to which it implicitly refers. The facts speak for themselves. In August 1640 the Scots routed the English forces at Newburn and remained squatting in the Northern counties for a full year. In September 1640, in a response to their presence, Charles reluctantly took the advice of the peers and issued the writs for the Long Parliament. In October the treaty (or, more strictly, the cease-fire) of Ripon was concluded, and by the next month, when parliament assembled, the negotiations for a full treaty were resumed in London—an action that Clarendon later thought was one of Charles's great mistakes. Agreement was long delayed, often deliberately, and throughout the first seven months of 1641 there were innumerable complaints in and out of parliament about the expense of paying for both armies, and as many expressed hopes that the signing of the treaty was imminent. Petitions were presented and dropped, Strafford was executed and other ministers fled at the threat of impeachment, the root-and-branch bill appeared and disappeared, and the great milestones of the constitutional revolution were erected; but hanging over all parliamentary business, as a matter of the most urgent necessity, was the settlement with Scotland that still had to be arranged. Until that time the armies waited, and the country was in a state of armed truce that nobody could afford.[15] If the poem did not contain more specific evidence that the treaty had been accomplished before Denham conceived his poem, we should never be quite sure if the praise of Charles " Who has within that Azure Round confin'd, / Those Realms which nature for their bounds design'd " (109-10) was a panegyric on the union itself or a piece of hopeful and wishful thinking, written perhaps as early as October 1640. However, the most natural interpretation, not only of the emblematic Garter but of the entire contrast between Charles's wisdom and Edward's ignorance, would always be that Denham was rejoicing in Charles's eventual success, in which the *concordia discors* of his nature had resolved the discords of his own warring realms.[16]

Charles' "better Fate" (93), however, was not only to have

[15] "The vast burden of the two armies" (I, 342) looms over Clarendon's account of the period. The main facts are recorded in S. R. Gardiner, *History of England* (1899-1900), Vol. IX, hereafter cited as "Gardiner."

[16] The "Tryumph" to which Denham refers (line 75) and which brought the kings of France and Scotland together as prisoners is probably the great joust held in Smithfield in 1357-58. See Stow's *Annales* (1631), p. 263.

made peace by peaceful means, but to have brought about the conditions in which the foreign crusade denied to Edward became again possible. The dream of a protestant war in Europe was an English fantasy that William III came closest to realizing during the seventeenth century, and it always appealed most to the imagination when affairs were going badly at home and the need arose for a distant object that all parties could agree was theoretically desirable. In 1640-42 the ready-made cause was the Elector Palatine's, the recovery of whose possessions had influenced the foreign policy of two reigns.[17] After the meeting of the Long Parliament one of the earliest statements that a foreign war might aid in the resolution of domestic differences was made by the Earl of Bristol, the chief English negotiator of the Scottish treaty, in a " pithie and a judicious speech " on 12 January 1641: " Hee did hope alsoe that God would soe farre blesse us that we should wiselie and happilie compose the present differences soe as both nations being happilie conioined in one Monarchie againe, and setled in peace and obedience under one and the same soveraigne, wee might soon pitch upon some great action that should fullie restore our glory."[18] In February the king announced the forthcoming marriage of his daughter to William of Orange, which occurred on 2 May, and gave as his third reason for the match " the Use I may make of this Alliance towards the Establishing of my Sister and Nephews,"[19] but it was not until 5 July that the subject came to the foreground and seemed for a long moment to become a national preoccupation. On the very morning on which he abolished the Star Chamber and reminded parliament of his many previous concessions and of the necessity of his journey to Scotland, Charles issued his Manifesto on behalf of the Palatinate. If treating at Ratisbon failed, he said, he would go to war.[20]

The abolition of Star Chamber made 5 July one of the big days in the revolution, but Gardiner underestimated the effect of the Manifesto: " The Houses listened gravely and gave a decorous

---

[17] See the index to Gardiner, Vol. X, under "Palatinate."
[18] D'Ewes, ed. Notestein, p. 247.
[19] Rushworth, IV, 188ʳ. Calybute Downing was the principal parliamentary pamphleteer for the cause.
[20] Rushworth, IV, 308-10. Also in July, Sir Francis Wortley in his *Dutie* wrote eight pages of heroic couplets in commiseration with the Queen of Bohemia.

answer: but the hearts of the members were no longer in the Palatinate. They had the dread of that ill-starred visit to Scotland before their eyes."[21] True, the House never lost its caution where Charles was concerned, but the Manifesto gave it one of its rare excuses to reaffirm its goodwill towards the king. The Commons considered and approved the document in a debate on 7 July, and at a conference between both Houses on 9th Holles's speech was typical of the general reaction: "*My Lords,* The Loyal Subject of *England* is so well tuned in a sweet agreeing Harmony to the Person of his Prince, that he is affected with the least Touch upon any part of the Princely Offspring, and answers it instantly with a Sound proportionable. . . . This then is enough to make us zealous for the Redress of the Prince Elector's Wrongs."[22] On 28 August Rudyard was objecting to sending troops to France or Spain on the grounds that they would depress the affairs of the Elector,[23] and on the same day the Manifesto was read and passed in the Scottish parliament. Lord Loudoun was still talking about it at the end of September as offering a miraculous opportunity to unite England and Scotland in a common cause,[24] and as late as November Abraham Cowley and a few others welcomed the king back to London with memories of this happy possibility.[25] As Holles had also said in July, both "Point of Policy and Reason of State" directed England to sup-

[21] Gardiner, IX, 405; C. V. Wedgwood in *The Great Rebellion: The King's Peace 1637-1641* (New York, 1956), pp. 436, 448, 457-58, gives evidence that the Manifesto was contemptuously received in some quarters as an obvious excuse for Charles to raise an army for use against his own people.

[22] Rushworth, IV, 316, who also prints similar speeches by D'Ewes and Rudyard, pp. 311-15; also *Parl. Hist.*, II, 870-80.

[23] Rushworth, IV, 381-82. Printed also as a separate, and much referred to.

[24] *A Second Speech Made by the Lord Lowden . . . the 24 of Septemb. 1641* (1641), pp. 4-5, misnumbered 6-7; see also *The Lord Lowden his Learned and Wise Speech . . . September 9 1641* (1641), pp. 3-4 [Thomason E 199 (13 & 14)]. *The Calendar of State Papers, Domestic Series 1641-43* [CSPD] contains many letters concerning the Palatinate. See especially a letter from the Earl of Bristol on 28 August, in which he notes that "the whole kingdom take[s] that business so much to heart" (p. 106); also letters of 9 September and 2 October, pp. 120, 130-31. The Earl of Northumberland and the Queen of Bohemia had lost hope of immediate help for the cause by the end of November: see pp. 165, 172. The Manifesto was taken very seriously by the Scottish parliament; also by Robert Baillie in July, in *Letters and Journals*, ed. David Laing (Edinburgh, 1841), I, 357, 387.

[25] *Irenodia Cantabrigiensis* (Cambridge, 1641), sig. K1ᵛ; also John Cragge, *Great Britains Prayers . . . Together with a Congratulatory for the Entertainment of His Majesty out of Scotland* (1641), sigs. A3ᵛ-A4ʳ.

port her allies, " to advance this Kingdom to the highest Pitch of Greatness and Reputation, to make us formidable abroad to the Enemies of our Church and State, and so enjoy Peace and Safety, and Tranquility at home." [26]

In all these discussions there is an implicit connection between the Scottish treaty and the foreign war, a connection that Denham himself exploited in *Coopers Hill*. Charles had succeeded, and could succeed, in schemes which Edward's greedy belligerence had put beyond his reach, but once again the protracted recurrences of the Palatine dream give us no certain clues about the date at which Denham was writing. Like the rest of the section on Windsor, however, it leads to the probability of post-midsummer composition, and in so far as the bad news on 1 November tended to make Ireland, not Germany, the foreseeable site of a foreign war, we can tentatively assume for the time being that the poem was first conceived during the four late summer and autumn months. Guidelines are useful at this stage because the section that follows on the problems of religion introduces a subject so central to the revolution that Denham's generalized treatment of it offers no help at all with the dating question. It is crucial, nevertheless, for determining the kind of royalism that Denham espoused.

By contrasting the " Lethargicke dreame " of religion in the reign of Henry VIII with the " worse extreame " of the contemporary fervor for religious reform, and by observing the implicit similarities between Henry's " Luxury or Lust " and the " too Active " and " devouring " zeal of his own times,[27] Denham pointed to that " temperate Region ... Betweene their frigid & our torrid Zone " (151-52). By no stretch of the historical facts, however, should this middle ground between religious extremes be identified with Laudian policies,[28] or with any of the most conservative reactions to the clamor for the root-and-branch extirpa-

---

[26] Rushworth, IV, 316. Both Houses agreed on 9 September that soldiers should not be permitted to serve the Elector's enemies abroad. John Nalson, *An Impartial Collection of the Great Affairs of State* (1683), II, 479-81 (Hereafter " Nalson "). The next year the cause was frequently bruited again, and became the seventeenth of parliament's *XIX Propositions* on 1 June.

[27] The radical Sir John Wray urged on 8 February 1641 " that hee conceived wee might as well meddle with Bishopps now as H. 8 did with Abbeies in his time " (D'Ewes, ed. Notestein, p. 336). It had also been suggested that the money collected for repairing St. Paul's be used to pay off the Scots. Sir Roger Twysden, in August, also lamented Henry VIII's greed. See *Archæologia Cantiana*, II (1859), 177-78.

[28] O Hehir, p. 194.

tion of the ecclesiastical hierarchy. The contours of moderation, like those of more radical positions on either side, shifted under the pressures of events, but they always encompassed a measure of necessary reform that was intended to placate the puritans and satisfy the more general sense that innovations had indeed crept into the church and needed to be expunged. The commonest distinction, employed by the king himself as early as January 1641, was between the correction of abuses and the overturning of a settled state. "Now I must tell you," said Charles to both Houses, " That I make a great Difference between Reformation and Alteration of Government; tho' I am for the first, I cannot give Way to the latter. If some of [the bishops] have over-stretched their Power, and encroached too much upon the Temporality, if it be so, I shall not be unwilling these Things should be Redressed and Reformed, as all other Abuses, according to the Wisdom of former Times; so far I shall go with you." [29] These remarks, which filled D'Ewes with apprehension " in case his Majestie should bee irremooveablie fixed to uphold the Bishops in ther wealth pride and Tyrannie," [30] preceded the great debate on the church on 8 February that Gardiner regarded as a prophetic taking of sides, and the first day on which parties stood clearly opposed.[31] Falkland on that occasion ended his speech by calling for a lopping of the branches rather than a rooting up of the tree, and others like Pleydall, Grimston, Digby, Colepeper, Rudyard, Selden, Hopton, and Hyde were to follow him.[32] As Hyde wrote later, those who knew the constitution of the kingdom knew also " that the bishops were no less the representative body of the clergy than the House of Commons was of the people, and, consequently, that the depriving them of voice in Parliament was a violence, and removing landmarks, and not a shaking (which might settle again) but dissolving foundations, which must leave the building unsafe for habitation." [33]

These were the metaphors that adorned the debate throughout the year, and in June Edmund Waller was arguing that the House

[29] Rushworth, IV, 155. A different version of the speech occurs in the *Journals of the House of Lords* [LJ], IV, 142. Nalson's version is closer to Rushworth's. Notestein comments on the variations in D'Ewes, pp. 279-80.
[30] D'Ewes, ed. Notestein, p. 281.
[31] Gardiner, IX, 281.
[32] Rushworth, IV, 186; Gardiner, IX, 281.
[33] Clarendon, I, 406.

should resolve "'To reform', that is 'not to abolish Episcopacy'," and that as the church's horns and nails had been pared already, the time had come to consider its right use and antiquity.[34] Denham's praise for Waller's defense of the church in the second draft of *Coopers Hill* was in itself a political act that served to identify the poet with the professedly moderate stance that Waller had adopted and vigorously maintained. Waller later became one of the principal spokesmen for the group that resisted the challenge of the Grand Remonstrance, and in June he was clairvoyant about the consequences of meddling with religion too much. Episcopacy was intrinsically mingled with English law like wine and water, and if scripture was offered as an excuse for separating them " I am confident that, whenever an equal division of lands and goods shall be desired, there will be as many places in Scripture found out, which seem to favour that, as there are now alleged against the prelacy or preferment in the church."[35] Even in his first draft, Denham placed himself squarely in the camp of Waller and the other opponents of root-and-branch when he prayed that " may no such storme / Fall on our tymes, where Ruyne must reforme " (127-28), but he thereby also revealed his own commitment to the redress of the worst grievances. " Ruyne " in the historical context meant " root-and-branch,"[36]

[34] *Parl. Hist.*, II, 826-28. Lord Digby's speeches in February, and Rudyard's, were in the same vein. Rushworth, IV, 170-74, 183-84.

[35] *Parl. Hist.*, II, 827-28.

[36] For a full account of the debates, see William A. Shaw, *A History of the English Church During the Civil Wars* [etc.] *1640-1660* (1900), I, 29-118. Denham repudiated anger and shame as appropriate responses to the present crisis (lines 161-62), but his concluding fear for " what's too neere " was not exaggerated. The root-and-branch bill, together with a drastic but unpresbyterian scheme for the reorganization of the church, had been adopted by the House in July and rested in committee, to be revived only briefly after the recess. " The fright occasioned by Charles's journey to Scotland drove the matter into the background " (Shaw, I, 99). On p. 65 he suggests that 3 June, when the Lords rejected the " Bishops' Bill," marked the end, unintentionally, of " all dreams of a moderate Church reform." Wormald in *Clarendon*, p. 14, observes that the possibility of a reconciliation in the late summer of 1641 was hindered mainly by ecclesiastical radicalism and fear of the king. The fear was brought to a head by the Scottish visit " and actually operated to restrain the radicalism. . . . [It] probably in the end led to the dropping altogether of the Root-and-Branch Bill." In view of evidence to be presented later, Sir Edward Nicholas' letter to the king on 19 September is of great interest. He reported rumors of the clergy favoring popery and hoped that Charles would take strong steps to enforce a " tymely moderac'on " and " to declare for " reddines to reforme what shalbe thought amisse in it by yor clergy & Parliam^t " *Diary and Correspondence of John Evelyn, to which is Subjoined the Private correspondence between King Charles I and Sir Edward Nicholas*, ed. William Bray [1889-91],

but there is nothing in the first draft which declares that Denham would have opposed the abolition of the bishops' temporal powers, or their exclusion from the House of Lords. He may or may not have objected to such legislation, and he probably viewed with alarm the impeachment of the bishops and the provocative ecclesiastical Orders that the House passed before its recess in September, but his main position is clear, and is no more Laudian than Falkland's or Hyde's, although it was easy for root-and-branchers to ignore the distinction. His concern was lest desires, under the banner of reform, should get out of hand, and his historical account of earlier calentures led him to wish for a moderate solution that could only be achieved by restraint and compromise. Like the earlier description of Windsor, therefore, the section on St. Ann's hill and Chertsey Abbey offers reasons that could be said to appeal to the widest possible spectrum of political opinion, doubtful as it was of the direction in which Pym was leading the parliament, but not royalist or episcopal in any die-hard sense.

An important piece of evidence for the dating of the poem occurs in the next section on "King Thames," in which "an inconsequential but grotesque eight-line simile," as the editor calls it,[37] is spliced between couplets which explicitly compare the river with a prudent and a wise king (179-86).

> Nor with an Angrey & unruly wave,
> (Like Profuse Kings) resumes the Wealth he gave:
> Noe unexpected inundations spoyle
> The Mowers hopes nor mocke the Plowmans toyle
> And as a parting lover bids farewell
> To his Soules ioy, seeing her Eyelidds swell
> He turnes againe to save her falling teares,
> And with a parting kisse secures her feares:
> Soe Thames unwilling yet to be devorc't
> From his lov'd channell, willingly is forc't
> Backward against his proper course to swell,
> To take his second, though not last farewell.
> As a wise king first settles fruitefull peace
> In his owne Realmes & with their rich increase
> Seekes warre abroade & then in triumph brings
> The Spoyles of Kingdomes, & the Crownes of Kings,

IV, 72). The king could best show his good faith by appointing thoroughly protestant bishops to the vacant sees.

[37] O Hehir, p. 217. He does not discuss the simile in his analysis of Draft I.

> So Thames, to London doth at first present
> Those tributes, which the neighbouring Countreys sent.
> (175-92)

Alan Roper has suggested to me that the simile may be less grotesque than it first appears if the river's two goodbyes correspond to the ebb and flow of its tidal waters, but it remains sufficiently unsatisfactory to compel our attention to the meaning that Denham was trying to convey by his awkward image. In Denham's own terminology for his poem, he saw the Thames more perspicuously with his mind than with his eye, and what he really saw was the king's two goodbyes to his parliament in August 1641.

Charles's departure for Scotland aroused, in Gardiner's words, " an overpowering sense of danger " which tended to make the parties forget their differences: " they were united as yet, as they were never again to be united till 1660, in their resolution that, as far as in them lay, there should not be a military despotism in England." [38] Having obtained one previous delay of the journey which would take Charles through the two armies in the North, the majority in the Commons fought desperately until the very last moment to obtain another postponement. On Saturday 7 August they were still hoping for another fourteen days, but, to cut off further petitions, Charles went to the House of Lords that same afternoon, summoned the Commons, and passed a number of bills, including two concerning forests and ship-money that were important. "After this the lord keeper made a short speech, and then the king bid the parliament farewell, and so departed." [39] Unwilling to take no for an answer, the House took the unprecedented step of sitting all day Sunday, but were unable to deflect Charles's determination to leave for more than one day, from Monday to Tuesday.[40] His decision could only have been strength-

---

[38] Gardiner, IX, 418; previous quotation p. 415.

[39] *Parl. Hist.*, II, 898; also *LJ*, IV, 349.

[40] Sir Ralph Verney, *Verney Papers*, ed. John Bruce, for the Camden Society (1845), p. 115. The House attended the king at Whitehall at 4 p.m., he says. The Lords had agreed with the Commons the previous day to petition the king for a delay of fourteen days " if it may stand with the Engagement he has made to that Kingdom; howsoever, that he may stay till *Tuesday* Night Six of Clock, which they are sure will stand with his Engagement " (*Journals of the House of Commons* [*CJ*], II, 244-45; also *LJ*, IV, 349-50). Charles's measly concession was in response to the Lords' pressure. The Scots' commissioners had been appealed to for support, but they naturally refused.

ened by the extremely gloomy sermon about mutability and God's punishments to which he had listened that morning.[41] On Monday the House received a message "that when his Majesty upon Saturday, bid the Lords severally Farewel, his Intent then was to both Houses, which if they did not so understand it, his Majesty now commanded to signifie it as his Intention therein."[42] On Tuesday 10th, however, having stayed up all night, the king again went to parliament at 10 a.m. " to take his second, though not last farewell,"[43] and to sign in person the pacification between England and Scotland. An hour later he was on his way to Edinburgh with the Elector Palatine in the coach beside him. Charles Louis's presence there has the precision of a metaphor actualized in experience, because the hopes of the cause he represented were dependent on an Anglo-Scots alliance, and the continuation of Denham's simile compares the Thames with a " wise king [who] first settles fruitefull peace / In his own Realmes & with their rich increase / Seekes warre abroade." I must return to the implications of Denham's political attitude, which the later sections of the poem clarify further, but three comments can be made here: first, that Charles's love of parliaments (" his Soules ioy ") was a fiction that he and his friends invariably sought to maintain, and he could in truth point to the Triennial Act and the Act perpetuating the Long Parliament to substantiate his claim. The image of the Thames, puzzling at the literal level, is conceptually uncomplicated: although Charles was unwilling to leave parliament, his " proper course," as he repeatedly insisted, was to visit Scotland. He therefore " willingly " delayed his departure in order to take a second farewell, and with his " parting kisse " signed the treaty and secured the fears of those who dreaded the object of his journey.

[41] *A Sermon Preach't to His Majesty, at the Court of White-hall. Aug. 8* (1641). Everyone was involved in the national sin, although "this wild variety of Sects, and lawlesse *independencies*" were perhaps most to blame (p. 24). Hall's sermon, which is as portentous as any to which Charles listened while awaiting execution, suggests that the feeling at court was nearing despair.

[42] Nalson, II, 437.

[43] On the two goodbyes, see *The Parliamentary or Constitutional History of England* (1753), IX, 476: "Then the King took his Leave a second Time of the Parliament, telling them 'That he hoped to use good Expedition in disbanding of both Armies, and would make all Haste he could to return before *Michaelmas*.'" Also Parl. Hist., 900; *The Diurnall Occurrences, or Dayly Proceedings of* . . . *Parliament* (1641), 331, 336; LJ, 349, 357. Accounts vary about the time at which Charles left London.

Second, of course, his leaving did no such thing, and Denham was nowhere more "royalist" than in his glossing over the fears that the king's absence enhanced for two or three weeks. By putting the most hopeful construction on the event Denham was himself bathing the swollen "Eyelidds" of the forsaken parliamentarians by emphasizing the positive achievement of the successful treaty, by evoking the possibility of a protestant war, and (this is the third point) by appealing to the widespread hope for the restoration of foreign trade. The complaints in 1641 about the decay of trade were far too numerous to catalogue here, but the title of Henry Robinson's pamphlet in August neatly voices the opinions not only of city merchants but of apprentices, parliamentary committee-men, country burghers, and petitioners across the country: *Englands Safety in Trades Encrease.* Or, as Sir Thomas Roe said in the House of Commons, the only way to stop the flow of money abroad was "by peace and Trade."[44] Such blessings could reasonably be expected to ensue upon the Scottish treaty, especially if men would refrain from questioning the king's motives and "behould his shore."[45] A reflective reader might also have wondered if the Thames who temperately refused to "resume the Wealth he gave" was not a reformed character since the days of ship-money and other "unruly waves." In view of the fact that "inundations," as I show later, were always associated with the exercise of prerogative power, the Thames in its peaceful

---

[44] *Sir Thomas Roe his Speech in Parliament* (1641), p. 5. See also, e.g., Lewes Roberts, *The Treasure of Traffike* (1641) and *The Humble Petition of Divers Citizens of London,* 24 April, in Rushworth, IV, 233-34. Robinson said, p. 17, that "The decay of trade is in everybodyes mouth" and both wealth and safety were thereby declining.

[45] I do not insist upon it, but this is the most likely meaning of the line "Search not his bottome, but behould his shore" (172), which appears to be a version of the thought expressed in the following passage: "What Glass hath this unhappy divided Kingdom from his Majesty's Presence and Audience to contemplate the fair and ravishing Form of his Royal Intentions in, but in the clear and diaphanous Administration of his Justice? And what do these traiterous and illegal Practices aim at, but ... to multiply, as by a Magick Glass, the Royal Dispensation of his Favours, into the ugly and deformed Visage of their Suppression of the Liberties [etc.] of his Loyal Subjects" (Captain Audley Mervin on 4 March 1641, in Rushworth, IV, 216). The exactly opposite thought is expressed a little later in the poem: "The Streame is so transparent pure & Cleare / That had the selfe enamoured youth gaz'd here, / So fatally deceav'd, he had not beene, / While he the bottome, not his face had seene" (219-22). Here Denham is arguing that had the king's true intentions been perceived there would have been no cause for alarm about them. The self-enamored youth can see only the intentions and desires written on his own face. Wise nature made this harmony, but the ignorant cannot perceive it.

JOHN M. WALLACE

role had conformed to the constitutional revolution and flowed evenly in the channel dictated by law. Its digression now from the shores of Westminster was only temporary and the future looked even brighter than the present.

The Thames slides into a passage, marginally noted in the mss. as " Windsor forrest," the main feature of which is a disquisition on nature's wonderful *concordia discors*. The river continues to figure in the harmony, but only as one of the " huge extreames " that nature has united, and the section concludes with a strange reference to " our angry supercilious Lords " who frown on the humble poor as the hill frowns on the stream. The editor has taken the opportunity to write the most learned account of *concordia discors* that we possess, noting specifically that " the word *harmonia* in Greek *always* denotes a means of connection between *a pair of opposites,* not a general agreement among many diverse things. As a result, even in non-Greek discourse on the topic, down to the time of Pope, the word ' harmony ' and its substitutes, including ' concord ' and ' variety,' usually imply a dyadic, not a multiple, agreement." [46] His observation is supported by everything in *Coopers Hill* so far: by the antitheses combined in Windsor hill and the king's person; by the dialectic between knowledge and ignorance, innocence and desire, that defines a safe center between extremes in politics and religion; and by the implicit celebration throughout the sections on Windsor and the Thames of the newly achieved harmony between England and Scotland. In the immediate historical context, the great example of *concordia discors* in a world otherwise jarred by furious dissonance was the Anglo-Scots treaty, and it is a curious fact that the only statements of the idea of balanced opposites that can be found in the political literature of 1641 refer precisely to that event. The most official pronouncement came from the Speaker of the House of Commons in a speech before both Houses on 2 December, the first day that Charles attended parliament after his return from the north. It began:

The Observation taken from the unlike Compositions and various Motions of the World made the Philosopher conclude, *Tota hujus mundi Concordia ex Discordibus constat.*

[46] O Hehir, p. 172, his italics. Earl R. Wasserman's analysis of *concordia discors* in his chapters on Denham and Pope in *The Subtler Language* (Baltimore, 1959) is also valuable, and his emphasis on perfect political balance remains correct.

The happy Conjuncture of both these Nations in the Triumph and Joy of Your Sacred Presence, extracted from the different and divided Dispositions and Opinions, gives us Cause to observe and to admire these Blessed Effects from such contrary Causes. We may without Flattery commend Your Sacred Majesty, the Glorious Instrument of the happy Change, whose Piety and Prudence, directed by the Hand of God, hath contracted this Union from these various Discords.

The Story of these Times will seem Paradoxes in following Generations, when they shall hear of Peace sprung from the Root of Dissention, of Union planted upon the Stock of Divisions, Two Armies in the Field, both ready to strike the first Blow, and both united without a Stroke.

Nothing can reduce these Truths into a Belief but the Knowledge of Your Piety and Justice, who have accomplished these Acts of Wonder by Goodness and Gentleness, without Force and Violence.

This Way of Conquest, this *Bellum incruentum*, hath been the Rule of the most valiant and puissant Monarchs, advancing Your Glory in Safeguard of One Subject more than in the Death of a Thousand Enemies.

Thus have You erected a Monument of Glory to Your Sacred Memory for all Generations.[47]

In his disastrous reply, Charles acknowledged Lenthall's speech to be " Learned " while contradicting its content with a complaint about the jealousies, frights, and alarms with which his people were still bitten. However, if he had read the eulogistic volumes issued by the university presses to welcome him home, he would have been well prepared for the Speaker's learning. Fellows and students alike burnished their metaphors for the occasion, the most common being those of the head or the soul returning to the body, the spring coming in winter, and the sun dispersing the factious mists. Because of his absence, Charles had had to wait three months for the public encomia he might have expected in August, but it was too late to hide an awareness of the Irish problem which infected the shallow rejoicing with some gloom. Jasper Mayne's panegyric was a typical tune whistled in the dark:

> You now returne, as when you did at first
> Receive this Crowne, and find in us like thirst
> Of your Approach; since by this progresse we
> One people of Two late divided see.

[47] *LJ*, IV, 459; also in Rushworth, IV, 453-54, and published as a separate. I cannot resist the speculation that Lenthall had seen *Coopers Hill*, since he bases the concord so firmly in Charles's character. Lenthall was also a friend and neighbor of Falkland's at Burford and hence in touch with the Great Tew circle, which also included Waller.

> One Forme againe doth spread it selfe through all;
> And adverse Hemispheeres become one Ball.
> And though in some things we walk feet to feet,
> Yet that we in our oppositions meet,
> And that from this Diversity we grow
> Entire, is your great worke; The Heavens move soe;
> Where Orbes wheeling 'gaynst Orbes, doe yet agree
> In the first Mover, and make Harmony.
> And those Iarres, which seemd Discords to our eares,
> Compos'd by you, grow Musick in the spheares.[48]

Denham's lines on *concordia discors* are an extension of his praise of the river (" O could my lines fully & smoothly flow, / As thy pure flood " [etc.]) and carry that praise to the recognition that King Thames is the embodiment of all-wise nature's divine law. The progress from the " grotesque " simile about Charles's departure, to the reflection about the wise king who first settles fruitful peace in his own realms, to the statement that the river is his theme, to the final celebration of *concordia discors* is an ascending series of generalizations on the subject of the king's wisdom in bringing peace out of discord. Although a shoulder-note in the text indicates that " Windsor forrest " enters the poem at line 203 we do not catch even a glimpse of the trees until line 215, and only then in an unfavorable comparison between " the steepe horrid roughnes of the wood " and " the gentle Calmenes of the flood." Denham's transition here from the Thames as a total image to Thames as part of an image of *concordia discors* arranged by nature is less difficult to follow if we perceive that the peace-loving and peace-making river continues as the harmonious element even after the roughness of the wood and the roughness of the bellicose hill have been introduced. He needed the transition because he wished to emphasize the opposi-

---

[48] *Eucharistica Oxoniensia* (Oxford, 1641), sig. a1r-v. See also *Irenodia Cantabrigiensis*, already cited, and John Bond, *King Charles his Welcome Home* (1641). The longest account of Charles's reception, *Ovatio Carolina*, is printed in *Somers Tracts*, ed. Sir Walter Scott (1810), IV, 137-51, and in *Harleian Miscellany* (1810), Vol. V. Provincial welcomes are recorded in *Five Most Noble Speeches Spoken to His Majestie Returning out of Scotland* (1641), Thomason E 199 (32). The most extravagant and metaphorical celebration of the treaty was John Thornborough's *A Discourse Shewing the Great Happinesse, that Hath and May still Accrue to his Majesties Kingdomes of England and Scotland, by Re-uniting them into one Great Britain* (1641). Thornborough himself, however, had died in July at the age of ninety, and his tract (which went into three editions) was merely a slightly updated reprint of two pamphlets he had written in 1604 and 1605. It probably did not appear before November.

tion that the king's efforts had overcome. "Such huge extreames, when nature doth unite / Wonder from thence results, from thence delight." The magnitude of Charles's achievement in the treaty was very much on Denham's mind, although in terms of the landscape he was viewing the harmony could be attributed only to nature's handiwork.[49] The angry supercilious lords with whom the frowning hill is compared were the lords of the privy council, who had been responsible for many years, often with considerable resentment and haughtiness, for seeing that the people were properly mulcted of their ship-money. By introducing tangentially a recollection of their Star Chamber activities Denham managed to dissociate the king from the most heinous offenses of his council, and to proclaim once again that he, the poet, was no supercilious royalist himself.[50]

Denham saw the stag-hunt, which has become the crux of the poem, solely with his "quicke poeticke sight," so the event took place in his conceptualizing mind's eye rather than within his vision. The hunt is an imaginary, invented, and wholly poetic example, suggesting that the poet has finally succeeded as he promised in making Cooper's Hill his Parnassus.[51] The boundlessness of his fancy has outdistanced his eyesight altogether, and a contemporary reader would have realized that Denham was most inspired, and spoke with his highest authority as a poet, when he claimed such autonomy of perception. It is a little dis-

[49] Both Wasserman and O Hehir feel the passage is unsatisfactory, and it is probably another case of Denham seeing more clearly with his mind than with his eye. The uniting of vast extremes, effected by the river, makes the hill an intrinsically Scottish mountain, not a Surrey hillock, with which "*our* [i.e. English] angry supercilious Lords" are compared. Later in the poem Denham reveals more anti-Scots bias, and his concern with their treatment of the king.

[50] Dr. Derek M. Hirst, after one glance at the context, identified the supercilious lords when I was investigating a far less likely possibility. The Grand Remonstrance was stuffed with notices of their iniquities; see especially Rushworth, IV, 445: "Multitudes were called to the Council-Table, who were tired with long Attendances there for refusing illegal Payments. The Prisons were filled with their Commitments: Many of the Sheriffs summoned into the *Star-Chamber*; and some imprisoned for not being quick enough in levying the Ship-Money, the People languished under Grief and Fear, no visible Hope being left but in Desperation." For an actual illustration of their surliness see Rushworth, III, 1182. M. D. Gordon, "The Collection of Ship-Money in the Reign of Charles I," *Trans. Royal Hist. Soc.*, Third Series, 4 (1910), 141-62, and Cora L. Scofield, *A Study of the Court of Star Chamber* (Chicago, 1900) remain useful accounts of the lords' activities, and Henry E. I. Phillips, "The Last Years of the Court of Star Chamber 1630-41." *TRHS*, Fourth Series, 21 (1939), 103-31, links the attack on the court to "the general movement against the episcopacy."

[51] See O Hehir's excellent paragraph on the "poeticke sight," p. 202.

concerting, therefore, to be told that the stag is a metaphor for the Earl of Strafford, and the hunt a " quasi-allegorical " account of his rise and fall.[52] To the most moderate of the editor's comments, that the hunt " bears several overtones reverberatory of the fall of the Earl of Strafford,"[53] no exception need be taken, but there are a number of objections to saying more than that. 1. All the records of Strafford's fall testify to his extraordinary courage, whereas the stag alternates between bravery and fear. 2. As O Hehir says, " Strafford was not *like* a declining statesman [line 255]; he *was* one."[54] 3. If Denham was a " committed royalist " or a sympathizer with the fifty-nine " Straffordians " then one would expect him to have shown more disapproval of the stag's end. Certainly, Strafford seemed " glad & proud to die " and exonerated Charles from the responsibility, but how could a royalist have summed it up as an " Innocent & happie chase " or ever have suggested that Charles was " hunting " Strafford in any sense?[55] 4. Finally, it has not been made clear what the function of the episode is in the developing argument of the whole poem; its didactic intention is automatically obscure, because, if the stag is chiefly Strafford, then Denham's royalist position is ambiguous, and we cannot be certain how the stag's death contributes to *concordia discors*. On an ethical level, nature's lesson " to shew how soone / Greate things are made, but sooner farre undone " may be a sufficient explanation for the hunt, especially as Denham punned wittily on the technical term (" to undo ") for the flaying and cutting up of a dead stag;[56] alternatively, we

[52] O Hehir, pp. 203-06.
[53] *Ibid.*, p. 211.
[54] *Ibid.*, p. 204.
[55] O Hehir argues, pp. 205-06, 224, that because the chase is not an allegory but a true hunt, the killing of the stag is more innocent and happy than the pursuit of liberty by tyranny; also that Charles's dooming of Strafford was more innocent than the barons' action " because its intention was Strafford's intention, to reestablish a ' blessed agreement ' between the King and his subjects." The stag hunt is an allegory and there is a much simpler explanation of the lines. For similar objections, and others, see Herbert Berry's review of O Hehir in *Ren Q*, 24 (1971), 416-17.
[56] *The Master of Game*, ed. William A. and F. Baillie-Grohman (1904), pp. 23, 201; [Juliana Berners], *The Gentlemans Academie, or, the Booke of S. Albans* (1595), p. 35. " Rous'd " (line 246) was the correct technical term for breaking or starting a stag, and the river to which a hart fled was called " the soil." A stag was sometimes distinguished from a hart as a younger beast, four or five years old. All royal forests existed solely for the pleasure of kings, " to put away from them the remembrance of their labouresome toyle." See John Manwood, preface to *A Treatise of the Lawes of the Forest* (1615); and also p. 33r for the king's " burden of cares in matters of common-

can import from the "B" text the sententious moral that Denham gave to the scene in 1655, "uncertain waies unsafest are, / And Doubt a greater mischief than Despair" (299-300), but the problems are not thereby solved.

They vanish, however, if we make a slight shift in the question we ask: not "Is the stag Strafford?" but "What did Strafford stand for?" O Hehir has shrewdly observed that on the day of Strafford's death the House of Commons authorized the publication of the second part of Coke's *Institutes* containing his commentary on Magna Charta, but this act was no more symbolic than the drama it concluded. Strafford was the symbol of arbitrary power, as countless references both inside and outside the courtroom testify, and his death warrant was signed by the king's commissioners, just as Charles was later to sign into law the other bills that marked the demise of unconstitutional government. The monarch of the glen was the obvious choice of a metaphor for absolute rule, partly because of his despotism over the herd, and partly because he was the most privileged of beasts and existed wholly for the king's will and pleasure. In calling him the "Royall Stagge" (245) Denham was also aware that "royal" when applied to the king's power meant the prerogative power that parliament could not lawfully control.[57] Royal power was the authority that Denham calls "boundles" at the end of the poem, or those inalienable rights of the crown, which should

---

weale." This explains how Charles came to be hunting "when greate affaires / Give leave to slacken & unbend his Cares" (243-44). Turbervile cites Pliny to the effect that a hart will prefer to yield to a man rather than the hounds, and moralizes one disastrous hunt: " This example may serue as a mirrour to al Princes and Potestates, yea and generally to all estates, that they brydle their mindes from proferyng of vndeserued iniuries, and do not constrayne the simple sakelesse man to stand in his owne defence . . . but as by all Fables some good moralitie may be gathered, so by all Histories and examples, some good allegorie and comparison may be made." *Turbervile's Booke of Hunting 1576* (Oxford, 1908), p. 125.

[57] E.g. Justice Hutton's argument in Hampden's case: the king "governeth his People by Power, not only Royal, but also Politick: If his Power over them were only Royal, then he might change the Laws of his Realm." Croke countered by saying that the writ was "not to be maintained by any Prerogative, or Power Royal, nor allegation of Necessity or Danger" (Rushworth, III, Appendix, 164, 181; see also p. 171). Sir John Holland at the beginning of the Long Parliament acknowledged that they had been summoned "by the Royal Power" but complained of "the late Inundations of the Prerogative Royal, which have broken out, and almost overturned all our Liberties, even those which have been best and strongest fortified, the Grand Charter it self" (Rushworth, IV, 27-28). It was extremely common to talk about arbitrary power in the abstract, because nobody wished to refer to the king's personal tyranny.

nonetheless, if the king were wise, be drawn " Within the Chanell & the shoares of Lawe."

If the stag is read as a personification of arbitrary power, or tyranny, or " lawless power " as Denham called it in 1655 (line 326), then none of the previous difficulties arise, and the likeness of the stag to Strafford is explained, as well as the analogy about the declining statesman—which recalls Strafford more easily than the other victims of parliament's vendetta. The irresolution of the stag was unquestionably true of the policies of arbitrary government over the years: two wars, two pacifications, ship-money, the Short Parliament, the dissolution, Charles's rejection by the council of peers at York, the calling of the Long Parliament, and the history of concessions and resistance there. Which (if any) of these actions are reflected in the stag's failure to find help in " neither speede nor Art, nor frends nor force " (263) it is difficult to say, although his final standing at bay in the river is likely to be a metaphor for the destruction of arbitrary government in the Long Parliament. The " Streame . . . more merciles " than the stag's pursuers is perhaps a rendering of the fairly common image of the " stream " of law, of which the king was the " fountain " and the judges the " cisterns."[58] The High Court of Parliament would satisfy the associations of the metaphor, and the overflowing of the stream at the end of the poem was another common adaptation of it. Given the predominance of Scotland in the background of *Coopers Hill*, a conceivable allegorization of

[58] Falkland, accusing Finch, stated that he had " pursued his hatred to this fountain of justice, by corrupting the streams of it, the laws; and perverting the conduit pipes, the judges " (*Parl. Hist.,* II, 695; also in Rushworth, IV, 139). Cf. William Smith in October 1641: " The Law [would fix the king to his crown] if it might runne in the free current of its purity, without being poysoned by the venemous spirits of ill-affected dispositions " (*Diurnall Occurrences,* p. 398). Also Bagshaw in Nov. 1640: " if the Stream of Justice be by Unrighteousness turned into *Gall* and *Wormwood* . . . those which drink of those Brooks must needs dye and perish " (Rushworth, IV, 26). A similar analogy occurs in the prosecution of Strafford (Rushworth, *The Tryal of Thomas Earl of Strafford* [1680], p. 722), and was used by Strafford himself, p. 650, and by St. John, p. 679. I think it highly probable that Strafford's brave death colored Denham's portrayal of the stag's last stand, but the stag cannot *be* Strafford, however, without compromising both Charles and the balance of the poem. Since Strafford was the greatest example of arbitrary power, readers can still insist on his presence behind the episode, but only if they concede that Denham was making a " parliamentary " statement by approving of his death. Such a combination of attitudes was quite possible to someone like Hyde in the autumn of 1641. The lengthening of the stag hunt in the subsequent revision suggests that Denham was personifying the abstraction rather than the man.

the stag's behavior would be to identify his first hesitant resolution that " tis better to avoyde, then meete " with the pacification of Berwick in June 1639 which narrowly averted a pitched battle; the trying of his friends could then become the Short Parliament, and his later assumption of courage in despair would be the confrontation with the Scots in August 1640.[59] The stag hunt represents the culmination of Denham's inspiration and his argument, but if we can only guess at the possible meaning of his details, he *tells* us that the stag is arbitrary power at the conclusion of the scene:

>This a more Innocent & happie chase,
>Then when of ould (but in the selfe same place)
>Faire Liberty pursu'd & meant a prey
>To Tyrany, here turn'd & stood at Bay   (281-84)

The lines simply exchange the figures of the chase, and it was naturally more innocent and happy for liberty to chase tyranny (as in the stag hunt) than for the situation to be reversed (as at Magna Charta). The stress is on " Liberty," which instantly transposes the new hunt for the old. The law of *concordia discors* dictates the alteration of extremes, and Magna Charta was a mirror image of the hunt which had ended when Charles passed the constitutional reforms into law. Denham, like parliament when it published Coke's *Second Institute,* was quite conventional in juxtaposing the Charta and arbitrary power, since a reference to one often triggered the name of the other, but he was convinced that tyranny was now dead, slain by the king's own " unerring hand," and it was time to realize how empty were the pretensions that he still ruled by his prerogative or royal powers. " The happier Stile of King, & Subiect " would never replace the epithets " Tyrant, & Slave " unless further demands ceased forthwith. Charles had already " All marks of Arbitrary power [laid]

[59] The fundamental difficulty in allegorizing the details of the stag hunt is that we have no means of knowing if a strict chronological scheme is operating and, if so, where it begins historically. As Dr. Hirst again points out, it is hard to see the Lords in the Short Parliament as shunning either Charles or Strafford (although the appeal to parliament for help failed), and easier to see the friends who " from him flye " as fugitives like Finch and Windebanck, and those who " chase him from thence " as the monopolists and courtiers who saved themselves by turning on their old masters. The unquenchable thirst for blood of " those lesser beasts " may suggest the craving for further constitutional reforms. In any case, the rapidity with which arbitrary government had been undone was regarded even by the parliamentarians as no less than a miracle.

downe" (line 294) by killing the stag, but the country was in danger of catapulting itself into the opposite extreme from the one it had just escaped. Whether tyranny hunted liberty, or vice versa, the result would be the same, and the evil which resistance had set out to destroy would be revived if all parties did not moderate their desires and remember that enough was enough. As Sir Benjamin Rudyard was to say in anguish just before the outbreak of war, England three years earlier would have thought it a mere "*Dream of Happiness*" to have a parliament at all, or to abolish monopolies, Star Chamber, and the High Commission: "Wherefore, *Sir*, let us beware we do not contend for such a hazardous unsafe Security, as may endanger the loss of what we have already. Let us not think we have *nothing*, because we have not *all* we desire; and tho we had, yet we cannot make a Mathematical Security, all humane Caution is susceptible of Corruption and Failing; Gods Providence will not be bound, Success must be his." [60]

Magna Charta, believed to have been confirmed more than thirty times in subsequent history, symbolized at this date the freedom of persons from unjust imprisonment and the rights of private property, but it also raised the difficult question of the subject's rights of resistance:

> When in that remedy all hope was plast,
> (Which was or should at least have beene the last)
> For Armed Subiects can have no pretence,
> Against their Princes, but their iust defence:
> And whether then or no I leave to them
> To iustifie, who els themselves condemne;
> Yett might the fact be iust if we may guesse
> The iustnes of an Action from successe.   (285-92)

Denham's "equivocal" attitude, his "highly limited and conditioned acceptance of the barons' actions" [61] is not hard to understand, because he was also thinking about the armed resistance that the Scots had recently offered to the crown. There was no need, except to keep the discourse historical and impartial, to look back to the barons when a topical analogy was so near to

[60] Rushworth, IV, 753.
[61] O Hehir, p. 206. Denham's tone is echoed by Thomas Wiseman writing to Sir John Penington on 26 August: "For my part, all that I shall say of them [the Scots] is, they have carried away our money, and left us a disjointed and distempered kingdom; and whether the remedy they have given it be not worse than the disease they found it in, I am yet to be satisfied" (*CSPD 1641-43*, p. 105).

hand, and Denham quoted from the Scots' *Six Considerations of the Lawfulness of their Expedition into England Manifested*, published in August 1640. Their "iust defence," as Denham smartly summarized it, was a combination of the usual arguments from justice and necessity that were to be thrown back in their teeth when Cromwell invaded Scotland in 1650. They concluded, " Neither have we begun to use a military Expedition to *England,* as a means for compassing those our pious ends, till all other means which we could think upon have failed us, and this alone is left to us as *ultimum & unicum remedium,* the last and only remedy." [62] Having ennobled and accepted the death of the stag, Denham could raise the question whether the opposition to the king himself, which the opposition to tyranny involved, was not a violation of a sacred duty to obey. He also raised a doubt— probably a popular one with readers who had heard too much about the Scots for too long—if the final remedy had been actually called for, but he acquiesced in so far as the " successe " of that resistance had led within twelve months to a reconciliation. Whether the action was right or wrong on principle would not be known until its success had been tested, and the innocence and happiness of the chase had been determined by the outcome. If, like the " Counterparte " to Magna Charta, the union led to the taking of further advantages, then peace would lead to future bloodshed. The sincerity and justification of the " Armed Subiects " depended ultimately on their willingness to accept the victory they had already won. The new charta established by the treaty had yet to be ratified by the moderation of all those committed to the peace. Thus it is less Denham's ambiguity in these lines that leaves the final impression than his scrupulous fairness in balancing the dangerous extremes of tyranny and resistance.

The precariousness of the mean between them, still a potential rather than an actualized reality in the continuing crisis, is underlined by the concluding image of the deluge that may yet engulf the country. So rapidly can one extreme lead to the other that, like the stag who " All Safety in dispaire of safety plact. / Courrage he then assumes," the king might be driven to reassert his tyrannical power and his " courrage from dispaire recall " (306). The overflowing river is the royal stag in another metaphor, and Denham's last warning that the extinction of arbitrary govern-

[62] Rushworth, III, 1227.

ment will be followed by its revival if the mean is not kept. Hyde was fond of the image, and in his much-printed speech at the impeachment of three barons of the exchequer in July he said: " 'Tis no Marvel, that an irregular, extravagant, arbitrary Power, like a Torrent, hath broke in upon us, when our *Banks* and our *Bulwarks,* the *Laws,* were in the Custody of such Persons. Men who had lost their *Innocence,* could not preserve their *Courage.*" [63] St. John, arguing against ship-money, had said that the laws are " the Sea-walls, and Banks, which keep the Commons from the Inundation of the Prerogative," [64] and Strafford at his trial, on the very day that Denham appeared as a witness, balanced the king's prerogative and the people's " propriety " in these terms:

And Kings are as Gods on Earth, higher Prerogatives than can be said, or found to be spoken of the Propriety or Liberty of the Subject; and yet they go hand in hand, and long may they do so, long may they go in that Agreement and Harmony, which they should have done hitherto, and I trust shall be to the last, not rising one above another in any kind, but kept in their own wonted Channels. For if they rise above these heights, the one or the other, they tear the Banks, and overflow the fair Meads equally on one side and other. And therefore I do, and did allow, and ever shall, for my part, desire they may be kept at that Agreement and perfect Harmony one with another, that they may each watch for, and not any way watch over the other.[65]

The metaphor of inundation was employed most often by the opposition, because it probably derived from Sir Edward Coke,[66] but Strafford could use it too, so Denham closed with a threat and a *sententia* that everyone would have understood. Charles had " endured " the curtailment of his prerogatives, but he was also to

---

[63] Rushworth, IV, 333; cf. his speech against the Court of York which had " so prodigiously broken down the Banks of the first Channel in which it ran, as it hath overwhelm'd that Country under the Sea of Arbitrary Power, and involved the People in a Labyrinth of Distemper, Oppression and Poverty." Rushworth, III, 1336. Also Clarendon, I, 372.

[64] Rushworth, III, Appendix, 257.

[65] Rushworth, *Tryal* (1680), p. 182.

[66] Professor Carolyn A. Edie generously sent me a copy of two notes she had taken at the Yale Center for Parliamentary History. In The Massachusetts Historical Society's copy of *The True Relation* newsletter, Coke is reported as saying on 3 April 1628 " in this poynt the prerogative is like a river, without which men cannot like [live?], but if it swell too high it may loose its own channell." In another account of what was probably the same speech, though dated 2 April, Harleian Ms. 1601 records " the prerogative of the Kinge like a river but if a river swell you will hardly find a channel." See also Sir Thomas Barrington's speech in *Speeches and Passages of this Great and Happy Parliament* (1641), p. 501, and Sir John Holland, quoted in note 57.

blame for initiating the cycle, since "kings by grasping more then they could hould, / First made their subjects by oppression bould" (317-18). The danger now appeared from the opposite quarter, and although Denham distributed his final advice with an entirely equal hand to both king and parliament, his argument rested on the assumption that Charles had already made the necessary concessions, and the time was ripe for the people to make theirs.

Before conclusions are drawn, the question about the poem's date must be settled. The negative evidence is stronger than usual, and it is inconceivable that Denham composed the first draft after Charles's next departure from London on 10 January 1642, which was indeed his "last farewell," as he was not to enter the city again until his trial and execution. The attempt on the five members on 4 January 1642 is another terminal point, because by that one grievous error Charles altered the whole complexion of political affairs, and destroyed the basis of the argument that Denham had been able to advance on his behalf. Some kind of a case, however, could be constructed for a date in November or December, coinciding with the king's return to London and the beginning of the next phase of the revolution, in which party lines were drawn with a new firmness. The fact that Charles's supporters were vociferous in their poetic welcome, and that one of their themes was the benefit he had bestowed by the *concordia discors* of the Anglo-Scots treaty, at least raises the possibility of Denham's participation in their chorus; but most of the evidence suggests an earlier month between August and October.

First, *Coopers Hill* is not a coming-home poem. Not only is there an absence of the slightest reference to, or sense of, the king's return (as one would expect if the poem, like the others, was associated in any way with the propaganda surrounding that event), but the "grotesque" simile of the Thames specifically calls attention to his departure. Denham's reworking of the simile in the second draft [67] cuts out the allusion to a second fare-

[67]
"Then like a Lover he forsakes his shores,
Whose stay with iealous eyes his spouse implores,
Till with a parting kisse he saves hir teares,
And promising returne secures her feares." (192-96)
Parliament as the spouse of the king was one of the most traditional of images, and is implied but not stated in the longer simile in Draft I.

well, presumably because it was neither necessary nor comprehensible. Charles's double goodbye to parliament in August could have had no relevance four months later after he had already returned, and no capital or interest could have been gained by referring to it. Moreover, for a poet of Irish birth with an Irish mother, there is a strange and utter silence about Ireland in *Coopers Hill*, although after 1 November the news of the rebellion was a subject of ubiquitous concern that even the king's panegyrists could not ignore. *Coopers Hill* is about peace, and had Charles's remaining realm already exploded before Denham wrote, it would have been damaging to his argument to have suppressed a notice of the balm with which Charles would heal the latest wound. The emphasis on a foreign crusade is also less anachronistic for the months preceding the Irish outbreak. No significance can be attributed to the traditional close of the stag-hunting season on Holyrood Day, 14 September (the modern season extends from 10 August-10 October), but there are other reasons for an " early " date.

The intriguing lines at the beginning of the poem, " And as Courts make not Kings, but Kings the Court, / So where the Muses & their Troopes resorte / Pernassus stands," can be explained more simply than by the claim that Denham referred tendentiously to the king's power to create prerogative courts.[68] The muses, like kings, create their courts wherever they happen to be; if they " resorte " elsewhere they take their courts with them. The lines need paraphrase, not explication, but the idea of removing from one place to another is implied, and the natural inspiration for such a thought is, once again, Charles's departure for Scotland, where he installed a court and addressed his Scottish parliament. A close analogue can be found in a pastoral dialogue with which F. Palmer of Christ Church greeted Charles on his return; during the king's absence Arcadia seemed dispeopled, and suffered the discord that he went to slay: " Nor is't a wonder; for where he resorts, / He creates Kingdomes too, as well as Courts." [69] Denham's analogy between king and poet is completed by the suggestion that each has recently removed his court, and the likelihood that he alluded to the Northern trip is strengthened by the fact that it had precipitated a fierce debate about the status

[68] O Hehir, pp. 181-84.
[69] *Eucharistica Oxoniensia*, sig. à1ᵛ.

of the parliament he had left behind. Could it function in his absence, or was the appointment of a *custos regni* a necessity? Nalson wisely observed of the debate that the *locum tenens* " was fairly pusht by the Faction, and had they gained this point, they would by his Authority, which they had not yet learnt to separate from his Person, as afterwards they did, have left him little besides the name of a King before his return out of *Scotland*." [70] D'Ewes recorded in his journal that " it was generallie taken for granted " that a *custos regni* would be needed,[71] although the failure of the House to secure more than a commission with very limited powers led to its adoption of D'Ewes's own notion that it could pass ordinances during the sovereign's absence. Denham's lines are neutral enough; they posit no more power for the king than was usually allowed, and they reinforce the impression that he was out of town when the poem was composed.

Another point in favor of a pre-October date is the sting in the poem's tail. Denham made his threat as impersonal as he could: not " Charles " but " kings " are " by their fall / Reinforc't, their courrage from dispaire recall." Now all authorities are unanimous that the danger of Charles returning at the head of an army was the fear that inspired the frenzy over his departure, and the frantic efforts to secure a delay. If Denham, therefore, having spent most of his poem allaying that fear and praising the king's wisdom and humanity, then chose to remind his readers that the danger was real after all, he must have been writing before the king's return empty-handed, and before the possibility of raising an army had failed. Gardiner believed that the king's hope of armed assistance had been crushed by 12 October,[72] but he also observed that after Charles had passed through both armies in August without incident " the natural result was that those of the Parliamentary leaders who had learned enough to predict evil were looked on as scared alarmists, who might have been trying to trouble the waters for their own ambitious ends. . . . The tide of feeling, which had been running so strongly against Charles,

---

[70] Nalson, II, 425.

[71] B. M. Harleian Ms. 163, fol. 425ᵛ. Important debates about the *custos regni* took place on 28-29 July and 5-6 August. See *CJ*, II, 227, 230, 238, 240; also *Parl. Hist.*, II, 891-93, 897-98, and Sir John Holland's diary, Bodleian Ms. Rawl. D. 1099, fol. 177, 179ᵛ, 181-82. For the judges' quandary, see Nalson, II, 430.

[72] X, 28.

was on the turn." [73] Nicholas on 23 August warned the king of the "great ielousies" in London lest he "make use of some of ye armyes to ye preiudice of ye Parliam^t," and Clarendon, besides confirming jealousies at this time, recorded others after 19 October when news of the "Incident" reached London on the eve of parliament's reassembly.[74] Denham sought to capitalize as discreetly as possible upon the fears that Charles's departure had aroused; if the opposition wouldn't listen to reason, it might respond to the threat of force, especially as he was expressing its own sense of danger rather than his. Denham's rhetorical maneuver would have been most effective when the fears were still real, and before it had been proved that the king's renewal of his power was not so easy a matter as he had hoped, or as his enemies feared. By the middle of September the armies had been disbanded and it was possible to feel that the danger of the Scottish visit had been exaggerated, but had not altogether vanished.[75]

Three additional facts, far too curiously related to Denham to be coincidental, to my mind clinch the matter. We know that Denham had a private interest in the first of the two parting kisses with which Charles forsook his parliament, because the "Act for the Certainty of Forests, and of the Meets, Meers, Limits and Bounds of the Forests"[76] which he signed on 7 August directly affected Denham's property at Egham. The village lies within the Hundred of Chertsey in the Bailiwick of Surrey, and by an action of the court held in 1632 at Bagshot by the Earl of Holland, Chief Justice in Eyre, it had thus been ruled a part of Windsor forest.[77] Denham had every reason to be relieved by the Act

---

[73] X, 8-9.

[74] Evelyn, ed. Bray, IV, 52, and Clarendon, I, 380, 391, 395. See also Nicholas's letter to the Earl of Arundel, 21 August, in *The Nicholas Papers*, ed. George F. Warner, for the Camden Society (1886), I, 22.

[75] However, delays in making the final payments caused the English commissioners in Edinburgh some concern, since the Scots refused to disband their army completely without them. Sir Philip Stapleton and John Hampden wrote to Pym on 13 September asking for immediate action. See *The True Copy of a Letter Sent from Thomas Earle of Arundell .... Whereunto is Added the Coppy of Another Letter Sent to Mr. Pym from the Committee in Scotland, Sep. 13 1641* (1641). Nicholas told the king on 9 September that four regiments remained to be disbanded (IV, 85), and on 29th he reported to Penington that two remained (*CSPD, 1641-43*, p. 125).

[76] The text is in Gardiner, *The Constitutional Documents of the Puritan Revolution 1625-1660*, 3rd ed. (Oxford, 1958), pp. 192-95.

[77] Owen Manning and William Bray, *The History and Antiquities of the County of Surrey* (1804), I, xii-xiii.

voiding the court itself, because, as Clarendon said, it was " a great benefit and ease to the people, who had been so immoderately vexed by the Justice in Eyre's seat ... that few men could assure themselves their estates and houses might not be brought within some forest; the which if they were, it cost them great fines."[78] Denham had, as it were, his personal assurance that the king had moderated his prerogatives by righting the wrongs committed during the period of his arbitrary government. Other inhabitants of Egham, however, reckoning they were already liberated by the Act, decided to go on the rampage. Writing to Charles on 31st, Nicholas reported " There hath bene some of yor Maties deer killed in Windsor forrest neer Egham by ye inhabitants of that town & of ye parishes adioyning, who hunted in ye day tyme, by 80 & 100 in a company: S^r Ar. Maynwaring hath bene amongst them, and wth good words & promises hath made them forebeare for ye p^{e}sent." [79] Unaccidentally, in the same letter Nicholas requested permission to reside at his house in Thorpe, three miles from Egham. Charles was angry at the information, and the Lord Keeper arranged a meeting at his country house " to consider of ye ryot com'itted in yor Maties forrest of Windsor, & of some fitting course to prevent ye killing of any more deere there." [80] On 8 September the House of Commons ordered the tumults to be suppressed but promised to vindicate the rights of the subject according to the new forest law.[81] The cause of the riot was stated by D'Ewes, and can be confirmed from the issuance of a writ on 14 September to Sir Arthur Manwaring, John Denham, and others " for inquiring into the bounds of the Forest of *Windsor* within the bailiwick of *Surrey,* as they stood in 20 *James* I." [82] The application for a writ, its terms of reference, and the appointment of

---

[78] Clarendon, I, 375.

[79] Evelyn, ed. Bray, IV, 60. The villagers' grievances had been exacerbated by further recent enclosures and deer-slaughtering had occurred. In May some of the more moderate parishioners " who have a respect as well to his Majesty's right as to their own," had petitioned the Earl of Holland for redress (*CSPD 1641-43,* pp. 318-19).

[80] Evelyn, ed. Bray, IV, 64. Besides Littleton, the committee consisted of the Chief Justice of the Common Pleas (Sir John Banks), the Attorney-General (Sir Edward Herbert), Sir Arthur Manwaring, and Nicholas himself.

[81] *CJ,* II, 282.

[82] Manning and Bray, I, xiii, who incorrectly dated the writ 17 September. See note b for Denham. D'Ewes reported that the deer had been killed " under pretence of the late statute which passed for the limitation of ... Forrests." He added " Divers spoke to it " (Harl. Ms. 164, fol. 96^v). The correct date of the writ is given in the document cited in note 90.

Denham as one of the commissioners of inquiry all stemmed from the provisions of the Act of 7 August.

The episode was subsequently complicated by the slaughter of two more " Great Stags " on 14 October by four men from Egham with their accomplices. The House of Lords discussed the business on 27 October and planned a conference with the Commons the next day,[83] which never occurred because the Commons voted on 28th to consider only bills of general concernment.[84] Following the escape of the arrested men the Lords issued a warrant to the sheriff of Surrey on 11 November.[85] On 13 December they ordered Manwaring's commission to adjourn its inquiry from 16 December until after 6 January 1642, and on 5 January they postponed it again until 9 February.[86] In flagrant violation of the order, the commission met on 7 January and ruled the bailiwick to be outside the forest.[87] On 11th the Lords stopped all proceedings on the commission's findings, and on 27th they instructed the keepers to take special care of the king's deer.[88] The order of 11 January was not finally vacated, and the commission's ruling allowed to stand, until 1 January 1648.[89] Since Denham was one of the twelve commissioners before whom the indenture was made on 7 January,[90] he was guilty of civil disobedience in a parliamentary cause after he had written *Coopers Hill*. Many years later, Nalson made the same reflection on the forest incidents that Denham had made at the end of his poem: " how unfit it is for Loyal Subjects to ask, and for Princes sometimes to part with things which seem little or indifferent. . . . But it was no wonder to see [the common people] follow the Example of their Superiors, who committed daily Riots upon the King's Prerogative and Reputation."[91] The

[83] *LJ*, IV, 406-07.
[84] *CJ*, II, 297.
[85] *LJ*, IV, 434.
[86] *LJ*, IV, 473, 503-04.
[87] Manning and Bray, I, xiii.
[88] *LJ*, IV, 506, 547. For other forest riots, see *LJ*, 595, 602, 608, 652.
[89] *LJ*, IX, 622. An account of all these proceedings is to be found in Tighe's and Davis's *Annals of Windsor*, II, 157-62. Frederic Turner's account (in *Egham, Surrey: A History of the Parish under Church and Crown* [Egham, 1926], pp. 150-54) is misdated and garbled, but he states that the Forest Commission would have met at Egham on 25 October if the Earl of Holland had not absented himself. I suspect that Turner had read at least one document that I was unable to find in the Public Record Office.
[90] *Forresta de Windsor, in Com. Surrey* (1646), p. 12. The B.M. call number for this pamphlet, which prints the commission's judgment, is 8122.b.131.
[91] Nalson, II, 625. On p. 499 he noted of the October disturbances that the rioters

real stag hunt, like the one in the poem, was an assault on tyrannical power.

With the rest of the evidence leading in the same direction, the actual but lawless version of the stag-hunt in his own village must surely have entered into Denham's conception of his poem at, or shortly following, the end of August. He was certainly at work on it during September, because it was during that month that the news started to leak back that the king was being forced " to give / More then was fitt for subiects to receave" (319-20). " The Subiects Arm'd," whom Denham had already hinted were the Scots, "the more theire princes gave, / But this advantage tooke the more to crave: / And as by giving the Kings power growes les, / So by receaving, their demands increase" (299-302). Charles was paying a high price for Scottish friendship by capitulating to their insistence that they approve the choice of his ministers, and on 5 September Thomas Webbe wrote to Nicholas that " Ther is something in this businesse more then I can understand; for, when they sent this demand to ye King at London, it was soe hopelesse a one that they gave order to ther Commissioners not much to stick uppon it, but to take any answer ye King would make to it, and now, when this is granted, they would have more. . . . Ther is noe buckler safe enough to feare, nor for ye ill deserver. Therefore they will never be secure." [92] Oh for a king with more power, he added. Endymion Porter took up the lament: " his majesties businesses runn in the wonted channell, suttle designes of gaineing the popular opinion and weake executions for the upholding of monarkie. The King is yet perswaded to howlde owte, but within twoo or three dayes must yeld to all." [93] Webbe wrote again on 7 September, " For ye kings answer goeing farther then was asked made them presume to aske more, but now they have ther owne desir they are against ther wills concluded, unlesse they can start out how their desir ought to be interpreted, which we shall know tomorrow." [94] The

were pretending that the deer were not within the bounds of the forest. See also *LJ*, IV, 406.

[92] *Nicholas Papers*, ed. Warner, I, 38-39.

[93] *Ibid.*, p. 40. On 11 September Porter continued (p. 45): "there is nothing of newes, but one and the same delaye, to bring the King to bee wearie of stayeing here and soe to yeld to all theye desier (which hee is most apt to doo)."

[94] *Ibid.*, p. 41. The elder Vane in Edinburgh reported ironically to Sir Thomas Roe on 5 September that "Yesterday his Majesty in his wisdom conceived a paper con-

same letter enclosed a copy of the king's official submission, and by 17th the Venetian ambassador in London was sending notice of Charles's difficulties to the Doge in similar terms.[95] By that time Nicholas had departed for Thorpe and wrote to Charles that " All things here are in a great still, every one being busy in listening after the proceedings of the Parliam^t in Scotland, where Mr. Th'rer writes the people are stiffe, & seem to be resolute not to recede from their proposic'ons, wch in my poore iudgem^t is bad newes, and of very ill example to us here." [96] It was indeed an ill example, and Hyde concluded later that Charles " seemed to have made that progress into Scotland only that he might make a perfect deed of gift of that kingdom, which he could never have done so absolutely without going thither." [97]

Denham was particularly struck by the fiasco of the king's

cerning [the nominating of officers of state] which he sent to the Parliament, and has thereby given them great satisfaction " (*CSPD 1641-43*, p. 116). From a Scottish point of view the concessions were gained with great difficulty. See Baillie's *Letters and Journals* (Edinburgh, 1841), I, 389-90. On the 16th when Charles completed his capitulation (*Acts of the Parliament of Scotland*, V, 354-55) the members of the Scottish Parliament " all arrose and boued themselues to the ground." Sir James Balfour, *Historical Works* (Edinburgh, 1824), III, 65. Sir Patrick Wemyss wrote a full account of Charles's misery during the week of 18-25 September, when it might appear that Charles knew he had made a grave mistake: " What will be the event of these things God knows; for there was never King so much insulted over. It would pity any man's heart to see how he looks; for he is never at quiet amongst them, and glad he is, when he sees any man that he thinks loves him; yet he is seeming merry at meat." *A Collection of Original Letters and Papers, Concerning the Affairs of England 1641-1660*, ed. Thomas Carte (1739), I, 4.

[95] " Private letters confirm all this, but they add that the Scots, not content with all that the king has granted them ask that he shall not in future distribute the offices of the crown to any individual before the kingdom has supplied his Majesty with information about the abilities and merits of the persons to whom he proposes to give them. This demand is certainly an indication that even in the midst of all these official signs of affection they do not lose hold of the intention of encroaching more and more upon the royal authority. I am advised that his Majesty is disposed to gratify them even over such an important request, with the sole object of securing the affections of that nation, and so to deprive the English of the hope of enjoying their efficacious assistance any longer " (*CSPV 1640-42*, p. 221). Ten days must be subtracted from the date of the ambassador's letter to get the date used in England. On 21 September Webbe wrote (*Nicholas Papers*, I, 49) " others swore ye King could not be denied finally, if his Majesty would propose it like a man and stand uppon it. And by ye way, these swearers say that ye King might carry everything, if he did not undoe himselfe by yealding." Many lords had " intreated him to be constant, or at least but to leave them to themselfes and they would carry ye businesse in despite of the opposers."

[96] Evelyn, ed. Bray, IV, 70-71. Letter dated 18 September.

[97] Clarendon, I, 415.

policy in Scotland, and his criticism and anxiety about Charles's mistaken generosity is barely hidden in the first draft. The Londoners, however, were no less greedy than their Northern brethren, because they too preyed on others to supply their wants, "Yet all in vaine, increasing with their Store / Their vast desires, but make their wants the more" (23-24). Both the beginning and the end of *Coopers Hill* refer to the idea that filled the great stillness which awaited the paquets from Edinburgh. By the end of the first week in September, and in London by 10th, the themes of Denham's poem were complete, and a political climate existed in which all the conditions I have described were simultaneously fulfilled. I should be very surprised if by the date that Denham was instructed to inquire into the bounds of Windsor forest—that is, into the limits of the royal prerogative [98]—he was not also deeply engaged in his own inquiry into the state of the kingdom. Holyrood Day is the poem's ideal date. The close season should begin on political stag hunting, and it is a coincidence too curious to omit that not only had Charles established his court at Holyrood House during his Scottish visit but that a famous legend attributed the foundation of the abbey to David I's miraculous rescue from a huge white stag when he was impiously hunting on 14 September.

Denham played his small part in trimming the flowers of the crown, and the Egham riot is as nice an example as could be found of the situation on which his poem reflected. He could be grateful to parliament, and to John Selden in particular, for introducing the bill that freed his parish from an incubus, and he could be grateful to the king for confirming his constitutional intentions; yet the gratitude of the village had been to commit an outrage against the sovereign, and what more proof did one need that the people's desires were insatiable? The drama in Egham was a microcosm of the state of England, as Nalson observed, and the justice of Denham's analysis can be seen in the fact that when parliament met on 7 September to hold a public thanksgiving for the treaty, it heard two sermons by Stephen Marshall and

---

[98] Falkland had made the analogy in his speech against Finch: "He practised the annihilating of Ancient and Notorious Perambulations of particular Forests, the better to prepare himself to annihilate the Ancient, and Notorious Perambulations of the whole Kingdom, the Meets and Bounders between the Liberties of the Subject, and Sovereign Power" (Rushworth, IV, 140). The connection is so obvious that Denham could not have missed it.

Jeremiah Burroughes that were as ungenerous as the spirit of provocation could devise: barely a word of thanks to the king, very little about the treaty, but a great deal about the glorious victories of this "mirabilis annus" and the triumphs that were to come. "Wee now see," gloated Burroughes, "the *goates* stand on the left hand, and the *sheepe* stand on the right: we never in our dayes nor our forefathers before us, ever sawe the day of judgment so resembled in our nation."[99] Pym could hardly have announced more clearly than by these sermons that he was going ahead with the revolution, and that Charles's concessions meant nothing to him. Denham rejected not only the preachers' animus but their tone, and his remarkably equable voice managed to suppress most of the hostility he felt towards the parliamentary desires. The interests of peace called for a peaceable poem, and the minimizing of the differences that Pym still sought to inflame.

Five years later, when Hyde looked back on these late summer months, he saw only a sequence of errors, accidents, misjudgments, and meddling by the Commons with "the highest matters both in Church and State."[100] The king's impatience had "hurried him to that expedition without well weighing and preparing how to comport himself through it."[101] When Thomas May recalled the same period he noticed, with less style but more detachment, the growing disaffection with the Commons, the standstill of parliamentary business during Charles's absence, and Falkland's support of the Palatinate cause.[102] Like all later historians, Clarendon and May placed their emphases where they naturally fall, on the extremely busy negotiations and legislation of July, and on the reactions to the Irish rebellion and the Grand Remonstrance in November and December. During the interim the center of political concern shifted to Scotland, and the London scene was left as a comparatively empty stage on which Pym was making preparations for the next act of the tragedy. It is of immense significance, as Wormald remarks, that Hyde himself laid no plans for what was to become

[99] *Sions Joy* (1641), p. 25. Marshall's sermon was *A Peace-Offering to God* (1641). J. A. R. Marriott, *The Life and Times of Lucius Cary*, 2nd ed. (1908), p. 213, notes "It was this growing confidence in the King's good faith which Pym set himself steadfastly to combat." The many historians who believe that Pym was justified in seeking further guarantees can easily discount my royalism here. I am reacting principally to the sermons, which I dislike.
[100] Clarendon, I, 382.
[101] *Ibid.*, I, 368.
[102] *The History of the Parliament of England* (Oxford, 1854), pp. 112-21.

his new role when parliament reconvened.[103] Yet it was during the late summer, after the completion of the constitutional revolution on 5 July and 7 August that the movement began towards the king on the part of men like Hyde, Falkland, Colepeper, Dering,[104] Sir John Strangways, and Sir Benjamin Rudyard. Mrs. Keeler classifies forty-four M.P.s as "reformers who became royalists," although some of them did not change until 1642.[105] The recess, therefore, is of vital importance in the formation of the group often known as the "constitutional royalists." The inadequacy of the term has been explained by Wormald, who observes that in October 1641 "to suppose that Hyde was less 'parliamentarian' or any more 'royalist' [than he had been before] is to introduce categories that are both irrelevant and misleading."[106] The phrase has probably come to stay, but it would be quite as just to call the king's new supporters "revolutionary constitutionalists," because in their own minds they fully accepted and approved of the reforms so far achieved, and had only recently become worried about the direction in which both politics and religion still continued to move. The stag hunt alone in *Coopers Hill*, not to mention the attitude towards the church or the explicit precepts throughout the poem, make it absolutely clear that Denham was voicing the opinions of a growing body of thoughtful men whose principles were equally parliamentarian and royalist. To emphasize one principle more than the other is to destroy the balance that they thought had now precariously arrived, and on which their hopes for future stability were founded. The doctrine of *concordia discors* dissolves instantly into warring antitheses when harmony is identified with one of its components, and we do not hear it sung again very strongly until Marvell argued for Cromwell's kingship in 1655.

[103] *Clarendon*, p. 18.
[104] See Derek M. Hirst, "The Defection of Sir Edward Dering, 1640-41," *The Historical Journal*, 15 (1972), 193-208, in which he attributes Dering's change in large part to the increasing disturbances in the county during the summer. William Sanderson, *A Compleat History of the Life and Raigne of King Charles* (1658), p. 431, compares the rioting and freedom of the people during the king's absence in Scotland to "The late Comedy, *The World turn'd up side down.*"
[105] Mary Frear Keeler, *The Long Parliament, 1640-1641* (Philadelphia, 1954), p. 12. Valerie Pearl, *London and the Outbreak of the Puritan Revolution* (Oxford, 1961), p. 122, discovers that the City government "was becoming openly sympathetic to the crown" in August and September.
[106] *Clarendon*, p. 18.

Coopers Hill has been honored as a poem for three centuries, but it deserves to be more famous as a historical document. It is the only statement in this phase of the revolution to give a comprehensive and coherent account of the "new Royalism"[107] at the moment of its inception. Our present knowledge of the phenomenon is a reconstruction from a thousand sources, the most important of which is Clarendon's *History;* but letters, diaries, county archives, Guildhall records, and diplomatic correspondence have all contributed a little to the received narrative. *Coopers Hill* is unique in being the single contemporary writing that attempts to fit all the pieces together and to present a unified argument for the new position. It confirms the accuracy of recent descriptions by Wormald and Zagorin, but it makes more vivid, as only poetry can, the strength of the feelings to which Denham appealed. At their center lay a patriotic regard for England, the monarchy, and the person of the king; no less formidable was the desire for peace, recently symbolized by the treaty, and a wish for a reformed episcopacy between the alternative extremes. By holding out the hope of greater economic prosperity Denham flattered self-interest and the City, and by suggesting the possibility of a foreign war he encouraged religious unity and sentiments of English grandeur. At the same time he called discreetly upon a latent hostility to the Scots, and threatened the radicals and the doubters with a return of prerogative government. Peace with Scotland would bring either a blessing or a curse, depending on England's response to it, and he perceived the dangerous analogy between the demands to which Charles was surrendering in Edinburgh and the unappeasable appetites of the opposition at home. Since it was common knowledge that parliament intended to model its future policy on Charles's concessions to the Scots, *Coopers Hill* was aimed at countering the maneuver. Calls for unity were frequent among the king's friends at this time, and the urgency with which they besought his early return to London revealed their fear that the Grand Remonstrance, or something like it, was in the offing. Denham's ideas were the more persuasive in that he presented them in the interests of national

---

[107] The phrase is Perez Zagorin's in *The Court and the Country* (1969), p. 331. Zagorin's account of events in London during 1641 is excellent, and I have consulted it frequently. I do not know if the phrase "parliamentary royalism" was used earlier than in John L. Sanford's *Studies and Illustrations of the Great Rebellion* (1858).

security, with the impartiality of a detached observer in the county, and under the guise of ordinary moral truisms about innocence, knowledge, and desire. Above all, in the stag hunt and in his criticisms of Edward III, Henry VIII, and the supercilious lords, he revealed his abhorrence of arbitrary government and his attachment to what he believed were the courses of moderation and agreement. His stress on *concordia discors* was an addition to the terminology of the great debate, which may have been influential the following year when Falkland and Colepeper wrote the king's *Answer to the XIX Propositions*.[108]

Denham's father, by writing a brief supporting opinion in the minority judgment in Hampden's case, was one of the early heroes of the revolution, so his son was qualified by birth to write the manifesto of parliamentary royalism. In his " Elegy on the death of Judge Crooke," written after *Coopers Hill,* he renewed his vows of allegiance to the achievements of the revolution in no uncertain terms. Croke had been " The Atlas of our Liberty. . . . The best of Judges in the Worst of Times. / He was the first who happily did sound / Unfathomd Royalty and felt the Ground." [109] Nor was Denham compromised by his appearance at Strafford's trial, when he had merely brought one of his father's papers which was not admitted in evidence.[110] His poem " On the Earl of Strafford's Tryal and Death " was a tribute to the Earl's courage and eloquence that even his enemies recognized, but it stated that

---

[108] The *Answer,* which Corinne Comstock Weston (in *Eng. Hist. Rev.,* 75 [1960], 426-43) has shown to be influential in the debate on the mixed monarchy, is the statement that comes closest to making Denham's position official, although it goes further in emphasizing the balance between the three estates: " . . . the Balance hangs even between the three Estates, and they run joyntly on in their proper Chanell (begetting Verdure and Fertility in the Meadows on both sides) and the overflowing of either on either side raise no deluge or Inundation " (1642 ed., p. 18). I have discussed the development of Denham's royalism, apparent in his somewhat later drama *The Sophy,* in " Examples are best Precepts," *Critical Inquiry,* I (1974), 273-90.

[109] *The Poetical Works of John Denham,* ed. Theodore H. Banks (New Haven, 1928), p. 157.

[110] Denham was listed as a defense witness from 23-29 March (*Harmony from Discords,* p. 28), but his name appears in Rushworth's transcript only on the fifth day of the trial, 26 March, when Strafford defended his care in preserving his own authority as Deputy and that of his council. Strafford said he would quote King James's instructions and produce a legal opinion: " I desire a Book may be read, a Book in the hands of Mr. *Denham,* containing certain Answers given by the Lord *Chichester* [former Deputy], to certain Complaints made against the State, and written with Mr. Baron *Denham's* own hand, which on debate, was Resolved not to be read, being written only for a private Remembrance." Rushworth, *Tryal* (1680), p. 179.

"the glory of thy fall / Outeweighes the Cause" of the execution; his bravery made him "our nations glory" but the cause "our nations hate."[111] Denham's local ties also were largely parliamentarian, because Surrey was one of the most radical counties, and had returned twelve out of fourteen members to parliament who were ardent reformers.[112] The evidence for thinking that Denham had personal reasons for resenting the excesses of the prerogative has already been given, although it might be added that the M.P.s who applied for the writ to inquire into the bounds of the forest were as radical a group as could have been put together. By defying an order of the House of Lords the commissioners later demonstrated their determination to rescue their bailiwick from the clutches of the crown. Nothing that we can infer either from Denham's other poems at this time, or from his known actions and associations, is inconsistent with the attitudes in *Coopers Hill*. The poem proclaims a balance, the keeping of which (while balance was still feasible) would always require some judicous concessions by both sides. In its historical context *Coopers Hill* is a poignant document, because the hope on which it rested was so transitory. Many historians, I think, have felt that Charles was unlucky as well as disingenuous; civil war might have been averted had there been no "Incident" in Scotland, no Irish rebellion—had there been, in fact, a little more time for confidence in the king to be restored. Clarendon's bitterness as he thought back was justifiable, because the understanding between king and parliament for which he argued so eloquently was a mature and rational point of view, that circumstances as well as people thwarted unmercifully. To compare *Coopers Hill* with the Thanksgiving sermons on 7 September is to feel that Denham was right, and that the objectives of Pym's party, comprehensible though they are, had been too narrowly defined and relentlessly pursued. With less fear of contradiction, it can at least be said that one of the reasons for the enduring fame of the poem is that it expresses a permanent ideal in English political life that was not realized in the seventeenth century until fifty years later.

I hope at another time to consider the serious critical problems arising from the fact that a poem composed with an irenic, albeit polemical, intention was published nearly a year later when Den-

[111] Denham, ed. Banks, p. 153.
[112] Keeler, pp. 65-66.

ham's animus against the parliament had greatly increased. *Coopers Hill* was written with the valid supposition that an accommodation could be reached and appeared in print as strictly royalist propaganda after all hopes of peace had been dashed. In particular, the evaporation of any conceivable benefit to be derived from the Scots alliance leaves one wondering what the poem " means " in 1642. It is a test case for an intentionalist theory of criticism. In the meantime, having asserted the preëminence of *Coopers Hill* as a document, I will conclude with a related suggestion about its originality as a poem.

Edmund Waller has always been credited with initiating the topographical-political genre, although O Hehir's texts prove that it was not until Denham's second draft that he praised " Upon His Majesties repairing of Pauls." The evidence that he had read Waller before composing the first draft consists in an echo of one of Waller's lines in his own elegy on Strafford, and the " evidence " that Waller was writing not later than 1639 is that the portico to which he refers was completed in 1637-38. The oddity of this assumption about Waller's precedence is that he had for many years been an active opponent of the court, and as late as September 1641 was regarded as sufficiently parliamentarian to be assigned to the important Recess committee in the Commons. Not until 29 October did Edward Nicholas inform the king that Falkland, Strangways, Waller, Hyde and Holborne had been defending the royal prerogative in the House.[113] In spite of his defense of the church at midsummer, it is unlikely that Waller would have written a poem in overt praise of Charles's policy until he became deeply involved in the defense of the Anglican establishment during the last two months of 1641, and the Horatian motto which he later appended to the poem (" Thus the favor of kings was sought in Pierian measures ") announced a purpose for its composition that would have been less presumptuous at Christmas 1641 than in June.[114]. Nor was the question to which he spoke—a reformed vs. a reconstructed church—a burning issue until the

---

[113] Letter quoted in Donald Nicholas, *Mr. Secretary Nicholas* (1955), p. 144. On 7 October, as Derek Hirst informs me from Egerton 2533, f. 243, Waller was busy helping to disband the Carlisle garrison.

[114] None of the copies of the 1645 editions of *Poems* (and the unauthorized *Workes*) that I have seen contains the quotation from Horace. It was apparently added for the second edition in 1664, although O Hehir has printed it as if it derived from his 1645 copy-text.

JOHN M. WALLACE

great debates of 1641. Denham's and Waller's poems were almost certainly products of the same year, and the simplest explanation of their relationship is that Waller wrote his after seeing Denham's elegy on Strafford and the first draft of *Coopers Hill*, and that Denham returned the compliment by putting him into the second. Denham not only wrote then of Waller's " *late* theame " (my italics) but acknowledged the success of a rival muse:

> Soe to this height exalted I looke downe
> On Pauls, as men from thence upon the towne.
> Pauls' the late theame of such a Muse whose flight
> Hath bravely reacht & soar'd above thy height.
> (Draft II, 17-20)

Coopers Hill, as John Scott long ago demonstrated, is full of syntactic ambiguities and inexact expressions. Certainly, in this passage, Waller's muse has flown higher than St. Paul's, but Denham himself was " to this height exalted " far above the cathedral, and the point of the conceit was that Waller's muse (" the best of Poetts ") had the better wings. Denham was recognizing that he had been outstripped, but seems to have rather carefully reserved the credit of the first flight to himself (" Hath bravely reacht & soar'd above thy height "). The comparison was between muses. Neither was he exaggerating when he suggested that St. Paul's was now " Secure, while thee the best of Poetts sings / Preserv'd from ruine by the best of Kings," because the root-and-branch propositions were dropped in the Grand Remonstrance and it was only mildly hyperbolic to suppose after the recess that the church had been saved.

I suspect that there was considerably more cohesion among the king's new-found friends than the remaining evidence proves, but even if Denham had no previous acquaintance with Waller, the occasion which he would have needed to excuse his showing the senior poet his verses was provided by Waller's appointment on 8 September to the committee entrusted with writing a letter to the sheriffs about the forest riots.[115] The committee, with Selden as chairman, was composed exclusively of lawyers, and the letter clearly implied a legal investigation into the facts of the case. Within one week of each other, Denham and Waller were officially

---

[115] See note 81. Tighe's statement in *Annals of Windsor*, II, 158, that Thomas Waller was appointed is incorrect. He had been elected for New Windsor, but was disqualified, and Edmund Waller was the only man of that name sitting in the House.

required to consider the proper boundaries of Windsor forest. Should Waller have needed a special incentive to write about the church, beyond the recent stimulus to its preservation and reform, it would be easy to find one in the commotion from November 1641-February 1642 about Inigo Jones's procedures in the restoration of St. Paul's.[116] Among " those State-obscuring sheds " he had pulled down had been St. Gregory's church, and the parliamentarians were determined to harass him as part of their campaign against the bishops. They eventually let their impeachment lapse, but not before they had given an occasion for anyone to reflect " Upon His Majesties repairing of Pauls." O Hehir himself has noticed that " in truth the poem . . . seems more to typify the strength attributed to Denham than the sweetness ascribable particularly to Waller's earlier verse [etc.]," and we can see now a new point and an implicit timing in Waller's remark that Denham " broke out like the Irish rebellion, three-score thousand strong, when no body was aware, or in the least suspected it."[117]

The University of Chicago

---

[116] The matter was first raised and a conference requested on 19-20 July. The Commons brought a charge against Jones, which, on 19 November, the Lords ordered to be read on 10 December. He appeared on that day and was given time to reply. On 21 December he pleaded Not Guilty to the charge " in such Manner and Form as therein is expressed." On 31 January 1642 he was ordered not to leave the country, but after arrangements for further hearings the impeachment was dropped. See *LJ*, IV, 319, 321, 447, 469-70, 472, 485, 554, 586; Vol. V, 6, 30, 53, 57.

[117] O Hehir, *Harmony from Discords*, pp. 21, 26. This essay began as a diversion while I held a John Simon Guggenheim Memorial Foundation fellowship in 1969-70, and an Overseas fellowship at Churchill College, Cambridge; it was completed with the aid of a grant from the American Council of Learned Societies in the summer of 1973. I am deeply indebted to all three foundations. The paper has profited from the careful scrutiny of Professors Alan Roper and Janel Mueller, and from criticisms it received in seminars at the University of California at San Diego, at the Clark Library, and at the University of Chicago. I am grateful, as usual, to the encouragement of Mr. Quentin Skinner and Professor J. G. A. Pocock, and to a very illuminating letter from Mr. M. J. Mendle about politics in London during the summer of 1641. My notes referring to Dr. Derek Hirst reflect my debt and thanks to him very inadequately. He has done his best to make an historian out of me, and the information he has provided would fill a book. Earl R. Wasserman was the True Founder of the contemporary interest in *Coopers Hill*, and of my own.

A NOTE ON WITTGENSTEIN AND LITERARY CRITICISM [1]

BY M. H. ABRAMS

Two years ago I published an essay, "What's the Use of Theorizing about the Arts?" directed against certain tendencies in the recent philosophy of aesthetic criticism, and especially against the rejection of all critical theory on the ground that it is a logical fallacy, since its impossible aim is to prove an essential definition of art. Some of my claims in that essay have been queried by a number of commentators, both in reviews and in colloquia on the philosophy of literary criticism. In response to these objections, I want to expand and justify what I said in the essay about the bearings of Wittgenstein's later philosophy on literary criticism, and then to consider briefly questions that have been raised about the implication of my views with respect to truth and subjectivity in aesthetic criticism.

I

We know, from the account by G. E. Moore and from recently published notes by several students, that Wittgenstein discussed aesthetic and critical topics in his lectures of 1930-33 and again in the summer of 1938.[2] The *Brown Book* that Wittgenstein dictated in 1934-35, as well as the *Philosophical Investigations* that he wrote between 1945 and 1949, include a number of passing comments about music, pictures, novels, and poems. In addition, a variety of Wittgenstein's more general philosophic concepts

---

[1] Based on a paper for a colloquium, "Wittgenstein and the Philosophy of Literary Criticism," April, 1974, at the University of Warwick, England. References are to two essays distributed in advance to participants in the colloquium: M. H. Abrams, "What's the Use of Theorizing about the Arts?" in *In Search of Literary Theory*, ed. Morton W. Bloomfield (Ithaca: Cornell University Press, 1972); and J. R. Bambrough, "Literature and Philosophy," in *Wisdom: Twelve Essays*, ed. J. R. Bambrough (Oxford: Blackwell, 1974).

[2] G. E. Moore, "Wittgenstein's Lectures in 1930-33," in *Philosophical Papers* (London, 1959); Cyril Barrett, ed., *Wittgenstein: Lectures and Conversations on Aesthetics, Psychology and Religious Belief* (Berkeley, 1967).

and procedures have been applied to aesthetics, sometimes in greatly expanded form, by a number of critics and writers about criticism. Chief among these are Wittgenstein's family-resemblance view, of course; what he says about the linguistic expression of feelings and of states of mind; his insistence that the use of a language involves "a form of life"; and most extensively, his discussions of "seeing as" and of the relation between the physical properties and the perceived "aspects" of a visual object.

My present concern, however, is not with Wittgenstein's particular aesthetic or philosophical concepts. I want instead to raise the question of the overall tenor of Wittgenstein's language-philosophy, and of its broad bearing on the characteristic uses of language and processes of reasoning that we find in critics of literature and the other arts. A number of philosophers about criticism who have been influenced by Wittgenstein have, on logical grounds, denied the validity of some standard critical practices and the aesthetic pertinence of some others. My essay in effect proposed that these philosophers—for convenience of reference I call them "metacritical analysts"—are mistaken in much of what they deny; that they are mistaken, however, not because they are Wittgensteinian, but because they are not Wittgensteinian enough.

In his account of the lectures, G. E. Moore stressed Wittgenstein's repeated insistence that his discussions of language were not intended to be comprehensive, but were directed only to those misunderstandings about the way language works which have led to important philosophical "errors" or "troubles" (Moore, 257, 324). This clearly remained Wittgenstein's orientation throughout his later lectures and writings. He undertook, that is, to expose the typical mistakes of traditional philosophy (including the mistakes in his own earlier *Tractatus*) by showing that they are vain attempts to solve "a muddle felt as a problem," or the results of inappropriate pictures, misused analogies, and "a misinterpretation of our forms of language,"[3] or efforts to solve what seem to be problems about matters of fact but are actually expressions of "deep disquietudes" and inner torments. All such undertakings, Wittgenstein says, constitute a "disease of thinking," for which his demonstrations of the way language

[3] *The Blue and Brown Books*, ed. Rush Rhees (New York, 1965), pp. 6-7, 43; *Philosophical Investigations*, translated by G. E. M. Anscombe (Oxford, 1953), No. 3.

works are intended to serve as "therapies" that will cure us of the compulsion to pose the pseudo-questions (*Brown Book* 143; *PI* III, 133, 593). Given this corrective orientation of Wittgenstein's discussions of language, it is understandable that his early effect on philosophers was mainly to stimulate a demolition project against philosophical errors in various linguistic enterprises including traditional aesthetics and literary criticism.

Wittgenstein warns us many times about the danger of analogy; at the same time, he is himself an inveterate deviser of striking analogues. He says, for example, that his kind of philosophy reveals the "bumps that the understanding has got by running its head up against the limits of langauge" (*PI* 119). Now this figure might suggest that language is an invisible cage which impedes our quest for knowledge but from which, unfortunately, there is no escape. But no simile, Coleridge remarked, "runs on all fours," and as Wittgenstein said, the danger in the use of any analogy is that it "irresistibly drags us on." One of Wittgenstein's ways of avoiding dragging in irrelevant features of any one of his similes for the uses and abuses of language is to supplement it with a variety of others, and a number of his alternatives emphasize not the limitations but the resources of language. One of his most revealing similes is this one: "The confusions which occupy us arise when language is like an engine idling, not when it is doing work" (*PI* 132; cf. 88). This figure is aligned with Wittgenstein's many comparisons of the component words of a language to "tools," to "instruments characterized by their use" (e. g., *Blue Book* 67; *PI* II, 569). The distinction between language when it is idling and when it is doing work comports also with Wittgenstein's repeated assertions that diverse forms of expressions are simply different ways of putting something, and that any manner of speaking is acceptable so long as we "understand its working, its grammar," and therefore is "all right so long as it doesn't mislead us when we are philosophizing" (*Blue Book* 7, 41). "I am at liberty to choose between many uses, that is, between many different kinds of analogy" (*Blue Book* 62) — provided I don't make the mistake of translating the form of any particular way of talking into a picture of the facts. "Does it matter which we say, so long as we avoid misunderstanding in any particular case?" (*PI* 48). He insists also on the requisiteness of many concepts "with blurred edges," for "isn't the indistinct [concept] often exactly what we need?"—and this is especially the case, he goes on to say, for "our concepts in aesthetics or ethics" (*PI* 71, 77; cf. 88).

In many observations like these, Wittgenstein indicates the powers rather than the limits of language; he also suggests the indispensability, in many areas of human concern, of fluidity and variability in our ways of speaking. The view that the justification for a linguistic procedure is not what forms of expression it uses, but whether it is really "doing work," is neither inhibitive nor prohibitive, but liberative. And such a view may be taken to confirm—not in details, but overall—the very diverse ways that our best literary critics have in fact used language in order to achieve their profitable discoveries and conclusions, as against what some recent analysts claim that the critics have done, or should instead have done.

II

Now I can restate what I had in mind in saying that some recent philosophers of aesthetics who follow Wittgenstein's lead are not Wittgensteinian enough. Instead of emulating Wittgenstein's openness about accrediting the diverse ways of speaking that have demonstrated their capacity to do profitable work in the criticism of the arts, they codify certain of Wittgenstein's concepts and set up paradigms of the "logical grammar" of fixed classes of critical expressions. In other words, they tend to establish for criticism rules of procedure that Wittgenstein called "calculi." Such calculi are modeled on the "ideal" languages (formal logic, mathematics, the exact sciences) which have been constructed to achieve highly specialized and limited purposes; but, Wittgenstein warns us, they apply only rarely to the loose and informal "grammar" that characterizes other forms of language.

Years ago I was struck by the fact that some of my young philosophical friends, in arguing a question, persistently referred to what they were doing as "moves." When one put forward an assertion, he called it "a move," and he tended to anticipate— often correctly—a philosopher's response as a "counter-move." It dawned on me that these philosophers had been "dragged on," as Wittgenstein put it, by his carefully delimited analogy between using language and playing chess, to the degree that their own philosophizing followed the model of the game of chess, with its rules that strictly define all possible moves and its single purpose—which, in their instance, was to win the game by checkmating an opponent's philosophical king. These philosophers were not following Wittgenstein's flexible and resourceful example, but instead were playing a new philosophical game—a *Wittgenspiel*.

Such early abuses of the innovations of a great and original philosopher are to be expected, and are not in the long run dangerous because they are easily detected. Much more difficult to detect are the subtler distortions of Wittgenstein's procedure that we find in philosophers of criticism who have much to say that is important and enlightening. In my essay I sketched some of the ways in which philosophical metacritics seem to me to have hardened Wittgenstein's concepts into calculi. For example, they convert Wittgenstein's family-resemblance concept—a striking way of showing, by analogy, how some words in ordinary use refer to a great variety of things which may, or may not, have shared features—into a Geiger-counter for detecting the fallacy of " essentialism " in order to reject, as logically abortive, procedures that many of the best critics and theorists have employed in pursuit of their profitable undertakings. They succumb also to the temptation that Wittgenstein calls " the tendency to sublime the logic of our language " (*PI* 38), by imposing simplified logical models on the complex ways in which critics actually talk. All the intricate goings-on of the myriad expressions and sentences in critical discourse—fluid, multiform, interinvolved, in which the component parts exhibit a continuum of subtle differences in ever-shifting and interchanging logical roles—are thereby forced into a few fixed classes of " irreducible " logical grammars, such as " description," " interpretation," " evaluation," and " theory." There is, I would agree, an indispensable use for such class-terms in discussing what happens in criticism; to be serviceable rather than inhibitive, however, such terms need to be kept open, adaptive, and overlapping instead of being treated as rigid, mutually exclusive, comprehensive of all logical roles in critical language, and applicable to a given expression outside its use in a particular context. Expressions with bounded and codifiable logical roles are not frequent in fluid critical discourse, nor can they be if a critic is to do his proper job.

III

In my essay I pointed to another bias in our thinking against which Wittgenstein warns us—the tendency in describing something, and in setting up norms for dealing with it, to replace the complex facts and their variable circumstances by a simplified and invariable picture or model. The use of such a picture can be the servant of understanding, so long as we remain aware that we are using it and for what purpose; but if its presence and its influence on our thinking are hidden, it readily gets out of hand and becomes, in Wittgenstein's metaphor, a picture that holds us captive (*PI* 114-15).

At the present time a widely prevalent explanatory picture is one that we can call the confrontation model of aesthetic criticism. This hidden picture lurks behind such assertions (cited in my essay) as that *the* function of critism is to teach us "what to look for and how to look at it in art," or that the critic "is a mere spectator . . . it is only required that he should see the object exactly as it is"—an object whose "peculiar features . . . remain constant and unaffected by the spectator's choices and priorities." The model represents the paradigmatic critical situation as an isolated person confronting a single work of art; this work is almost always, explicitly or implicitly, a painting which, hanging there on the wall, is fixed in the present moment and is consistently cut off from its surroundings by a frame. In terms of the implicit model, therefore, a critical eye is fixed on a given object and proceeds to detect and communicate the particular features which are already, although more or less patently, there.

Such a picture has, in recent aesthetic history, proved itself a fruitful one for fostering concepts that serve limited critical purposes; but if it is not to prevent us from discovering matters relevant to other and equally important critical purposes, we must remain ready to put the simplified model of critical activity back into its complex and variable surroundings. When we do so, we find that the most important thing the model leaves out is the role played in the transaction by language—both by the general system of language and by the characteristic language of the individual critic. In terms of the model, language comes into play only insofar as the critic, having made his aesthetic discoveries, proceeds to render his visual perceptions in words.

What a purely visual experience of a painting might be like I can't imagine; but that isn't the present issue. What concerns us is that the critic has thought about art before he looks, and also thinks while he looks; that what he says to himself is essential both to what he thinks and what he sees; and that the result of this process doesn't become criticism until he tidies up the syntax of what he says to himself, elaborates and organizes it, and makes it public in the mode of a sustained utterance.

Consideration of the part played by the critic's language breaks down the seeming isolation both of the critic and of the painting by putting them into a variety of contexts. For example, the general language that the critic uses belongs to a system that he inherits, and is subject to the loose and elusive, yet effective, control of rules or criteria that he may alter, but not evade, if what he says is to be intelligible and coherent. His language, furthermore, includes groups of expressions—subsets of ordinary language—which have in the course of time become more or less specialized to the critical enterprise. Most expressions in these specialized subsets, as I tried briefly to show in my essay, have been introduced into the available critical vocabulary by those aesthetic theorists who are given short logical shrift by analytic philosophers, and many of the expressions had an indubitably metaphysical, or even theological source; but without recourse to such expressions, with their built-in valencies, a critic would be able to say little or nothing that we would count as criticism. (By its "valency" I mean not only the appraisive weight of a term, but also its tendency to consort with certain terms and to clash with or exclude others.) It is also worth noting that many of these critical terms had a moral provenience in ordinary language, and that they maintain a moral valency when used to bring out an aspect of a work of art. Some good critics try to eschew such quasi-moral terms; for others, no less high in the widely accepted critical hierarchy (including Dr. Johnson, Arnold, Leavis, Trilling), they are central and pervasive components in the critical lexicon.

The individual also brings to the critical transaction an immense amount of applicable information. He does not, usually, see simply a painting, but an identifiable painting—let's say, he knows that it is the Arnolfini marriage portrait, painted in the 1430's by Jan van Eyck. His knowledge of the repertory of conventions and devices current in that time and place, as well as the repertory specific to Van Eyck himself, brings out aspects of the painting of which he would otherwise remain unaware. When he looks at the Arnolfini painting, for example, what he would otherwise see simply as carefully rendered realistic objects in formal relationships—a burning candle, a little terrier, a casually discarded pair of white pattens, the carved figure of a saint on the back of an armchair standing next to the nuptial bed—he now sees as invested also with rich and subtle symbolic significances. Furthermore, he sees the material and symbolic objects as related to an overall subject which only his historical information about Flemish marital customs of that era enables him to identify, not as a newly married couple, but as a couple in the very act of marrying themselves before the eyes of the artist as a legal witness, who accordingly inscribes the painting " Johannes de Eyck fuit hic. 1434."

No less important is the context of the total essay or book in which we ordinarily find the critic's analysis of a particular painting. In that larger context, the types of expressions the critic habitually uses and the kinds of things he says (as well as the many alternative types of expressions he doesn't use and the kinds of things he doesn't say) manifest his critical perspective and guiding principles—no less effective when they are implicit than when they are expressed in the theoretical mode of definitions and systematic generalizations—which, by fostering certain types of critical expressions, bring out, in a critical confrontation, those aspects and values of the painting that he detects, inter-relates, and communicates.

The limitations of the confrontation model become even plainer if we bring to mind the act of criticising, not a painting, but a work of literature. When the medium of arts is words, and the apprehension of a work of art extends over a long period of time, the claim that the critic " is a mere spectator " who " should see the object exactly as it is " becomes a very distant metaphor. Consider, for example, what you in fact do when what you are told to " look for " and " look at " in a novel is a character-trait, a type of plot, a specified style, a mode of irony, or a distinctive authorial voice.

I have saved for last a prime inadequacy of the confrontation picture of the critical act, and that is, that only a very small fraction of actual criticism corresponds to the normative model, according to which the critic limits himself to assertions about particular features of a single work of art. Random leafing through the pages of any critic whose writings we find illuminating will reveal how large a part of what he says involves, by various linguistic means, classifying features of the work in hand with those of a shifting variety of other works—works written by the same author, or written by other authors in the same period, or else types of works produced over many periods. The conspicuous tendency in the last fifty years or so, fostered especially by the New Criticism, to focus on single works or passages for close critical commentary is in this respect misleading. For what the close critic typically does is to bring to bear on the particular item diverse classes of other items which, by their similarities or oppositions, serve in concert to bring out aspects of the work that seem, after their discovery, to have been there in all their particularity all the time. The physical features of the work do not change; but it is only when we compare one critical analysis with an analysis of the same work by another critic, equally rewarding in his discriminations, that we recognize how much the evocation of particular aesthetic aspects is the result of a critic's deployment of linguistic devices for classifying and cross-classifying things in any number of distinctive, unpredictable, and illuminating ways.

I have emphasized what many will probably agree is the obvious; but my point is, that circumstances which are obvious on any particular occasion are apt to drop out of view when we deal with the general terms " the work of art " and " aesthetic criticism "; for these terms, by being inclusive, are radically omissive, and invite us to suppose that a simple normative model is adequate to account for the transactions between them. It seems evident, furthermore, that certain elements in my description of critical encounters with a work of art will evoke objections from some analytic philosophers of criticism, and we can anticipate, from typical assertions in their writings, what they might say. " But some uses of language that you describe are irrelevant to criticism—the application of terms that have a moral source and significance, for example, or the assertion of critical judgments that depend on extraneous information about the individual artist or about the historical and social circumstances at the time when he made the work of art. Criticism precludes the use of non-aesthetic terms and the reference to external circumstances, for criticism is disinterested and concerns itself solely with what is distinctively art, with the qualities of art *qua* art, which are given in the work and are to be judged by criteria internal to the work." This is an interesting and involuted logical maneuver. It sets a narrow boundary around the application of the term " art "—a boundary which certainly does not coincide with the wide range of historical and current uses of that family-term; then it refers to the term so bounded in order to draw another boundary, equally at variance with the range of common uses, around the term " criticism."

To philosophers so alert to symptoms of the essentialist fallacy, the temptation is to retort, "Aha! essentialism! " In my essay I succumbed to this debater's temptation to turn the tables. But in fact, I see no fallacy in setting up definitional boundaries of artifice in this way, or even in the seemingly logical eddy of positing an arbitrary boundary for one term in order to establish a boundary for one's use of a correlative term. Some such stratagem, indeed, seems indispensable if we are to talk to any purpose about matters signified by terms so vague and diverse as " art " and " criticism." The provisos are, that we had best be aware of what we're doing, and why; and above all that we use the bounds we stipulate for these terms not as ruling definitions, but as working definitions, to block out in a preliminary way what we undertake to talk about and how we propose to talk about it. Or in Wittgenstein's metaphor, the crucial issue is whether the way we use a seemingly essential definition is language idling or language doing work.

IV

My debater's stance in opposition to some of the procedures and claims of analytic philosophers disguises the extent to which I concur with their general approach to critical language and with many of their particular discoveries. These philosophers have taken a decisive step by rejecting the narrow logical-positivist views of rationality—based on formal logic and on empirical reasoning in the physical sciences—and have directed our attention from such highly specialized models to what able critics in fact do, in pursuing their indispensable cultural enterprise. To the discursive processes by which critics achieve their illuminating judgments, relate them to a variety of general assertions, and support them by pertinent reasons, it is absurd to deny rationality. The rational thing is instead to enlarge the criteria of rationality so as to encompass the diverse procedures which have again and again demonstrated their power to achieve valuable results. Wittgenstein's later thinking has helped recent philosophers to recognize and to explore the consequences of this approach to the uses of language in various humanistic pursuits, including literary criticism. My demurral is simply that they have stopped too soon and, by imposing premature logical limits, have denied rationality to a number of profitable critical procedures. Coleridge once warned us not to pass an act of uniformity against poets; no more should we against critics.

I shall close by considering briefly a recurrent objection to this point of view; that is, that by my broad conception of what constitutes valid rational procedures in criticism, I have eliminated the possibility of any general criteria for distinguishing beween true and false critical assertions and between good and bad critical procedures. I have done so, it is claimed, by making all important critical judgments relative to the individual critic, and in two different ways: a critic's judgments (1) are conceptually relative to his elected theoretical frame or perspective, and (2) are "subjective," in the sense that they are relative to his own temperament and taste.

(1) With respect to the charge of conceptual relativity, I was struck by some things that Mr. Bambrough said in his essay on "Literature and Philosophy." It is, he said, a mistake to assume (prior to investigation) that, in philosophy or in discussions of literature, a generalization necessarily disqualifies a conflicting, or even a seemingly contradictory, generalization. In such areas there is no one totally satisfactory way of putting something in words; different ways of putting it may in fact constitute alternative perspectives on the matter in hand; and only the superposition of views from diverse vantage points will yield what Bambrough strikingly describes as a "vision in depth" or "multi-dimensional description." To guard against the seeming suggestion of a sceptical relativism, Bambrough also reminds us "that what a thing is like from this point of view and from that point of view is all part of what the thing *is* like, and that if that is what we want to know we are not at liberty to choose

part of it and represent it as being the whole." These remarks apply precisely to the function I attributed to the diversity of profitable critical theories: each of the theories serves as a critical perspective which does not conflict with, but supplements the alternative perspectives. The use of such diverse but complementary conceptual vantages seems to me to be not only rationally justifiable, but necessary to the understanding of art, and indeed of any subject of humanistic inquiry; and I would say that the resulting vision in depth is a characteristic feature of humanistic truth, as distinguished from mathematical or scientific truths.

(2) Mr. Bambrough himself, however, has in a recent letter raised a different but related issue, and one in which other commentators on my essay have concurred. The claim is that what I say implies that critical judgments are "subjective," in that they are relative to inherent differences in the temperament of individual critics, so that there are no objective criteria for deciding between conflicting judgments.

Now, I do say a number of things that might be taken to suggest some such view. I say, for example, that once an assertion is adopted as the premise of a critical theory, "its origin and truth-claim cease to matter," for its validity is to be measured by its demonstrated power to yield valuable critical insights; that the particular theoretical perspective employed by a critic not only selects, but in some fashion alters the features of a work of art (in Wittgenstein's terms, the perspective affects both what he is apt to see and what he sees it *as*); that some range of disagreement in literary interpretations and judgments of value is endemic to criticism; that the ultimate standards of valid critical judgments are not sharp-focus, but soft-focus standards which we signify by terms such as sensibility, good sense, sagacity, tact, insight, and that the application of such standards allows "room for the play of irreducible temperamental differences"; and also that the term "certainty" does not without special qualification apply to most critical conclusions about a work of art. It may seem that as a consequence I am committed to the view that all aesthetic judgments are equally sound, that there's no disputing about taste, and that one should leave one's critical language alone.

This is a matter of concern to me, especially since much that passes for criticism in the present age strikes me as uncommonly irresponsible, so that we can ill afford to minimize the availability of standards for discriminating between sound and unsound procedures in critical reasoning. I don't, however, hold the relativistic opinions I have just described, nor do I think that they are entailed by anything I have said. I in fact believe that we possess valid criteria for judging when criticism is good and when it is bad, and that we are able to disqualify many aesthetic judgments out of hand. But I also think that it is a mistake to assume, and self-defeating to pretend, that these criteria are simple and obvious, or that they are similar to the criteria for distinguishing between a right and wrong answer to a mathematical problem or to a question of empirical fact.

Misunderstanding on this issue is in some part a result of what my essay undertook to do; if it had set out to expose what's wrong in bad criticism, rather than to justify what's right in good criticism, its emphases would have been quite different. But in large part the risk of misunderstanding is inherent in the nature of critical problems and of the language we have evolved for dealing with them. Wittgenstein, in the closing pages of *Philosophical Investigations* (227-228), made some remarks which are very much to that point. He is discussing the reasons why we get general agreement in " judgments of colours " but fail to get such agreement in answer to the question whether someone's " expression of feeling is genuine or not." He points out that we may reasonably argue about whether the expression of feeling is or is not genuine, but " we cannot prove anything "; that, on the whole, better judgments will be made by those who are expert, but that this expertise is not acquired through a course of systematic instruction but only " through 'experience'," and can only be described by a vague expression such as having a " better knowledge of mankind "; that such knowledge can be taught, yet not as " a technique," but only by giving someone " the right *tip* "; that " there are also rules, but they do not form a system," so that " unlike calculation rules," only " experienced people can apply them right "; and finally that, while " it is certainly possible to be convinced by evidence," the term " ' evidence ' here includes ' imponderable ' evidence," and " what does imponderable evidence *accomplish?* " And Wittgenstein exclaims, poignantly: " What is most difficult here is to put this indefiniteness, correctly and unfalsified, into words."

I think that the important critical questions are not like the question, "What color is it?" but much more like the question, "Is this expression of grief genuine?" A persistent dilemma for the philosopher of criticism is how to give due recognition to the indefiniteness of the evidence for an answer, yet not be taken to deny that there are sound, and often convincing reasons that support one answer rather than another. Because of this difficulty in putting the matter "correctly and unfalisified into words," a monologue is not a very satisfactory way of conducting a philosophical inquiry into aesthetic criticism. To get progressively clearer as to the multiple and interdependent discriminations involved requires the evolving give-and-take of dialogue. Mr. Bambrough applies to such dialogue the ancient philosophical term "dialectic," and says (citing F. R. Leavis) that the most to be expected is that when a proponent says, "This is so, isn't it?" his interlocutor will reply, "Yes, but . . ." That is in the nature of all humanistic discourse, and a reason why the search for humanistic truth has no ending.

Cornell University

MOST HOLY FORMS OF THOUGHT: SOME OBSERVATIONS ON BLAKE AND LANGUAGE *

BY ROBERT F. GLECKNER

In an extraordinary passage at the end of Blake's greatest achievement, *Jerusalem*, he describes more fully than anywhere else in his works the apocalypse—the reachievement of four-fold unity, the marriage of Albion (the Grand Man) and Jerusalem (his emanation), the reintegration of the four zoas, the four senses, the four faces of man, the four compass points, the four elements—all that had been sundered by the Fall. It reads in part:

The Four Living Creatures Chariots of Humanity Divine Incompre-
    hensible
In beautiful Paradises expand These are the Four Rivers of Paradise
And the Four Faces of Humanity fronting the Four Cardinal Points
Of Heaven going forward forward irresistible from Eternity to Eternity

And they conversed together in Visionary forms dramatic which bright
Redounded from their Tongues in thunderous majesty, in Visions
In new Expanses, creating exemplars of Memory and of Intellect
Creating Space, Creating Time according to the wonders Divine
Of Human Imagination, throughout all the Three Regions immense
Of Childhood, Manhood & Old Age; & the all tremendous unfathom-
    able Non Ens
Of Death was seen in regenerations terrific or complacent varying
According to the subject of discourses & every Word & Every Character
Was Human according to the Expansion or Contraction, the Trans-
    lucence or
Opakeness of Nervous fibres such was the variation of Time & Space
Which vary according as the Organs of Perception vary & they walked
To & fro in Eternity as One Man reflecting each in each & clearly seen
And seeing: according to fitness & order. And I heard Jehovah speak
Terrific from his Holy Place & saw the Words of the Mutual Covenant
    Divine
On Chariots of gold & jewels with Living Creatures starry & flaming

---

* A different version of this paper was delivered to a Blake symposium at the University of Tulsa.

With every Colour, Lion, Tyger, Horse, Elephant, Eagle, Dove, Fly, Worm,
And the all wondrous Serpent clothed in gems & rich array Humanize . . .[1]

These redemptions are the product of an enormously complicated sequence of events chronicled in the total poem, which itself is the product of the equally complex process of Blake's regeneration of himself, particularly in the poem *Milton*, so that he might become *the* poet, *the* prophet, the "Inspired Man." The sum total of these redemptions is the awakening of man from 6000 years of brutish, nightmarish human history, the annihilation of the total Creation (which was a colossal error born in the mind of the archetypal fool), and the regeneration of the fallen physicality of all things, gathered together once again into the imaginative-human forms from which they were all rudely and tragically abstracted.

All Human Forms identified even Tree Metal Earth & Stone. all
Human Forms identified, living going forth & returning wearied
Into the Planetary lives of Years Month Days & Hours reposing
And then Awakening into his Bosom in the Life of Immortality.
(99: 1-4)

In that life of life, as the opening of *The Book of Urizen* describes it,

> Earth was not: nor globes of attraction
> The will of the Immortal expanded
> Or contracted his all flexible senses.
> Death was not, but eternal life sprung. (3: 36-39)

All of this is so incredibly grand—and bold—a conception that paradoxically we seem to have little difficulty following it, grasping it all, if not in its minute particulars, at least in its totality. For it is the fond wish of all men however debased our imaginations.

But one aspect of this cosmic rehabilitation has received less attention than is its due—that of language, words. Concomitant with the Blakean Fall into disintegration, fragmentation, and dislocation, is the fall of the Word into words, the degeneration

---

[1] Plate 98, ll. 24-44. All Blake quotations are from *The Poetry and Prose of William Blake*, ed. D. V. Erdman (New York, 1965), noted by plate and line numbers (or, for *The Four Zoas*, page and line numbers).

ROBERT F. GLECKNER

of "Visionary forms dramatic" into language, the compromising of the free, translucent, imaginative interconversation of the Eternals into a time-bound, space-bound syntax that passively mirrors the shattered mind and the excruciatingly finite limits of fallen sense perception. This is, of course, Urizen's world, the world of eternity bereft of its fundamental humanness, and peopled by what Blake calls "human shadows" which are produced by man himself "begetting his likeness, / On his own divided image" (*Bk. of Urizen* 19: 15-16). "Cruel enormities" is what Urizen, his residual humanity stunned at the fallen condition of his eternal creations, himself calls them:

> And his world teemd vast enormities
> Frightning; faithless; fawning
> Portions of life; similitudes
> Of a foot, or a hand, or a head
> Or a heart, or an eye, they swam mischevous
> Dread terrors! delighting in blood.   (23: 2-7)

Thus on the one hand Blake sees the process of the Fall as all but endless, a dizzying and sickening inner strife which produces finally not merely "portions of life" or portions of men, but even worse, only *similitudes* (a word borrowed, appropriately enough, from Locke) of a foot or a hand or a heart or an eye. On the other hand, this horrible process is exacerbated by shrinkage as well:

> . . . their eyes
> Grew small like the eyes of a man
> And in reptile forms shrinking together
> Of seven feet stature they remaind
>
> Six days they. shrunk up from existence
> And on the seventh day they rested
> And they bless'd the seventh day, in sick hope:
> And forgot their eternal life.   (*Bk. of Urizen* 25: 35-42)

What is perhaps least obvious about this Fall is that the physical creation of space and time, of the solar system and earth, and of mankind all are preceded by the utterance of the first words,[2] now separated from the imaginative significations of

---

[2] Cf. Heidigger's point that although language became actualized as "conversation" and seemingly as a consequence the gods acquired names and a world appeared, in reality "the presence of the gods and the appearance of the world are not merely a consequence of the actualisation of language, they are contemporaneous with it"

Eternity's "visionary forms dramatic." In *The Book of Urizen*, Urizen is first seen as "a shadow of horror," as yet unrealized and unrealizable:

> Dark revolving in silent activity:
> Unseen in tormenting passions;
> An activity unknown and horrible;
> A self-contemplating shadow,
> In enormous labours occupied. (3: 18-22)

Out of this portentous silence,[3] the auditory equivalent of voidness, emerge two sounds: a trumpet, heralding Blake's remarkable parody of the apocalypse, and the utterance of "Words articulate," bursting in thunders that rolled on the tops of Urizen's mountains—words which emanate, as Urizen himself says,

> From the depths of dark solitude. From
> The eternal abode in my holiness,
> Hidden set apart in my stern counsels
> Reserv'd for the days of futurity. (4: 4-9)

And those words he immediately freezes into solid form and sets down for the edification (and enslavement) of all futurity:

> Here alone I in books formd of metals
> Have written the secrets of wisdom
> The secrets of dark contemplation
> . . . .
> Lo! I unfold my darkness: and on
> This rock, place with strong hand the Book
> Of eternal brass, written in my solitude.
>
> Laws of peace, of love, of unity:
> Of pity, compassion, forgiveness.
> Let each chuse one habitation:
> His ancient infinite mansion:
> One command, one joy, one desire,
> One curse, one weight, one measure,
> One King, one God, one Law. (4: 24-40)

(quoted in Robert W. Funk, *Language, Hermeneutics. and the World of God* [New York, 1966], p. 40).

[3] Portentous in the sense that it heralds noise, non-communication, but also, in a typically Blakean paradox, this silence is reminiscent of the "silence" of eternity, its visionary forms dramatic and most holy forms of thought. Similarly Joseph Mazzeo reminds us in *Renaissance and Seventeenth-Century Studies* (New York and London, 1964) that according to Ignatius Martyr the Incarnation was a descent from silence into "speech" or *logos* and Christ was thus "his word proceeding from silence" (pp. 22-23). See also Mazzeo's interesting chapter on St. Augustine's "Rhetoric of Silence."

And one *Word*, we might add, the ultimate perversion of the Word, which in Urizen's world, despite his laws, becomes the gibberish of the tower of Babel or mere similitudes of the Word—that is, nouns, verbs, adjectives which arrogate to themselves the divine wisdom, truth, and reality of Eternity's cosmic syntax.

Therein lies the central problem of the poet—for without words is no prophecy, and without prophecy is no apocalypse. How then is the poet to regenerate or redeem the Word via the use of the fallen elements that "signal their complicity with that which makes the [Word] unrealizable,"[4] and that therefore require regeneration and redemption themselves? How can language be unBabelized and still remain comprehensible to or apprehensible by fallen man—the reader? Given the necessity of speaking words in time, or writing words in linear space, how can the poet annihilate the very temporal and spatial confines which make verbalization possible in the first place? With Urizen's original utterance of "words articulate" in mind, and his writing them down in his book of metals, how can the poet be Urizenic and at the same time prophetic, that is, Blake's Los?

In two earlier papers I attempted the beginnings of an answer to these questions. In the first (to be published in a special issue of *Communication*) I suggested that the Romantic poets twisted and strained language in such fashion that it finally militated against its own existence, aspiring toward that totality of unverbalizable communication, that act of pure intellection which we call (with a certain helplessness) silence. For example, Shelley (who, more often than not, is the best example) writes in *The Defense of Poetry* that "Poetry is a sword of lightning, ever unsheathed, which consumes the scabbard that would contain it." And in one of the most daring of metaphors for this linguistic self-immolation, in his Preface to *The Cenci* he writes: "Imagination is as the immortal God which should assume flesh for the redemption of mortal passion." Thus, the poet creates words (poetry) which in their self-annihilative power flash upon the imagination the truths (or reality) of which they are but the imperfect and evanescent conductors. Or to put it another way, as George Steiner does in his remarkable book *Language and Silence* (New York, 1967; 1st ed. 1958): "Light, ... instead of making syntax translucent with meaning ... seems to spill

[4] Frederic Jameson, *The Prison-House of Language* (Princeton, 1972), p. 88.

over in unrecapturable splendor or burn the word to ash " (p. 40). For the Romantic poet, however, and—as the poet so fervently hoped—for the imaginative reader, that splendor is not only not unrecapturable; it is as inextinguishable as the burnt words are consumable.[5]

While such a formulation may be conceptually acceptable in a general way, the operative particulars clearly are not—perhaps inevitably, since to talk about wordlessness even theoretically is to compromise conceptuality with the impoverished reality of words. In a recent fine essay on Shelley's veil imagery [6] Jerome McGann provides a useful metaphorical means of discussing the dilemma. In *The Prelude*, for example, Wordsworth wrote of his soul (for which we may here read " poetry " or " language ") putting " Off her veil and, self-transmuted," standing " Naked, as in the presence of her God " (IV, 150-52). While we can recognize that for hundreds of years language was thought of as the clothing of thought, it is difficult, if not impossible, to conceive of thought naked of its dress. Nevertheless Wordsworth's veil (or any number of its synonymous metaphors in other poets— masks, mists of light, curtains, clouds) has to be seen as his tacit assumption that *some* manner of articulation is necessary to make the silence of pure imaginative cognition or intellection humanly conceivable.[7] The poet thus creates the veil of language while coinstantaneously stripping off that veil—creator and destroyer both. Blake typically makes the point in its most extreme (and apocalyptic) form: " God becomes as we are, that we may be as he is " (*There Is No Natural Religion*)—which is

---

[5] With the ideas in this paragraph (and elsewhere in this paper) compare Stanley E. Fish's provocative thesis in *Self-Consuming Artifacts* (Berkeley and Los Angeles, 1972). For example: "A self-consuming artifact signifies most successfully where it fails, when it points *away* from itself to something its forms cannot capture "; and: " art, like other medicines is consumed in the workings of its own best effects " (3-4). Professor Fish's argument is far too complex to be summarized here; but while I am not fully persuaded by his emphasis almost wholly on " what is happening in the reader " rather than " what is happening on the page," his book deserves a reading by all Blake students, especially the chapter on Herbert's poetry.

[6] "Shelley's Veils: A Thousand Images of Loveliness," in *Romantic and Victorian: Studies in Memory of William H. Marshall*, ed. W. P. Elledge and R. L. Hoffman (Rutherford, N. J., 1971), pp. 198-218.

[7] Cf. Frederic Jameson's point about Dante's *Paradiso* in *The Prison-House of Language*: " the content of the *Paradiso* turns out to be a series of investigations of how paradise could have content; that the events of the poem are 'nothing more' than a series of dramatizations of the pre-conditions necessary for such events to be conceivable in the first place " (p. 88).

another way of saying that The Word must be made flesh, must be articulated, so that its existence may realize itself, wordless, in our unarticulatable imaginations. But the central paradox involved here is most neatly set out by Shelley. On the one hand he writes: " Poetry lifts the veil from the hidden beauty of the world "; and poetry " strips the veil of familiarity from the world, and lays bare the naked and sleeping beauty, which is the spirit of its forms." On the other: " Poetry . . . arrests the vanishing apparitions which haunt the interlunations of life, and veiling them, *or* in language *or* in form, sends them forth among mankind "; and, more succinctly: poetry " spreads its own figured curtain, *or* withdraws life's dark veil before the scene of things " (*The Defense of Poetry*). "Whatever can be Created can be Annihilated," Blake insisted (*Milton* 32: 36) —except what he called " forms," that is, their eternal realities or identities. " The Oak is cut down by the Ax, the Lamb falls by the Knife / But their Forms Eternal Exist, For-ever . . . (*Ibid.* 32: 37, 38). On the other hand he writes with marvelous circularity and a touch of humor that is less rare than most of us allow him:

> . . . What seems to Be: Is: To those to whom
> It seems to Be, & is productive of the most dreadful
> Consequences to those to whom it seems to Be . . . .
> *(Jerusalem 32: 51-53)*

In a second paper [8] I tried to demonstrate that in certain poems, at least, Blake's verbal and syntactical strategies become as much a symbol of the world the poetry presents (whether fallen or unfallen) as are the images, actions, plot, and characters for which the words are the vehicle. Further, the Fall (as Blake interpreted it) is not only equal to the fall of the Word into words but also to the disintegration of non-discursive unity into normal syntactical patterns. Blake's linguistic problem in this sense was to create emblems of disjunctiveness while at the same time providing us the paradigmatic conjunction or identification of All by which the disjunctiveness can become meaningful. He saw quite clearly that it was not enough simply to rely on the reader's perception of the difference between abnormal or disjunctive syntax and the normal linear flow of meaningful

---

[8] "Blake's Verbal Technique," in *William Blake: Essays for S. Foster Damon,* ed. A. H. Rosenfeld (Providence, R. I., 1969), pp. 321-32. The substance of the following three paragraphs is taken from this essay.

words—for then we would merely be measuring one aspect of the Urizenic fallen world (disintegration) against another aspect of the same world (excessive order—" one King, One God, one Law "). The challenge was to construe what Harold Bloom calls a " grammar of imagination," a language that can imaginatively assume the condition of oneness and interchangeability of grammatical forms and functions, the loss of which it not only describes but enacts.

A fine example of this is from the " Preludium " to *The Book of Urizen*:

> Of the primeval Priests assum'd power
> When Eternals spurn'd back his religion;
> And gave him a place in the north,
> Obscure, shadowy, void, solitary.

If in the fallen world the priest has appropriately a " place," imaginatively there is no place; it is " void." Further, the adjectives in the last line ambiguously modify both " place " and " him," thus linking together the mutual imaginative unreality of character and landscape while ostensibly supplying them a solid context. Similarly, the four lines together form a grammatical fragment, an illusory verbal context within which the words jostle uncertainly—in a sense to be " spurn'd back " by the imaginative reader in emulation of the Eternals. But to pursue the particulars a bit further, as the " place " is " obscure," so the priest's vision is obscuring or obscured; if the " place " is " shadowy," the priest also is unsubstantial, a delusion. Blake's call for " swift winged words," then, is for the fire to do battle with Urizen's " Words articulate " (4: 4) which will be ensconced in his " Book / Of eternal brass " (4: 32-33) as

> Laws of peace, of love, of unity:
> Of pity, compassion, forgiveness.
> . . . .
> One command, one joy, one desire,
> One curse, one weight, one measure
> One King, one God, one Law.   (4: 34-40)

And one syntax, the fallen unwinged word of lead that unfledges all flights of fire.[9]

The first chapter of *The Book of Urizen* merely expands this

[9] Cf. Shelley's *Epipsychidion*, ll. 588-90.

technique of Urizenically asserting space as well as physical identity and coinstantaneously denying them. Urizen is "a shadow of horror," "Unknown, unprolific! / Self-closd, all-repelling," a "form'd" void or vacuum (3: 1-5). That is, he is unknowable imaginatively but he is "self-known" just as he is imaginatively sterile but self-prolific, his "enormous labours" productive of "self-begotten armies," "phantasies," "horrible forms of deformity," "cruel enormities," all ultimately but "similitudes / Of a foot, or a hand, or a head / Or a heart, or an eye ... (3: 22, 5: 16, 10: 14, 13: 43, 20: 50, 23: 4-6). Closing himself in and repelling all so that he may self-create his identity, Urizen exemplifies paradoxically his own illusoriness by way of Blake's contrapuntal imaginative syntax which undoes the Urizenic universe at its very borning. Or to put it another way: Urizen's imaginative unreality becomes the symbol for all that he is not; and conversely, his emergence as a palpable reality is annihilated by the imaginative voidness of his realization.

While I am still persuaded by the broad outlines and general directions of these two papers, the demonstrative particulars leave a good deal to be desired partly (at least) because of the inadequacies of any critical vocabulary to talk about the adequacies or inadequacies of poetic language to vehicularize ineffability whether that be conceptualized as nothingness or everythingness. In any case I am more and more convinced that Blake (as well as, of course, the other Romantic poets) quite deliberately and consistently struggled toward a transcendant or translucent syntax, whose formulations invite us to imaginatively perceive their own self-destructiveness. For while "space undivided by existence" strikes horror into all imaginative souls (*Bk. of Urizen* 13: 46-47), "What can be Created Can be Destroyed" (*Laocoön*), and such annihilation of the error constitutive of "existence" is "The whole Business of Man" (*Laocoön*). In this spirit, then, let me here hazard some further observations relative to the total context and ramifications of the problem.

Though it may seem outrageously simplistic and sweeping let me suggest at the outset that everything Blake says about Man, the Universe, society, imagination and the senses—in fact, everything that he says about anything—is translatable into a comment upon language, words, the poet's task, poetry.[10] Put that

[10] Interestingly James Rieger recently came to the conclusion that *Milton* "exists

way, the subject of Blake's language assumes proportions as forbidding as the intricacies of his mythology—into which we have not yet stopped probing and are unlikely to do so in the near future. My focus, however, will be on only three aspects of the total problem:

(1) What was Blake's conception of the language of Eternity, the ur-linguistic condition so to speak?
(2) What are the linguistic implications of the fall from this condition and how does Blake present " fallen " language other than merely using it himself?
(3) How does he conceive of the redemption of language, the reassumption of the reality and primacy of the Word, the reintegration of Babel into not merely one language but into that language that requires no temple, no building to signify it?

Initially we must recognize that Blake with two notable exceptions (*Bk. of Urizen* 3: 36-39; *Jerusalem*, plates 97-99) gives us no vision at all of Eternity (or undifferentiated Imagination). He describes it, names it (precisely as Adam names the creatures in Genesis), talks about it, but its imaginative allness eludes his pen or graver. The reasons are obvious. By its very nature Eternity is neither describable nor representable. Any image (or set of images), any words, by their very nature, would compromise its imaginative (or mental) reality. He said once, in *Milton*:

> Every Time less than a pulsation of the artery
> Is equal in its period & value to Six Thousand Years.
>
> For in this Period the Poets Work is Done: and all the Great Events of Time start forth & are conceived in such a Period Within a Moment: a Pulsation of the Artery. (28: 61-29: 3)

From this perspective the only poem of Eternity possible must occupy no more time than this pulsation—and presumably no more space than Eliot's still point. Given the patent absurdity of such a conception Blake had to find other means of annihi-

---

on four levels of discourse," the utterances of each higher realm being " only partially intelligible to the inhabitants of the worlds below it. That is the central stylistic problem of the poem "—" ' The Hem of Their Garments ': The Bard's Song in *Milton*," in *Blake's Sublime Allegory*, ed. S. Curran and J. A. Wittreich (Madison, Wis., 1973), p. 277.

lating space and time while at the same time perforce capitulating to their insidious and resistless demands. Yet we do learn *about* Eternity, as I've said, and about its language, about the constitution of the Word. In Chapter IV of *Jerusalem*, for example, Blake writes:

> When in Eternity Man converses with Man they enter
> Into each others Bosom (which are Universes of delight)
> In mutual interchange—(88: 3-5)

a rather startling echo of Wordsworth's marvelous phrase in *The Prelude*, " an ennobling interchange." The Word then is not so much a linguistic unit as an event, a sharing, an act of love, a coming together.[11] Blake used the splendid word " cominglings " to describe it:

> Embraces are Cominglings: from the Head even to the Feet;
> And not a pompous High Priest entering by a Secret Place.[12]

The quotation from *Jerusalem* with which this paper began accents the point:

>   & every Word & Every Character
> Was Human . . .
>   & they walked
> To & fro in Eternity as One Man reflecting each in each
> & clearly seen
> And seeing . . .

Thus Eternity is in the form of a man, and the Word is a man, and all things are human-formed, each in each without separation, mergeable identities interpenetrating without end.

One of Blake's finest lyrics dramatizes this conception in terms of the poet's own four-fold vision. Standing on the shore at his retreat in Felpham he feels his eyes expanding

> Into regions of air
> Away from all Care
> Into regions of fire
> Remote from Desire

---

[11] Cf. Peter Brooks' interesting essay on nineteenth-century French melodrama, " The Text of Muteness," *NLH* (1974), 549-64, especially his notion of mute gesture as "immediate, unarticulated language of presence: a moment of victory of expression over articulation."

[12] *Jerusalem* 69: 43-44. Cf. 66: 56. " He who will not comingle in Love, must be adjoind by Hate "—that is by the pomposity of lexical analyses which arrive at meanings through " adjoinings." Also *Jerusalem* 88: 6-7, where cominglings produce "thunders of intellect."

>   The Light of the Morning
>   Heavens Mountains adorning
>   In particles bright
>   The jewels of Light
>   Distinct shone & clear—
>   Amazd & in fear
>   I each particle gazed,
>   Astonish'd Amazed
>   For each was a Man
>   Human formd. Swift I ran
>   For they beckond to me
>   Remote by the Sea
>   Saying. Each grain of Sand
>   Every Stone on the Land
>   Each rock & each hill
>   Each fountain & rill
>   Each herb & each tree
>   Mountain hill Earth & Sea
>   Cloud Meteor & Star
>   Are Men Seen Afar (Letter to Butts, Oct. 2, 1800)

And then miraculously, epiphanically, apocalyptically, time and space are annihilated, the doors of perception are expanded infinitely, and the mental reality of Eternity is realized: [13]

>   My Eyes more & more
>   Like a Sea without shore
>   Continue Expanding
>   The Heavens commanding
>   Till the Jewels of Light
>   Heavenly Men beaming bright
>   Appeard as One Man
>   Who Complacent began
>   My limbs to infold
>   In his beams of bright gold
>   Like dross purgd away
>   All my mire & my clay
>   Soft consumd in delight
>   In his bosom Sun bright
>   I remaind. (*ibid.*)

Aside from the loveliness of this poem (which must surely have been lost on the patient, generous, but plodding and pedestrian

---

[13] Cf. Roger Easson's argument that Blake's use of the " sublime " is related to the fact that " to sublime " in chemistry means the passing of a substance " from solid to gas without passing into the intermediate liquid state " (" Blake and His Reader in *Jerusalem*," in *Blake's Sublime Allegory*, p. 316).

Butts), it serves admirably to remind us that for Blake Eternity exists within the timelessness and infinity of the human mind. Blake's visions of Eternity—and its language—then, are visions of his own mind, the mind of the totally imaginative man. "Mental Things are alone Real," he insisted in *A Vision of the Last Judgment*; "what is Calld Corporeal Nobody Knows of its dwelling Place it is in Fallacy & its Existence an Imposture Where is the Existence Out of Mind or Thought Where is it but in the Mind of a Fool." Thus just as "Eternity Exists and All things in Eternity Independent of Creation" (*ibid.*), just as the Word is expressed in Eternity as "Visionary forms dramatic which bright / Redounded from [the tongues of the Four Zoas or the Divine Humanity] in thunderous majesty, in Visions / In new Expanses"—so Blake explodes to the man he accused of being hired to depress art, Sir Joshua Reynolds: "All Forms are Perfect in the Poets Mind. but these are not Abstracted nor Compounded from Nature but are from Imagination" (Annotations to Reynolds).

The poet's mind, then, is not merely the image of Eternity, or its analogue, but is precisely that infinite reality of which nature is the mere shadow. As such, the mind contains not only all forms—perfect—but all words and the Word, Imagination complete (which is to say infinitely expanded sense perception, or, mythologically, the fourfold unity of the Four Zoas). The Fall in this regard is thus the shattering of the Human Imagination into the disparate and woefully limited senses, the turning of mental reality inside out, the descent of the Word (and all perfect forms) via the viscera and pulp of the Tongue into what Blake variously calls "fabricate[d] embodied semblances" (*Four Zoas* 90: 9); "similitudes / Of a foot, or a hand, or a head / Or a heart, or an eye (*Bk. of Urizen* 23: 4-6); "the rotten rags" and "filthy garments" of Bacon, Locke, and Newton (*Milton* 41: 4, 6); the linguistic world of Urizen's iron book of laws and the Tower of Babel; the poetry of Pope, Dryden, and the endless unarticulated babblings, gnashings, groanings, screamings, and ravings of Blake's own mythological fragments of man's total being.

But the fallen state of language is less easily described, for the total Fall itself in Blake is an incredibly complex and omniverous affair. Initially, we recall, the Fall is not into Creation directly but rather into non-entity, the world of eternal Death:

> Sund'ring, dark'ning, thund'ring!
> Rent away with a terrible crash
> Eternity roll'd wide apart
> Wide asunder rolling
> Mountainous all around
> Departing; departing; departing:
> Leaving ruinous fragments of life
> Hanging frowning cliffs & all between
> An ocean of voidness unfathomable.   (*Bk. of Urizen* 5: 3-11)

This Dali-esque landscape Blake describes variously as "space undivided by existence," the "eternal Abyss," the "dark void," the "Non-Ens." *The Book of Los* presents one of his most succinct enactments:

> Falling, falling! Los fell & fell
> Sunk precipitant heavy down down
> Times on times, night on night, day on day
> Truth has bounds. Error none: falling, falling:
> Years on years, and ages on ages
> Still he fell thro' the void, still a void
> Found for falling day & night without end.
> For tho' day or night was not; their spaces
> Were measur'd by his incessant whirls
> In the horrid vacuity bottomless.   (4: 27-36)

Aside from the parodic eternity and infinity of the Fall before a limit is placed to it by "the Divine Hand" or "Eternal Mind," the importance of this conception lies in the formlessness of error prior to the creation. Linguistically, then, the fall of the Word and its shattering of Truth (or reality) into endlessly multiplied fragments of words constitute and define error. But even that is not quite correct—for this error has no bounds. Like Urizen the Word during the Fall is

> Unknown, unprolific!
> Self-closd, all-repelling . . .
>   . . . .
> Dark revolving in silent activity:
> Unseen in tormenting passions;
> An activity unknown and horrible;
> A self-contemplating shadow,
>   In enormous labours occupied.   (*Bk. of Urizen* 3: 2-3, 18-22)

Enormous labours, of course, to no end but a perpetuation of the fall into non-entity.

The creation of the Universe, then, of the earth, of mankind, and of language is the giving of form to what otherwise would remain an eternal abstraction (and therefore unredeemable) — the limit of contraction and the limit of opacity. Accordingly the Creation is an act of mercy,

> by mathematic power
> Giving a body to Falshood that it may be cast off for ever.
> (*Jerusalem* 12: 12-13)

Somewhat differently:

> ... whatever is visible to the Generated Man
> Is a Creation of mercy & love, from the Satanic Void.
> (*ibid.* 13: 44-45)

Or again, Los and his sons (the artisans of this world) are portrayed as

> Creating form & beauty around the dark regions of sorrow,
> Giving to airy nothing a name and a habitation
> Delightful! with bounds to the Infinite putting off the Indefinite
> Into most holy forms of Thought ... (*Milton* 28: 2-5)

Or, finally and most elaborately, in the first chapter of *Jerusalem*:

> Lo!
> The stones are pity, and the bricks, well wrought affections:
> Enameld with love & kindness, & the tiles engraven gold
> Labour of merciful hands: the beams & rafters are forgiveness;
> The mortar & cement of the work, tears of honesty: the nails,
> And the screws & iron braces, are well wrought blandishments,
> And well contrived words, firm fixing, never forgotten,
> Always comforting the remembrance: the floors, humility,
> The cielings, devotion; the hearths, thanksgiving:
> . . . .
> The curtain, woven tears & sighs, wrought into lovely forms
> For comfort. (12: 29-40)

It is in this sense, of course, that "Eternity is in love with the productions of time" (*Marriage of Heaven and Hell*).

But, while Los, the eternal artificer, can do all this to provide both the hope and the possibility of redemption and a reassumption of Eternity, the Creation is Urizenic after all:

> ... the land of woven labyrinths:
> The land of snares & traps & wheels & pit-falls & dire mills:
> The Voids, the Solids, & the land of clouds & regions of waters:

With their inhabitants: in the Twenty-seven Heavens beneath Beulah:
Self-righteousness conglomerating against the Divine Vision:
A Concave Earth wondrous, Chasmal, Abyssal, Incoherent!
(Jerusalem 13: 48-53)

Put somewhat crudely and not entirely accurately, what Los creates Urizen rules over and commands—so that the wars of Blake's mythology directly pit the poet (the human imagination) against the non-poet (the sense-dominated reason-controlled man). More to the point, that war takes place within each man. As his imagination strives to produce "most holy forms of thought" for the redemption of his total being, his reason produces space-bound, time-bound monsters which struggle for personal dominion and enslave that portion of man whose vision of Eternity remains at least a glowing ember. Reason, then, which Blake describes as "once fairer than the light till foul in Knowledges dark Prison house" ("Then She Bore Pale Desire"), along with its cohorts, the fallen infinite and innumerable senses now shrunken to four, produces "A Pretence of Art: To Destroy Art" (Annotations to Reynolds)—its human agents being Bacon, Newton, Locke, Reynolds, Gainsborough, Rembrandt, Titian, Rubens, Pope, Dryden—and all who are not, in Blake's definition, artists. The major products of their infernal creations are two: the law and bad art (which are the same thing). Blake's metaphors for these abominations are several. Bad poets are, for example, "the destroyers of Jerusalem,"

> Who pretend to Poetry that they may destroy Imagination;
> By imitation of Natures Images drawn from Remembrance
> These are the Sexual Garments, the Abomination of Desolation
> Hiding the Human Lineaments as with an Ark & Curtains.
> *(Milton* 41: 21, 23-26)

They are the blotters and blurrers of the minute particulars of Eternity, creating instead

> Harmonies of Concords & Discords
> Opposed to Melody, and by Lights & Shades, opposed to Outline
> And by Abstraction opposed to the Visions of Imagination.
> *(Jerusalem* 74: 24-26)

Their counterparts—the readers, perceivers, or listeners—are equally debased:

> The Ear, a little shell in small volutions shutting out
> All melodies & comprehending only Discord and Harmony

> The Tongue a little moisture fills, a little food it cloys
> A little sound it utters & its cries are faintly heard
> Then brings forth Moral Virtue the cruel Virgin Babylon.[14]

Even more terrifying perhaps than the moral law and bad poetry, which are spun out of the entrails of Urizen and recorded in his books of iron and brass, are Blake's mechanistic metaphors for fallen language.[15] Words are described in *Milton* as being laid

> in order above the mortal brain
> As cogs are formd in a wheel to turn the cogs of the adverse wheel.
> (27: 9-10)

In *The Four Zoas* this epic machinery is seen as quite literally warring with itself—devastatingly all within man's mind:

> Terrific ragd the Eternal Wheels of intellect terrific ragd
> The living creatures of the wheels in the Wars of Eternal life
> But perverse rolld the wheels of Urizen & Luvah back reversd
> Downwards & outwards consuming in the wars of Eternal Death.
> (20: 12-15)

In *Jerusalem* those wheels are enmeshed neatly with the loom of Locke that cocoons the human imagination (linguistically the words which clothe the thought),[16] and fashions the nets that envelope all bodies and all minds, inducing "single vision and Newton's sleep":

> I turn my eyes to the Schools & Universities of Europe
> And there behold the Loom of Locke whose Woof rages dire
> Wash'd by the Water-wheels of Newton. black the cloth
> In heavy wreathes folds over every Nation; cruel Works
> Of many Wheels I view, wheel without wheel, with cogs tyrannic
> Moving by compulsion each other: not as those in Eden: which
> Wheel within Wheel in freedom revolve in harmony & peace.
> (15: 14-20)

---

[14] *Milton* 5: 23-27. Blake's later version of this passage, in *Jerusalem*, is:
> The Ear, a little shell, in small volutions shutting out
> True Harmonies, & comprehending great, as very small:
> The Nostrils, bent down to the earth & clos'd with senseless flesh.
> That odours cannot them expand, nor joy on them exult:
> The Tongue, a little moisture fills, a little food it cloys,
> A little sound it utters, & its cries are faintly heard. (49: 36-41).

[15] Cf. Morris Eaves' interesting explication of "The Title-Page of *The Book of Urizen*" in *William Blake: Essays in Honour of Sir Geoffrey Keynes*, ed. M. D. Paley and M. Phillips (Oxford, 1973), pp. 225-30.

[16] See Rieger's discussion of this in *Blake's Sublime Allegory*, espec. pp. 278-80.

The total effect of these wheels and cogs upon man is predictable, but what is perhaps startling is that the wheels produce in man's brain words. In *The Four Zoas*, for example, men are

> bound to sullen contemplations in the night
> Restless they turn on beds of sorrow. in their inmost brain
> Feeling the crushing Wheels they rise they write the bitter words
> Of Stern Philosophy & knead the bread of knowledge with tears
>   & groans.   (138: 12-5)

Los' task is to combat all this, just as the human imagination must contend with the fetters of reason, the petrified forms of the law, and the vague general forms of the debased artist. Not only is he Blake's eternal artificer; he is also appropriately Time.[17] For,

> Time is the mercy of Eternity; without Times swiftness
> Which is the swiftest of all things: all were eternal torment.
>   (*Milton* 24: 72-73)

And we recall, of course, that it is in the pulsation of an artery that the poet's work is done. Although Los laments endlessly that

> Reasonings like vast Serpents
> Infold around [his] limbs, bruising [his] minute articulations
>   (*Jerusalem* 15: 12-13)

it is his, the poet's, the imagination's job to create these minute articulations of error so that they may be annihilated. Thus in Chapter iii of *Jerusalem* the Eternal Great Humanity urges Los to his task,

> Crying: Compell the Reasoner to Demonstrate with unhewn Demonstrations
> Let the Indefinite be explored. and let every Man be Judged
> By his own Works, Let all Indefinites be thrown into Demonstrations
> To be pounded to dust & melted in the Furnaces of Affliction:
> . . . .
> The Infinite alone resides in Definite & Determinate Identity

---

[17] For a useful analysis of Los' various significations and functions see E. J. Rose's "Los, Pilgrim of Eternity" in *Blake's Sublime Allegory*, pp. 83-99. Particularly related to the point of this paper are pages 89-90 where Ros describes the artist's initial act as the same as the "visionary's effort to delineate form on indefinite space—to mercifully give time to space, to draw a line."

> Establishment of Truth depends on destruction of Falshood
> continually
> On Circumcision: not on Virginity. . . . (55: 56-66)

Accordingly Los works unceasingly and heroically with his hammer, anvil, and fires—both to give form to error that it may be annihilated, and also to re-reveal the minute particularity of a vision of Eternity:

> & in his ladles the Ore
> He lifted, pouring it into the clay ground prepar'd with art;
> Striving with Systems to deliver Individuals from those Systems.
> (*Jerusalem* 11: 3-5)

Perhaps not extraordinarily, then, Los creates (in addition to all else he creates in his cosmic, enormous labors)

> English, the rough basement.
> Los built the stubborn structure of the Language, acting against
> Albions melancholy, who must else have been a Dumb despair.
> (*Jerusalem* 36: 58-60)

And with that rough basement Blake (and *all* poets) must work—building enormous structures which at once embody error in annihilable form ("giving to airy nothing a habitation and a name") and provide the possibility of organizing the minute particularity of vision in order to reconstruct Eternity. "I rest not from my great task," Blake cries in propria persona in *Jerusalem*,

> To open the Eternal Words, to open the immortal Eyes
> Of Man inwards into the Worlds of Thought: into Eternity
> Ever expanding in the Bosom of God. the Human Imagination.
> (5: 17-20)

And again:

> Therefore I print; nor vain my types shall be:
> Heaven, Earth & Hell, henceforth shall live in harmony.
> (*ibid.* 3: 9-10)

That printing will be, as *The Marriage of Heaven and Hell* reminds us, "in the infernal method, by corrosives . . . melting apparent surfaces away, and displaying the infinite which was hid."

These reformulations of familiar material bring us to the key question (my number 3 above): what can Blake do, even with all his multi-artistic genius, to redeem language—or at least to make his language susceptible of redemption and a renewal of the primacy of the Word. It is both a matter of perception (predictably) and of action (rather than a matter of merely reading). To take the latter point first, reading is not a human (i. e. imaginative) activity to Blake. It is as Urizenic as all other aspects of the fallen Imagination. For example, in *The Four Zoas*

> ... Urizen gave life & sense by his immortal power
> ....
> Thus in the temple of the Sun his books of iron & brass
> And silver & gold he consecrated reading incessantly
> To myriads of perturbed spirits thro the universe
> They propagated the deadly words the Shadowy Female absorbing
> The enormous Sciences of Urizen ages after ages exploring
> The fell destruction. (102: 14, 23-29)

Or: " Los reads the Stars of Albion! the Spectre reads the Voids / Between the Stars " (*Jerusalem* 91: 36-37). Or, as " the Shadowy Female howls in articulate howlings " of the woven garments of life,

> I will have Writings written all over [them] in Human Words
> That every Infant that is born upon the Earth shall read
> And get by rote as a hard task of a life of sixty years.
> (*Milton* 18: 12-14)

Reading, thus, is performable only by fallen man: it is the mere scanning of objects, the tracing of " dreadful letters " (*Four Zoas* 78: 2), the accumulation of data, the obverse of Adam's " naming." It is a sense experience. In *Jerusalem* Blake chides us directly:

> You accumulate Particulars, & murder by analyzing, that you
> May take the aggregate; & call the aggregate Moral Law:
> And you call that Swelld & bloated Form; a Minute Particular.
> But General Forms have their vitality in Particulars: & every
> Particular is a Man; a Divine Member of the Divine Jesus.
> (91: 26-30)

The bloated " aggregate," of course, is the " meaning " that the reader abstracts from the particulars—and then permits to assume a reality of its own—in precisely the same way that the priests in *The Marriage of Heaven and Hell* abstract deities from their objects and then pronounce them the only realities. Words thus become part of the vast machine of the physical world, cogs in a cerebral wheel to turn the adverse wheel of the reader's mind in a kind of perpetual motion machine producing nothing—which is to say, producing mere images drawn from Nature. From these, laws are abstracted that men impose upon themselves; and gods are invented, as the source of the laws, before which men then prostitute themselves. The viciousness and self-enslavement of the reading process could not be made more graphic.

At the same time Blake clearly regarded his words as the embodiments, the formalizations, the deabstractifications of error. "There is not an Error," he wrote in *A Vision of the Last Judgment*, "but it has a Man for its Agent that is it is a Man." And again, from the same work: "Error is Created Truth is Eternal Error or Creation will be Burned Up & then & not till then Truth or Eternity will appear it is Burnt Up the Moment Men cease to behold it." We are thus thrown back upon the nature of perception: not only *how* one sees, but which direction one looks. If one sees merely the words, in order arranged, settled neatly into the time and space of the page, one sees precisely as Blake's idiot questioner who cries out irritatedly: "When the Sun rises do you not see a round Disk of fire somewhat like a Guinea"? Blake's answer is what his poems demand our answer to be: "O no no I see an Innumerable company of the Heavenly host crying Holy Holy Holy is the Lord God Almighty."[18] To see the words on the page as linguistic constructs (or even metaphors and symbols)[19] is to see one's self only. One is reminded of the quip about great poetry being as a mirror: if an ass peers into it, he can hardly expect an angel to peer out. So, for Blake, his words are intended to circumscribe and circumcise "the excrementitious / Husk & Covering into Vacuum evaporating revealing the lineaments of Man" (*Jerusalem* 98: 18-19) and the minutely discriminated particulars of vision—which are apparent to all who turn their eyes *inward* "into the Worlds of Thought: into

---

[18] *A Vision of the Last Judgment*. It is worth noting here that Karl Barth's hermeneutic methodology (as presented in the Preface to the second edition of *Römerbrief*) "is to *live* with the text until it disappears and one is confronted with the divine word itself" (Robert W. Funk, *Language, Hermeneutics, and the Word of God*, p. 11). Cf. Merleau-Ponty's distinction between the "accomplished work" and "the work which exists in itself like a thing" (Funk, p. 234).

[19] Cf. Jerzy Peterkiewicz's notion in *The Other Side of Silence* (London and New York, 1970) that metaphors are structurally "scaffoldings around invisible reality" (p. 45).

Eternity / Ever expanding in the Bosom of God" (*Jerusalem* 5: 19-20). To "read" in such fashion is to see not words at all but human forms acting out the drama of fall, redemption, and apocalypse that takes place within one's own mental universe.

Blake's advice to us is appropriately pointed. We must arm ourselves, as he did,

> With the bows of my Mind & the Arrows of Thought
> My bowstring fierce with Ardour breathes
> My arrows glow in their golden sheaves.
> (Letter to Butts, Nov. 22, 1802)

So armed, we must engage with the words in mental strife, entering into their worlds (which are "universes of delight") in "Mutual interchange."[20] For

> every Word & Every Character
> [Is] Human according to the Expansion or Contraction, the
> Translucence or Opakeness

of our "Nervous fibres" or senses (*Jerusalem* 98: 25-37).

This intellectual intercourse (clearly the external analogue of sexual intercourse) makes clear Blake's otherwise seemingly peculiar notion that the sense of touch (the Tongue) is the "Parent Sense" (*Jerusalem* 98: 17). Without such engagement and comingling Blake's poetry seems much wind and splutter, intellectually fascinating but cranky, and perhaps finally irrelevant to *my* situation. But Blake did not say lightly (he repeated it seven times), through the Bard of *Milton*: "Mark well my words! they are of your eternal salvation."

His poetry, then, is not an "impossible enterprise" however shabby its "equipment."[21] "If," he writes in *A Vision of the Last Judgment*, "the Spectator could Enter into these Images in his Imagination approaching them on the Fiery Chariot of his Contemplative Thought if he could Enter into Noahs Rainbow or into his bosom or could make a Friend & Companion of one of

---

[20] *Jerusalem* 88: 4, 5. Cf. John M. Hill's interesting thesis about *Pearl* in "Middle English Poets and the Word," *Criticism*, 16 (1974), 153-69, especially: the dreamer "speaks of a melting mind . . . which suggests that to say truly 'of that syght' requires baffled reason and melting consciousness. Comprehension, then, would mean an entering into rather than an observation of and reference to mystical domain" (p. 166).

[21] Jameson, *The Prison-House of Language*, p. 158; T. S. Eliot, *East Coker* V.

these Images of wonder which always intreats him to leave mortal things as he must know then would he arise from his Grave then would he meet the Lord in the Air & then he would be happy." And then he will recognize the dross of language to be the Baconian-Newtonian Lockean-Urizenic illusion that obscures, debases, and falsifies, but never hides the "Visionary Forms Dramatic" redounding *from* the plate or page as they do from all unfallen tongues and minds. Thel was told about the grave: " 'Tis given thee to enter / And to return; fear nothing." In the sense that I have been attempting to develop, Blake's linguistic text, indeed the whole of each grand plate, is our "grave." It is not much to ask us to enter, but it is everything. On page 67 of his manuscript notebook, he wrote: " 23 May 1810 found the Word Golden." It's clearly worth the search.

University of California
Riverside

THE MORALIZED SONG:
SOME RENAISSANCE THEMES IN POPE

BY KATHLEEN WILLIAMS [*]

Our greatest poets have often much in common with one another in the broader aspects of their work, its vision and attitudes, despite the differences which time and circumstances make inevitable. It is the differences, in the end, that form the individual poem, but it is useful sometimes to consider that organically developing whole of which many poets seem to have felt their work to be a part, "episodes to that great poem, which all poets, like the co-operating thoughts of one great mind, have built up since the beginning of the world." So Shelley puts it in *A Defence of Poetry*, and the poets of earlier periods were certainly not less likely to think in that way. Renaissance and post-Renaissance poets, indeed, are ready to point very carefully to details for which they have drawn upon Theocritus, Virgil, Homer, and later upon Spenser or Milton. Their intention appears to be not merely to tell us that they are writing in a great tradition and believe they have a claim to belong to the ancient and august body of poets, but to direct us, often with considerable precision, to the way *this* poem should be read, to what is different and particular about it as well as to what it shares with the past.

Pope, of course, from the *Pastorals* on, elaborately relates his work to past achievement. The *Homer* and the Horatian poems spring first to mind. But if Pope thinks of himself in relation to Greece and Rome, as did Milton and Spenser, he also like them remembers his British heritage. He adapts Chaucer and Donne; the *Pastorals* are full of British as well as Greek and Latin echoes; in *An Essay on Man*, *Paradise Lost* is a presiding presence, and one that Pope carefully emphasizes. That the *Essay* is a modern parallel to Milton's poem is part of its meaning, but so is the

[*] This is to record with deep regret the death of Kathleen Williams on December 5, 1974.

fact that it is not, and could not be, *Paradise Lost,* since in Pope's time such matters are best dealt with in another manner. Milton's lofty port is no longer appropriate, as everlasting Blackmore demonstrated by attempting it, and ending up as a dunsical character in a poem in which Pope does choose, gloriously, to be Miltonically lofty. *The Dunciad* is incomparably the finest Miltonic poem of a very Miltonic century, but it does implicit homage also to Dryden, and this is typical of Pope's way, which is to bring the Renaissance tradition, British and classical, together at one place of intricate precision.

Dryden apart, Milton is the great modern predecessor with whom we associate Pope, and rightly so. If I attempt here to draw attention to certain Spenserian affinities, it is not to suggest that these are of comparable importance or even that they exist in isolation. As always the mature Pope, like Dryden, sees himself as the point at which the whole poetic company, the voice of civilization, is presently operative. Pope's early life was parallel to Milton's, and with the gift for symbolic living which has been so sensitively shown us by Professor Mack he must have felt the parallel as not only pleasing but meaningful. Living in the country like Milton, but like Milton not too far removed from that aspect of civilization which embodies itself in the city, in civic responsibility and sophisticated art, the young Pope devoted himself to becoming a poet. And in those quiet days he wrote, as other young aspirants did, verses " in imitation of " Waller, Cowley, Rochester, Spenser. The Spenser imitation, " The Alley," is a kind of burlesque, something like Swift's " City Shower " though not comparably effective. It shows a good ear and eye for Spenser's surface techniques, but one does not look here for profound Spenserian affinities, any more than one looks at " Presenting a Lark " or " The River " for that response to Cowley which is evident in the mature retirement poetry. One finds Spenser (though it is only proper to add not Spenser alone, but Spenser as a Renaissance epitome) in better work than this. Yet even " The Alley " may suggest, given the hindsight that later poems afford, something more than a facility in metrical effects.

Its subject is the poor and squalid area common to Thames-side villages and towns, from the most workmanlike to the most elegant, from " *Wapping,* smelling strong of Pitch," to Twickenham

> which fairer scenes enrich,
> Grots, Statues, Urns, and *Jo—n's Dog* and *Bitch* (49-50)

and more elegant and more august places still, like

> *Richmond's* self, from whose tall Front are ey'd
> Vales, Spires, meandering Streams, and *Windsor's* tow'ry Pride.
> (53-54)

When we look back from *Windsor Forest*, even this small jeu d'esprit suggests an early awareness that part of Spenser's theme in *The Faerie Queene, Prothalamion, The Ruines of Time, The Teares of the Muses*, is the nature of England, what it is, has been, and could be. Spenser's England, of course, is seen in a context larger than itself; insofar as it is orderly or chaotic, admirable or deplorable, it is so in relation to general assumptions of what behavior, private and public, should be, just as is the England of Pope's major poetry. "The Alley" is faithful to this. It is set in the country's symbolic center, the lower reaches of the Thames, the home of a variety of activities so vital to the country's existence that they become symbolic of it: "Deptford, Navy-building Town," Woolwich and Wapping; the influential see of Lambeth, "Envy of each Band and Gown," Twickenham with its pleasant houses on the river and Richmond with its view of Windsor, home of kings. Even these places have their sordid alley. The poem is, in its joking way, an epitome of the country, and it establishes its meaning by its choice of places and by the presence of the generalizing figure of Obloquy, who is firmly rooted in Thames-side reality despite her abstract name. She is an allegorical fishwife,

> who in her early Days
> Baskets of fish at *Billingsgate* did watch,
> Cod, Whiting, Oyster, Mackrel, Sprat, or Plaice:
> There learn'd the Speech from tongues that never cease.
> (29-32)

She is an evocation of the meaner side of man as it is shown in Pope's own time and place, for malice and envy exist not only among the poor and "low," where they may have some excuse, but in the Thames-side villas, the houses of the aristocratic and the well-to-do. Pope refers us sharply to the world and his satire (in a couplet presumably added later)[1] in the comment on his

---

[1] The poem is dated in the Twickenham edition as "before 1709," but though

neighbor, James Johnston, former Secretary of State for Scotland, of whose public character he and his friends had a very low opinion. Johnston was a considerable gardener and was " reckoned to have a very good taste,"[2] that is, he aspired to that life of virtuous retirement, the cultivation of simple things, which was a recognized value of the time and which is so much a part of Pope's later poetry. Yet while Pope (at least in his poetic being) listens peacefully at home to the sound of the London traffic as the din but

> Rolls o'er my Grotto, and but sooths my Sleep[3]

his neighbor, for all his pretensions to taste, displays among the symbolic objects of retirement (" Grots, Statues, Urns ") a pair of leaden animals which by Pope's choice of words[4] display how close their owner still is to the leaden snarlings of Obloquy, and to Envy, like a spitting cat, and Malice, like a cur. Pope the satirist and Pope the celebrator are both present, at least in embryo, and they are present in what is, for all its burlesque quality, a genuine enough Spenserian way.

We are accustomed to think of Pope as a satiric, and Spenser as a celebratory poet, and overall of course we are right. But to some degree each is both, and naturally enough if the Renaissance was right in thinking that praise and dispraise are two sides of the same thing. *Windsor Forest* is an obvious (and magnificent) example in Pope, and another is *An Essay on Man*, but there are fine passages of praise in the formal satires too. As for Spenser, the other side of the coin is present in *Mother Hubberd's Tale*, which is not only intelligent, flexible, and inventive, but even amusing, in an age when most satire is heavy going. Pope does not mention the poem, and there is no need to suppose that he gave it much attention. Beginning as what could be a formal satire like Wyatt's, *Mother Hubberd's Tale* develops into an extremely funny beast fable, and this is not Pope's way, unless the fable is as brief and illustrative as Horace's story of the country mouse. He may well have thought of the *Tale*, as Gabriel

---

Johnston lived at Twickenham from 1702, Pope did not move there until 1718. The lines could have been added before publication in 1727.

[2] Quoted in the *Dictionary of National Biography*.

[3] *Imitations of Horace*, Sat. II, i, 124.

[4] " *Dog and Bitch* " is as obvious and ordinary a phrase for degradation as Swift's " Dog and Cat " of " Phyllis, or The Progress of Love."

Harvey of *The Faerie Queene,* that Hobgoblin, regrettably, had run away with the garland from Apollo. When he adapts Renaissance satire he turns to Donne's Horatian poems as if to emphasize that this, the central Roman tradition, is where he feels himself to belong.

Yet it would be interesting to know Pope's opinion of the lively dialogue of Spenser's satiric fable and, even more, of the opening passage which, though Chaucerian in style, is Horatian, one might even say Popean, in its strategy. We are set, quickly and economically, in a situation much like that of the *Epistle to Dr. Arbuthnot,* in the hottest and most disease-ridden time of year, the mad dog-days, when Pope is made sick by the ravening would-be poets who leave him no peace. In Spenser the "hot Syrian Dog"

> Corrupted had th' ayre with his noysome breath,
> And powr'd on th' earth plague, pestilence, and death.
> Emongst the rest a wicked maladie
> Raign'd emongst men, that manie did to die,
> Depriv'd of sense and ordinarie reason. (7-11)

In both cases, the world has run mad and the poet suffers as a result, and this is why he must write his medicinal satire, with the hope not so much of curing the mad dogs who now appear to populate the world as of helping his own sickness by coming to terms with the external madness which has caused it. Satiric poetry makes its own sense of that which is "Depriv'd of sense and ordinarie reason," removes it to a distance at which it can be contemplated instead of merely suffered. Pope's use of the actual as a metaphor in his similar satiric strategy is of incomparable brilliance; the sick poet, desperately doctoring himself, discusses his case with one of his dearest friends, the actual doctor, John Arbuthnot. Spenser's strategy is less consummate than this, but it is from the same world. The sick poet has, like Pope, a friend, an *adversarius,* and she too is in her homely way a doctor, for the "good old woman" Mother Hubberd has come with other friends to solace him in his illness. She does so by herself becoming the satirist, effecting for the poet what Pope, in *Arbuthnot,* effects for himself. She tells him a tale of the adventures of two comic villains on the make, the fox and the ape, who move through the public world of the sixteenth century and its now tattered hierarchy. In the end they are exposed by the kingly lion, awakened from his long sleep; but the inspiriting quality of the fable, which helped the poet so much in his heavy depression that he is now telling it to us, is not in this provisional and tentative happy ending, but in the sense it gives of a healthy mind making meaning, even gaiety, out of a lunatic baseness. The *Tale* is very much a topical poem concerned with a real situation and with at least some real people, but its medicinal quality is in its detachment, its laughing demonstration that the ambitious ape and fox, " guilefull and most covetous," have always been with us; they sum up the lowest qualities of man but have never yet wholly prevailed, for there are still poets and good old women to absorb them into a greater sanity.

Still more, one expects that Pope would have understood *Colin Clouts Come Home Againe*, an astonishingly sure-footed poem which is a kind of pastoral but also a kind of satire and a kind of celebration, with each element somehow undiluted by the others but all working together to make a comprehensive statement about the relations of the poet to the world, of poetry to facts, of retirement to the world of action, of good to evil. All these are subjects very close to Pope's heart, and he has his own complexities in bringing them together. I wish there were—as there are not—any grounds for saying that Pope read *Colin Clout* attentively and observed how Spenser was working, for here these two poets do seem oddly close. Nothing of this kind could be as dazzling in its flexible speed of movement as Pope's later satires, but here Spenser too is dazzling, a term that one does not normally feel called upon to use in his case. To dazzle is not usually to his purpose. But here there is a similar speed of movement from one stance to another before any one has weakened in our minds as we read, flickering yet vivid, the pieces settling into momentary shape before our eyes. All the ways of looking at things are there together, chaotic and even contradictory, approximately our own shifting processes of seeing, feeling, thinking. As Pope says in the *Epistle to Cobham,*

> the diff'rence is as great between
> The optics seeing, as the object seen. (23-24)

The effect is of an inclusive truth to the reality of our reactions. One relation a poem can have to facts is to include them all, as they are refracted through a single, normally changeable mind, not selecting prematurely but letting the mind sift impressions into a working shape which makes its own wry sense of them as it must in ordinary life. Thus the poet is a shepherd, living in a simple world of retirement and peace, looking for no gain, devoted only to his song, to goodness, to humaneness. But this admirable state of affairs has its limitations. It leaves out too much of what really goes on, too much of the movement of mind, and this can be for poetic ill as well as poetic good. In short, the shepherd-poet can be something of a fool in his ignorance and his simple assumptions of good; Colin (Spenser's name for himself in poetry) and Coridon show this to exquisite comic effect. Similarly, Cynthia the Queen and Rosalind are both cruel and kind, the English court is both ideal and corrupt, English poets are both fine and base, Ireland is both lovely and wretched, according to where one stands at the moment and to where they stand at the moment. The complications of feeling, of judgment, of understanding and communicating with one's fellows or with the world at large, are nowhere simplified.

The way this is done is, of course, chiefly through dialogue, through Colin's talk with the shepherds and shepherdesses and his reported talk with the sea-shepherd Raleigh. There are more persons than in Pope's formal satires, but in both cases the movements of the mind are developed through talk with foils invented for the purpose. Pope's magnificent use of the " Friend " in various guises need hardly be commented upon further than to say that, like Colin's friends, he is there to enable the poet to organize a variety of points of view, of moods even, which are representative of the shifting viewpoints of us all. Both poets have a strong sense of the complications and changes of any human being, and the similar complications and changes of the world he lives in, and satire is not the only form suited to the expression of that sense. One of the poems that embodies it most completely is the *Metamorphosis*, in which theme and method in perfect unity show the whole universe of men and creatures and things as shifting, merging, changing perpetually; and Pope and Spenser, like so many of our poets, respond deeply to Ovid.

Spenser's feeling for mutability, which is for good and ill the central fact of the mortal, living world, is apparent everywhere, and of this state of ceaseless flux man is a part. Or is a part so long as he is in any real sense alive. The worst thing that can happen to Spenser's characters is to get caught in an unnatural stasis, like the people in Dante's hell. In the story of Malbecco, Paridell, and Hellenore in Book III of *The Faerie Queene*, this happens to all three characters. Paridell has become an automatic seducer; he is incapable of escaping from the mold into which he has poured his considerable powers (for he has good qualities, intelligence, charm, bravery) and he is becoming nothing more than an accomplished "learned lover." Hellenore, lady of the castle, becomes nothing but an avid receiver of sexual potency, refusing to leave the satyrs by whom she is held in common as a fertility figure, a May lady. Malbecco shows the process, or the cessation of process, in its completest form, for he ceases to be a human being at all, and becomes a personification of the jealousy with which he has identified himself. The comparison with Pope's great satiric characters is one that can justly, I think, be made; Sporus or Atticus is caught forever in these unchanging and obsessive characteristics with which he has chosen to identify himself, which he has almost chosen to become. Even good people, as Atticus partly is, must beware of this cessation. Spenser's Amoret, though loving and kind, becomes nothing but a figure in an allegorical masque, surrounded by unreal personifications, until she is released into the living and moving world by Britomart, who is herself one of Spenser's best-drawn figures of change, of becoming, of learning to react flexibly and openly to the mutable in others, in events, in herself.

Something like this is what Pope wants for Patty Blount, the "free Innocence of Life" of the charming "Epistle to Miss Blount, with the Works of Voiture":

> Too much *your Sex* is by their Forms confin'd . . .
> Custom, grown blind with Age, must be your guide . . .
> By nature yielding, stubborn but for Fame . . . (31-35)

Miss Blount is the only genuinely alive person in "The Epistle to a Lady." "Woman's at best a Contradiction still" (270) but the women of the poem are set in contradictions as automatic as Paridell's responses. Pope does not name his people as personifications, but then Spenser does not either, except in special cases like Malbecco whose name becomes "Gelosy." His "Paridell" or "Amoret" are of the same nature as Pope's "Sporus" or "Narcissa"; we relate Sporus to Hervey, but we do not identify them, and Pope is entirely accurate in using not the actual name but one that, by its connections and its unreality in a contemporary context, suggests that this is the point at which Hervey is likely to become fixed. Thus in the " Epistle to a Lady " Miss Blount is surrounded by fixed Narcissas and Flavias, but the closing paragraphs, with their affectionately warning tribute, portray her as flexibly accepting her changing nature. She will need "Fix'd Principles, with Fancy ever new," shaken together, if she is to avoid some version of the terrible fate of the women who live only in the memory of their conquests, circling for ever in the same place. Or die in that memory; for they are not even personifications, they are ghosts, set forever in a changeless reality, in Pope's terrible, pitying lines:

> Still round and round the Ghosts of Beauty glide,
> And haunt the places where their Honour Dy'd. (241-42)

There is a strong feeling in Pope as in Spenser for the flow of life, which it is a dangerous human instinct to check. Spenser's Cymodoche tries to avert danger for her son by creating a static situation, but she succeeds only in so limiting what he can be that he is removed from life, and avoids death only by freeing himself to change. "The terms of mortall state," as Spenser says, are "tickle," shifting and uncertain, and our only course is to go with them. His image of the mutable nature of life is, frequently, water. Colin Clout crosses the destructive element of the sea, the image of death itself, it seems to him, to find that the ship can move safely and lightly on the water and bear him to a world of experience unknown to the simple rustics at home. The ship is strange and magical to the landsman Colin; it comes

> Dauncing upon the waters back to lond,
> As if it scorn'd the daunger of the same;
> Yet had it armes and wings, and tead and taile,
> Glewed togither with some subtile matter,
> Yet had it armes and wings, and head and taile,
> And life to move it selfe upon the water.
> (*Colin Clouts Come Home Againe*, 214-19)

A fragile thing, made by the art of man, as a poem is, but ship and poem can make their own way by moving with the mutable elements. Colin even finds that the sea, so frighteningly unstable compared with "land, our mother," is not without its shepherds. Cynthia has her flocks by sea and by land, and in *The Faerie Queene* Proteus himself, the very image of metamorphosis, is yet called the shepherd of the sea. Water, as myth (and mythographers) insist, is the source of life as well as of death, and there is no more frequent image of the changing course of life, in poetry of all periods, than the river. Water flows often through Spenser's work, from *The Ruines of Time*, where it chanced the poet to be beside the shore " Of silver streaming Thamesis," to the most famous of his refrains, " Sweete Themmes, runne softly, till I end my song." *Prothalamion* is, indeed, shaped by the streaming of the river. As in *The Ruines of Time*, the poet has walked forth to forget his worries

>Along the shoar of silver streaming Themmes, (11)

and the poet's art cooperates with the changing experiences that the river symbolizes to make one of the richest and most perfectly articulated of the shorter poems of Elizabethan England. This and the marriage of the Thames and the Medway in Book IV of *The Faerie Queene*, are the most fully developed of Spenser's uses of the water metaphor, and we shall return to them.

But first it will be useful to revert to that sense of flux and movement which Pope shares with Spenser, and which the river figure expresses so well. The " Epistle to Cobham " is an extended example. Its theme is the inevitability of change within the living human mind, hence in the way we appear to each other; the metaphors which develop the theme are frequently from nature, of which man is felt to be a part: roses and diamonds and trees, scientific observations of the " Peculiar in each leaf and grain " (l. 15), of the experiments of optics, and perhaps most effective of all, the river.

>Our depths who fathoms, or our shallows finds,
>Quick whirls, and shifting eddies, of our minds?
>Life's stream for Observation will not stay,
>It hurries all too fast to mark their way. (29-32)

We are hurried along in the stream of life, but also we help to compose it. Our minds, our actions, contribute endlessly to the movement. There is some clue to understanding one another in the ruling passion, with its tendency to draw the shifting eddies into its mainstream, but even this is a merely external guide which operates for characters moving towards stasis, and the impression left by the poem is one of mutability. " Comets are regular, and Wharton plain " (209) is a syntactically positive statement, but what it presents is a working hypothesis like Newton's or Ptolemy's or the hypotheses which enable us to predict the recurrence of comets. It is less a statement of truth than an idea one can work with in one's relation to people, as in one's relation to comets. As a hypothesis of recurrence in change, indeed, it has something in common with Spenser's " eterne in mutabilitie." Only those who cease to live cease to change.

An Essay on Man too affects us chiefly in its evocation of a changing world in which the sadness of loss is a necessary part of that process of metamorphosis which sustains all life in multiplicity and richness.

> See dying vegetables life sustain,
> See life dissolving vegetate again:
> All forms that perish other forms supply,
> (By turns we catch the vital breath, and die)
> Like bubbles on the sea of Matter born,
> They rise, they break, and to that sea return.   (III, 15-20)

The outline in the first book of creation's range and just gradation, from the green myriads in the peopled grass to " Man's imperial race " and beyond, is a huge exulting celebration of the mutable world which a Renaissance poet like Spenser would have been proud to write, though he might have done so in more mythological terms, as he does in the third book of *The Faerie Queene* and the *Mutabilitie* Cantos. "ALL subsists by elemental strife" (I, 169) would have been taken for granted for centuries before Pope. Subsists by it, but can be destroyed by it if the exquisite balance of the self-sustaining universe is once upset.

> This light and darkness in our chaos join'd,
> What shall divide? The God within the mind.   (II, 203-04)

The world of meaning which the human mind makes in cooperation with its surroundings can be unmade, and the close of *The Dunciad*'s fourth book is a magnificently traditional use of the microcosm-macrocosm figure by which Pope's predecessors had expressed their sense of the precariousness of the balance of productive change and the responsibility of man to see to it that that change did not revert to the lifeless chaos of its beginnings. The dunces in writing, and becoming, nonsense destroy more than themselves. One of the things that the wonderfully unified picture of a dying world seems to say is that in letting our own minds and our arts fall back into primeval night we are letting the whole universe fall, since we deprive it of that meaning it depends on us to give it, to see in it.

In the same way Spenser's beautiful but crass Mutabilitie understands the world quite differently from Nature, and as she remarks, "What we *see* not, who shall us perswade?" (*F.Q.*, VII, vii, 49). Things can be seen by us as meaning or as meaning nothing, as creating or as collapsing perpetually into the dark, as life or death. Mutabilitie presents her pageants of times and seasons as proof that all is under her own purposeless sway, but there is another way of seeing them, as the change without which life could not be, and could not be so absorbingly full. Spenser makes the point finally in his own way, through the appearance of Life and Death as persons, as personifications, we sometimes dismissively say. In fact such figures suggest what Pope suggests in *An Essay on Man* and *The Dunciad* by a different technique. Pope's images hold together man's imperial race and the rest of animate and inanimate creation so that we feel them as interdependent; meaning is meaning for us, the intelligible can only be the humanly intelligible, that which assumes the shape of ourselves because it is our selves which see and respond to it. At best "'Tis but a part we see, and not a whole" (*EM*, I, 6), the part we as humans are equipped to see; but we must use that equipment with all the intelligence we can muster. So with Spenser's life and death, who are two persons, Life and Death, because only man can really look at them. They bring to a close Mutabilitie's case before Nature and the assembled creatures who wait to hear what their own meaning "is," is seen to be. A triumphant close, Mutabilitie thinks, since it ends in the ultimate change of death. Yet the procession turns out, after all, to end in life. "And after all came Life, and lastly Death," yet somehow Death is not there, for though he is "with most grim and griesly visage seene"

> Yet is he nought but parting of the breath;
> Ne ought to see, but like a shade to weene,
> Unbodied, unsoul'd, unheard, unseene. (VII, vii, 46)

The death's head fades into nothingness, and what we see at the pageant's end is Life, young, lusty, "Full of delightfull health and lively joy," vividly present with his golden wings and his wreaths of flowers, briefest of things yet perpetually renewed. It depends on what we see, and what, after all, do we really see but life? To put together the *Mutabilitie* Cantos, *An Essay on Man*, and the fourth book of *The Dunciad* is to see that indeed great satire presupposes a capacity for great celebratory praise.

In *Windsor Forest* the kinds of theme and attitude that I have related to Spenser's practice by way of emphasizing their traditional quality are especially noticeable. Of course *Windsor Forest* derives in part directly from the Georgics, and from such poems as Denham's. But the georgic-type poems of the seventeenth and eighteenth centuries have close connections with those earlier poems which in slightly different ways do essentially the same thing: celebrate the public values of a close knit society, on great estates or in the country as a whole, in terms that subsume the private values of pastoral. *Windsor Forest*, one might roughly say, is a heroic pastoral, a poem that contains the pastoral values of personal serenity and disinterestedness and art, and merges them in, shows them contributing to the public dignity and peace of a great and developing country, and reaching even beyond that country. So Dryden had written in his poem to his cousin John Driden, so Jonson in some of his finest poems, and before them (in a manner closer to Pope's in *Windsor Forest* than to theirs) had Spenser.

Prothalamion is an example. Like *Windsor Forest* it is not only public and national (though also private) it is, even, specifically political. Pope looks to Queen Anne, in whom the native royal line has replaced the foreign conqueror, and he celebrates the Tory peace. Spenser looks to Essex, a controversial figure who, if Elizabeth will make right use of his powers, may make England safe from " forraine harmes " and the name of Elizabeth ring through all the world. Both poems flow with the river, the river of change which is also the Thames, one of the most powerful symbols (as great rivers always are) of the being and potential of the country, and flowing through some of the most idyllically beautiful landscapes towards the places of power; Windsor, Westminster, Essex House. The long intricate stanzas of *Prothalamion*, with their flows and pauses, are almost the river itself, which is to run softly until the poet's song is ended, and into this gentle onward movement are drawn the related figures which have their being as part of it. It is very much a celebratory poem, celebrating more than the double marrriage of

Elizabeth and Katherine Somerset, celebrating rather the Thames itself and all that it means. Yet it begins in frank sullenness and discontent, a disaffection towards "princes court," in fact in the materials of satire. The poet goes out to the river bank in the hope he may feel better among the meadows and variable flowers. And so he does, for the river, like an image of his mind, focuses for him a vision in which the busy public national issues of the court and the calm beauty of the country, heroic and pastoral, become one. The nymphs sing and gather their roses and daisies, and two pure white swans, so exquisitely and intricately related to the pure water that they seem a part of the river with which they move, are at the same time the representatives of one of the great houses of England and in their freshness and beauty and their coming marriage, an image of hope for England, for the future, for the poet himself. The nymph's song asks, as a wedding song should, for endless peace, blessed plenty, and fruitful issue "Which may your foes confound," and this is a hope for England too.

So the swans go quietly down the river of England which approves of them and loves them, and the flow of the poem takes them to "merry London, my most kyndly nurse," the heart of the poet's life as it is of the country's, and to its heroic and public places, the bricky towers of the Temple, home of the Knights Templar, the Knights of St. John, and now of the law, and to the house where the poet's patron, the great Leicester, had lived and where Essex lives now. In the meeting of the swan-brides and Essex, "Great Englands glory and the worlds wide wonder," the Thames has brought the poet from discontent with the public case and his own to a future hope; he goes on with the river. The confounding of foes, the peace and plenty of the marriage verse become the peace and plenty of England, freed from foreign attack by the hero of Cadiz. The Thames and its meadows become a *locus amoenus*, a pastoral center from which good flows through the country so that England in its turn becomes a center of good, the muses singing the peace of Elizabeth through all the world.

Looked at in this way, *Prothalamion*, despite obvious differences, can be felt to be part of the tradition of which *Windsor Forest* is so late and so fine an example. Windsor is an epitome of the rightness of creation, where all things are, but are related and balanced, elemental strife issuing in ordered fecundity, not chaos-like "But as the World, harmoniously confused." Its nature as an emblem of what is right and good in the world and in the country is expressed first in pastoral terms, and the paradisal connections which always haunt pastoral are here explicit:

> The Groves of *Eden*, vanish'd now so long,
> Live in Description, and look green in Song:
> *These*, were my Breast inspir'd wih equal Flame,
> Like them in Beauty, should be like in Fame. (7-10).

The lines look back to Milton and to Marvell's garden poems, and beyond them to Spenser; for Pope, in whose life and work the theme of virtuous country retirement is so dominant, is as well aware as they that the "Rural Scene" is "A Type of Paradise," as he puts it in some lines "On Solitude and Retirement" written for insertion in a poem of Wycherley's on the same subject. Like his Renaissance predecessors, however, he not only remarks upon the paradisal peace and purity of country life, but organizes his Rural Scene in a way that makes it an emblematic center of the world. The garden planted eastward in Eden was, for its brief time, such a center of divine intention and of human responsiveness. Now that it has vanished we make our own approximate Edens, in which the strife and trouble of a lapsed world is drawn, however precariously, into a unity. Thus Marvell's garden is not unaware of civil war, but brings it into relation with a more peaceful, playful strife. Spenser's sweet Thames with its nymphs and flowers and swans comes to include war with Spain and the rival amibitions of Essex and his enemies, and in the Garden of Adonis the very source of life is seen as indeed the "joyous paradize" of Venus, but a paradise in which love and peace are inextricable from strife, joy from sorrow, life itself from death, and the "great mother" herself laments the passing of her brood:

> there is the first seminary
> Of all things that are borne to live and dye,
> According to their kynds . . .
>
> But were it not, that Time their troubler is,
> All that in this delightfull gardin growes
> Should happy bee, and have immortall blis . . .
>
> There is continuall spring, and harvest there
> Continuall . . . (*F. Q.*, III, vi, 30-42)

That the imperfect is our paradise is true of course; a *locus amoenus*, a world center, less inclusive than these would be a false one, like Acrasia's bower. In *Windsor Forest* " tho' all things differ, all agree," and the fruitful fields arise " midst the Desart." The past history of English forests under the first Norman Kings, when nature and its human creatures were alike wasted, is the measure of our imperfection; the replacement of tyranny and war by " hunting, commerce, retirement, poetry, and contemplation." [5] and the balanced and fruitful life for which Windsor is a figure, suggest what we, with nature, can still do. Such inclusiveness seems an urge in Pope. He is as aware as his predecessors of the questions that pastoral poses, but his assumption, natural enough in the eighteenth century, that it is a form remote from our world and concerned wholly with the Golden Age, makes it difficult for him to work out as they did appropriate ways of including what " we at this day really are." [6] Even so, the opening passages of " Spring," " Summer," and "Autumn " already attempt something of what *Windsor Forest* achieves in the georgic kind. The opening address to Trumbull does more than compliment a distinguished older friend, for Trumbull is seen as himself an example of balanced wisdom achieved through a proper relation of private and public.[7] A retired statesman, he has retreated to Windsor, the place of his birth, to

> Enjoy the Glory to be Great no more,
> And carrying with you all the World can boast
> To all the World Illustriously are lost! (" Spring," 8-10).

He is now a pastoral figure tuning his lyre to sing, a nightingale to Pope's thrush, but the cares of the public, the heroic (or the failed heroic) world have not been ignored. Garth is a noted healer, Wycherley " a famous Author of Comedies," a worldly

[5] Ronald Paulson, " Satire, and Poetry, and Pope," *English Satire* (William Andrews Clark Memorial Library, 1972), p. 62.

[6] *A Discourse on Pastoral Poetry, Poems*, Twickenham ed., vol. I, p. 25.

[7] The retired great man is not only an admired figure of Roman history and literature; he appears in Malory's Lancelot or in Spenser's hermit, once a knightly redresser of wrongs but now retired to a sanctified oneness with nature. The tradition extends into *Windsor Forest*, where the " Happy the Man " passage, praising both the man who serves his country and him who retreats " to these Shades," blends the eighteenth century virtuoso with the medieval-Renaissance hermit who, like Spenser's, gathers herbs for healing and " draws the Aromatik Souls of Flow'rs " as well as studying, equally traditionally, astronomy and history.

wit who, like Garth, has made his satiric comment on the follies of the outside world.

Already Windsor, the improbable scene of Pope's competing or lamenting shepherds, is becoming a center of meaning. The series begins

> First in these Fields I try the Sylvan Strains,
> Nor blush to sport on Windsor's blissful Plains:
> Fair Thames flow gently from thy sacred spring . . .
> ("Spring," 1-3)

The first two lines are Virgilian, the third is one of many echoes of Spenser. Pope's addition is to make the Thames a sacred spring, a figure for Helicon. In "Summer" the poet himself, "A Shepherd's Boy" like Spenser/Colin, and no longer Damon or Daphnis, sings "along the silver Thame," playing mournfully the flute which Colin himself bequeathed. In "Autumn" Hylas begs in language reminiscent of the *Pollio* or of Pope's own *Messiah* that an earthly Paradise may arise for Delia in the familiar fields.

> Let opening Roses knotted Oaks adorn,
> And Liquid Amber drop from ev'ry Thorn. (36-37)

The attempt to find ways in which the actual forest, the actual Thames can become a center (a "temple" in Angus Fletcher's word) in pastoral, paradisal and Hesperidean terms is clear enough, but it is *Windsor Forest* that achieves the inclusiveness Pope aims for in a form that unifies (as Spenser's and Milton's poetry had done) the pastoral and the heroic. Pope suggests as much, of course, when in the closing lines, after a soaring prophecy, he echoes the opening lines of "Spring":

> There cease thy Flight, nor with unhallow'd Lays
> Touch the fair Fame of *Albion's* Golden Days.
> The Thoughts of Gods let *Granville's* Verse recite,
> And bring the Scenes of opening Fate to Light.
> My humble Muse, in unambitious strains,
> Paints the green Forests and the flow'ry Plains,
> Where Peace descending bids her Olives spring,
> And scatters Blessings from her Dove-like Wing.
> Ev'n I more sweetly pass my careless Days,
> Pleas'd in the silent Shade with empty Praise;
> Enough for me, that to the list'ning Swains
> First in these Fields I sung the Sylvan Strains. (423-34)

The suggestion of "Spring," where the address to Trumbull links public and private wisdom, the world and the lyre, is here fully developed, and the vision of Windsor as a figure for what public, private, and poetic creativeness can achieve is beautifully integrated. For Windsor's metaphorical power resides only potentially in it, in the forest and the castle. The potential is brought to actuality by the poet who is native to it and co-operates with it to achieve an exalted vision of what could be, the Virgilian and biblical promise of a time when conquest and slavery shall cease. Windsor is "At once the Monarch's and the Muse's Seats" (2), a place made famous by great warrior kings but also by poets, "Majestick Denham," "noble Surrey," and now Pope himself.

Two of the facets of Pope's inclusive picture of Windsor, "as the World, harmoniously confus'd," are of particular interest in relation to the Spenserian tradition. One, of course, is the use of myth or rather the creating of myth. Pope is one of the few poets of his century for whom a myth, like but not identical with the myths of classical poetry, can be the most natural way of expressing poetic reality. Like his predecessors in this way of writing, he can make meaningful myth because he responds to the meanings in the old poems. For the Renaissance the meaning of myth comes chiefly through Ovid, no mere storyteller but an Orphic poet of profound insight into cosmic, human, and poetic nature; and as Professor Paulson has remarked, in the essay already cited, "in *Windsor Forest* the georgic readjustments are posed in terms of metamorphosis. The central one is of Lodona, fleeing from Pan, transformed into a river, her flight into a smooth-flowing, contemplative mirror of nature, as war is transformed into peace."[8] The nymph transformed into a river is one of the forms of Ovidian metamorphosis that the Renaissance found most expressive, and it is a favorite with Spenser, whose vision of nature is deeply Ovidian. The metamorphic river-swans of *Prothalamion* are close to Greek myth, and in *The Faerie Queene* there are several nymphs who become rivers or streams. These stories in Spenser express through the details of their treatment a variety of responses to the nature of things, but one response is common to them all. Through the nymph, one of the closest of the creatures of myth to the human creature and to human powerlessness before the Olympians, and through the

[8] Paulson, p. 62.

merging of the nymph in the water, a merging of the life in animate and inanimate nature makes itself felt. A river is a very living thing in its movement and sound and change, and all rivers, like all people, are different though they share a pervading existence. "A river is particular,"[9] and especially open to our human way of seeing our own values embodied in the things that surround us. When we know a river, we know the nature of its nymph or its god seen in human terms; conversely the story of the nymph puts in words the kind of thing this particular river is for us. The metamorphosis is a way of suggesting the oneness of human and non-human, as with Spenser's own river in *Colin Clouts Come Home Againe*, " Mulla mine " and her lover Bregog; a sad little story, humanly loving and humanly disastrous.

The version of this recurring metamorphic myth that is closest in Spenser to Pope's Lodona story in *Windsor Forest* is the tale of Mulla's sister, Molanna, in the *Mutabilitie* Cantos, where it is part of the description of Arlo hill, once a paradise, a center where Nature herself before the gods and the creatures gave judgment on Mutabilitie. Arlo is Spenser's hill, " the highest head ... Of my old father Mole," as Windsor is Pope's forest; both are homes of poetic vision. Windsor merging with the New Forest as an epitome of the land, was once a desert and a desolation and is now a rich creative place of peace whose influence may yet reach out to embrace the world. " Unbounded *Thames* shall flow for all mankind, and the freed Indians in their native groves shall once more enjoy their pastoral paradise. Arlo reverses the process, but to the same effect. Desert or paradise depends upon human effort and understanding. Both poets are making a myth of the meaning that only man can give to human or to natural life.

In Spenser Arlo once, in the good days of holy Ireland, was the loveliest of places, chosen by Cynthia, or Diana, for her resort. Molanna was one of her nymphs and a river beautiful even now, in her fallen state. Diana used to bathe in Molanna's " sweet streams " until the day when foolish Faunus, a comic Actaeon, bribed the nymph—but in this idyllic world only with queen apples and red cherries—to hide him so that he could watch the naked goddess. He is captured and punished, and Molanna is " whelm'd with stones." It is this betrayal of godhead that leaves

[9] Elizabeth Sewell, *The Human Metaphor* (Notre Dame, 1964), p. 90.

her stream encumbered with boulders, and leaves Arlo under Diana's curse, the haunt of wolves and thieves. It is a story of the waste and misery of the Irish wars, but still more of the human error that has brought about all such wars, a story of the fall of man and the fall of all men as it is seen in the poet's own world. Rivers, hills, forests, can be places of natural goodness, but natural goodness depends also upon the nature of man. We make such places what they are. So Penshurst, Nunappleton, Cooper's Hill, Windsor Forest, are all places in which man has helped nature to fulfill itself, but man can also (and in *Windsor Forest* has in the past done so) prevent or destroy that goodness. Nature in the Renaissance tradition, is a figure for, and is dependent on, the values and achievements of man; and the poet, because of his special capacity has here a special responsibility. It is Spenser who (helped by Dan Geffrey Chaucer) can see the lost paradise in wretched Arlo hill, as Milton was to see the lost Eden in the island of orcs and sea-mews, and as Pope sees the thoughts of gods, the " fair Fame of *Albion's* Golden Days," in Windsor Forest. In Pope's poem too, Diana used once to hunt in the forest as on Arlo, and Lodona was her follower until, straying beyond her bounds, she was pursued by Pan. As she lies melting in tears, she is dissolved into a silver stream, the cold and weeping Loddon whose clarity reflects the forest in terms of balanced art as does the poem, and which flows into the Thames, the English river. Nature, and humanity and art which are also nature, come together in all their potential for good and evil. They can make or destroy an approximation to paradise, and given the nationality of the two poets the paradise is thought of as English, or Irish. So Milton thought, and Blake; for a paradise, to be a practical ideal, must be as " particular " as a river. But England or Ireland become in their turn like Arlo or Windsor, images of what is or could be true for all the world of men.

In the integrated figuring of *Windsor Forest* and *The Faerie Queene* Lodona and Molanna lead to and are another facet of what, for want of a more adequate expression, I called the inclusive metaphor, for they image change, possibility for harmony or destruction, the world eternal in its flowing. Like man they begin as a spring of innocence and move towards castles, courts, cities, to reach the sea. They mirror as one the moving mind of man and the world it moves in. Spenser's most consummate use of rivers is the marriage of Thames and Medway in *The Faerie Queene*. Here Britain, embodied in its rivers, becomes a developing entity with their capacity to move, change, become; and the British rivers are in their turn part of the whole world of the waters in which they and all life began, part of an unceasing creativeness. It is at the marriage celebration that Florimell and Marinell, who exist on the border of the human and the natural, or, rather, are at that point at which nature and human meaning are one, come together, and the whole magnificent scene shows us the natural world existing in relation to us. At the end the poet himself, contemplating the fecundity and the promise, exclaims in delight at the impossibility of recounting the huge abundance of the sea. All the sea-gods are present for the wedding, and the heroes who were their sons, including Neptune's son,

> mightie Albion, father of the bold
> And warlike people which the Britaine Islands hold.
> (*F. Q.*, IV, xi, 15)

Arion is there with his harp, delighting the sea creatures and the sea itself, and reminding us (for he is second only to Orpheus as a figure for the power of poetry) that it is the poet who is enabling us to see Britain as part of this joyous vision. Thames's wedding feast is also the meeting place of the great rivers of the world and of history: Ganges, Euphrates, Indus, Meander, Tiber and, lately known to Europe, the "huge river" of the Amazons, bringing us to the very present of Britain and to its destiny as a sea power. The friend of the sailor Raleigh, through a stanza as practical as it is passionate, exhorts the sons of Albion to follow up Raleigh's Guiana expedition by claiming "that land of gold" which is part of the sea's bounty:

> But this to you, O Britons, most pertaines,
> To whom the right hereof it selfe hath sold;
> The which, for sparing little cost or paines,
> Loose so immortall glory, and so endlesse gaines. (IV, xi, 22)

There follows the procession of the bride and groom, preceded by Arion. Thames's ancient parents come first, Thame, bowed with the learned weight of Oxford, and Ouse or Isis, almost too crooked, weak and blind to make her way at all, and helped by Churne and Charwell. Their son is young and fresh, carrying easily a cornet of Troynovant's castles and towers, like the turreted crown of Cybele, fecund mother of the gods. Around him attend the "chaulky Kenet," the "morish Cole," the "wanton Lee," and he is followed by the many rivers of England and Wales and of Spenser's Ireland, all individual.[10] Then comes the Medway described in terms of water, its "deawy humour" which is the breeding place of life, and its moving glittering surface like water chamelot. This is the quintessential river. The description modulates into that of the sea, beginning and end of rivers, in the form of the fifty daughters of Nereus who rule and guide the waves.

The river list is a popular Renaissance method of ordering material, and it has classical origins; Pope's catalogue, for instance, draws on Ausonius as well as Spenser. Spenser's is a particularly fine example of this convention in its rich centering of meanings, and even the accomplished (and much longer) treatment of his devoted disciple Michael Drayton cannot equal it. Nonetheless Drayton's Fifteenth Song in *Poly-Olbion*, on the marriage of Tame and Isis, and the Seventeenth and Eighteenth Songs, which deal with the lower reaches of the Thames, " the Iles emperiall Flood," contribute certain details to the tradition which Pope was to draw upon. Drayton's poem is in intent a kind of extended version of what is done more concisely by Denham; it treats not only of metaphoric geography but of historical events and great men. As he follows the rivers, Drayton comes to Windsor, the "place of the great English Kings, The Garters royall seate," and later Thames himself recites a further catalogue, that of the kings. An explanatory "Illustration" of the line "And by a fatall dart, in his *New Forest* slaine " (Song XVII, 120) discourses upon the brutality of William I, who was thought to have brought divine vengeance upon his son Rufus

[10] Spenser's rivers, like Drayton's later, express in human form their natures as these may appear to us not only from personal experience but from their appearance on a map. Thus the Ouse is a slow and crooked stream, and at Oxford the river, on maps of the time, does look bowed by the weight of the outlined city. Thames, on maps, is crowned with special elaboration. Such maps help us in responding to Spenser's and Drayton's rivers, and in some degree still to Pope's, though Pope's Thames adopts the more classical urn. See, for example, the maps in Drayton's sumptuously illustrated *Poly-Olbion* of 1613, where the rivers are especially notable, all with their nymph or city-crowned god (*Works*, ed. J. W. Hebel, IV [Oxford, 1961]). The maps are alive with such creatures, including sea-gods like Spenser's. I am reminded by my colleague Professor John B. Vickery that the list of rivers has survived to our own day in *Finnegans Wake* (I, viii. "Anna Livia Plurabelle").

by his destruction of churches " to make dens for wild beasts." [11]

The excellence of Pope's management of the Thames and the other rivers to embrace cosmic, moral, and political themes has been discussed by Earl Wasserman in his essay on *Windsor Forest* in *The Subtler Language,* and it needs no comment here. My intention has been only to treat in more detail the way in which Pope has compressed a complex Renaissance tradition into one comparatively brief poem. The editors of the Twickenham edition point to places in which Pope has drawn on Spenser's descriptive details; it is interesting too to see how deeply Pope seems to have understood Spenser's intention. The Thames, with his supporting rivers and his urn with its picture of Augusta, Spenser's Troynovant, brings out his own poetic meaning more explicitly than Spenser's river, but to the same effect. His prophecy relates his own stream to the historic rivers of the world, to Tiber at the center of the Roman peace, to Hermus with its tides of gold and the rich harvests of Nile. All these and more shall, through the blessings of trade, be subsumed; the Thames shall bring richness, peace, fertility home to Augusta, and more, shall confer its benefits on the world.

Of all rivers, Thames was most meaningful to Pope, whose life interacted so purposefully with his art. A passage from a letter of 1722, to Bathurst, shows how easily he thought in terms of the Spenserian tradition, in which a marriage of rivers can express the potential of the country in trade and navigation for all kinds of national good, and make this itself an image of the goodness of creation.

> How much I wish to be her Guide thro' that enchanted Forest, is not to be exprest: I look upon myself as the Magician appropriated to the place, without whom no mortal can penetrate into the Recesses of those sacred Shades. I could pass whole Days, in only describing to her the future, and as yet visionary Beauties, that are to rise in those Scenes: The Palace that is to be built, the Pavillions that are to glitter, the Colonnades that are to adorn them: Nay more, the meeting of the *Thames* and the *Severn,* which (when the noble Owner has finer Dreams than ordinary) are to be led into each other's Embraces thro' secret Caverns of not above twelve or fifteen Miles, till they rise and openly celebrate their Marriage in the midst of an immense Amphi-

---

[11] *Works,* ed. Hebel, IV, 343.

theatre, which is to be the Admiration of Posterity a hundred Years hence. But till the destin'd time shall arrive that is to manifest these Wonders, Mrs. *Digby* must content herself with seeing what is at present no more than the finest wood in *England*.[12]

Pope, it is true, inherits much from metaphysical poetry. He also inherits and understands the Spenserian line; and when he wishes to write of England as myth it is to that tradition that he turns. Not without significance did he borrow his famous phrase on the moralizing of his song from *The Faerie Queene*.

University of California, Riverside

---

[12] Quoted by Pat Rogers, "Pope and the Social Scene," *Writers and Their Background: Alexander Pope* (London, 1972), p. 113.

THE ROLE OF IMPROVISATION IN *CORINNE*

BY GEORGES POULET

Corinne begins with an anomaly. In this book to be devoted with exceptional brilliance to the deeds and exploits, to the feelings and thoughts of an extraordinary heroine, it is not the latter who opens the narrative, but one who is in the final analysis a secondary character, Oswald, Lord Nelvil. Corinne herself makes her entry rather late, long after the reader has been accustomed to knowing her solely mediated through the feelings she inspires in others. How is this peculiarity to be explained? Why is an individual who is intended to occupy a supereminent place in the narrative not established in it as of the first moment?

The answer to this question is quite clear. *Corinne* is not a typical novel. Like *Jean-Christophe*, it is a work of imagination having as its protagonist an individual of genius. But while Romain Rolland's work presents this individual to the reader from birth onward in the progression of his genius, Mme. de Staël portrays a person who, like Minerva, is already endowed with a mature genius the moment she appears on the scene. Moreover, she describes this person not only in her intimate life, but also and primarily in the actions and words by which her quality of genius outwardly manifests itself. In a sense nothing could have been more difficult to achieve. For how is the reader to be persuaded that the character being presented to him is a genius, if this character's utterances and behavior do not carry with them something authentically brilliant? Therein reside the difficulty of such an enterprise and the reason for which, nearly every time it has been attempted, it has failed. Only a writer of genius can confer genius on a character of his own invention, and even then he can confer only the particular sort of genius that is his own. It is true that this difficulty would hardly have hampered Mme. de Staël. Brilliant herself, nothing prevented her from infusing her character with the genius she herself enjoyed. Thus Corinne is endowed with the very qualities that brought renown to Mme. de Staël. Here ways of sensing, thinking, imagining, speaking are exactly those of her author. Corinne *is* Germaine de Staël: she is so by a profound natural identity, by an exact correspondance between the inner life of her creator and the inner life attributed to her by the latter. But she is so also by the external manifestation as it were of that intellectual brilliance. Corinne offers herself to the eyes of all in the midst of a chorus of ecstatic expressions of admiration. Such was obviously the case for Mme. de Staël herself. Whatever her personal misfortunes and however directly they may have been caused by her own exceptional gifts, there was at least one misfortune in her existence which was spared her, that of going unrecognized. The intensity of her fame rose from the start to equal that of her genius. The same is true for the heroine whom she presents, and in whom she represents herself. In writing *Corinne*, Mme. de Staël not only shows herself in all the radiance of her brilliant personality; she also makes us aware of the extent of the field over which this radiance exerts itself.

Briefly, what she reveals to us in *Corinne* is not only a person of genius; it is the effulgence of the glory that surrounds this person like a halo.

Now to describe an individual in his own glory is not to describe him in his inner life, however exceptional it may be. It is rather to show him from the outside, in the sort of current that his genius sets up around him. Glory is not to be confused with the inward sense of being glorious. It consists in the epiphanic relationship that arises between the eminent individual and a certain public that accords him this eminence as his due. Hence a novel which proposes as its subject a person's glory could hardly be entirely introspective. It must necessarily be oriented toward the external world or at least toward that privileged sector of the external world from which emanates, in response to the spontaneous kindling power of genius, the equally spontaneous reaction of enthusiasm. From its very first pages, *Corinne* is precisely such a novel. First to appear is not the heroine herself, but a character who is marked to become the most attentive witness of her glory, and the one most entranced by her exalting influence: Oswald, Lord Nelvil. The moment the novel begins, he is charged with a function without which the novel would lose greatly in scope. It is through Oswald as intermediary, and through his feelings, that the heroine is to be approached by the reader. His first actions serve no other purpose. They permit us to come into contact with Corinne, not as yet in her actual person, but in the acclaim that rises around her. Only when this phase is completed can Oswald penetrate the inner circle surrounding the heroine. Before seeing and hearing her he must learn of her existence and her talents from hearsay. His knowledge of her must be indirect and peripheral before she can become the object of his admiration and, soon, of his love.

Of crucial importance therefore is the fact that *Corinne* effectively begins only when, in the company of the witness-character, Lord Nelvil, we have covered a rather long itinerary. This itinerary leads from objectivity to subjectivity. Everything in this novel begins by movements of crowds, by shouts of admiration, by cheers, in other words, by the tumult rising up about an individual who is not to be seen but who commands the center of attention. A name resounds, a strain of music is heard, a procession begins to move, a chariot drawn by white horses traverses the streets of Rome. Such are the first indications Mme. de Staël chooses to give us about a heroine who is herself. Before revealing herself in her thoughts and in her emotions, it is her intention to be seen through her most external qualities. As yet invisible she arouses in passing a multitude of admiring reactions. She then shows herself in person, but at a distance: a feminine form clothed in a long draped white tunic, recalling the style of Domenichino's sibyl. This description is designed to present us with the exterior aspect of the subject, the aspect offered to the assembled public. Next takes place the ascent of the Capitol, the ediles' reception, and finally the solemn eulogy of the heroine. Is is not curious that Mme. de Staël, intending to write a great novel within which she would portray herself without reserve in the depths of her genius, begins not by transporting us directly into the interior of that genius, but on the contrary, by placing us far away from herself? The reason is precisely that she desires at first to reveal herself to us in her renown before initiating us into her inner life, source of that renown.

It would thus be difficult to find a beginning better arranged to reveal to us the physical and loudly acclaimed character of an extraordinary being. The visible majesty is brilliantly presented, placed at the heart of a distant perspective as the most wondrous object to be discerned there. But even more brilliant is the consciousness of self to which the author attains by dividing herself in two, in order to place herself on the outside and consider herself as an object worthy of contemplation and admiration. For we must not be deceived by the presence of the witness-character whose function it is to observe the spectacle offered by the homage paid to Corinne. Mme. de Staël presents herself here in the process of contemplating herself. She contemplates herself, not in the habitual manner of a consciousness gazing into its inner depths, but such as she appears to others, even though this perspective is ordinarily withheld from those who are the object of it. Corinne is Mme. de Staël apprehending through contrivance that thing which is exterior to herself, her own personal eminence. Thanks to the particular disposition of her novel, she beholds herself simultaneously as subject and object, in the interiority of her genius, and in the exteriority of her fame.

It is true that this consciousness of oneself as object of admiration is accomplished by Mme. de Staël through the intermediary of Oswald's point of view. But Oswald's gaze blends with the gaze of the throng. Mme. de Staël perceives herself universally as the object of universal esteem. She exists in a sort of collective emotion, a general thrill that concerns her directly. She is the substance of everyone's thought. What is more, this consciousness on the part of others in which her fame is reflected is the very object in which she beholds the accomplishment of her dream. In the guise of Corinne, as in her own person, Mme. de Staël is devoured by the " universal desire to please." Thus the admiration of the crowd finds its echo in a mind rejoicing in the realization of its most ardent wish. I, Corinne, I, Germaine de Staël, obtain the highest consciousness of myself through the image of myself that I communicate to those around me. I display myself and find myself admirable. The relationship existing between me and my circle is thus one of great clarity: it is typically narcissistic. I admire myself in the consciousness of the admiration I arouse and inspire. The world and I commune in the same elevated consciousness of my self.

But the look of the other is not uniquely defined here with a value of universality. It is a particular look as well, that of an individual admirer, on the point of becoming a lover. Oswald as lover differs little from Oswald as simple admirer. To love is to admire more intensely, more totally, the being whom one admires. Likewise, the exalting sensation of being admired finds its complement in the even more exalting awareness of being loved. Various episodes in the narrative furnish ample proof of this. Hence, once the bond between the two lovers has been definitely established, what matters most to Corinne in the moments when she abandons herself completely to the impulse of artistic inspiration, is the sight of Oswald, himself entranced by the rapture that animates her: " How exquisite it was to know that the one she loved was there when she felt that moment of exaltation which only poetry can give."

The most intense pleasure experienced by the artist in the moment when she finds herself lifted to the summit of her genius derives from the conviction that this brilliant manifestation of herself immediately wins the lover's passionately enthusiastic assent, which is coextensive with the sentiment of love. It will be appropriate to determine whether this belief is well-founded or calamitously illusory. For the moment let us concentrate on the fact that the relationship established here concerns two individuals, one of whom acts primarily on the other by the power of speech. Corinne's verbal gifts, like those of Mme. de Staël, require the presence of a listening consciousness that they address by a sort of dedication. Neither Corinne nor Germaine belongs to that group of romantic individuals who live their experience in the depths of forests or on the banks of streams in solitary silence. The Staëlian genius is essentially communicative. Whatever heights it may attain, it always remains within hearing range of an audience. Such genius is thus at one and the same time a marvel of inspiration and a marvel of elocution. Inspired thought instantaneously becomes inspired speech. It does so, not by an inner movement under the impulse of which the romantic poet " takes up his lyre and begins to sing," but rather by an eccentric movement, vocal and social in nature, a movement by which a sublime thought strives to reveal itself to others at the same time and with the same force as it does to the inspired mind in which it springs forth. The form most appropriate to the Staëlian genius is thus the monologue. In many of the writings of Mme. de Staël, and especially in her letters, we can find indications of the extraordinary power she was able to exert on others through spoken language. Hence nothing could be more fitting than to confer on her heroine the distinctive quality that was her own. Corinne is portrayed in the novel as an *improvisatice*, that is, as a person whose function and even whose profession it is to produce an extemporaneous discourse on any and every occasion. Such a discourse implies in the mind of the speaker a certain reciprocity. It is conversation, comprising a part which is spoken, but also a part which is heard. Every discourse thus assumes the existence of interlocutors. It is true that Corinne's speech, like that of Mme. de Staël, often ends up as a simple soliloquy. It runs on in silence, requiring only attention and admiration on the part of others: "One might say," says Corinne on the subject of her art, "that improvisation is like an animated conversation for me. Rather than limit myself to a particular subject, I abandon myself to the impression produced upon me by the mood of my audience." Hence on the one hand, around Corinne, there are those who listen to her, just as on the other, in the center of the circle they form, there is Corinne who speaks to them. But this improvisation carried on by its author in the surrounding silence nonetheless remains a conversation joining participants together. An exchange is produced. There can be no discourse without a consciousness of the interest aroused in others by that discourse. A double exchange is in the process of taking place. The inspired enthusiasm arising in the mind of the artist is communicated to the audience; by a refluent movement it is then carried back to her. Thanks to the participation of others, she takes sustenance from the emotion she engenders.

Thus everything in *Corinne* becomes language. Thought charges itself with emotion, and emotion becomes speech. Speech in turn flows immediately back to the one who produces it. Almost the entire narrative structure of the novel consists in the description of certain major moments when the heroine, either at the Capitol, before the monuments of Rome, or in the presence of the natural beauties of the Gulf of Naples, begins to speak. The difficulty of such a subject resides entirely in the awkwardness of continuously having a single person speak. It becomes literally necessary from time to time to allow her to rest. Whence a series of diversions whose purpose is to take Corinne, her lover, and sometimes her circle of listeners from one end of the peninsula to the other. So that it would not be incorrect to say that the oral novel begins to become a visual novel, since words give way to scenes. But the scenes in *Corinne* are constituted not so much to be viewed as to be spoken or sung about. Their unfailing effect is to arouse the heroine's poetic fervor. She enters into a trance; ideas flood her imagination, and they must necessarily be translated immediately into speech. Thus the underlying reason for which Mme. de Staël leads her heroine from monument to monument, from site to site, is not to transform her into an enlightened *cicerone* of the beauties she reveals; it is rather in every case to place her in the presence of an object worthy of inspiring her with new subjects for talk.

Yet for Mme. de Staël or Corinne, discourse need not always take the form of a series of words. Corinne is not content merely to speak. She also dances, and even performs tragedy. One of the most significant episodes of the novel describes a dance she performs before her admirers, with the aid of a tambourine. "Whenever Corinne danced," writes the author, " she transmitted whatever she was feeling to the hearts of the spectators, as though she had been improvising, playing the lyre, or sketching; all was language for her." Dance for Corinne is simply a new type of improvisation, hence yet another form of language. The same holds true for dramatic art. At one point in the novel Corinne plays the part of Shakespeare's Juliet. Throughout the performance she transmits to Oswald, looking on, those ideas and emotions that correspond to their own personal story. Her every gesture, intonation, and look appeals to him, speaks to him: " The tone of voice, the glance, and slightest movements of an actor truly moved, truly inspired," remarks Mme. de Staël, " are a continual unveiling of the human heart."

It is immediately obvious that such a manner of acting (and communicating) is diametrically opposed to Diderot's paradox of the actor. Mme. de Staël in no way seeks to remain immune to the emotional disquiet that seizes her in the course of a dramatic portrayal. She does not, for the sake of a better performance, endeavor to maintain a detached calm. On the contrary, the intensity of her emotions seems to have the immediate effect of engendering within her an infinity of ideas and feelings that otherwise would never have come to light. Describing Corinne's state of mind at Cape Miseno, about to begin the most celebrated of her improvisations, Mme. de Staël makes the following observation: " If this talent were to be forever lost, she wanted its last light, before flickering out, to shine for the one she loved. This desire brought her to discover in the very turbulence of her soul, the inspiration she had been seeking."

Inspiration and its effect, the improvised discourse, are caused by a deep-seated agitation of the subject's very being. It is as if, with Mme. de Staël as with her heroine, at certain privileged moments a rush of ardent emotion overwhelms the person, simultaneously initiating within an impulse tending toward language. There are doubtless in both cases certain detectable elements that persist or recur, thus maintaining a certain continuity. Corinne is in love with Oswald, and finds a way at every new occasion to express her love once more. But this love is itself not continuous. It corresponds neither to a permanent elevation of thought, nor to a constant sublimity of mood. The type of love in question here is an agitation, that is, an intermittent and spasmodic movement. In other words, it is an emotion that depends entirely on the particular affective tonality experienced by the subject in the momentary present. In love Corinne goes from exhilaration to exhilaration, much as she goes from scene to scene and from improvisation to improvisation. Within the domain of love as within that of admiration, she lives from instant to instant. Nothing is lasting in a purely affective existence, just as nothing is durable in a constantly improvised language. Thought flies from summit to summit, and the heart partakes of successive moments of happiness that are neither anticipated nor, once superseded, afterwards missed.

"As her disposition lacked considerably in foresight," Mme. de Staël remarks of Corinne, " she was happy with the present as it was, although it was impossible for her to know what was to follow." In a later text she says similarly, " She was more passionate than prudent, dominated by the present but remaining unconcerned about the future."

Such then is the way time tends to assert itself in *Corinne* In contrast to *Adolphe*, in which the immediacy of the love experience is so to speak consumed once and forever, and reduced to cinders almost at the instant it blossoms, such experience in *Corinne* organizes itself in the form of an indefinitely repeated revitalization of the momentary present. "At once apathetic and impassioned, she fancied it sufficient to gain time ..." The phrase sums up Corinne's attitude toward love. Like poetic exhilaration, like the billowing of fame, like the springing forth of inspiration, and finally like the movement of language itself, love is a passion experienced from day to day, from hour to hour, and even from moment to moment. Thus, no more with Corinne than with Mme. de Staël, is it possible to find traces of an erosion of sentiment. Passion never slows its tempo. Like the phoenix it always emerges intact and as ardent as before. Corinne and Mme. de Staël are sustained by an emotion that at every successive moment finds a way to rekindle itself with undiminished vigor.

But while such is the case for Mme. de Staël and her heroine, while passion for the one as for the other is an affective movement constantly renewed without loss, the same does not hold for the object of that passion, whether his name be Oswald or Benjamin Constant. For the author of *Corinne* as for the central character, love, according to its ideal development, strives to unfold itself in the form of a *circulus amorosus*. The lover exerts ever anew his heady influence on the loved one, who in turn repays his intoxication by transforming it into grateful adoration. To the ardor of the seductress corresponds the ardor of the seduced. One engenders the other. Love becomes then a special type of relationship, in which one of the two lovers perpetually affirms himself as the causal principle of the emotion he arouses in the other. If, in the novel, there were only the heroine plus an obeying receptive principle, the emotional flux would never be in danger of waning. It is in the assurance of such a premise with Corinne acting and Oswald merely submitting, that nearly the entire first half of the novel consists in a lyrical effusion incessantly renewing itself, in which the heroine, in the capacity of creative power, holds a preponderant role, and the hero—if Oswald can be so called—a position on the contrary extremely diminished.

This situation is utterly changed in the second half of the novel. There, Oswald's pure passitivity transforms itself into a contrary and even hostile disposition. Whence, by a necessary consequence the crumbling of the lyrical novel and the rupture of the enchanted circle inside which the woman thought to have imprisoned the man. The novel dominated by Corinne, buoyed by poetic enthusiasm, transported by passionate love, and radiant with personal glory gives way to the novel defined by the character of Oswald, weary of the overshadowing eminence of the other, paralyzed by his own irresolution, and growing gradually colder: "Sentiment is weakened by the very dominion encroached on it, and the power of tears too often exercised cools the imagination." The manner in which the novel changes is hence clearly visible. Having at first been the perpetual conquest of the other by all the marvellous powers of genius, this narrative now presents the discovery by the seductress of the increasing ineffectiveness of her charms. Rather than offering the perspective of mutual comprehension, it now demonstrates the impossibility henceforward of true communication. The magic of poetic exaltation is lost in the slackening of its feverish pitch; as the temperature cools, the radiant energy of public approbation can no longer be converted into amorous steam.

Mme. de Staël wrote with moving expressive force this second "novel," so completely opposed to the first. She of course reproduced in it her own personal experience, as she had done not only in *Delphine*, another novel, but also, in a more abstract and generalized fashion, in her theoretical work entitled *On the Influence of Passion*. Like *Adolphe*, *Corinne* is divided into two parts differing radically from each other; one being the novel of passion, the other of passion lost. But while *Adolphe* describes this rupture from the point of view of the individual who no longer loves and endeavors to break away, *Corinne* describes it in the perspective of the one who, while continuing to love, finds herself forsaken. Ardor yields to anguish and longing. Formerly sustained in the momentary present by her enthusiasm, the subject can now only turn toward a past all the more nostalgically cherished as it is beyond reach. Rather than remaining a living presence, love becomes the continually renewed sensation of an absence. The creative force that in happy moments spawned such spiritual wealth now, by an intolerable quickening of mental activity, engenders a swarm of torturing notions, each one of which inflicts its wound.

Thus the novel of the rapturous subject is transformed into that of the self-rending subject. But it nonetheless remains the novel of the exceptional individual, the person of genius. The incessantly renascent agony which tortures Corinne is not that of an ordinary being, but that of a conscience who while suffering persists in rising above the ordinary. "When a person of genius," writes Mme. de Staël, "is endowed with true sensibility, his sorrows are multiplied by his very faculties." It is this proliferation of pain that we witness in the second half and *dénouement* of *Corinne*. Just as the first half contains a series of joyous affirmations, the second is filled with cries of suffering. The tonality of the work has certainly changed, but not the form in which it is expressed. Corinne is characterized from the beginning by her possession of an essential gift, that of improvisation. Improvisation for her is an inexhaustible source of fertile and resplendent thought, of intense and marvellously contagious emotion. Misfortune—itself requiring invention and language—cannot annihilate this talent for improvisation. In an atmosphere of fever and delirium, the entire second half of *Corinne* consists in the expression of an endlessly repeated cry of pain, "ultimately monotonous," remarks Mme. de Staël, "like that of birds in the night."

(Translated by Kevin Clark and Richard Macksey)

University of Nice

THE PROBLEM OF *AMELIA*: HUME, BARROW, AND THE CONVERSION OF CAPTAIN BOOTH

BY MARTIN C. BATTESTIN

> ... it is our business to discharge the part of a faithful historian, and to describe human nature as it is, not as we would like it to be.
>
> Fielding in *Amelia*

Most readers agree that *Amelia* (1751), though his " favourite Child," [1] represents a decline in Fielding's powers as a novelist. In less than three years' time the feast of life that he had celebrated in *Tom Jones* (1749) appears to have staled for him. His tone has become darker, more monitory, in keeping with his subject—no longer the follies of men, but their errors and cupidities and the doubtful efficacy of those institutions, the law and the church, which were meant to preserve the social order. His narrator, whose genial, controlling presence in *Tom Jones* attests to the power of art to dispel confusion, less frequently makes his appearance upon the stage, and his voice, wavering between anger and a maudlin sentimentality, no longer inspires confidence.

The qualities that make *Amelia* Fielding's most disconcerting novel, however, are those as well that make it, intellectually, his most interesting and ambitious work, the product of his maturest thinking about human nature and about the grounds of order in society. As the opening chapters declare, from one point of view the institutions of society are Fielding's principal subject—from " the state of matrimony," [2] that smallest unit of the polity, to the English " constitution " itself, by which he meant both the laws and the essential character and temper of

---

[1] *The Covent-Garden Journal* (25 January 1752).

[2] *Amelia*, ed. George Saintsbury, 2 vols. (London and New York: Everyman's Library, 1950), I.i; I, 3. Quotations from *Amelia* will be from this accessible reprint; citations will be by Book and Chapter and by volume and page. On the theme of marriage in the novel, see A. R. Towers, "*Amelia* and the State of Matrimony," *RES*, N.S., 5 (1954), 144-57.

the nation.[3] Reinforcing our sense of *Amelia* as a social document to be distinguished from Fielding's previous comic "biographies" is the narrator's remarkable strategy of withholding the identity of his hero until the third chapter. The story of Captain Booth and his wife is framed by episodes whose function it is, through negative and positive examples, to establish the importance of laws and their proper execution to the health of the body politic: Justice Thrasher, ignorant and venal, sounds this theme, giving way in the closing scenes of the novel to another magistrate, very much resembling Fielding himself, who, as the mob surges through the streets threatening to burst the dykes of civilization, distributes justice and restores innocence to its rightful estate. Cooperating in this work of redemption, moreover, is another agent of social order, the good priest Dr. Harrison, who serves as Fielding's spokesman throughout. Booth, infidel and debtor, is at a stroke released from prison and from his subtler bondage to error, and to him Dr. Harrison asserts the Christian faith in Order which Fielding's happy endings implicitly affirm: "Providence hath done you the justice at last which it will, one day or other, render to all men" (XII.vii; II, 299).

For the better part of twelve books *Amelia* is the record of corruption, oppression, and disorder both in society at large and in the private sphere, but, like Booth's "dream" (XII.viii; II, 305), the novel ends with the sudden transition of its principal characters from misery to joy—a comic apocalypse affirming that fiction is the mirror of a higher reality than life's tragic muddle. As Dr. Harrison understands, the justice done to Booth and Amelia is a paradigm of that which will ultimately be meted out to all, transforming the nightmare of actuality into perfection and vindicating God's ways to man. What has seemed "real" to our limited vision will one day prove an illusion. This paradox is one province of the novelist's art as Fielding conceived it, and is playfully rendered in the penultimate chapter when Dr. Harrison substantiates Booth's "dream" of redemption by reading aloud from a newspaper, that humblest amanuensis of daily history.

Though this conception of the ways in which art imitates reality informs Fielding's earlier fiction, it has a special relevance

---

[3] For these two senses of the word, see Fielding's *An Enquiry into the Causes of the late Increase of Robbers* (1751), Preface.

to the problem of his final novel, for *Amelia* at the profoundest level was written to substantiate a dream—no less, indeed, than the Christian humanist vision on which the meaning and coherence of Fielding's world was founded, and which, as he wrote, was being challenged by a new scepticism in religious matters and a new empiricism in morality, whose formidable champion was David Hume. To Hume, who more than any other writer of the century precipitated History's own sudden transition from traditional to Modern conceptions of reality, that vision *was* a dream. If so, as one of his critics prophetically observed, " It is a delusion so essential to the interests of society, that it should be preserved by the strictest sanctity, from the least violation, as a sacred Palladium upon which the fate of our world depends." [4] As I mean to show in the course of the present essay, this crisis of belief may be seen to define the problem of *Amelia,* reflected not only in the hero's hard progress from doubt to faith, but in Fielding's strange new conception of his art.

If, as I have argued elsewhere,[5] the design and narrative movement of *Tom Jones* gave the consummate expression to the Augustan faith in Order, whether in the universe at large or in the moral life, *Amelia* is the troubled adumbration of an age less certain of the traditional grounds on which that faith was founded. With respect to Fielding's own intellectual development, it is as if the year 1750 marked precisely that " great caesura " between the old world and the new which Leo Spitzer saw occurring more gradually in the middle decades of the century.[6] The problem of *Amelia* which critics have noted and variously explained— in particular, the apparent urgency of its Christian didacticism and that extraordinary emphasis throughout the novel on sentiment and the passions—may be better accounted for, I believe, not in the conventional ways: not, for example, as the regrettable effect of a sudden access of piety on Fielding's part, or as the crotchet of a man weary of the spectacle of human depravity parading before the bench at Bow Street, or even as the consequence of the novelist's attempt to bend his talents to the uncongenial mode of his rival, Richardson. The hypothesis I wish

---

[4] James Balfour, *A Delineation of the Nature and Obligations of Morality* (Edinburgh, 1753), p. 172.

[5] See *The Providence of Wit: Aspects of Form in Augustan Literature and the Arts* (Oxford, 1974), Chs. v-vi.

[6] *Classical and Christian Ideas of World Harmony* (Baltimore, 1963), p. 76.

instead to propose is that the awkwardness one senses in reading *Amelia* derives from an intellectual drama unfolding in the novel—a drama residing in Fielding's anxious response to a new and particularly disturbing species of philosophical scepticism whose cogency, in part, he seems to have felt. To this philosophy, whose essential tenets were the denial of Providence and of the liberty of moral agents and whose eloquence and logical clarity made it all the more likely to contaminate the minds of the faithful, Fielding opposed the traditional arguments of Christian humanism.

In *Amelia* this drama is enacted in the story of Fielding's hero, achieving a tenuous and unconvincing resolution in Booth's conversion from the errors of atheism and fatalism. Its true antagonists, however, are the opposing ideologies of Fielding's latitudinarian Christianity—the Christianity, in particular, of his " favourite " divine, Isaac Barrow [7]—and the scepticism of David Hume. Barrow's importance to the spiritual health of Amelia and Booth is plain enough from the narrative: besides the histories of Bishop Burnet and a few English plays and poems, Barrow's works are the only reading Fielding allows his heroine (VI.vii; I, 288); and it through perusing Barrow's sermons on the Apostles' Creed that Booth is rescued from infidelity (XII.v; II, 287). Indeed, the probable influence of Barrow has been traced in *Joseph Andrews* (1742) and *Tom Jones*,[8] and, closer still to *Amelia*, it is especially notable in *The Covent-Garden Journal* (1752), where Fielding alludes to this famous divine in six of his leaders and quotes liberally from his sermons.[9] On the other hand, the case for Hume's influence on *Amelia* is obscure and will require, in due course, a thorough review of the evidence.

It will first be necessary to consider in detail the nature of the philosophic problem to which Fielding addressed himself in *Amelia* and to mark the curious ambivalency of his attitude toward the solution he proposes, vacillating between the confident affirmation of conventional Christian stoic doctrine, as in the

---

[7] *The Covent-Garden Journal* (11 April 1752), ed. Gerard E. Jensen (New Haven, 1915), I, 305.

[8] See Battestin, *The Moral Basis of Fielding's Art: A Study of "Joseph Andrews"* (Middletown, Conn., 1959), pp. 30-39 and *passim*; and *The History of Tom Jones, a Foundling*, edd. Battestin and Fredson Bowers (Oxford and Middletown, Conn., 1974), pp. 95 n, 96 n, 566-67 n.

[9] See *The Covent-Garden Journal* for 14 January, 24 March, 11 April, 16 May, 2 June, and 4 November 1752.

opening chapter, and the contradictory assertion in the narrative itself of a sensationalist psychology scarcely distinguishable from the "fatalism" he means to repudiate. We may begin at the beginning, with Fielding's declaration in the "exordium" that Fortune is an "imaginary being" (I, 3), that our happiness or misery is a function of how well we have mastered "the ART OF LIFE" (I, 4), learning to control our passions through the exercise of prudence and the will.[10] These ideas will be familiar enough to readers of *Tom Jones*: there Fielding's good-natured, impetuous hero had come to maturity as a moral agent through the hard-earned acquisition of prudence, learning to discipline his passions and to accept responsibility for the calamities that have befallen him. As the prison doors open which had symbolized Jones's captivity to error, virtue is seen to require not only the benevolent energies of the heart, but the rational exercise of the judgment and the will; and what Jones and the reader have mistaken for the effects of blind Fortune are revealed as the wise dispositions of Providence. This theme seems again to be the burden of Fielding's final novel:

> To speak a bold truth, I am, after much mature deliberation, inclined to suspect that the public voice hath, in all ages, done much injustice to Fortune, and hath convicted her of many facts in which she had not the least concern. I question much whether we may not, by natural means, account for the success of knaves, the calamities of fools, with all the miseries in which men of sense sometimes involve themselves, by quitting the directions of Prudence, and following the blind guidance of a predominant passion; in short, for all the ordinary phenomena which are imputed to Fortune; whom, perhaps, men accuse with no less absurdity in life, than a bad player complains of ill luck at the game of chess. (I, 3)

The narrator enforces the point by applying to the life of man, the microcosm, an analogy used by philosophers and divines alike to discredit the epicurean notion that the world is the product of chance, not of art: "Life," he observes, "may as properly be called an art as any other; and the great incidents in it are no more to be considered as mere accidents than the several members of a fine statue or a noble poem" (I, 4).

These reflections are appropriate enough to the story of the

---

[10] For an authoritative discussion of these themes, see D. S. Thomas, "Fortune and the Passions in Fielding's *Amelia*," *MLR*, 60 (1965), 176-87.

philosophical Captain Booth, who, impatient in adversity, holds with Epicurus that chance, not Providence, governs circumstance, and who believes with Hume that the charcters and actions of men are determined by passions which reason is powerless to control. The doctrine Fielding opposes to these errors is the conventional wisdom of Christian stoicism, deriving ultimately from Cicero and Seneca, for whom virtue was the *ars vivendi*.[11] Within this tradition, for example, Barrow anticipates Fielding's theme in the "exordium," denying the existence of Fortune, rebuking those who abandon themselves to passion, and commending the stoic view that virtue is an art to be acquired only by opposing reason to our natural impulses and inclinations:

> We are apt [writes Barrow], when any thing falleth out unpleasant to us, to exclaim against fortune, and to accuse our stars; or to inveigh against the second causes which immediately offend us, ascribing all to their influence; which proceeding in us doth argue in us a *Heathenish* ignorance and infidelity, or at least much inconsiderateness and impotency of mind; that our judgment is blinded and clouded, or perverted and seduced by ill passions; for that in truth there is not in the world any occurrence meerly fortuitous, or fatal (all being guided and wielded by the powerful hand of the All-wise and Almighty God) . . . .[12]
>
> . . . .
>
> What *Seneca* saith in general of virtue (*Nature giveth no virtue; it is an art to become good*) is most true of this virtue [i. e. contentment]; it is an art, with which we are not born, no more than with any other art or science; the which, as other arts, cannot be acquired without studious application of mind, and industrious exercise: No art indeed requireth more hard study and pain toward the acquiry of it . . . We have no great capacity, no towardly disposition to learn it; we must, in doing it, deny our carnal sense, we must settle our wild fancy, and suppress fond conceits; we must bend our stiff and stubborn inclinations; we must repress and restrain wanton desires; we must allay and still tumultuous passions; we must cross our humour and curb our temper; which to do is a hard chapter to learn. . . .[13]

[11] See Cicero, *De Finibus*, V.vi.16; and Seneca, *Epistulae Morales*, XC.27, 44, quoted below by Barrow: "Non enim dat natura virtutem; ars est bonum fieri."

[12] Sermon V, "Of Contentment," in *Works*, 5th ed. (1741), III, 38. A copy of this edition was in Fielding's library: see item 452 of the Catalogue, reprinted as an Appendix in Ethel Margaret Thornbury, *Henry Fielding's Theory of the Comic Prose Epic*, University of Wisconsin Studies in Language and Literature, No. 30 (Madison, 1931).

[13] Sermon VI, "Of Contentment," *ibid.*, III, 46.

These same assumptions, furthermore, later inform Hume's characterization of the Stoic, classical exemplar of the rationalist tradition which his own passional psychology was designed to discredit. For the Stoic, Hume writes, "the Man of Virtue" is he "who governs his Appetites, subdues his Passions, and has learn'd, from Reason, to set a just Value on every Pursuit and Enjoyment."

> For is there an Art and Apprenticeship requisite for every other Attainment? And is there no Art of Life, no Rule, no Precepts to direct us in this principal Concern? Can no particular Pleasure be attain'd without Skill; and can the whole be regulated without Reflection or Intelligence, by the blind Guidance of Appetite and Instinct? [14]

Like the good man of Barrow or Fielding, Hume's Stoic despises Fortune, "that unstable Deity," and, secure in his virtue, withdraws from her "Dominion" (p. 209). Appropriately for our present purpose, Hume seems deliberately to invite the antithesis between this philosophy and his own that Fielding develops in *Amelia*; for in *Essays Moral and Political* (1741-42) the character of the Stoic stands in opposition to that of the Sceptic, the latter comprising what Professor Mossner calls "a popular statement" of Hume's own philosophical principles.[15] For Hume's Sceptic, as for Captain Booth before his conversion, character is determined by the passions and temperament, which "cannot be forced or constrained by the utmost Art and Industry," and "Human Life is more govern'd by Fortune than by Reason ..." [16]

Having in his opening remarks defined his subject generally in the terms of Christian stoicism, Fielding withholds the precise problem he means to analyze until Chapter III, whose title, "Containing the inside of a prison," points as well to the controlling metaphor of the novel, the hero's crippling spiritual bondage to a false philosophy. As defined in Booth's encounter with the gambling philosopher Robinson, Fielding's specific targets are the correlative errors of infidelity and fatalism: on the one hand, that particular species of atheism which, while acknowledging the existence of a Deity or First Cause, denies the supervision of Providence in human affairs; on the other

---

[14] From Essay XIX, "The Stoic," in Hume's *Essays Moral and Political*, 3rd ed. (1748), p. 206. References to this work will be abbreviated, *Essays*.

[15] Ernest Campbell Mossner, *The Life of David Hume* (Oxford, 1970), p. 141.

[16] Essay XXI, "The Sceptic," in *Essays*, pp. 238, 245.

hand, the doctrines of necessity in moral actions. Two distinct versions of these positions are under inspection, however—one represented by Robinson; the other, to be developed at length in the novel, represented by Booth. It is essential to distinguish between them, not only because it is Booth's error that Fielding regarded as particularly seductive, and therefore more likely to infect society, but because it is the distinctive content of Booth's philosophy that, I believe, demonstrates Hume's influence upon *Amelia*.

Robinson, Booth's fellow prisoner and free-thinker, is a fatalist who takes comfort in the belief that, since all things are irresistibly determined by the mechanical concatenation of cause and effect, men cannot be held responsible for their actions. By this view even the Deity himself is powerless to control the universal machinery he has set in motion. Accordingly, Robinson encourages Booth to bear his misfortunes with indifference:

> ". . . for what is, is; and what must be, must be. The knowledge of this, which, simple as it apears, is in truth the height of all philosophy, renders a wise man superior to every evil which can befal him. I hope, sir, no very dreadful accident is the cause of your coming hither; but, whatever it was, you may be assured it could not be otherwise; for all things happen by inevitable fatality; and a man can no more resist the impulse of fate than a wheelbarrow can the force of its driver." (I, 13-14)

This gentleman, Fielding remarks, " was what they call a free-thinker; that is to say, a deist, or, perhaps, an atheist; for, though he did not absolutely deny the existence of a God, yet he entirely denied his providence. A doctrine which, if it is not downright atheism, hath a direct tendency towards it; and, as Dr. Clarke observes, may soon be driven into it " (I, 14). As A. R. Towers has pointed out,[17] Fielding is here most probably recalling the first of Samuel Clarke's categories of deism as defined in the Boyle lectures for 1705.[18]

---

[17] " Fielding and Dr. Samuel Clarke," *MLN*, 70 (1955), 257-60.
[18] Cf. Clarke's *Discourse concerning the Unchangeable Obligations of Natural Religion* (1706): " Some Men would be thought to be *Deists*, because they pretend to believe the existence of an Eternal, Infinite, Independent, Intelligent Being; and, to avoid the name of Epicurean Atheists, teach also that this Supreme Being made the World: Though at the same time they agree with the Epicureans in this, that they fancy God does *not at all concern* himself in the *government* of the World, nor has any regard to, or care of, what is done therein. But, if we examin things duly, this Opinion must unavoidably terminate in *absolute Atheism* " (p. 19; cf. also pp. 20-24).

For those of Fielding's readers who were acquainted with the polemical divinity of the first three decades of the century, moreover, the allusion to Clarke would instantly have supplied the context and sources of Robinson's philosophy. Though the doctrine of fatalism originated in antiquity and was opposed by, among others, Cicero in *De Fata* and Boethius in the *Consolation*, it was Clarke who, among Fielding's contemporaries, made the extirpation of this dangerous philosophy a special cause. In the Boyle lectures for 1704 he identified it specifically with the necessitarianism of Hobbes and, most especially, of Spinoza, " the most celebrated Patron of Atheism in our Time," [19] whose main purpose was " to make us believe that there is no such Thing as *Power* or *Liberty* in the Universe, but that every particular thing in the World is by an Absolute Necessity just what it is, and could not possibly have been in any respect otherwise . . ." [20] In 1716 Clarke resumed his refutation of this doctrine in an epistolary dispute with Leibniz.[21] Perhaps more relevant to Fielding's characterization of Robinson, the " freethinker," however, is Clarke's quarrel with the deist Anthony Collins over this same issue. Collins, whose *Discourse of Free-Thinking* (1713) gave prominence to the " sect " of which Robinson is a member, published in 1717 a defense of the necessitarian position to which Clarke replied in the same year, concluding with an appeal to his adversary to heed the inevitable debilitating consequences of such a doctrine to the moral order:

> . . . according to This Supposition, there is nothing *intrinsically good* or *evil*, there is nothing *personally just* or *unjust*, there is no *Behaviour of rational Creatures* in any degree *acceptable* or *unacceptable* to God Almighty. Consider the Consequences of This . . . *Religion* there can be None, without a *Moral Difference of Things*: A *moral Difference of things there cannot be*, where there is no place for *Action:* And *Action* there can be none, without *Liberty*.[22]

[19] *A Demonstration of the Being and Attributes of God*, 2nd ed. (1706), p. 41.

[20] *Ibid.*, pp. 78-79. Clarke's attack on the fatalism of Hobbes and Spinoza had been anticipated by another of the Boyle lecturers, John Harris: see *A Refutation of the Atheistical Notion of Fate, or Absolute Necessity* (1698).

[21] See *Correspondance Leibniz-Clarke*, ed. André Robinet (Paris, 1957).

[22] From Clarke's reply to Collins, *Remarks upon a Book, entituled, A Philosophical Enquiry concerning Human Liberty* (1717), pp. 44-45. Though it is unlikely that Fielding wished to associate Robinson's version of fatalism with any one philosopher, it is worth noting that during the early 1730's, the period in which *Amelia* is set, Collins, having waited for Clarke to die, again drew public attention to his doctrine

As with Clarke, we may be sure, Fielding's interest in the doctrine of fatalism was owing to a fear of the destructive consequences for religion and morality should the arguments of Collins and his kind prevail—consequences dramatically rendered in the character and inglorious demise of Robinson, who, after a temporary reformation, reverts to "the dark paths of vice" and is hanged for taking a purse on the highway (XII.ix; II, 310-11).

Though equally a species of infidelity and moral necessitarianism, Booth's errors are fundamentally different from Robinson's, and, with respect to religion, as Fielding is careful to assure us, they are the effects of ignorance and misunderstanding, corrigible faults, rather than of a perverse inclination to injure the established order. Booth, we are told, "was in his heart an extreme well-wisher to religion (for he was an honest man), yet his notions of it were very slight and uncertain" (I, 14). His experience of the world's all too obvious inequities has "led him, who (though a good classical scholar) was not deeply learned in religious matters, into a disadvantageous opinion of Providence" (I, 14). Like Claudian, whom Fielding quotes in order to define the specific problem he wishes to explore, Booth finds himself spiritually in a "wavering condition," a sceptic whose "way of thinking, or rather of doubting," is prompted by the mistaken apprehension that mere chance, not a just and kindly design, governs human affairs. By relying on experience alone as a guide in religious matters, Booth has fallen, in other words, even against his will,[23] into the error of Epicurus. Since it is a clue to Booth's spiritual condition, we may recall the entire passage from Claudian's *In Rufinum* to which Fielding alludes:

> My mind has often wavered between two opinions: have the gods a care for the world or is there no ruler therein and do mortal things drift as dubious chance dictates? For when I investigated the laws and the ordinances of heaven and observed

by publishing *A Dissertation on Liberty and Necessity . . . With Some Remarks on the late Reverend Dr. Clarke's Reasoning on this Point* (1729). He was answered by John Jackson (*A Defense of Human Liberty*, 2nd ed. 1730), by Phillips Gretton (*Remarks upon Two Pamphlets Written by the late A. C. Esq.; concerning Human Liberty and Necessity*, 1730), and by George Berkeley (*Alciphron*, 1732).

[23] It is important to note that in quoting from the Delphin edition of Claudian (Paris, 1677), his probable text, Fielding departs from the original by typographically emphasizing the phrase "non sponte," as if to stress the fact that Booth is only reluctantly a disbeliever. A copy of the 1677 Delphin edition was in Fielding's library, No. 411 in the Catalogue.

the sea's appointed limits, the year's fixed cycle and the alternation of light and darkness, then methought everything was ordained according to the direction of a God . . . But when I saw the impenetrable mist which surrounds human affairs, the wicked happy and long prosperous and the good discomforted, then in turn my belief in God was weakened and failed, and even against mine own will I embraced the tenets of that other philosophy [epicureanism] which teaches that atoms drift in purposeless motion and that new forms throughout the vast void are shaped by chance and not design—that philosophy which believes in God in an ambiguous sense, or holds that there be no gods, or that they are careless of our doings.[24]

Professor Rader has helpfully pointed out that Fielding's application of Claudian in this context may have been prompted by Ralph Cudworth,[25] who had used this same passage to illustrate the atheist's objection to the idea of Providence:

If the World were made by any Deity, then it would be governed by a *Providence*, and if there were any *Providence*, it must appear in Humane Affairs. But here it is plain, that all is *Tohu* and *Bohu, Chaos* and *Confusion:* Things happening alike to all, to the Wise and Foolish, Religious and Impious, Virtuous and Vicious. . . . From whence it is concluded, that all things float up and down, as they are agitated and driven by the Tumbling Billows of Careless Fortune and Chance.[26]

Though Cudworth probably inspired Fielding's use of Claudian,[27] the identification of this erroneous opinion of Providence as a principal cause of infidelity is, of course, at least as old as Boethius and it was a commonplace among the divines whom Fielding read—to be found, for example, in Barrow, South, Tillotson, and James Foster, most of whom associate the doctrine specifically with epicureanism.[28] Barrow, especially, is worth quoting on this

---

[24] *In Rufinum*, trans. Maurice Platnauer (Loeb Classical Library, 1922), I. 1-19.
[25] See " Ralph Cudworth and Fielding's *Amelia*," *MLN*, 71 (1956), 336-38.
[26] *The True Intellectual System of the Universe* (1678), I.ii.17; p. 79. To illustrate this argument Cudworth quotes from Claudian on the following page. A copy of this edition of Cudworth was in Fielding's library, No. 463 in the Catalogue.
[27] Tillotson, however, invokes Claudian in the same context, quoting a different passage from *In Rufinum*: see Sermon CXL, " The justice of God in the distribution of rewards and punishments," in *Sermons* (1757), VIII, 196-97.
[28] See, for instance, Barrow's Sermon XXXII, " The Reasonableness and Equity of a Future Judgment," quoted below; South's Sermon XXXII, " The fool hath said in his heart, There is no God," in *Sermons Preached upon Several Occasions* (Oxford, 1823), VI, 169; Tillotson, Sermon CXL, *Sermons*, VIII, 195-97; and Foster, Sermon VI, " Of the abuses of free-thinking," in *Sermons*, 5th ed. (1755), I, 135-39 (an earlier edition of Foster's *Sermons* was in Fielding's library, No. 331 in the Catalogue).

point, since his remarks occur in the series of sermons on the Apostles' Creed that eventually disabuse Booth of his errors and bring about his conversion: the observation that justice seldom prevails in this world, Barrow writes, "hath been a huge scandal to religion, which hath caused many to stumble, hath cast some quite down into the gulf of *Atheism*, or *Epicurism*; hath brought some men to doubt, hath induced others flatly to deny, that there is a God, that is, a most wise, powerful, just, and good being, every-where present; or that he, being, doth preside over, or any-wise concern himself in our affairs."[29] The orthodox answer to Booth's "disadvantageous opinion of Providence"—an opinion which brings even Amelia to suspect her husband of being "little better than an atheist" (X.ix; II, 214)—is of course the doctrine of futurity, of a future state of rewards and punishments in which all the inequities of this life will be redressed. "Providence," Dr. Harrison exclaims to Booth, whose liberty and happiness have been restored, "hath done you the justice at last which it will, one day or other, render to all men."

That Fielding should have considered this ancient question to be of timely interest to the readers of *Amelia*, to the extent of writing it into the characterization of his hero, may be better understood, I believe, if we are aware that, as he began to compose the novel, the old empirical arguments against a particular providence and a future state had been revived and shrewdly elaborated by Hume in the *Philosophical Essays concerning Human Understanding* (1748), the work that first called the atheistical implications of his philosophy to the public attention. In Essay XI, "Of the Practical Consequences of Natural Religion"—to which, for the 1750 edition, he gave the more explicit title, "Of a Particular Providence and a Future State"—Hume allowed an Epicurean philosopher to supply at length the empirical reasoning against a belief in providential order that led Booth to scepticism:

> *Are there any Marks of a distributive Justice in the World?* If you answer in the Affirmative, I conclude, that, since Justice here exerts itself, it is satisfy'd. If you reply in the Negative, I conclude, that you have then no Reason to ascribe Justice to the Gods. If you hold a Medium betwixt Affirmation and Negation, by saying, that the Justice of the Gods, at present, exerts

---

[29] Barrow, Sermon XXXII, II, 338-39.

itself in Part, but not in its full Extent; I answer, that you have no Reason to give it any particular Extent, but only so far as you see it, *at present*, exert itself.[30]

Part of Fielding's purpose in *Amelia* was to disabuse his hero of the epicurean doctrine that Hume in this celebrated essay so persuasively advocates.

Just as Booth and Robinson differ in their reasons for denying a Providence, so too their opinions of moral determinism must be carefully distinguished; for the implications of this most remarkable aspect of Booth's philosophy affect the novel in profound and surprising ways. Replying to his companion's assertion that men are powerless to shape their destinies, Booth

> ... declared himself to be of the same opinion with regard to the necessity of human actions; adding, however, that he did not believe men were under any blind impulse or direction of fate, but that every man acted merely from the force of that passion which was uppermost in his mind, and could do no otherwise. (I, 15)

"A discourse," Fielding remarks as he brings the chapter to a close, " now ensued between the two gentlemen on the necessity arising from the impulse of fate, and the necessity arising from the impulse of passion, which, as it will make a pretty pamphlet of itself, we shall reserve for some future opportunity."

A recurrent topic in the narrative, Booth's " doctrine of the passions " stands in direct contradiction of the stoicism recommended by his author in the " exordium "; for it represents all men as compelled to follow " the blind guidance of a predominant passion," granting no efficacy to the rational " directions of Prudence." Curiously, however, though we are evidently meant to regard Booth's doctrine as contributing to his frailty as a moral agent, the narrator's attitude toward it is more respectful than ironic. Only once in the novel are these antithetical philosophies allowed to clash openly, as Booth converses with a fellow prisoner in the spunging house who extolls the virtues of a system based upon Aristotle and " the Stoics " (VIII.x). Booth clearly prevails. Through a " long course of meditation " on the vanities and vicissitudes of life, his companion claims to have gained a complete victory over his passions—over " all eager wishes and abject fears, all violent joy and grief concerning objects which cannot

---

[30] *Philosophical Essays* (1748), p. 219—so abbreviated hereafter.

endure long, and may not exist a moment" (II, 100); secure in his virtue and indifferent to circumstance, he believes himself "superior to all the attacks of fortune" (II, 101). The gentleman's philosophy deserts him, however, when the bailiff threatens to dispatch him to Newgate, his terrors serving to vindicate Booth's more empirical estimate of human nature:

> ... however true all this may be in theory [Booth had objected], I still doubt its efficacy in practice. And the cause of the difference between these two is this: that we reason from our heads, but act from our hearts.... Nothing can differ more widely than wise men and fools in their estimation of things; but, as both act from their uppermost passion, they both often act alike. (II, 100-101)

If, as an explanation of human nature, Booth's doctrine seems preferable to the quixotic rationalism of the Stoic gentleman, it must also be distinguished from the cynical philosophy of (as Miss Matthews calls him) "that charming fellow Mandevil" (III.v; I. 114), whose theory of the passions it has been said to resemble.[31] Though Mandeville's credo, announced in the Introduction to *The Fable of the Bees*, seems close enough to Booth's own—"*I believe Man*," Mandeville declares, "... *to be a compound of various Passions, that all of them, as they are provoked and come uppermost, govern him by turns, whether he will or no*"[32]—yet nowhere during the course of that work does he systematically develop this premise to the point where it may be equated with Booth's conception of "necessity arising from the impulse of passion." In allusions elsewhere to Mandeville, Fielding never attacked this aspect of his philosophy, presumably because he did not think it distinctive or dangerous enough to trouble with.[33] It is rather Mandeville's cynical reduction of human nature to the single motivating principle of self-interest that invariably drew Fielding's criticism, as it does Booth's, who, in reply to Miss Matthews, emphatically dissociates his own doctrine from that of his friend's favorite philosopher:

---

[31] See, especially, F. Homes Dudden, *Henry Fielding: His Life, Works, and Times* (Oxford, 1952), II, 824; A. R. Towers, *MLN*, 70 (1955), 260; C. H. K. Bevan, "The Unity of Fielding's *Amelia*," *Renaissance and Modern Studies*, 14 (1970), 91-110; and Eustace Palmer, "*Amelia*—The Decline of Fielding's Art," *Essays in Criticism*, 21 (1971), 135.

[32] *The Fable of the Bees*, ed. F. B. Kaye (Oxford, 1924), I, 39.

[33] For a summary of Fielding's attitude toward Mandeville, see Battestin and Bowers, edd., *Tom Jones*, p. 268, n. 2.

"Pardon me, madam," answered Booth; "I hope you do not agree with Mandevil neither, who hath represented human nature in a picture of the highest deformity. He hath left out of his system the best passion which the mind can possess, and attempts to derive the effects or energies of that passion from the base impulses of pride or fear. Whereas it is as certain that love exists in the mind of man as that its opposite hatred doth; and the same reasons will equally prove the existence of the one as the existence of the other." (I, 114).

That Booth should find a model for his doctrine in an author he thus despises is most unlikely.

It may be seen, however, that his analysis of human nature, combining as it does the rejection both of stoic rationalism and of Mandevillean cynicism, corresponds exactly to that of Hume. As Booth in his dispute with the Stoic philosopher excludes reason from the province of morality, so Hume had repudiated the traditional premises on which Fielding's exhortations in the "exordium" are founded:

> NOTHING [Hume writes] is more usual in philosophy, and even in common life, than to talk of the combat of passion and reason, to give the preference to reason, and to assert that men are only so far virtuous as they conform themselves to its dictates ... On this method of thinking the greatest part of moral philsophy, ancient and modern, seems to be founded; nor is there an ampler field, as well for metaphysical arguments, as popular declamations, than this suppos'd pre-eminence of reason above passion. The eternity, invariableness, and divine origin of the former have been display'd to the best advantage: The blindness, unconstancy, and deceitfulness of the latter have been as strongly insisted on. In order to shew the fallacy of all this philosophy, I shall endeavour to prove *first*, that reason alone can never be a motive to any action of the will; and *secondly*, that it can never oppose passion in the direction of the will.[34]

For Hume, anticipating Fielding's hero in the most famous assertion of the *Treatise* (1739), "Reason is, and ought only to be the slave of the passions, and can never pretend to any other office than to serve and obey them" (p. 415). This celebrated declaration, overturning classical ethics at a stroke, is, of course, the essential tenet of Hume's moral philosophy. Yet equally essential is the correlative doctrine that he opposes to the school of Hobbes

---

[34] *A Treatise of Human Nature* (1739), II.iii.3 ("Of the influencing motives of the will"); in L. A. Selby-Bigge, ed. (Oxford, 1888), p. 413.

and Mandeville: this is the view that "the soul or animating principle" of all the passions, love and hatred among them, is "sympathy."[35] Accordingly, in his essay "Of the Dignity of Human Nature," Hume denies the Mandevillean view that "the selfish and vicious Principles of Human Nature" predominate, observing instead "that the social Passions are by far the most powerful of any, and that even all the other Passions receive from them their chief Force and Influence."[36] Like Hume, then, Fielding's hero rejects on empirical grounds as equally fallacious both the Stoic's claims for the superiority of reason and Mandeville's notion that all motivation is reducible to the principles of pride and self-interest.

Throughout *Amelia* Booth finds his theory of the passions confirmed in his own behavior and in the actions of his acquaintance. For him reason and the will have no part in the moral life; the passions alone, over which the individual has no control, determine conduct. Of these one usually predominates—whether pride or benevolence or lust, avarice or fear or ambition—defining "character" according to our natural dispositions; but all mingle in the soul and affect behavior as their objects at any given moment are more or less compelling. To Booth, therefore, the actions of anyone are predictable if his circumstances and ascendant passion are known: the generosity of Colonel James seems "proof" of his doctrine (III.v; I, 113); the charity of Sergeant Atkinson shows that "Love, benevolence, or what you will please to call it, may be the reigning passion in a beggar as well as in a prince" (III.vii; I, 125); Miss Matthews's vanity, "plainly her predominant passion," is the key to wooing her successfully (IV. vi; I, 187).

What is more, the Christian stoic injunction, *vince teipsum*, which Fielding had recommended in *The Champion* (2 February 1739/40) and which informs the message of the "exordium" to *Amelia,* is to Booth meaningless, for according to his doctrine, there can be no victory over the self, the innate essential character of a man. To speak of "resolution" in temptation, of "mastering" or "subduing" or "conquering" the passions is to speak "nonsense." All one can hope for is that, when one is moved

---

[35] *Ibid.,* II.ii ("Of Love and Hatred"), p. 363.
[36] *Essays,* p. 125. See also Essay I, "Of the different Species of Philosophy," in *Philosophical Essays,* pp. 14-16 n.

by dishonorable desire, a nobler passion will prevail. In this way, for example, Booth analyzes his own behavior, recalling his ineffectual struggle to deny his love for Amelia:

> " I abstained three days from seeing her; to say the truth, I endeavoured to work myself up to a resolution of leaving her for ever: but when I could not so far subdue my passion—But why do I talk nonsense of subduing my passion?—I should say, when no other passion could surmount my love, I returned to visit her . . ." (II.ii; I, 59)

During the interview, Booth continues, Amelia's beauty and innocence proved an almost irresistible temptation to confess his passion:

> " Upon my soul, if ever man could boast of his resolution, I think I might now, that I abstained from falling prostrate at her feet, and adoring her. However, I triumphed; pride, I believe, triumphed, or perhaps love got the better of love. We once more parted. . . .
> " I now had, I thought, gained a complete victory over myself; and no small compliments did I pay to my own resolution. In short, I triumphed as cowards and niggards do when they flatter themselves with having given some supposed instance of courage or generosity; and my triumph lasted as long; that is to say, till my ascendant passion had a proper opportunity of displaying itself in its true and natural colours." (I, 60-61)

Similarly, Booth later describes the psychomachia even in Amelia's soul, whose love for him and fear for his safety on the eve of his departure for Gibraltar cannot be subdued by Dr. Harrison's reasoned appeals to her pride:

> " Though the doctor could not make pride strong enough to conquer love, yet he exalted the former to make some stand against the latter; insomuch that my poor Amelia, I believe, more than once flattered herself, to speak the language of the world, that her reason had gained an entire victory over her passion; till love brought up a reinforcement, if I may use that term, of tender ideas, and bore down all before him." (III.ii; I, 102)

In such passages Fielding, by dramatically rendering Booth's doctrine in all its implications, draws our attention to a crucial question of contemporary ethics to which, by the 1750's, Hume had given a new prominence and urgency: this was the question of the " Liberty " or " Necessity " of moral agents, which Hume, both in the *Treatise* and in the *Philosophical Essays*, had considered at length and decided in favor of necessity.[37] Rejecting the distinction between moral and physical agency on which Clarke had insisted in refuting Spinoza and Collins, Hume maintained that the relation between the motivating passions and human behavior was as invariable as that between cause and effect in nature. Anticipating Booth's dispute with Robinson over "the necessity arising from the impulse of fate, and the necessity arising from the impulse of passion," Hume, moreover, insisted on the novelty of his analysis of cause and effect and its application to the passions, carefully distinguishing his own "new definition of necessity" from conventional fatalism.[38] Sharing Hume's scorn for the "fantastical system of liberty,"[39] Booth denies the freedom of the will and lapses into a kind of moral paralysis and impotency; for, as he recalls to Dr. Harrison, "as men appeared to me to act entirely from their passions, their actions could have neither merit nor demerit" (XII.v; II, 288).

An awareness of this issue adds an important dimension to the theme of *liberty* in *Amelia*, a word that Fielding plays upon in all its variety of meanings, from the opening sentence of the narrative, which places the action "within the liberty of Westminster," to Booth's discussion of the dubious "liberty" of Englishmen liable to be imprisoned for debt under an imperfect constitution (VIII.ii; II, 61-62), to the "charms of liberty" (VIII.i; II, 58) of which the inhabitants of Newgate and of Mr. Bondum's spunging house have been deprived.[40] It is, I would suggest, Booth's "errors"—his "disadvantageous opinion of Providence" and particularly his theory of "necessity arising from the impulse of passion"—that account for one of the most remarkable manifestations of this theme in the novel: the fact that, from the moment he is introduced until the moment of his spiritual enlightenment and conversion in the final Book, Fielding's hero is literally without his liberty. Whether in Newgate or the

---

[37] See *Treatise*, II.iii.1-2 ("Of liberty and necessity"), and Essay VIII, "Of Liberty and Necessity," in *Philosophical Essays*.

[38] See, for example, *Philosophical Essays*, p. 157. In his *Abstract* (1740) of the *Treatise*, Hume emphasized the novelty of his arguments in this respect (pp. 28-31).

[39] *Treatise*, II.iii.1; p. 404.

[40] The word is used in other senses as well: e. g., as indicating physical freedom from constraint (I.iii; I, 11); or freedom from social decorum (V.ii; I, 219); or, ironically, freedom of movement in a prison (VIII.ii; II, 61). Examples in all categories are numerous.

spunging house or his own lodgings, he is a man confined; even when he is not actually incarcerated, his movements are restricted to the area within the Verge of the Court. With this curious circumstance in mind, one recent critic has shrewdly remarked that the prison is "the unifying symbol" of *Amelia*.[41]

That Fielding should consciously have intended this means of objectifying Booth's spiritual predicament gains a certain probability from the intellectual tradition whose validity he wishes to affirm. Within that tradition the notion of bondage or imprisonment is, as Tillotson declares, "one of the principal metaphors"[42] by which to render the errors of infidelity and the condition of those who abandon themselves to passion. The *locus classicus* of this symbolism, of course, is the *Consolation of Philosophy*, wherein Boethius's exile and imprisonment render emblematically the confusion of his soul, particularly those doubts concerning the justice of Providence and the freedom of the will which Philosophy must dispel. Similarly, release from captivity is Locke's figure for the man who is "determined in willing by his own thought and judgment" rather than by passion or circumstance: such a man alone "is perfectly at liberty," having "his chains knocked off, and the prison doors set open to him . . ."[43]—a passage, one may suppose, to which Hume archly alludes in limiting the definition of liberty to freedom of movement only, which "is universally allow'd to belong to every Body, who is not a Prisoner, and in Chains."[44] But the relevance of the metaphor to Booth's spiritual condition is most clearly seen in the homiletic tradition which supplied the Christian basis of Fielding's fiction. In his sermon, "True liberty, the result of Christianity," for example, Tillotson expounds the view that the gospel "frees us from the bondage of ignorance, and error," from "the slavery of our passions and lusts."[45] The scriptural text most frequently cited by the divines who develop this figure is John 8: 32 ("And ye shall know the truth, and the truth shall

---

[41] Peter V. LePage, "The Prison and the Dark Beauty of 'Amelia,'" *Criticism*, 9 (1967), 337-54. Cf. also Allan Wendt, "The Naked Virtue of Amelia," *ELH*, 27 (1960), 146.

[42] Sermon CCXLVII, "True liberty, the result of Christianity," in *Sermons* (1757), XII, 169.

[43] *An Essay concerning Human Understanding*, II.xxi ("Of Power"); ed. Alexander Campbell Fraser (Oxford, 1894), pp. 346, 348.

[44] *Philosophical Essays*, p. 150.

[45] Tillotson, Sermon CCXLVII, XII, 169, 174.

make you free "). Thus, in his sermon on this text entitled, " Of the Liberty of Moral Agents," Samuel Clarke asks: " If a man's Body be under confinement, or he be impotent in his Limbs, he is then deprived of his *bodily* Liberty: And for the same Reason, if his *Mind* be blinded by sottish Errors, and his Reason over-ruled by violent Passions; is not This likewise plainly as great a Slavery and as true a Confinement? "[46] To Benjamin Hoadly and Bishop Berkeley, moreover, there was a delicious irony in the paradox that those deists (Anthony Collins, for example) who most strenuously denied the liberty of the will had styled themselves " *free*-thinkers."[47] Finally, within this Christian context there is a further appropriateness in Fielding's characterization of his hero as a debtor, the technical cause of his confinement; for, as Parson Adams knows in *Joseph Andrews* (III.iii), *debtors* is Christ's own metaphor for mankind, who have omitted our duties to him and offended against his Word.[48] At the moment of Booth's conversion, Dr. Harrison makes explicit the meaning of this figurative system in the novel: " at present," he assures his friend, " as the devil hath thought proper to set you free, I will try if I can prevail on the bailiff to do the same " (XII.v; II, 288). Disabused of his errors, his debts forgiven, Booth gains his liberty at last.

The problem of *Amelia*, however, is not resolved by the hero's conversion, for the true and *felt* dilemma of the novel is Fielding's own. The moral and psychological—even, as I would suggest, the aesthetic—realities of the narrative remain in radical contradiction of the stoicism of the " exordium," and the reader, at

---

[46] Sermon XII, in *Sermons*, 8th ed. (1756), II, 200. See also Robert South, citing this text in his sermon on II Thessalonians 2: 11 (*Sermons* [Oxford, 1823], III, 265-66). Two other divines, John Jackson and John Orr, develop an analogy between civil and moral liberty, which depend, respectively, on the rule of law and the government of reason over the passions: see Jackson, p. 79; and Orr, Sermon XIV, " The Spiritual and Moral Liberty of Men," in *Sermons*, 2nd ed. (1750), I, 384-87. A copy of the 1749 edition of Orr's *Sermons* was in Fielding's library, No. 171 in the Catalogue.

[47] See Hoadly's " Queries Recommended to the Authors of the late Discourse of Free-Thinking," in *Works*, ed. John Hoadly (1773), I, 143; and Berkeley's *Alciphron*, Dialogue II, in which Crito completes his characterization of a free-thinking necessitarian: " this curious piece of clock-work, having no principle of action within itself, and denying that it hath or can have any one free thought or motion, sets up for the patron of liberty, and earnestly contends for *free-thinking* " (in *Works*, A. C. Fraser [Oxford, 1901], II, 115-16).

[48] On the significance of this metaphor, see Barrow, " Exposition on the Lord's Prayer," in *Works* (1741), I, 490, and Sermon XXXIII, " The Certainty and Circumstances of a Future Judgment, from Divine Revelation," in *ibid.*, II, 354.

least, finds no release from the tension generated by this ambivalency. That Fielding, interested as he was in the preservation of social order, should wish to cure Booth of his scepticism is understandable, and, if one cannot claim that the scene in which he accomplishes this is successfully managed, yet the choice of a vehicle for his purpose is logical enough. Barrow's sermons on the Creed open with an analysis of infidelity which is especially relevant to Booth's situation and which underscores the pernicious consequences to society of atheism in all its forms: " IF," Barrow declares, " the causes of all the sin and all the mischief in the world were carefully sought, we should find the chief of all to be infidelity; either total or gradual." The " great masters and patrons " of infidelity, he continues, by denying everything " immaterial, or immortal " in man, so turn him " into a beast, or into a puppet, a whirligig of fate or chance ": " They ascribe all actions and events to necessity or external impulse, so rasing the grounds of justice, and all virtue, that no man may seem responsible for what he doth, commendable or culpable, amiable or detestable."[49] That Booth, whose scepticism Fielding carefully attributes to his ignorance of " religious matters," should be disabused of his errors by reading Barrow's eloquent exposition of the Creed is both consistent with his character and appropriate to Fielding's social theme.

What is remarkable, however, is that the *grounds* of Booth's scepticism (though not of course the atheism they had seemed to him to imply) are accepted as valid both by Dr. Harrison, Fielding's spokesman in the novel, and, as we shall see, by the narrator himself:

> " Indeed [Booth declares], I never was a rash disbeliever; my chief doubt was founded on this—that, as men appeared to me to act entirely from their passions, their actions could have neither merit nor demerit." " A very worthy conclusion truly! " cries the doctor; " but if men act, *as I believe they do*, from their passions, it would be fair to conclude that religion to be true which applies immediately to the strongest of these passions, hope and fear; choosing rather to rely on its rewards and punishments than on that native beauty of virtue which some of the ancient philosophers thought proper to recommend to their disciples." (XII.v; II, 288. Emphasis added.)

[49] Sermon I, " Of the Evil and Unreasonableness of Infidelity," in *ibid.*, II, 1, 10.

Instead of answering Booth's theory of the passions and his necessitarianism by asserting the stoic formula Fielding had expounded in the " exordium "—by urging, that is, the efficacy of " Prudence," the "ART of LIFE," in directing the passions to virtuous ends—Harrison wholly concurs in the doctrine, insisting only that, given this truth about human motivation, the moral order can best be preserved by a religion whose ultimate appeal is not to reason, but to the selfish affections. His argument is by no means novel. Though its specific source is probably another of Barrow's sermons in the series that converted Booth,[50] it was a commonplace among the divines, who sensed with Robert South that " hope and fear are the two great handles, by which the will of man is to be taken hold of, when we would either draw it to duty or draw it off from sin."[51] As Hume understood, however, this truth confirmed rather than damaged the necessitarian doctrine on which Booth's " chief doubt " was founded. In his essay " Of Liberty and Necessity " he observes:

> All Laws being founded on Rewards and Punishments, 'tis suppos'd as a fundamental Principle, that these Motives have a regular and uniform Influence on the Mind, and both produce the good and prevent the evil Actions. We may give to this Influence, what Name we please; but as 'tis usually conjoin'd with the Action, it must be esteem'd a *Cause*, and be look'd upon as an Instance of that Necessity, which we would establish.[52]

The awkwardness one senses in *Amelia* is owing, in part at least, to the ambivalency of Fielding's own attitude toward the new psychology. On the one hand, it is clear from the " exordium " and from the conversion of his hero that the message of the book

---

[50] With Harrison's remarks compare Barrow in Sermon XXXII, " The Reasonableness and Equity of a Future Judgment ": since, Barrow writes, " an invincible principle of self-love " is natural to man, it follows " that hope and fear are the main springs, which set on work all the wheels of human action: so that any matter being propounded, if men can hope, that it will yield pleasant . . . fruits, they will undertake it . . . If it do appear, that virtue can pay men well for their pains, they, perhaps, may be her servants; but they will hardly wait on her in pure courtesy, or work in her service for nothing; if she bringeth visibly a good dowry with her, she may be courted; but her mere beauty, or worth, will draw few suitors to her " (*ibid.*, II, 334-35).

[51] South, Sermon on Hebrews XI.24-26, III, 136. Cf. also Clark, *Discourse*, pp. 281-85, and, as answers to Shaftesbury's preference of the natural beauty of virtue as an incentive to moral action, Berkeley's *Alciphron*, Dialogue III; Joseph Butler's *Analogy of Religion* (1736), I.v.36, vi.14-16; and Philip Skelton, *Ophiomaches: or, Deism Revealed* (1749), I, 238-40.

[52] *Philosophical Essays*, p. 154. Hope and fear are among the " direct passions " which Hume analyzes in the Treatise, II.iii.9.

is *meant* to be the reaffirmation of the Christian humanist tradition which Hume had placed in jeopardy. If Hume's scepticism prevailed, if his eloquent and carefully reasoned arguments reviving epicurean and necessitarian doctrines were allowed to undermine religion and the idea of moral responsibility, chaos would come again. As author and magistrate Fielding was well aware that the stakes were high in the intellectual contest between Hume, the modern *bête noir* as Mossner sees him,[53] and the defenders of orthodoxy. By having Barrow persuade Booth to abandon his scepticism and embrace the faith, Fielding implies that well-meaning men *are* capable of enlightenment, that the Christian religion is served by a sweeter eloquence and a higher reason than Hume's. And once at least in the novel, in contrasting the troubled conscience of Mrs. Ellison with the contentment of his heroine in affliction, he assures the reader that moral agents *are* at liberty to choose between villainy and virtue: " innocence," he declares, " is always within thy own power " (VIII.iii; II, 69).[54]

On the other hand, whatever comfort the reader may derive from such incidental reassurances in *Amelia*, they are finally unpersuasive, for the novel itself is the expression—in some respects, the embodiment—of a theory of human nature virtually indistinguishable from the psychology it ostensibly repudiates. Despite the message of the " exordium " Fielding seems no longer convinced by the notion developed in *Tom Jones* that morality resides in the power of prudence and the will to govern the passions; still less does he find, as in *Joseph Andrews*, that the energies of a good heart are sufficient as a moral imperative. The problem of *Amelia* is, I believe, largely attributable to the unresolved tension in the novel between the new psychology, to which Fielding no less than Booth implicitly subscribes, and the antithetical orthodoxy which he wishes to reaffirm. A theory of the passions very similar to Hume's is the informing principle of characterization in *Amelia*, as well as the aesthetic principle affecting the very mode of the book; Fielding's efforts to accom-

---

[53] Mossner, p. 223.

[54] Similar assurances occur elsewhere in Fielding's writings after *Amelia*, notably in *The Covent-Garden Journal* (25 February 1752) and in the revised version of *Jonathan Wild* (1754), p. 263. For discussions of the importance of the will in Fielding's ethics, a notion he was obviously reluctant to abandon, see Battestin, *Moral Basis*, pp. 60-62, and Henry Knight Miller, *Essays on Fielding's " Miscellanies": A Commentary on Volume One* (Princeton, 1961), pp. 217-18.

modate this theory within the intellectual matrix of Christian humanism could not easily succeed.

Though Fielding had earlier seen the passions as motivating human behavior, he had done so in the manner of Pope in the *Essay on Man* (1733-34) or of Locke in the *Essay concerning Human Understanding* (1690), allowing reason the artful function of governing their impulses.[55] In *Amelia*, however, passion alone determines character in accordance with what Fielding calls our "different natural dispositions" (VIII.ix; II, 93). In its essentials, his own view closely resembles the amalgam of subjectivism and passional psychology expressed by Booth, who explains to Amelia that the social affections, though real enough, are limited on the one hand by our private experience of the world, restricting our capacity sympathetically to identify with other men, and on the other hand, by the fortuitous composition of the soul itself:

> "Compassion [Booth observes], if thoroughly examined, will, I believe, appear to be the fellow-feeling only of men of the same rank and degree of life for one another, on account of the evils to which they themselves are liable. Our sensations are, I am afraid, very cold towards those who are at a great distance from us, and whose calamities can consequently never reach us."
>
> * * * * *
>
> "I have often told you, my dear Emily [he continues], . . . that all men, as well the best as the worst, act alike from the principle of self-love. Where benevolence therefore is the uppermost passion, self-love directs you to gratify it by doing good, and by relieving the distresses of others; for they are then in reality your own. But where ambition, avarice, pride, or any other passion, governs the man and keeps his benevolence down, the miseries of all other men affect him no more than they would a stock or a stone. And thus the man and his statue have often the same degree of feeling or compassion." (X.ix; II, 214)

Though these remarks confirm Amelia's suspicions that her husband is "little better than an atheist," we have seen that in substance they are acceptable to Dr. Harrison, and they clearly square with Fielding's own principles of characterization in the

[55] For the general background, see Bertrand A. Goldgar, "Pope's Theory of the Passions: The Background of Epistle II of the *Essay on Man*," *PQ*, 41 (1962), 730-43. On Fielding's view of the passions, see Battestin, *Moral Basis*, pp. 57-60, and Miller, *Essays*, pp. 113-18.

novel. Consider, for example, his elaborate anatomy of Colonel James, perhaps the book's most complex and fascinating character. James's early generosity to the Booths elicits from the author a panegyric on the apparent goodness of his nature—a "benign disposition," so rare that "scarce one man in a thousand is capable of tasting the happiness of others" (IV.iv; I, 178). As his character is more fully disclosed, however, we find that *eros*, that "all-subduing tyrant" (VI.i; I, 261), is the reigning deity in James's breast: though he gives Booth money, he hates him for succeeding with Miss Matthews where he had failed, and, when Amelia in her turn innocently provokes his lust, he plots to debauch her and to ruin her husband. The foundation of morality, the narrator declares, is the capacity for sympathy, an ingredient of character which James happens to lack; without it, furthermore, he is helpless *not* to indulge the vicious inclinations of his soul:

> In truth, the colonel, though a very generous man, had not the least grain of tenderness in his disposition. His mind was formed of those firm materials of which nature formerly hammered out the Stoic, and upon which the sorrows of no man living could make an impression. A man of this temper, who doth not much value danger, will fight for the person he calls his friend, and the man that hath but little value for his money will give it him; but such friendship is never to be absolutely depended on; for, whenever the favourite passion interposes with it, it is sure to subside and vanish into air. Whereas the man whose tender disposition really feels the miseries of another will endeavour to relieve them for his own sake; and, in such a mind, friendship will often get the superiority over every other passion. (VII.v; II, 79-80)

A few pages later, as James attempts to convert the good Sergeant Atkinson into a pimp in order to execute his designs on Amelia, Fielding enforces the notion of subjectivism that is a constant theme in the novel—the notion that our estimate of the world necessarily depends on our experience of it, as our knowledge of the human potential for virtue or vice is controlled by our sense of the natural disposition of our own hearts: "Few men, I believe, think better of others than of themselves; nor do they easily allow the existence of any virtue of which they perceive no traces in their own minds . . ." (VIII.viii; II, 92). James continues to the end the slave of his libidinous appetites, his condition of soul aptly dramatized in his fate: having separated from his wife, he last appears as the paramour of Miss Matthews, doting " on her (though now very disagreeable in her person, and immensely fat) to such a degree, that he submits to be treated by her in the most tyrannical manner" (XII.ix; II, 310).

In *Amelia* Fielding places greater stress than ever before on what he called in the " Essay on the Knowledge of the Characters of Men " (1743) " some unacquired, original Distinction, in the Nature or soul of one Man, from that of another " [56]—an innate and ineradicable stamp of character accounting, say, for the difference between Amelia and her sister Betty, as for the impulsive benevolence of Tom Jones or the malevolence of his half-brother Blifil. A man like James, Fielding assures us, would find utterly incomprehensible the love that Amelia inspires in Dr. Harrison, a disinterested affection founded in esteem: " to raise that affection in the human breast which the doctor had for Amelia, Nature is forced to use a kind of logic which is no more understood by a bad man than Sir Isaac Newton's doctrine of colours is by one born blind " (X.iv; II, 181).

Though good-nature in *Amelia* is still the warming sun of Fielding's moral universe, a truth of human nature as certain as the axioms of physics, it shines but faintly, if at all, in the breasts of many of his characters, and its energies, more often than not, are ineffectual. There is a new emphasis in the novel on the dark passions of cruelty and malice—the behavior, for example, of Betty Harris, or of Amelia's acquaintance who exult in her damaged beauty, or of Booth's envious neighbors who take pleasure in ruining him. But, together with Booth's denunciation of Mandeville, the examples of Dr. Harrison and Atkinson, of Amelia and even poor Booth himself, make clear that Fielding has by no means discarded his earlier conviction that, however rarely it may predominate, there is much goodness in the composition of man. Dismayed at her discovery that James's generosity to her family disguises his true designs against her virtue, Amelia exclaims to Dr. Harrison, " sure all mankind almost are villains in their hearts " (IX.v; II, 131). Dr. Harrison corrects her, however, again apparently echoing Barrow:

[56] Fielding's *Miscellanies, Volume One,* ed. H. K. Miller (Oxford and Middletown, Conn., 1972), p. 154.

> "Fie, child!" cries the doctor. "Do not make a conclusion so much to the dishonour of the great Creator. The nature of man is far from being in itself evil; it abounds with benevolence, charity, and pity, coveting praise and honour, and shunning shame and disgrace. Bad education, bad habits, and bad customs, debauch our nature, and drive it headlong as it were into vice. The governors of the world, and I am afraid the priesthood, are answerable for the badness of it." (II, 131-32) [57]

There are, he is convinced, speaking of James, "good stamina in the nature of this very man; for he hath done acts of friendship and generosity to your husband before he could have any evil design on your chastity; and in a Christian society, which I no more esteem this nation to be than I do any part of Turkey, I doubt not but this very colonel would have made a worthy and valuable member" (II, 132). At one time or another in the novel not only James, but other contemptible or villainous characters are similarly described as "good-natured"—Mrs. James, Colonel Bath, Mrs. Ellison, even Robinson.

But as Booth succumbs to his Dido and gambles himself ever deeper into debt, his "frailty" makes clear that good-nature alone is insufficient to insure either virtue or the stability of the social order. However reluctant she may be to encourage her husband in his theory of the passions, Amelia intuitively understands its validity, and, in educating her children, takes care to school them in habits of virtue by applying to their hopes and fears and sense of shame:

> This admirable woman never let a day pass without instructing her children in some lesson of religion and morality. By which means she had in their tender minds, so strongly annexed the ideas of fear and shame to every idea of evil of which they were susceptible, that it must require great pains and length of habit to separate them. Though she was the tenderest of mothers, she never suffered any symptom of malevolence to show itself

---

[57] With Harrison's remarks, compare Barrow in Sermon VII, "The Being of God Proved from the Frame of Human Nature." There remain, he declares, "dispersed in the soil of human nature divers seeds of goodness, of benignity, of ingenuity, which being cherished, excited and quickened by good culture, do, to common experience, thrust out flowers very lovely, yield fruits very pleasant of virtue and goodness." Later he observes that man's sociable disposition will flourish only "if well managed, if instructed by good discipline, if guided by good example, if living under the influence of wise laws and virtuous governors." Evil dispositions, on the contrary, "do grow among men (like weeds in any, even the best soil) and overspread the earth from neglect of good education; from ill conduct, ill custom, ill example . . ." (Barrow, II, 82-83.)

in their most trifling actions without discouragement, without rebuke, and, if it broke forth with any rancour, without punishment. In which she had such success, that not the least marks of pride, envy, malice, or spite discovered itself in any of their little words or deeds. (IV.iii; I, 174-75)[58]

Amelia's method of educating her children succeeds because, though no philosopher, she senses with Booth that men " act from [their] hearts," that passion, not prudence, is the sole determinant of conduct. This being so, as Dr. Harrison later asserts in acknowledging the truth of Booth's doctrine, only religion, by appealing to our hopes and fears with the promise of future rewards and punishments, can prevent anarchy in the moral order. Amelia herself is the embodiment of Fielding's ethical system in the novel, her chastity, as Harrison assures James, being " so strongly defended, as well by a happy natural disposition of mind as by the strongest principles of religion and virtue, implanted by education and nourished and improved by habit . . ." (X.ii; II, 174).

With respect to Fielding's career as a novelist and his conception of the art of the novel, *Amelia*, I would submit, is the strange and anomalous book it is because it is the expression of a new psychology: the belief—discernible in inchoate form in Fielding's earlier writings, but never before fully articulated in any work of fiction—that passion alone is the spring of human behavior. In dedicating his book to Ralph Allen, Fielding may be seen to make this conviction serve as the basis for a new aesthetic: he declares he will " promote the cause of virtue " not by provoking our laughter, but by affecting our hearts, giving us " pleasure . . . from a tender sensation " (I, xv). To a degree unprecedented in any of his previous fiction, the vocabulary of sentimentalism dominates even the linguistic texture of the novel, which abounds in scenes of tears and tenderness and where characters alternate between " venting " their passions and dissolving in " fits " and " raptures " of feeling. What is more,

---

[58] Fielding's sense in *Amelia* of the crucial importance of education in disciplining the natural dispositions of men has been recently discussed by C. R. Kropf, " Educational Theory and Human Nature in Fielding's Works," *PMLA*, 89 (1974), 113-20, esp. p. 119. Kropf stresses the probable influence of Locke's *Some Thoughts concerning Education*; he overlooks, however, an even better gloss on the present passage, Tillotson's series of sermons, " Of the education of children " (see Sermons LI-LIII, vol. IV). Also relevant is James Forrester's *Dialogues on the Passions, Habits, and Affections Peculiar to Children* (1748).

the rhetorical procedure of the book's internal narrators, Miss Matthews, Booth, and Mrs. Bennet—who seek to stir the emotions of their listeners by " 'running into too minute descriptions' " (I.ix; I, 40), replete with " 'too many particulars' " (II.i; I, 58) and " 'many little incidents' " (VII.i; II, 4) —is now, in many passages, Fielding's own and uncongenial strategy. It is this curious quality of the narrative that has puzzled two of his most perceptive critics, who observe that the solemn detailing of emotion in the novel marks a radical shift in Fielding's attitude toward sensation.[59] Professor Rawson, remembering Fielding's admiration for *Clarissa*, suspects that it is Richardson whose example has turned Fielding to a new mode and vitiated his comic art. But, as Fielding's sarcasm against his rival in the Preface to the *Journal of a Voyage to Lisbon* (1755) suggests, what appear to be "sub-Richardsonian elements"[60] in *Amelia* may be better accounted for by looking elsewhere—to a source enabling us to relate the distinctive sensationalism of the narrative itself to the conception of human psychology that the novel articulates.

It is worth noting in this respect that, considered even as a *literary* work, *Amelia* may be seen to coincide with Hume's critical interests. In his essay, "Of the Connexion of Ideas," for example, Hume insists that the supreme art of narrative or dramatic poetry is " that Communication of Emotion, by which alone [the author] can interest the Heart, and raise the Passions to their proper Height and Period."[61] With Fielding's puzzling experiments in retrospective narration in mind, as well as his choice of the *Aeneid* as a model, we may compare Hume's analysis of how Homer and Virgil maintained an intensity of emotional appeal by means of "oblique Narration," artificially achieving a sense of the immediacy of past events in order " to forward the Transition of the Passions ":

> Hence arises the Artifice of oblique Narration, employ'd in the *Odyssey* and *Æneid*; where the Hero is introduc'd, at first, near the Period of his Designs, and afterwards shows us, as it were in Perspective, the more distant Events and Causes. By this

[59] See Robert Alter, *Fielding and the Nature of the Novel* (Cambridge, Mass., 1968), pp. 166-70; and C. J. Rawson, *Henry Fielding and the Augustan Ideal under Stress* (London and Boston, 1972), pp. 88 ff.
[60] Rawson, p. 96.
[61] *Philosophical Essays*, p. 45.

means, the Reader's Curiosity is immediately excited: The Events follow with Rapidity, and in a very close Connexion: And the Concern is preserv'd alive, and continually encreases, by means of the near Relation of the Objects, from the Beginning to the End of the Narration. (pp. 39-40)

Indeed, the very premiss behind Fielding's unusual choice of a subject in *Amelia*—announced in the opening sentence as the " various accidents which befel a very worthy couple after their uniting in the state of matrimony "—would seem to be anticipated by Hume in his essay, " Of Polygamy and Divorces ":

The happiest Marriages, to be sure, are found where Love, by long Acquaintance, is consolidated into Friendship. Whoever dreams of Raptures and Extasies beyond the Honeymoon, is a Fool. Even Romances themselves, with all their Liberty of Fiction, are oblig'd to drop their Lovers the very Day of their Marriage, and find it easier to support the Passion for a dozen of Years under Coldness, Disdain and Difficulties, than a Week under Possession and Security.[62]

There are of course many sides to the problem of *Amelia*, Fielding's most puzzling work of fiction. In this essay I have focused on just two of the questions the book poses: What might have prompted Fielding, during the three years that separate *Tom Jones* from *Amelia*, to choose as a protagonist for his last novel a man whose particular spiritual predicament would dramatize the clash of opposing philosophies within his society— the clash, specifically, between scepticism and the new passional psychology on the one hand, and, on the other hand, the tradition of Christian humanism? What, during the same period, might have led him to modify so radically the form of comic narrative he had perfected in *Tom Jones* in favor of a darker, more sentimental mode? I suggest that the answer to both these questions may lie in his profound response to one of the major intellectual events of the century: the publication on 25 April 1748 of Hume's *Essays concerning Human Understanding*.

POSTSCRIPT: FIELDING AND HUME

Only once, in an unpersuasive essay published nearly half a century ago, has Hume's influence on Fielding been seriously

---

[62] *Essays*, p. 258.

proposed,[63] though in his more recent study of narrative form in Hume, Fielding, and Gibbon, Leo Braudy is tempted by the possibility.[64] Only twice in discussions of *Amelia* has Hume's name been incidentally invoked to illustrate the general background of Booth's theory of the passions,[65] the prevalent (and, as I have earlier shown, improbable) hypothesis being that Fielding's specific source was Mandeville. At first glance, certainly, there would seem to be good reason for dismissing Hume from considerations of Fielding's moral psychology, since Fielding nowhere mentions him by name, as he was usually ready enough to do in answering such intellectual antagonists as Hobbes, La Rochefoucauld, Mandeville, Shaftesbury, Whitefield, or Bolingbroke.[66]

What evidence is there, then—besides the general correspondence of ideas already examined—to support the contention of this essay that in *Amelia*, but in none of his previous works, Fielding may have been responding specifically to Hume's philosophy. To begin with, there is the fact that he owned, and therefore presumably read, a copy of the *Philosophical Essays* (1748), the controversial book that first made Hume's reputation as a sceptic and epicurean in religious matters and a necessitarian in morality.[67] It seems unlikely, furthermore, that Fielding would earlier have been acquainted with Hume's most important work, the *Treatise of Human Nature* (1739-40), of which the *Philosophical Essays* was a popularized redaction: by Hume's own admission the *Treatise* " fell *dead-born from the press*, without reaching such distinction, as even to excite a murmur among the

[63] See George Rogers Swann, *Philosophical Parallelisms in Six English Novelists* (Philadelphia, 1929), Ch. IV (" Fielding and Empirical Realism "), esp. pp. 59-64.
[64] *Narrative Form in History and Fiction* (Princeton, 1970), esp. p. 92 n. a.
[65] See Willi Erzgräber, " Das Menschenbild in Henry Fieldings Roman *Amelia*," *Die Neueren Sprachen*, N. S., 6 (1957), 108; and D. S. Thomas, *MLR*, 60 (1965), 184.
[66] The hypothesis that Hume's doctrine of necessity was the model for Booth's own may seem to run afoul of the further difficulty that Fielding has set his story in 1733 (see Dudden, II, 799), well before Hume began publishing. But Fielding was always more concerned to achieve a sense of topical immediacy in his fiction than to eliminate inconsistencies from his time-scheme. This motive explains, for example, several anachronisms in the narrative of *Tom Jones*, which are fully discussed in the introduction and notes to the Wesleyan edition (for references, see the Index, p. 1065, under " *Tom Jones* "). The most obvious of such inconsistencies in *Amelia* is the Noble Lord's plotting to seduce the heroine at a masquerade at Ranelagh, which did not open until 1742 (VI.v; I, 279, and VII.vi; II, 36)—an " error " in narrative chronology immediately detected by the reviewer in *The London Magazine*, 20 (December 1751), 303.
[67] See item No. 539 in the Catalogue of Fieldings's library.

zealots."[68] Though it is possible that Fielding was acquainted with Hume's *Essays Moral and Political* (1741-42), which was "favourably received," that work was too innocuous to provoke a reaction.

With the publication of the *Philosophical Essays* in 1748, however, several circumstances conspired to assure that Fielding's attention would be drawn to the book. In the first place, it was issued by Andrew Millar, Fielding's own bookseller, who from this year continued to act as Hume's chief London publisher.[69] In Millar, who personally had the warmest affection for Hume and who regarded his works "as Classicks," the two authors had a close mutual friend.[70]

Secondly, by 1749 (but not earlier) Hume found that, owing to the notoriety of the *Philosophical Essays*, his works, except for the "unfortunate" *Treatise*, "were beginning to be the subject of conversation";[71] by 1751, certainly, his reputation as a "fine and elegant," if controversial, writer had been established.[72] What is more, the man who led the attack on Hume throughout this period was Fielding's intimate acquaintance, William Warburton:[73] "I found," Hume wryly recalls, "by Dr. Warburton's railing, that the books were beginning to be esteemed

[68] *The Life of David Hume, Esq. Written by Himself* (1777), pp. 7-8; see also Mossner, pp. 139-40.

[69] See Mossner, p. 145. In 1748 Millar also brought out a new edition of the *Essays*.

[70] See Mossner, p. 230, and Austin Dobson, "Fielding and Andrew Millar," *The Library*, 3rd Ser., 7 (1916), 177-90. It is pleasant to note that upon his death in 1768 Millar bequeathed £200 each to Hume and to Fielding's sons, William and Allen (see Dobson, p. 190).

[71] See Hume's *Life*, p. 14, and Mossner, pp. 223v ff.

[72] See *The Monthly Review*, 6 (January 1752), 1. In his *Essays on the Principles of Morality and Natural Religion* (London: July, 1751), Lord Kames could observe of Hume: "The figure which this author deservedly makes in the learned world, is too considerable, to admit of his being past over in silence" (Edinburgh, 1751; p. 103).

[73] Fielding's friendship with Warburton is attested by compliments to his learning in *The Champion* (31 May 1742), *A Journey from This World to the Next* (1743), I.viii, *Juvenal's Sixth Satire Modernized in Burlesque Verse* (1743), line 81 n., and *Tom Jones*, XIII.i.

Warburton's "dogging" of Hume from 1749 onward is fully documented by Mossner (see esp. pp. 289-90, 323-27) and by A. W. Evans, *Warburton and the Warburtonians* (1932), pp. 213-16. He was probably responsible, moreover, for the only contemporary review of the *Treatise*, a typically arrogant and abusive performance appearing in *The History of the Works of the Learned*, VI (November-December 1739), 353-404. As Mossner points out, there is no evidence that Warburton knew of Hume's authorship of that work, which was published anonymously (Mossner, pp. 120-23, 618-19). Such secrets were seldom well kept in the eighteenth century, however, and the possibility

in good company." [74] In this connection, furthermore, it is worth remarking that Fielding's acquaintance with Warburton was owing to their mutual friendship with Ralph Allen, to whom *Amelia* is dedicated.

Warburton was implacable in his hatred of Hume. Privately, he denounced the *Philosophical Essays* as "a rank atheistical book," [75] and when he published his edition of Pope in 1751, it found a place in his commentary on *The Dunciad* (III, 224) as illustrating the line, "But 'Learn, ye DUNCES! not to scorn your God.'" He continued to hound Hume well beyond the period in question. Having succeeded in suppressing an earlier version of the *Four Dissertations* (1757), he conspired with Richard Hurd that same year to publish his *Remarks* on Hume's essay on "The Natural History of Religion," in which Hume and Bolingbroke are represented as the twin scourges of order in religion and morality, who labored "to exclude the Creator from his Works, and by the doctrine of an impious fatalism to emancipate people from the FEAR of GOD" (pp. 1-2). Even this late, Warburton was cherishing his bitterness againt the *Philosophical Essays* and its "Epicurean arguments against the being of a God" (p. 9). To Millar, who loved Hume, he wrote on 7 February 1757, expressing his outrage against the man who was so effectively undermining the grounds of faith: "You have often told me of this man's moral virtues. He may have many, for aught I know; but let me observe to you, there are vices of the *mind* as well as of the *body*; and I think a wickeder mind, and more obstinately bent on public mischief, I never knew." [76]

In Book IX, Chapter x, of *Amelia*, Dr. Harrison discusses with a proud young student of divinity the spreading climate of irreligion in the age. In accounting for this situation, they find at least one point of agreement:

> "Are not books of infidelity [asks the young man], treating our holy religion as a mere imposture, nay, sometimes as a mere jest,

---

cannot be ruled out entirely. By 1755, at least, John Bonar was referring to the *Treatise* in print as Hume's "compleat system" (see *An Analysis of the Moral and Religious Sentiments contained in the Writings of Sopho* [i. e., Lord Kames], *and David Hume, Esq*; [Edinburgh, 1755], p. 26).

[74] *Life*, pp. 14-15.

[75] See Warburton's letters to Richard Hurd (28 September 1749) and to Philip Doddridge (1750), quoted in Mossner, pp. 289-90.

[76] Quoted by Mossner, p. 326.

published daily, and spread abroad amongst the people with perfect impunity?"

"You are certainly in the right," says the doctor; "there is a most blameable remissness with regard to these matters . . ." (II, 157-58)

When Fielding wrote these lines, it was above all Hume in the *Philosophical Essays* whose scepticism and necessitarianism had, as Warburton put it, "crowned the liberty of the press"; it was a pernicious book, published "to the disgrace of all Government."[77] This, too, is the burden of other pious criticisms of Hume's philosophy which began to be heard more frequently in 1752.[78] These writers concentrated on three especially disturbing aspects of Hume's philosophy: (1) his "scepticism" and "epicureanism"—as evinced by his denial of miracles, of the distributive justice of Providence, and of a future state; (2) his "sentimentalism"—as seen in the theory that moral conduct is a function not of the exercise of reason, but of the passions only; and (3) his doctrine of "necessity." What all these critics understood was that Hume's philosophy was designed to explode the continuous tradition of Christian humanism that had ordered their world.

It will be apparent, then, that the particular "errors" which Fielding wrote into the character of Booth are precisely those which Hume had disseminated in the *Philosophical Essays* and which, from 1749, began to provoke public controversy. Though other models might be found for Booth's epicureanism or his general emphasis on the passions as motivating conduct, Hume alone can be considered a likely source for his doctrine of "necessity arising from the impulse of passion," on which Booth's "chief doubt" about religion and moral responsibility is

---

[77] See Mossner, pp. 289-90.

[78] The first published response to the *Philosophical Essays* was by Philip Skelton. who, in *Ophiomaches: or, Deism Revealed* (2 June 1749), attempted to refute Hume's essay "Of Miracles"; Fielding owned a copy of this work, No. 47 in the Catalogue of his library. My estimate of the reaction to Hume is based on the following works: William Adams, *An Essay in Answer to Mr. Hume's Essay on Miracles* (1752); James Balfour, *A Delineation of the Nature and Obligations of Morality* (Edinburgh, 1753); Robert Clayton, *Some Thoughts on Self-Love, Innate-Ideas, Free-Will, Taste, Sentiment, Liberty and Necessity, etc. occasioned by reading Mr. Hume's Works* (1753); anon., *An Estimate of the Profit and Loss of Religion* (Edinburgh, 1755—B.M. 4374.f.14); anon., *Some Late Opinions concerning the Foundation of Morality, Examined* (1753—B.M. 113.f.51); John Bonar; and John Leland, *A View of the Principal Deistical Writers of the Last and Present Century*, vol. II (1755).

founded.[79] Sensing the full and distressing implications of the *Philosophical Essays*, Fielding, I would suggest, responded to them in *Amelia* by attempting to accommodate Hume's passional psychology within the system of latitudinarian Christianity to which he was committed—declaring, with Barrow and Dr. Harrison, " that religion to be true which applies immediately to the strongest of these passions, hope and fear . . .." The essays of Hume's which seem most relevant to Fielding's concerns in the novel are those " Of Liberty and Necessity " and (to use the revised title) " Of a Particular Providence and of a Future State," and perhaps from the earlier *Essays Moral and Political* those contrasting the philosophies of " The Stoic " and " The Sceptic." But Hume's distinctive analysis of the passions, first presented at length in Book II of the *Treatise*, informs virtually every page of his later, more popular works, and it is all essential background to the sentimentalism of *Amelia*. Furthermore, besides the book's general strategy of appealing to the passions, it is evident that two of the most curious literary aspects of Fielding's novel— his choice of love in marriage as a subject and his experiments with retrospective narrators—coincide with Hume's own critical interests.

That Fielding should carefully avoid any mention of a writer to whom he appears to have responded so profoundly is odd. Once in *Amelia* (IX.ix) he may have Hume in mind when he declares " the truth of an observation which I have read in some ethic writer, that a truly elegant taste is generally accompanied with an excellency of heart; or, in other words, that true virtue is, indeed, nothing else but true taste " (II, 152); but this observation, though an axiom of Hume's ethics, may as easily be associated with Shaftesbury or with Hutcheson, say.[80] If this

---

[79] Lord Kames, Hume's friend and fellow sentimentalist, expounded a similar theory of necessity in his *Essays on the Principles of Morality and Natural Religion* (see Essay III, " Of Liberty and Necessity "); but this work, published in London on 6 July 1751, appeared too late to have had any important influence on *Amelia*.

[80] At the start of the *Philosophical Essays*, Hume himself credits Hutcheson with having " taught us, by the most convincing Arguments, that Morality is nothing in the abstract Nature of Things, but is entirely relative to the Sentiment or mental Taste of each particular Being; in the same Manner as Distinctions of sweet and bitter, hot and cold, arise from the particular Feeling of each Sense or Organ. Moral Perceptions therefore, ought not to be class'd with the Operations of the Understanding, but with the Tastes or Sentiments " (p. 15 n.). Later, summarizing his own system in the essay " Of the Academical or Sceptical Philosophy," Hume observes: " MORALS and Criticism are not so properly Objects of the Understanding as of Taste and

compliment was intended for Hume, one can say only that it is unique in Fielding's writings, and that the ambiguity of reference was prudent, given Hume's unsavory reputation. It is less easy to understand why Fielding should have refrained from indicting Hume publicly for the subversive tendencies of his philosophy. But two possible explanations suggest themselves. For one thing, considering his friend Millar's affection for Hume and his considerable interest in the success of Hume's publications, Fielding may have not wished to attack Hume openly, especially in a work that Millar was publishing. There is the further possibility that Fielding did not wish to add to the publicity that Hume was beginning to enjoy. Upon the early success of the *Philosophical Essays* this, at least, was an important motive to Warburton, who thought that a published attack on the work might only succeed in making its mischief the more virulent. To Hurd on 28 September 1749 he wrote:

> I have a great mind to do justice on [Hume's] arguments against miracles, which I think might be done in few words. But does he deserve notice? Is he known amongst you? Pray answer me these questions. For if his own weight keeps him down, I should be sorry to contribute to his advancement to any place but the pillory.

Given Fielding's silence in the matter, the case for Hume's influence on *Amelia* cannot be finally proved. It will remain an hypothesis only, founded, however, on what appears to be cogent presumptive and circumstantial evidence. As a way of accounting for some of the more puzzling features of the novel, it is at least worth entertaining.

University of Virginia

Sentiment. Beauty, whether moral or natural, is felt, more properly than perceived" (p. 255).

THE SOCIALIZATION OF CATHERINE MORLAND

BY AVROM FLEISHMAN

"And as to *most matters*, to say the truth, there are not many that I know my own mind about."[1] Every schoolboy knows Catherine Morland as an innocent who goes out to discover the world as romance and finds instead the harsh realities of the social nexus in which she lives. In the satirical plan of *Northanger Abbey*, the naïf finds that she has made her mind up not, like Elizabeth Bennet and Emma Woodhouse and Anne Elliot, on the basis of insufficient evidence, but on the wrong kind of evidence altogether—Gothic romance proving no appropriate model in a country neither medieval nor romantic. Yet like that greater naïf whose mind was turned by reading high-flown romances and who found them inapplicable to his time, the heroine—even in her mediocrity—reflects the grand ironies of human experience in the structure of her perceptions. Catherine, like the Don, is matched against not one or another of the antagonists encountered in the course of her travels, but against the entire network of tacit assumptions and habitual behavior which constitutes the individual's cultural milieu. How she learns to make her way in the world by acquiring the cultural forms under which its members order their own thought and conduct—this is the universal drama which *Northanger Abbey* instances.

The realm of literature is the most obvious exception to Catherine's disclaimer, quoted above; in literary matters, she well knows her own mind. Without her reading, which gives her a set of terms by which to order—erroneously, as it happens— some of her perceptions, she might not be aware of herself at all, much less know the external world in even a rudimentary way. It is not alone her scanty store of social facts but her flimsy equip-

---

[1] *The Novels of Jane Austen*, ed. R. W. Chapman (1923; rpt. London, 1965), V; Vol. I, ch. xv, p. 124. Further citations will be made parenthetically in the text, by chapter and page numbers; to conform with other editions, I have numbered the chapters of the second volume in sequence with those of the first (of which there are fifteen).

ment for grasping such facts that Jane Austen develops in the opening account of Catherine's difference from the heroines of romance. After detailing her superficial training and ineptitude in music, gardening, and other subjects, Austen says: "What a strange, unaccountable character!—for with all these symptoms of profligacy at ten years old, she had neither a bad heart nor a bad temper . . . she was moreover noisy and wild, hated confinement and cleanliness, and loved nothing so well in the world as rolling down the green slope at the back of the house" (i, 14). Austen will, of course, neither exult in the glories of childhood innocence nor prefer this variant of the natural man to civilized corruption. Instead, she will trace the stages by which this tomboy is made, not simply into an approximation of a heroine or a marriageable young lady, but into an adequately functioning member of her society. What Catherine does in the course of the action is to *make her mind up*, that is, to furnish it with abstractions, symbols, and patterns of understanding by which men are made distinctively human in the process of cultural formation. The story of this young lady's development is distinguished in the tradition of the *Bildungsroman* by its systematic exploration of the variety of forms which culture provides to constitute the individual mind—a culture including not only literature and moral dicta but esthetic norms, historiography, language, and several kinds of rhetoric. It is as if the tale of Tom Jones or Wilhelm Meister had been rewritten while holding in hand a copy of Cassirer's *Philosophy of Symbolic Forms*.[2] But

---

[2] Cassirer's formulation of the ways in which human life is given its specific and varied character by the cultural symbol-systems into which it is organized is probably so well known as to require no extended summary here. Unfortunately, Cassirer nowhere, to my knowledge, provides an account of the individual's acquisition of the symbols by means of which perception, thought and action in a given society proceed. His formulation of the functions of language, myth, art, historiography, science, etc. in constituting the shape of reality within civilization is given in *The Philosophy of Symbolic Forms*, 3 vols., trans. Ralph Manheim (New Haven and London, 1953). An abbreviated version of his thought is available in *An Essay on Man* (Garden City, N. Y., 1953). Social scientists, e. g., Sorokin, and other philosophers, e. g., Langer, have developed systems to describe the relation of the individual's mental world and the forms provided by his culture. Anthropologists, too, have addressed themselves to the derivation of ways of seeing from the models made available to the individual by society. A number of such studies are collected in *Socialization: The Approach from Social Anthropology*, ed. Philip Mayer, monographs of the Association of Social Anthropologists of the Commonwealth, vol. VIII (London, 1970); especially interesting is an account of the influence of art in Anthony Forge's "Learning to see in New Guinea," pp. 269-91.

Jane Austen did not need a philosopher to support her in establishing her vision of life as lived *sub specie culturalis*.

Austen refers facetiously to Catherine's development as her " training for a heroine " (i, 15), but the materials of her training conspire rather to confirm her in an isthmus of a middle state, destined to fill an ordinary social role among the lower or middle gentry. She is encouraged to make this adaptation by timely exposure to literature, the arcanum of her tribe: by Gray's churchyard maxim recalling the " flower . . . born to blush unseen " (quoted: i, 15), supported by sympathetic thoughts of the poor beetle who " feels a pang as great / As when a giant dies " (misquoted from *Measure for Measure*). In both cases, encouragement is given to accept one's middling lot, while claiming an inner life of sentiment equal to the greatest. Additional models for forming one's expectations of life and postures of response are provided; she is told of Pope's unfortunate lady, who " bear[s] about the mockery of woe " (quoted, i, 15), as contrasted with the less extravagant but equally artificial stance of the woman in love who seems ". . . like Patience on a monument / Smiling at grief " (from *Twelfth Night*). Catherine is here instructed in attitudes of resignation and emotional restraint, based on pictorial images for their bodily expression. Individuality is, on the other hand, given some scope by the application to her own youthful impulses of Thomson's lines on teaching " the young idea how to shoot " (from " Spring "; quoted: i, 15). Catherine's ideas can hardly be considered flowering, but such authority provides a sanction for the romantic impulses that emerge in her taste for the Gothic. In general, we can say that the unshaped mind picks up the formulae available to it in the literature of its social milieu, but selects and emphasizes according to the apparently fixed dispositions of age and temperament, i. e., there is a natural element at work amid the cultural process.[3]

In line with her acquisition of appropriate emotional stances by which to greet the eventualities of love and life, Catherine

---

[3] The Chapman edition's notes and appendices indicate additional literary allusions that play their parts in Catherine's education; they represent most of the major eighteenth-century authors—that is, the "best" near-contemporary texts to stock a young mind. Besides Pope, Gray and Thomson there are Prior and Gay; besides the Gothic romances there are Fielding, Richardson, Sterne, Burney and Edgeworth; and for style, there are (presumed) references to the *Spectator* papers, Johnson's *Dictionary*, and Hugh Blair's *Lectures in Rhetoric, and Belles-Lettres*.

is provided with a smattering of moral attitudes by her authority figures. Her home provides her with apt ethical reflections drawn from collections of maxims like Thomas Moss's *Poems on Several Occasions* and Henry Mackenzie's *The Mirror*. When she finds herself aflutter over the prospect of dancing with Henry Tilney at a Bath cotillion, Austen mimics the moralizing strain which has been imparted to Catherine: "What gown and what head-dress she should wear on the occasion became her chief concern. She cannot be justified in it. Dress is at all times a frivolous distinction, and excessive solicitude about it often destroys its own aim. Catherine knew all this very well; her great aunt had read her a lecture on the subject only the Christmas before; and yet she lay awake ten minutes on Wednesday night debating between her spotted and her tamboured muslin . . ." (x, 73). Moral dicta thus must compete with natural impulses, but they provide the forum of decision and the limits of conduct.

Catherine's chaperone, Mrs. Allen, makes efficient use of moral dicta to assuage her disapointment at the neglect with which she is met at Bath: "This sentiment ['how pleasant it would be if we had any acquaintance here'] had been uttered so often in vain, that Mrs. Allen had no particular reason to hope it would be followed with more advantage now; but we are told to 'despair of nothing we would attain,' as 'unwearied diligence our point would gain'; and the unwearied diligence with which she had every day wished for the same thing was at length to have its just reward . . ." (iv, 31). Meeting an old acquaintance, Mrs. Thorpe, may be accounted some reward for Mrs. Allen's patient hope, but the annoyance to Catherine and the misery of her brother which the Thorpes bring in their wake come to seem less than a providential " just reward." Yet such are the theology-laden terms by which the men and women of Austen's world define their feelings, expectations and fulfillments.

A more general way to describe such formulations would be to say that events, both social and psychological, hardly exist without a language to enunciate them. It is in keeping with this premise that much of Catherine's education consists of instruction in rhetoric. In one of the first conversations with Tilney, the subject of style is raised when Catherine confesses that she keeps no diary. He replies in his arch manner: "'Not keep a journal! . . . How are the civilities and compliments of every day to be related as they ought to be, unless noted down every evening in a journal? . . . it is this delightful habit of journalizing which largely contributes to form the easy style of writing for which ladies are so generally celebrated' " (ii, 27). Henry makes two points here: that the events of the day cannot—for the experiencer—fully be said to have happened until they are transcribed; and that the habitual activity of transforming experience into language gives its peculiar cast to the feminine style. Henry goes on to characterize that style as "'faultless, except in three particulars[:] A general deficiency of subject, a total inattention to stops, and a very frequent ignorance of grammar' "—but these satirical barbs are less profound than his grasp of the relation between the language of young ladies and their modes of assimililating experience.[4]

Henry is, to be sure, something of a pedant on young ladies' deficiencies, and when he catches Catherine up for a colloquial use of "nice" his sister reports on his frequent badgering of her for "incorrectness of language" (xiv, 107). But he does not confine himself to noting the sillier traits of feminine style, and looks instead toward a standard of intelligible and honest communication, from which the ladies' mannerisms are often a concerted deviation. It is striking that he finds his norm best represented in Catherine herself. When he chastises her for her naïveté in interpreting motives, she replies. ". . . I cannot speak well enough to be unintelligible" (xvi, 133). For Catherine's language, despite or because of her novice status in the arts of social relationship, represents a frank intelligibility—to the point of plain-dealing bluntness. She has already established as much with Tilney when, during the contretemps over their broken date, she names the anger which his facial expression reveals. Henry tries to mask not so much his feelings as the naming of them: "'I angry! I could have no right.'" But Catherine frankly declares the evidence: "'Well, nobody would have thought you had no right who saw your face.'" Henry's response is the mark of her victory and affirms the principle to which he himself sub-

---

[4] The view that thought and conduct are affected, perhaps determined, by the semantic structure of the language in which the behavior is conceived is so widespread that it has been called the "Humboldt-Boas-Cassirer-Sapir-Whorf-Lee hypothesis"; see David French, "The Relationship of Anthropology to Studies in Perception and Cognition," *Psychology: A Study of a Science*, ed. Sigmund Koch (New York, 1963), study II, vol. VI, 392. The entire article is useful as a review of research in this field.

scribes: "He replied by asking her to make room for him, and talking of the play" (xii, 95). That is, he is embarrassed into silence on the subject, but also more than ever attracted to Catherine for her rhetorical excellence.

The inclusion of ethical and linguistic norms in the educational activity of *Northanger Abbey* proceeds as a matter of course; rules for speech and social conduct are the first to be taught in any society. More specialized kinds of information are soon provided Catherine in her orientation to adult society—particularly in the realms of historiography and esthetics. The former is introduced in the course of discussing the novice's own special interest, fiction. Her preference leads her to make a sweeping rejection of works of history: "'history, real solemn history, I cannot be interested in . . . The quarrels of popes and kings, with wars or pestilences, in every page; the men all so good for nothing, and hardly any women at all—it is very tiresome: and yet I often think it odd that it should be so dull, for a great deal of it must be invention. The speeches that are put into the heroes' mouths, their thoughts and designs—the chief of all this must be invention, and invention is what delights me in other books'" (xiv, 108). Catherine's naïveté allows her to make two telling points about eighteenth-century historiography, which is most directly implicated: that its subject-matter is restricted to affairs of state, with a corresponding absence of cultural activities and with a predilection toward the so-called "crimes and follies" of historical personages; and the apparently paradoxical point that for all their preference for the factual, historians tend toward ideal reconstructions of states of mind, speeches, and even situations for which precise data is lacking. Catherine is here expressing more than a girlish preference for the romantic as opposed to the brute facts of life, or for fictional "best-sellers" rather than the "non-fiction" shelf of current reading. Her criticism implies a desire for an image of life that will be larger than the proceedings of statesmen and the movements of armies; she wants a picture of the actual life lived by men and women, the world of manners and morals that was later assimilated into historiography by nineteenth-century *Kulturgeschichte*.

The Tilneys, brother and sister, take up the argument in defense of history, but their assumptions do not deny those of Catherine. Eleanor defends the role of "embellishment" or imagination in historical writing, pointing to the success of Hume and Robertson in creating idealized speeches for their historical figures, but this is consistent with the desire for human interest—Catherine would doubtless welcome imaginative heightening if it did not pose as literal fact. Henry, meanwhile, grants the failure of lesser historians to fulfill the "higher aim" (xiv, 109) of history, which the more distinguished achieve. In his well-trained neo-classical parlance, the higher aim of history is "to instruct," but this moralistic abstraction might well accommodate the truthful picture of human life for which Catherine hungers. The close relationship between these ideas of history is never fully revealed to the participants in the debate, but there is an underlying fund of agreement on the need for both the revelation of human truths and the creation of an esthetically satisfying formulation of the past. Catherine is not yet of a mind to adopt historical instruction as a complement to her other modes of orientation to the world around her, but it remains a potentiality of her subsequent marriage to Tilney—in which the anticipated modification of her taste for the Gothic would bring about a more sophisticated awareness of the past.

The social value of esthetic tastes imparted by a girlish education may seem as meager as those of historiography, but the late-eighteenth and early nineteenth centuries were as insistent as our own times that a young person should know his mind about the arts. Landscape, architecture and painting (or drawing) were clearly matters of concern for the well-bred, and there are discussions throughout the Austen canon on these matters.[5] Landscape design does not play an important role in *Northanger Abbey*, where focus of discussion is on architecture. The inspiration for such discussion usually stems from Catherine herself, as she responds to townscapes and buildings with the imagined stuctures of Gothic romance in mind. Her interest in the unfortunate excursion to Blaize Castle with John Thorpe largely derives from anticipation that it is "like what one reads of" (xi, 85); similarly, her view of the spectacle of Bath and its surroundings is in accord with "what I have read about" (xiv, 106). The fullest image of what a medieval building *should* be is, of course, her conception of Northanger Abbey: "... she was to be for weeks

---

[5] A number of considerations have been made of landscape theory in Austen; the fullest is Alistair M. Duckworth, *The Improvement of the Estate: A Reading of Jane Austen's Novels* (Baltimore and London, 1971).

under the same roof with the person whose society she mostly prized—and, in addition to all the rest, this roof was to be the roof of an abbey!—Her passion for ancient edifices was next in degree to her passion for Henry Tilney—and castles and abbies made usually the charm of those reveries which his image did not fill" (xvii, 141). There is a strong suggestion that not only her anticipations of a social visit but her sexual vibration, too, is given its form in her mind—its "image" in her "reveries"—in the framework of the architectural models provided by her reading. Here is another indication of the power of acquired notions of form to shape even one's image of the beloved.

We are given a detailed account of the country house as Catherine explores it, first with General Tilney for a guide and then on her own. The rooms (including a billiard-room) are oppressively modern, the pre-Reformation cloister has become a mere "court," and only the original kitchen proves "rich in the massy walls and smoke of former days" (xxiii, 183). The genuine mystery of English country house architecture—its mixture of medieval and classical elements, and the roots of this mixture of styles in the tangled religious history of the country—all this is lost upon "the well-read Catherine." She is reduced to a simple target of satire as she builds up a mystery around the furniture of her room, according to the prescriptions Henry has set out for her; and she discovers a provocative document that proves to be a laundry list (chapter xxi). In general, Catherine's expectation is of the obscurity associated with antiquity and barbarism, and she takes this association literally enough to be disappointed when the Abbey proves not obscure but open to the light of day: "To be sure, the pointed arch was preserved—the form of them was Gothic—they might be even casements—but every pane was so large, so clear, so light!" (xx, 162).

Architectural taste, as often happens, leads to architectural principle, and Catherine is enlisted in the camp of the preservationists who have, for over two centuries, opposed the alteration (and even restoration) of the monuments of the past: "Catherine could have raved at the hand which had swept away what must have been beyond the value of all the rest [of the building], for purposes of mere domestic economy . . ." (xxiii, 184). As the visit proceeds, however, she comes to sense that personal comfort and contemporary style may be virtues, too: "They took a slight survey of all; and Catherine was impressed, beyond her expectation, by their multiplicity and their convenience" (xxiii, 184). There is, in fact, a process of social as well as architectural enlightenment at work during her stay at Northanger, which culminates in the revelation of the General's avarice and tyrannical manners. The heroine is engaged in a sequence of discoveries about the life lived in country houses, the relation of that manner of life to the visible structures, and the relationships that obtain between esthetic and ethical values. While Catherine is disabused of her belief in medieval models for men like General Tilney, she learns at the same time that a light and airy modern mansion may be the preferred domain of a man who can be crudely inhospitable to a suddenly unwanted guest.

Besides her grand ideas of architecture, Catherine has been urged to try her hand at drawing—" she did what she could in that way, by drawing houses and trees, hens and chickens, all very much like one another" (i, 14). But she is unable to appropriate visual models for the shaping of her personal life, particularly for her projection of a desirable lover: " Her greatest deficiency was in the pencil—she had no notion of drawing—not enough even to attempt a sketch of her lover's profile, that she might be detected in the design " (i, 16). This lack of a technique by which to form a conception of a lover is equalled by her lack of a terminology by which to see the countryside around her: the Tilneys " were viewing the country with the eyes of persons accustomed to drawing, and decided on its capability of being formed into pictures, with all the eagerness of real taste. Here Catherine was quite lost. . . . The little which she could understand however appeared to contradict the very few notions she had entertained on the matter before. It seemed as if a good view were no longer to be taken from the top of an high hill, and that a clear blue sky was no longer a proof of a fine day " (xiv, 110). If any confirmation be needed that cultural symbols can make rain and fine weather, we have it here: not only a good view but a fair day depend for their existence on what men expect them to be. While Catherine is facetiously granted an advantage in being able to attract a lover by her naïveté (" Where people wish to attach, they should always be ignorant "), her best weapon is her capacity to see the world as she is taught to see it: ". . . a lecture on the picturesque immediately followed, in which his instructions were so clear that she soon began to see beauty in every thing admired by him . . . Catherine was so hopeful a scholar, that when they gained the top of Beechen Cliff, she voluntarily rejected the whole city of Bath, as unworthy to make part of a landscape " (xiv, 111).

The most explicit acknowledgement that cultural forms determine the structure of reality for Catherine emerges from her discussion of flowers with Henry:

> ". . . What beautiful hyacinths!—I have just learnt to love a hyacinth."
> "And how might you learn?—By accident or argument? "
> " Your sister taught me; I cannot tell how. Mrs. Allen used to take pains, year after year, to make me like them; but I never could, till I saw them the other day in Milsom-street; I am naturally indifferent about flowers."
> . . . . .
> "At any rate, however, I am pleased that you have learnt to love a hyacinth. The mere habit of learning to love is the thing; and a teachableness of disposition in a young lady is a great blessing." (xxii, 174)

Two broad implications may be drawn from this dialogue: the fairly obvious one that the judgment of beauty and value is a product of education, involving relationships with other people and invoking their perceptual models; and secondarily, that " nature " plays a role in addition to the powerful force of culture, but that this role seems restricted to an openness to cultural influence, " a teachableness of disposition," rather than an inclination in a given direction. Catherine is " naturally indifferent," but this lack of disposition can be hostile to influence, preferring to be left neutral, or it can welcome instruction (especially if Henry's) and eventually acquire the " habit of learning to love." Human nature is seen here as best employed in opening itself to cultural formation—the virtue of naturalness lying not in effusions of pure feeling or freedom from artificial embellishments but in enthusiam for such acquired sensibilities as the love of flowers.

A further esthetic debate takes place in the novel, on the question of representation in painting, particularly of likeness in portraiture. The subject is the dead Mrs. Tilney's portrait and the General's attitude to it—heightened, of course, by Catherine's suspicions of its Gothic role in bearing witness to his presumed crime. The discussion opens before Catherine is shown the picture: Eleanor explains that her father was "dissatisfied" with it, but that she has hung it in her own room—"where I shall be happy to shew it you;—it is very like" (xxii, 181). Catherine's inference immediately follows: "A portrait—very like—of a departed wife, not valued by the husband! He must have been dreadfully cruel to her!" She focuses on the likeness as the mark which should recommend it to Tilney as a primitive substitute for the departed; yet it is precisely that likeness which she comes to question. After seeing the monument to Mrs. Tilney at church on Sunday, and marvelling at the General's coolness in facing up to this testimony to his presumed misdeeds, she confronts the portrait in Eleanor's room:

> It represented a very lovely woman, with a mild and pensive countenance, justifying, so far, the expectations of its new observer; but they were not in every respect answered, for Catherine had depended upon meeting with features, air, complexion that should be the very counterpart, the very image, if not of Henry's, of Eleanor's;—the only portraits of which she had been in the habit of thinking, bearing always an equal resemblance of mother and child. A face once taken was taken for generations. But here she was obliged to look and consider and study for a likeness. (xxiv, 191)

Catherine fails to confirm her previous inferences that the General's dismissal of a "very like" representation of his wife indicates his culpability, for the portrait is not to her mind representative of a Tilney face. But this defeated expectation leads her to go over the grounds of judging likeness.[6] She recognizes in herself a tacit assumption or desire that the portrait will resemble the man she loves (the latter itself a shorthand term for a complex cultural symbol, and a term which Jane Austen

---

[6] The social influence on perceptions of facial resemblance has been observed, not only by many a member of the younger generation receiving the prescriptions of family chroniclers, but also by observers around the world. The classic—and at some points amusing—account of a cultural formula for arriving at judgments of likeness has been Malinowski's: "Malinowski found a complicated but culturally uniform pattern of such perceptions. Among the Trobriand Islanders, children were perceived to look like their father but not at all like their mother. Furthermore, siblings, children of the same father, did not look like each other. Thus, two brothers might each be said to look just like their father; yet it would be vigorously denied that they looked like each other. Malinowski was very impressed with this surprising perceptual pattern—more surprised than the reader might be [—] for this was a matrilinear society that regarded the mother and child as 'blood' relatives, but not the father and the child"; M. H. Segall, D. T. Campbell, and M. J. Herskovits, *The Influence of Culture on Visual Perception* (Indianapolis, 1966), p. 26.

uses sparingly). This assumption depends in turn on previous experience, most of the portraits she has seen having been done on the principle that parents and children must resemble each other—"A face once taken was taken for generations." The esthetic or commercial conventions of a certain type of artist— probably of a social rank inferior to those whom the General and the higher gentry would employ—are thus found to be the determinants of her "habit of thinking." Yet they fail to act as determinants in this case: Catherine is honest and perceptive enough to find the likeness to her beloved absent; she is being introduced to the norms of another school of painting, in which the sitter's individuality is at a higher premium than confirmations of family unity. To sum up, she has transcended both her easy assumption that the portrait resembles Mrs. Tilney and is therefore an indicator of the General's guilt, and also her assumption that the portrait resembles Henry and will therefore call forth the adoring responses that she gives his appearance. Instead, she values the painting with a purer esthetic response, although touched by personal feeling: "She contemplated it, however, in spite of this drawback, with much emotion; and, but for a yet stronger interest, would have left it unwillingly" (xxiv, 191). We cannot say for sure, but she seems to respond to the human values of the portrait—perhaps to the image of Mrs. Tilney's individual being.

Another domain of cultural formation in which the heroine is given some training in getting through the world around her is that of politics. There are no elements of political theory, or even generalizations about political behavior, in the course of her education. But in a remarkable conversation—frequently quoted at length in the critical literature on this novel—a number of symbols are imparted by which Catherine may learn to make perceptions of contemporary affairs. The subject emerges from one of the debates on literature, and although punctuated by an amusing misunderstanding, the talk of politics becomes linked to the system of fictions which structure the heroine's world. Catherine looks forward to the next Gothic novel to "come out in London," which is to be "more horrible than anything we have met with yet" (xiv, 112), but Eleanor takes her to mean a "dreadful riot" in actual life. Henry quickly perceives the double entendres on "come out" and "horrible," and elaborates it into a joke on government: "'Government,' said Henry, endeavouring not to smile, 'neither desires nor dares to interfere in such matters. There must be murder; and government cares not how much.'" The play on words becomes a play on concepts, the most directly implicated being that of *laissez-faire*—government non-interference in private affairs is now extended from publication about murder to murder itself. When Henry explains his little joke, he only complicates it by bringing recent history into evidence:

> "... You [Catherine] talked of expected horrors in London—and instead of instantly conceiving, as any rational creature would have done, that such words could relate only to a circulating library, she [Eleanor] immediately pictured to herself a mob of three thousand men assembling in St. George's Fields; the Bank attacked, the Tower threatened, the streets of London flowing with blood, a detachment of the 12th Light Dragoons, (the hopes of the nation,) called up from Northampton to quell the insurgents, and the gallant Capt. Frederick Tilney, in the moment of charging at the head of his troop, knocked off his horse by a brickbat from an upper window." (xiv, 113)

The perhaps unconscious irony of Henry's satire on girlish exaggeration is that there is no exaggeration here: his account picks up the chief events of the Gordon Riots of 1780—within the lifetimes of the characters, assuming a setting contemporary with the writing of the novel. Moreover, as Dickens was to point out in his version of the Riots in *Barnaby Rudge*, one of the chief horrors was the ineffectuality of a government taking the *laissez-faire* stance in the midst of a near-holocaust.

In effect, Henry's ridicule of his sister's revolutionary fantasies anticipates his later disclaimer of Catherine's literary fantasy vis-à-vis his father's presumed crimes. In both cases the assumption that "it can't happen here" in enlightened, modern England rings a bit false. One of the best commentaries on this subtler note is that of A. Walton Litz: "The ironies of this misunderstanding are directed at complacent sense as well as exaggerated sensibility ... Gothic violence is not impossible in English society, only repressed and rigidly controlled ..."[7] Although Henry in both sessions provides Catherine with a full set of the favored pieties of English political mythology, he fails to overcome the strong influence of the Gothic symbols of underlying social crime.

[7] *Jane Austen: A Study of Her Artistic Development* (New York, 1965), pp. 64-65.

Indeed, his account of the Riots, together with his parodic predictions of her terror at visiting the Abbey, may provide indirect support for her sense of the comparable horrors of life and literature.

In this context, the celebrated satire of Gothic fiction in *Northanger Abbey* becomes but one phase—the decisive phase, to be sure—in a process of socialization. Catherine's enthusiasm for romantic novels is by no means a personal idiosyncracy to be removed by education; she is at the crest of the wave of public taste—especially for girls of her age and class. On the other hand, an exclusive attention to exotic scenes—let alone, extraordinary situations—may tend to unfit the novice for playing his roles in the social world. The heroine must therefore be instructed in the approved way of taking her literary experiences: not as simple schemes for perceiving the world around her, but as highly-charged symbols whose forms add shadow and depth to the prosaic. In the end she must learn to take the Gothic novels not as alternatives to the given but as enrichments and articulations of it. As Lloyd W. Brown writes, in making a similar point:

> The abbey has been endowed with its own individual personality, and the primary function of this identity lies in its stubborn resistance to the patterns of Gothic meaning that Catherine tries to force upon it. Simultaneously, the aura of imaginative splendor which overexcites Catherine serves to rebuke the crass materialism of the building's owner. In effect, Northanger Abbey is a satiric projection of the highly subjective nature of the symbolic process itself. Particularly in the cases of Catherine and General Tilney, it is emblematic of the way in which means of communication like symbols can also be psychological and moral experiences.[8]

A review of the heroine's use of her fictional experience in forming judgments is in order, before approaching her confrontation with the Abbey. While she does not indulge in Isabella's conventional effusions on true love—"'Every thing is so insipid, so uninteresting, that does not relate to the beloved object!'" (vi, 41)—Catherine does take a view of marriage along story-book

---

[8] *Bits of Ivory: Narrative Techniques in Jane Austen's Fiction* (Baton Rouge, 1973), pp. 80-81. See also John K. Mathison, "*Northanger Abbey* and Jane Austen's Conception of the Value of Fiction," *ELH*, 24 (1957), 147-49, which lists the primary ways in which the romances contribute to Catherine's orientation.

lines; when Henry attempts a witty comparison of marriage and dancing, she objects: "'People that marry can never part, but must go and keep house together. People that dance, only stand opposite each other in a long room for half an hour'" (x, 77). Similarly, when the first indications of Isabella's infidelity to her brother emerge, Catherine refuses to believe in the existence of deviations from plighted troth: when Henry sarcastically replies, "'I understand: she is in love with James, and flirts with Frederick,'" she rejects the reality: "'Oh! no, not flirts. A woman in love with one man cannot flirt with another'" (xix, 151). Yet at hearing of Mrs. Tilney's death, "Catherine's blood ran cold," in the appropriate literary phrase; "Could it be possible?—Could Henry's father?—And yet how many were the examples to justify even the blackest suspicions!" (xxiii, 186-87). How can we account for the shift in Catherine's notions of what is morally possible—from the conviction that "a woman in love with one man cannot flirt with another," to the assurance that her "blackest suspicions" are simple truth?

The answer would seem to lie not in the realities but in the symbols involved in these judgments of the possible. The belief that sexual indiscretion is impossible in a respectable girl derives from no generalizations about the conduct of others but only from a sense of what is conceivable in literary convention. Although wider experience of the world may lead her to modify her sexual conceptions, Catherine limits her view of the possible according to the select range of fiction in which such peccadillos are inadmissible. In the matter of wife-murder, on the other hand, Gothicism can widen her conception of the possible. In effect, all such conduct takes place for Catherine in a fictional realm, and it is to one corner of that realm that she consigns General Tilney. There is no great danger of wronging him because her judgment is less a moral than a literary one; her perceptions of his features are not judgments of ethical worth but of literary genre. In this way, she invests him with considerably more intensity and interest than he initially possesses; just as Catherine's visit to Northanger Abbey is heightened by Gothic associations, her image of its proprietor is given vigor and color by her literary sense.

When Catherine comes to reflect on Henry's explanation of the limited applicability of Continental depravities on the sceptered isle of England, she grasps a point about human nature that is far more convincing than his reliance on "the laws of the land, and the manners of the age." "Among the Alps and Pyrenees [she muses], perhaps, there were no mixed characters. There, such as were not as spotless as an angel, might have the dispositions of a fiend. But in England it was not so; among the English, she believed, in their hearts and habits, there was a general though unequal mixture of good and bad" (xxv, 200). Catherine is here in line for promotion in literary as well as ethical discrimination, for she is able to preserve her illusions about Latin extremes of character, yet accepts the Anglo-Saxon as the domain of complex men and women, a fit subject for literary realism. While the complexity of human character was well known to authors before the advent of nineteenth-century realism, it is a firm part of the network of assumptions that determine that literary tradition. In effect, Catherine—with Jane Austen—opts for the conventions of realism in dealing with English life, whatever grotesques of romanticism may be appropriate to Romance lands.

The climax of Catherine's development is no volte-face from romance to realism, but a strengthening of her powers of discrimination by combining the variety of modes of interpretation in which she has become practiced. Her inclination is not to remove the guiltless General from moral scrutiny but to refine her evaluation of him: "Upon this conviction [cited above], she would not be surprized if even in Henry and Eleanor Tilney, some slight imperfection might hereafter appear; and upon this conviction she need not fear to acknowledge some actual specks in the character of their father, who, though cleared from the grossly injurious suspicions which she must ever blush to have entertained, she did believe, upon serious consideration, to be not perfectly amiable" (xxv, 200). Given this mode of perception, she is capable of judging the genuine moral horror of his rough treatment of her—though its abruptness makes it a shock nonetheless. And when Henry tests her in her responses to Isabella's jilting of her brother, according to the literary models of feeling to which she might previously be expected to subscribe, she displays an accuracy of introspection that matches her newly acquired ethical sophistication. "'You feel [he suggests] that you have no longer any friend to whom you can speak with unreserve; on whose regard you can place dependence; or whose counsel, in any difficulty, you could rely on. You feel all this?' 'No,' said Catherine, after a few moments' reflection, 'I do not—ought I?'" (xxv, 207). Her lingering timidity is quickly rebuked by Henry, who delivers one of Jane Austen's finest affirmations of the Socratic imperative of moral intelligence: "'You feel, as you always do, what is most to the credit of human nature.—Such feelings ought to be investigated, that they may know themselves'" (xxv, 207).

In other ways, too, Catherine's literary sense of Northanger is not so much discredited as reworked into another, more complicated pattern. When Eleanor comes to her room to tell of the General's immediate dismissal, the scene is conceived Gothically: ". . . it seemed as if some one was touching the very doorway—and in another moment a slight motion of the lock proved that some hand must be on it. She trembled a little at the idea of any one's approaching so cautiously; but resolving not to be again overcome by trivial appearances of alarm, or misled by a raised imagination, she stepped quietly forward, and opened the door. Eleanor, and only Eleanor stood there. Catherine's spirits however were tranquillized but for an instant, for Eleanor's cheeks were pale, and her manner greatly agitated" (xxviii, 222-23). The first indications of a satirical control shaping this narration imply that the naïve Catherine is again to be reminded—or in this case to remind herself—of the disparity between fact and fiction. Elements of the two realms are melded indissolubly, however: Eleanor's hesitation at the door is motivated by genuine embarrassment and unwillingness to hurt her friend, while her appearance conforms to the melodramatic stance of a fictional character.

Again, the scene itself lends form to Catherine's response to the climactic event: "That room, in which her disturbed imagination had tormented her on her first arrival, was again the scene of agitated spirits and unquiet slumbers" (xxviii, 227). It is true that as the new disturbance is "superior in reality and substance," Catherine regards the "solitude of her situation, the darkness of her chamber, the antiquity of the building . . . without the smallest emotion"; but it is also true that her "contemplation of actual and natural evil" accords perfectly with such a setting—if not in the Gothic, then in the *penseroso* vein. Finally, the heroine's summation of the General, even after Henry's lucid explanation of his motives, employs her reading to provide a metaphoric construct, rather than a literal description, of his behavior: " Catherine, at any rate, heard enough to feel, that in suspecting General Tilney of either murdering or shutting up his wife, she had scarcely sinned against his character, or magnified his cruelty " (xxx, 247).

When the evidence of this fusion of moral, esthetic and other perceptual modes is taken together, we are better able to assimilate the artifice in Jane Austen's rapidly sketched denouement. Her facetious remarks and obtrusive presence have called denunciations down from those with expectations of a consistent realist style, but if the novel's traffic with cultural fictions is held in mind, strictures by reference to realist norms seem footless. *Northanger Abbey* moves beyond its initial parodic style into a fairly conventional satire of the beau-monde at Bath, finally arriving at a complex comic vision of the perceptual illusions involved in all human enterprises—of which a visit to a country house may be taken as a significant instance. In a keen insight into the connection of this mixture of genres with the denouement's artifice, Frank J. Kearful has written:

> The book thus ends by denying the autonomy of the illusion it has presented, as in a Prospero-like gesture the narrator disperses the creatures of her imagination and the world they inhabit. Those who object to the inconsistency of technique and structure in *Northanger Abbey* as well as those who reduce it to univocal form have missed the point of what they have read. . . . [Austen] is, rather, combining elements of all these [genres] in such a fashion as to make us aware of the paradoxical nature of all illusion—even those illusions by which we master illusion.[9]

We may add to this deduction from the novel's mixture of genres a reflection on the varied content of the work: the heroine moves from an unformulated openness to experience, through a naïve notion of the direct applicability of symbols (like those of the Gothic novels), to a more sophisticated use of cultural forms—which she treats no longer literally but metaphorically. When the heroine becomes aware that a literary convention does not predict or determine the behavior of those to whom it superficially

[9] " Satire and the Form of the Novel: The Problem of Aesthetic Unity in *Northanger Abbey*," *ELH*, 22 (1965), 526-27.

applies—and that it yet may be taken as a useful metaphoric construct by which to shape one's response to them, as Catherine does with regard to General Tilney—she has arrived at a peak of cultural self-consciousness, in which one both sees through the artificiality of all cultural symbols and yet remains an active and skillful participant in their processes.

Such playful remarks as those in which the narrative voice accepts the "credit of a wild imagination" (xxx, 243), hastens her characters "to perfect felicity" (xxxi, 250), and questions "whether the tendency of this work be altogether to recommend parental tyranny, or reward filial disobedience" (xxxi, 252), expose the author as a participant in the same symbolic processes by which Catherine's mind is formed in the course of the work. Just as the heroine molds the raw data of experience according to the forms provided in her culture, so the novelist forms the raw data of a fictional donnée by manipulating the conventions and expectations of the literary tradition in which he functions. If the latter are shown to be merely arbitrary, we can the more relish them as a special case of the complex cultural forms displayed in the action. We accept the necessity of, and the enrichment offered by, systems of cultural symbols; by the same token, we are invited to appreciate the artfulness of this most fictional of nineteenth-century fictions.

The Johns Hopkins University

CHARACTERISTICS OF DRYDEN'S PROSE

BY ALAN ROPER

I

Most of us now, when we read through Arnold's " The Study of Poetry," are moved to vindicate the eighteenth century from his charge that its poetry is too much like prose to be good. We rarely trouble to amplify the complementary praise he accorded Restoration and eighteenth-century prose in both " The Study of Poetry " and the earlier preface to his selection from Johnson's *Lives of the Poets.* Yet the praise is just and should be amplified. Johnson's style, Arnold tells us,

> is ours by its organism, if not by its phrasing. It is by its organism,—an organism opposed to length and involvement, and enabling us to be clear, plain, and short,—that English style after the Restoration breaks with the style of the times preceding it, finds the true law of prose, and becomes modern; becomes, in spite of superficial differences, the style of our own day.[1]

The " fit prose " established between the Restoration and the end of the eighteenth century exhibited " the needful qualities " of " regularity, uniformity, precision, balance," [2] and these qualities were Dryden's in abundance. But Dryden, " the puissant and glorious founder . . . of our age of prose and reason," was also " a man, on all sides, of such energetic and genial power." [3] Nearly seventeen years before " The Study of Poetry " Arnold had occasion to praise Jeremy Collier's translation of Marcus Aurelius. The translation, we are told, " deserves respect for its genuine spirit and vigour, the spirit and vigour of the age of Dryden." [4] Spirit and vigor—the " gay and vigorous dissertation " which

---

[1] *Complete Prose Works of Matthew Arnold,* ed. R. H. Super (Ann Arbor: University of Michigan Press, 1960-), VIII, 314.
[2] *Complete Prose,* IX, 180; VIII, 316.
[3] *Complete Prose,* IX, 180, 179.
[4] *Complete Prose,* III, 137.

Johnson found in Dryden's criticism [5]—do not combine easily and always with "regularity, uniformity, precision, balance." Johnson, indeed, perhaps measuring Dryden's prose against his own, found Dryden's clauses "never balanced, nor the periods modelled; every word seems to drop by chance, though it falls into its proper place." [6] Yet Dryden's prose exhibits multiple combinations of vigor and balance. If we can analyse some of those combinations, we will be able to amplify Arnold's praise.

"To how many of us," Arnold exclaimed, is Dryden a mere name, about whose "supposed characteristics of style we may have learnt by rote something from a handbook, but . . . of the power of [his] works we know nothing!" [7] A century later, we can congratulate ourselves on knowing more about the characteristics of Dryden's style than a little handbook information. Scholars have identified various social and intellectual forces which helped shape the prose of Dryden and others. Students learn to speak confidently of a plain style answering the needs of new science, political journalism, or Puritan suspicion of metaphor. Like men of the seventeenth century, we can classify styles as Ciceronian, Senecan, Tacitean, as periodic, loose, curt. We are familiar with the notion that good prose should sound like good talk. Nor have we neglected smaller things. Malone long ago supposed that the changes Dryden made when he revised *Of Dramatic Poesy* for a second edition could usefully illustrate "the progressive improvement of so great a writer." [8] Recent studies have proved him right, and we are aware of Dryden's attempts to banish prepositions from the end of clause or sentence and bring order to the teasing irrationality of relative pronouns. We understand much, then; know much that it's good to know. But our researches have principally confirmed Arnold's praise for a prose exhibiting "regularity, uniformity, precision, balance," and have added to that list, as chief modifier, the quality of conversational ease. By neglecting, as for the most part we have, the qualities of "spirit and vigour," we have insufficiently distinguished Dryden's prose from Addison's, say, to take a style often

---

[5] *Lives of the English Poets*, ed. George Birkbeck Hill (Oxford: Clarendon Press, 1905), I, 412.
[6] *Lives*, I, 418.
[7] *Complete Prose*, VIII, 310.
[8] *Critical and Miscellaneous Prose Works of John Dryden* (London, 1800), I, ii, 2nd. pag., 136.

linked with Dryden's as loose, gentlemanly, urbane. The reasons for neglect are not hard to find. We have classified Dryden's prose, but, except by linguistic study of prepositions and pronouns, we have not described its individuality. To discharge the latter task requires sustained, and seemingly exclusive, analysis of Dryden's prose in terms of itself, rather than explanation of it in terms of social and intellectual influences. It's hard to interest others and oneself in sustained analysis of prose style, in nice speculations upon diction and syntax. Moreover, if we wish to evaluate as well as describe (and who, with Dryden's prose before him, would not wish to evaluate?), we must at some stage be subjective, impressionistic, in order to be properly appreciative. We must concede the truth of Bouhours' proposition: "chacun a ses aversions & ses inclinations dans le langage, aussi-bien que dans le reste."[9] Vexed by those blunt instruments called critical terms, we long to exclaim with Johnson:

> Of all this however if the proof be demanded I will not undertake to give it; the atoms of probability, of which my opinion has been formed, lie scattered over all his works: and by him who thinks the question worth his notice his works must be perused with very close attention.[10]

Sighing that such splendid arrogance is now denied us, we must seek the proof through close perusal.

We must also try to restrain our impressionism (since we cannot banish it altogether), and restraint is hard, though not impossible, to apply when we analyse a prose solely in terms of itself. We merely compound the problem if we try to compare Dryden's style with Addison's, say. The unyielding maxim of Bouhours easily checks our rush to victory, because analysis of one style in itself or comparative analysis of two styles used to say different things in different ways makes it hard to keep distinct our properly objective description and inevitably subjective evaluation. Description should inform evaluation, but evaluation should seep as little as possible into description, else we stagger from our path, drunk with *de-gustibus* relativism. We can find what we need by comparing Dryden's prose with that of another who is trying to say the same thing in much but not precisely the same way. We

---

[9] Dominique Bouhours, *Doutes sur la Langue Françoise*, 2nd. ed. (Paris, 1675), p. 39.

[10] *Lives*, I, 418. Johnson's opinion here is that Dryden's learning was superficial.

must turn to the most neglected works in the canon, Dryden's prose translations. Many are barely acknowledged. I refer to the borrowings, sometimes plagiarisms, from such commentators as Casaubon and Segrais which are embedded in several of the later prefaces. But four are freestanding and acknowledged. One, *The Art of Painting* (1695), translates a French version of a Latin poem,[11] offering comparison too intricate for our purposes. The other three seem more germane: *The History of the League* (1684), from the French of Louis Maimbourg; *The Life of St. Francis Xavier* (1688), from the French of Dominique Bouhours; and the first book of the *Annals* of Tacitus (1698), Dryden's contribution to a translation "by several hands" of the *Annals, Histories, Germania,* and *Agricola.*

Some years ago L. W. Cameron devoted a long note to the translations of Maimbourg and Bouhours, arguing that "anyone interested in Dryden as a craftsman in prose" will find comparison of the French and English worthwhile.[12] Cameron was right, but for many more reasons than he could indicate in the space at his disposal, most of which he used to illustrate the anti-Ciceronian "ideals of urbanity and ease and propriety." In addition, Cameron emphasized the *Xavier*, the less interesting of the two translations. He argued, correctly, that Dryden found the syntax of Bouhours' French more congenial than Maimbourg's. Dryden was able to follow the order of Bouhours' words closely, and respected, for the most part, Bouhours' preference, so unlike his own, for a diction purged of metaphor. Bouhours' *Xavier* shows his adherence to a maxim he had enunciated some years earlier: "le style métaphorique n'est bon parmi nous ni en prose ni en vers."[13] Since, in Arnold's terms, Bouhours' style was more or less Dryden's "by its organism, if not by its phrasing," and since Dryden approximated the phrasing as best he could, his translation is at once too close to the French and too unlike his original prose for us to determine from it many interesting characteristics of his style. The case is otherwise with the translation of Maimbourg, even though that, too, is principally what Dryden called metaphrase, "or turning an Authour word by

[11] *Prose Works*, ed. Malone, III, 293-94.
[12] "The Cold Prose Fits of John Dryden," *Rev. de Litt. Comp.*, 30 (1956), 371-79.
[13] *Entretiens d'Ariste et d'Eugène*, ed. René Radouant (Paris, 1920), p. 51. *Entretiens* was first published in 1671, *Xavier* in 1682.

word . . . from one Language into another."[14] Where Bouhours sought models for good French in Caesar, Seneca, Tacitus,[15] Maimbourg aspired to the style of Livy.[16] Dryden described Maimbourgs's French as "rather *Ciceronian*, copious, florid and figurative; than succinct."[17] Dryden dispatched Maimbourg quickly, devoting little more than three months to a 160,000-word translation.[18] For the most part, nagged, we may suppose, by time, tedium, and quite probably ill health as well, Dryden translated mechanically, word by word, with only the minimum syntactical changes necessitated by differences between the languages. The result is English uncharacteristic of Dryden. But on scattered occasions he translated more freely, employing what he called paraphrase, " or Translation with Latitude, where the Authour['s] . . . words are not so strictly follow'd as his sense."[19] He retrenched, rearranged, and varied the diction. On such occasions we find English reminiscent of Dryden's best.

We may premise that paraphrastic moments in the translation represent freer adaptations of the French in the interests of what Dryden thought good English. Something like an act of choice is involved, and the style of a man who commands his language may properly be seen as the result of choosing, again and again, between available dictions and syntaxes. We can isolate the choices by comparing Dryden's paraphrase with what metaphrase of the same passage would produce. We have, moreover, abundant evidence from the rest of the translation of how Dryden would himself translate metaphrastically. I have said *something like an act of choice is involved*, and the qualification is important, for its omission might suggest a meditated translation remote from what we plainly have and contradicting what we know about the mood and circumstances of composition. An occasional paraphrase of knottily idiomatic French might represent some

---

[14] Preface to *Ovid's Epistles* (1680) in *The Works of John Dryden*, ed. H. T. Swedenberg, Jr., et al. (Berkeley and Los Angeles: University of California Press, 1956-), I, 114.

[15] *Entretiens*, pp. 60-61.

[16] *Histoire de l'Heresie des Iconoclastes*, 2nd. ed. (Paris, 1675), I, sigs. ã4ʳ, ẽ2ʳ.

[17] *The History of the League* (London, 1684), 2nd. pag., p. 48. Subsequent references to this edition are shown in the text.

[18] For the dating of Dryden's work and the edition of Maimbourg he used see my "Dryden's *The History of the League* and the Early Editions of Maimbourg's *Histoire de la Ligue*," PBSA, 66 (1972), 245-75.

[19] *Works*, ed. Swedenberg, et al., I, 114.

deliberation, some choosing of equivalent English. But for the most part we ought to assume that the praraphrase is largely unstudied, almost instinctive.

Maimbourg's intricate periodicity caused problems for Dryden, not all of which he solved satisfactorily. Something similar is true of his partial translation of Tacitus. Anyone who offers an English Tacitus must string a particularly tough bow. That studied brevity, the ellipses, the strong words pushed together, with humble connectives admitted rarely and grudgingly, are hard to catch in English at once close and idiomatic. Dryden's Tacitus is more consistently paraphrastic than his Maimbourg; it is also better English, reads more often like Dryden's original essays. Its usefulness for our purposes is consequently diminished by the too frequent gap between English translation and Latin original. But Dryden's Tacitus confirms some points yielded by his Maimbourg, and adds others. Tacitus also provides a valuable third term. Dryden noted that Maimbourg was not succinct; no more was Dryden. Dryden's adventures with succinct Tacitus and copious Maimbourg show us how to identify important features of Dryden's original prose, so different from theirs. The translations take us away from the Dryden suggested by the revisions in *Of Dramatic Poesy*: Dryden the father of English Augustanism, correct, conversational, well-bred, Dryden, indeed, as an English Bouhours. *The History of the League* and the first book of the *Annals* take us away from that Dryden and back to the Dryden which the eighteenth century itself recognized: elegant at times, it's true, but also negligent, even careless, vigorous, familiar, sometimes coarse.

II

To get a proper sense of Maimbourg's style and the problem it posed for Dryden, we should consider a complete sentence where Maimbourg's periodicity works well. Maimbourg is describing early attempts to establish a league in Picardy:

> Monsieur de Guise ayant envoyé son projet au sieur de Humieres duquel il se tenoit fort asseûré, se Seigneurs [Seigneur], qui outre son attachement à la Maison de Guise, avoit un interest particulier, & aussi grand que celuy de se maintenir dans son Gouvernement de Peronne, qu'on luy estoit [ostoit] par l'Edit de May, pour donner cette importante Place au Prince de Condé, fit si bien par le grand

credit qu'il s'estoit aquis dans toute la Province, que comme d'ailleurs les Picards ont toûjours esté fort zelez pour l'ancienne Religion, il obligea presque toutes les Villes & toute la Noblesse de Picardie à déclarer hautement qu'on ne vouloit point du Prince de Condé, parce que, disoit-on dans le Manifeste que l'on publia pour justifier ce refus[,] l'on sçavoit de toute certitude que ce Prince avoit résolu d'abolir la Foy Catholique, & d'établir universellement le Calvinisme dans la Picardie.[30]

A Bouhours could certainly find here one of those "grandes périodes . . . qui par leur grandeur excessive suffoquent ceux qui les prononcent."[21] But the sentence also supports Pierre Bayle's reproof of Bouhours for failing to realize that a writer often "se sert de periodes un peu longues" because he "veut étre court, & renfermer plusieurs pensées dans un même circuit de paroles."[22] We can see what Bayle means, and perhaps a little more, if we look closely at Maimbourg's sentence, in which a central act, "ce Seigneur . . . fit si bien," is preceded, interrupted, and followed by subordinate clauses. The grammar of the sentence gives us a single subject, Humieres, performing a single act by influencing the Picards to reject Condé. But its logic delivers the sentence as a complex answer to the question, " what caused the Picardy manifesto against Condé? " The machinations of Guise, political interests of Humieres, zealous Catholicism of Picards, public character of Condé, and provisions of the Edict of May cannot be properly expressed as a chronological sequence. Each starts from a different point in time, tending to a different conclusion, but intersecting with all the others at the crucial moment of the published manifesto. The sentence is a ganglion, each of its clauses a nerve of reason, cause, modification, or consequence, and thus provides a fine solution to the historian's problem of expressing, in at least a semblance of chronological sequence, matters not fully explicable sequentially.

Dryden's uneasiness with Maimbourg's style shows in his metaphrase of the sentence (pp. 33-34). Maimbourg uses an easy

[20] *Histoire de la Ligue* (Paris [i. e., The Hague], 1684), pp. 25-26. Simple errors in " Dryden's edition," a Dutch piracy with pseudonymous imprint, are followed by the reading of the quarto first edition (Paris, 1683); dropped words and punctuation are also restored from the quarto. Subsequent references are shown in the text.
[21] *Entretiens*, p. 129.
[22] *Critique Generale de l'Histoire du Calvinisme de Mr. Maimbourg*, 3rd ed. (Ville-Franche [i. e., Amsterdam], 1684), I, 53.

device for suspending the sense of a period: separation of subject and predicate by a series of clauses modifying the subject. In Dryden's version this series is enclosed in parentheses, presumably Dryden's, or just possibly the supervisor's, since the parenthesis is much too long to have been opened by a compositor. For Dryden these clauses and phrases, separating subject and verb, really are parenthetic, because they apparently do not gloss the main, grammatical action of the sentence. But for Maimbourg, I have argued, they are not at all parenthetic. However subordinate, even incidental, they may appear grammatically, they are correlatives in the logic of the sentence.

Maimbourg's style will not go easily into English at once close and idiomatic. French is much richer in pronominal conventions than is English, and Maimbourg ransacks its treasures to gratify his passion for the relative construction. Bouhours was certainly right to warn against ambiguous reference in relative and personal pronouns,[23] and ambiguity is even more likely in English than in French. As Swift observed to Hooke, " one of the greatest difficulties in our language, lies in the use of the *relatives*; and the making it always evident to what *antecedents* they refer." [24] The advantage of even a moderately inflected language like French over a virtually uninflected language like English is that it can rely upon the inflection to connect, say, a pronoun with a remote antecedent, or a verb with a remote subject.

But there is more to the matter than a grammatical difference between languages pushed to extremes by the stylistic habits of Maimbourg and Dryden. Maimbourg's style conveys a manner of apprehending experience quite distinct from Dryden's, as we can begin to see by comparing the French and English of a passage late in the history explaining why Sixtus V ceased to oppose Henry IV and accepted him. Here is Maimbourg's version:

> Car ayant fait de solides réflexions sur le passé, sans se laisser préoccuper, il avoit clairement connu le grand merite du Roy, qu'il taschoit alors de regagner à l'Eglise par la douceur; l'ambition des Chefs de la Ligue; les fourberies de leurs Agens, qui l'avoient si souvent trompé par leurs fausses relations; & sur tout les pernicieux desseins des Espagnols, qui pour l'engager tellement avec eux qu'il ne s'en pust

---

[23] *Doutes*, 4me. Partie, " sur la Netteté," *passim*.
[24] Spence, *Anecdotes*, ed. James M. Osborn (Oxford: Clarendon Press, 1966), I, 169.

> dédire, vouloient à toute force qu'il excommuniast tous les Catholiques qui suivoient le Roy, & qu'il s'obligeast par serment à ne le recevoir jamais dans le sein de l'Eglise, quelque soumission qu'il luy pust faire. (pp. 427-28)

Dryden translates thus:

> For having made solid reflections on the past, without suffering himself to be prepossess'd, he clearly understood the great merits of the King, whom he then endeavour'd to reconcile to the Church by gentle usage: The Ambition of the Heads of the *League*, the indirect dealing and cousenage of their Agents, (who had so often deceiv'd him by false Relations; and more than all the rest, the pernicious designs of the *Spaniards*, who that they might irrevocably ingage him in their Interests, were vehemently urgent with him to Excommunicate all the Catholiques who follow'd the King, and that he shou'd bind himself by Oath, never to receive him into the Bosom of the Church, what submission soever he should make;) had open'd his eyes, and caus'd him to take much other measures. (p. 823)

Dryden reworks Maimbourg poorly. He makes Maimbourg's first object—the merit of Henry IV—the sole object of "understood," and Maimbourg's remaining co-ordinate objects—the ambitions of the League heads, the lies of their agents, and the pretensions of the Spanish—co-ordinate subjects for a new predicate not in Maimbourg. Since this predicate must carry a great weight of subject, Dryden stretches it out by making it co-ordinate. The first part, "had open'd his eyes," is obviously suggested by the earlier main verb, "clearly understood," while the second exists as just so many words sufficient to conclude the rhythm of the sentence. Dryden effectively makes two sentences of Maimbourg's one, dividing them with a colon. Since he cannot manage the suspended sense of the second sentence, he tries to signal his intentions by opening a parenthesis to announce that the predicate will be delayed. But the parenthesis is opened for a relative clause modifying his second co-ordinate subject; it continues with his third subject, which is not parenthetic in his syntax. Despite the weakness of the English here, the translation points to what Dryden found most alien in Maimbourg's style. Maimbourg's four co-ordinate objects together explain how Sixtus V came to change his mind, an act which forms the substance of the preceding sentence. Dryden wants Sixtus to argue out his motives in sequence, not, as in Maimbourg, apprehend all things at once.

Dryden's difficulty with Maimbourg involves the difference between explanation or judgment thought out before being set down and explanation or judgment recorded while being formed. His difficulty with Tacitus (although it seems not to have troubled him greatly) involves the difference between explanation or judgment implied and made explicit. Tacitean judgment is clear, but, especially in the *Annals*, frequently unstated. Judgment often inheres in terse antithesis, an unelaborated coupling of base act and noble sentiment, say, or juxtaposition of bad conduct and good principle. Dryden responds by explicating the contrast, usually by dwelling upon the base member, rendering it more ignominious or scurrilous.

When the Pannonian veterans began to murmur, one Percennius encouraged them in dissidence:

> Is imperitos, & quænam post Augustum militiæ conditio ambigentes, impellere paulatim nocturnis conloquiis, aut flexo in vesperam die, & dilapsis melioribus, deterrimum quemque congregare.[25]
>
> (This man, [working upon] minds ignorant and doubting what the condition of military service might be after Augustus, gradually incited [them] by nocturnal conversations, or when day had turned into evening; and when the better had scattered [to their quarters], assembled all the worst.)

English cannot respect the syntax of this passage without adding a phrase or two. But English scarcely demands a version as free as Dryden's:

> This Man haunting the Conversation of the most Ignorant, and Silly, who were very inquisitive to know what their Condition was like to be under their new Emperour, debauch'd them by his Nightly Conversations with them, or at least when it grew late in the Evening; and when the more sober Party were withdrawn to Rest, assembled the Band of Mutineers.[26]

[25] *Annals*, I.xvi; subsequent references are shown in the text. Quotations from Tacitus follow the text of Johann Gronovius. I use an edition published in Amsterdam in 1685, which has the advantage, not common in early editions, of adopting chapter divisions almost identical with those in modern editions.

[26] *The Annals and History of Cornelius Tacitus* . . . 3 vols. (London, 1698), I, 48. Subsequent references are shown in the text. I have not included Dryden's chapter numbers, since they differ greatly from those of Gronovius and modern editions.

Tacitus offers a dispassionate account of what Percennius did, restricting judgment to the antithetical *melioribus, deterrimum*; for *imperitos*, with its sense of unskilled or inexperienced as well as ignorant, rather describes than judges the veterans. Dryden's contempt for seditious mobs shows in the intensification of judgment. "Most Ignorant, and Silly" combines with "very inquisitive" to make vacant fools of the disaffected, while those "Nightly Conversations" seem drunken when *impellere* becomes "debauch'd" and *melioribus* "the more sober Party." An English translator who respects the position of *is* must immediately anticipate *impellere*, but "haunting the Conversation of" (pressing for acquaintance with), while catching in part the process marked by *paulatim*, renders neutral adverb as furtive act. "The Band of Mutineers," proleptic in context, since the veterans are as yet only disaffected, not openly rebellious, makes of potential act a present judgment. Like any English translator, Dryden needs more words than Tacitus. We must call his version paraphrase, because the "words are not so strictly follow'd as [the] sense." Dryden added that, in paraphrase, the sense "is admitted to be amplyfied, but not alter'd." Yet we can see clearly that amplification involves considerable alteration of the spirit, and perhaps of the sense as well. Amplification, the extra words and phrases, renders the passage unlike Tacitus, substituting scornful judgment for dispassionate commentary.

Something similar is true of Dryden's tendency to offer the explanations Tacitus leaves unstated. Thus it is when Germanicus had crushed the mutiny of the fifth and twenty-first legions. The chastened soldiers persuaded Germanicus to lead them immediately against the unsuspecting Germans: *læti neque procul Germani agitabant* (I. 1) (the Germans were merrily occupied, and not far off). Dryden adds a clause: "the *Germans*, who were not far distant, pass'd their Time secure in Pleasure, while the War seem'd to sleep about them" (I, 100). *Læti* translates most easily into an adverb. Having made his adverb "secure in Pleasure," Dryden adds a clause explaining or glossing "secure," a clause begotten by the needs of a preceding word. At moments like this, prose from Dryden's last years respects a principle enunciated in his first published essay. A poet, he insisted, should so order his syntax "that the first Word in the Verse seems to beget the second, and that the next, till that becomes the last Word in the Line which in the negligence of Prose would be so." [27]

News of Germanicus' successes reached Rome, where *nunciata ea Tiberium lœtitia curaque adfecere* (I.lii) (announcement of this matter affected Tiberius with joy and anxiety). Once again, Dryden incorporates explanation: "when *Tiberius* had Intelligence of this, it fill'd him with excess of Joy; but the Pleasure was not so sincere, as not to be mix'd with great Disturbance" (I, 102). Tacitus goes on to explain the mixed emotions—joy that the mutiny was crushed, anxiety that Germanicus would gain in popularity and glory. Dryden's long paraphrase of *lœtitia curaque* does not, in any case, explain why Tiberius had mixed emotions. Rather, it explains how such emotions could be mixed; it explicates the curt antithetical pair. "Not so sincere, as not to be mix'd" is nearly tautologous (not so unmixed as not to be mixed). But "sincere," while in one sense preparing for, begetting "not . . . mix'd," implies in another sense "undissembled," and Tacitus repeatedly notes the dissimulation of Tiberius, as he does a few lines later. Moreover, the Tiberius of Tacitus experiences contrasted emotions simultaneously; Dryden's Tiberius experiences his emotions successively: first the "excess of Joy," then the admixture of "great Disturbance." The difference here is similar to that between the Sixtus of Maimbourg and of Dryden. In French, the Pope acts for reasons he apprehends all at once; in English, he argues his motives in sequence.

This tendency to substitute sequence for simultaneity shows even more in passages of physical description, accounts of a battle, riot, or procession. Such passages account for much of the paraphrase in *The History of the League*, perhaps because they appealed more to Dryden than did the long analyses of character, motive, event, and issues. One instance will suffice.

Maimbourg is recounting the preparations for the great battle of Coutras between the royalist forces under Joyeuse and Navarre's Huguenots. After describing the Huguenot battle lines, Maimbourg turns to the royalists:

> Cependant le Duc de Joyeuse ayant passé avec beaucoup de peine, & de desordre, causé par la jeune Noblesse volontaire dont on ne pouvoit arrester la fougue, certains fascheux défilez qui estoient entre son logis & la plaine, le Marquis de Lavardin

[27] Dedication of *The Rival Ladies* in *Works*, ed. Swedenberg, *et al.*, VIII, 100.

> son Mareschal de Camp, grand homme de guerre, sur lequel il se réposoit, y mit, comme il put, en bataille cette armée, qui ne montoit alors à gueres plus de neuf mille hommes, & gardoit tres-peu de discipline. (p. 141)

Dryden's version strikingly reorders the French syntax. especially of the long initial participle:

> In the mean time the Duke of *Joyeuse*, having pass'd through certain narrow and troublesome ways, which lay betwixt his last Nights Lodging and the Plain, and that with difficulty enough, which was caus'd by the disorderly March of his young Gallants, whose eagerness was not to be commanded; the Marquis of *Lavardin* his Marshal *de Camp* a great Souldier, on whom chiefly he rely'd, drew up his Army into Battalia, as well as the disorder wou'd give him leave; his whole Forces, at that time, not amounting to more than nine thousand men, and those ill Disciplin'd. (pp. 209-10)

The reason for Dryden's initial reordering is obvious: to eliminate the distance between the participle, "having pass'd," and its object. Dryden explodes Maimbourg's suspended syntax, rearranging its members into a cumulative sequence. He proceeds by accretion, dealing with one thing at a time. But Maimbourg, at least until he gets to "défilez," is always dealing with two things at once: the force of a modifying clause or phrase and the still to be completed significance of "ayant passé." Dryden's English reads more quickly than Maimbourg's French, because it does more of the reader's work for him. But Maimbourg's French recognizes far more clearly than does Dryden's English that we have yet to reach the main verb, because it reminds us all the time that we are reading through a participial phrase. The phrase, moreover, commences a sentence whose subject is not Joyeuse, but Lavardin, his experienced chief officer. The Joyeuse participle in Dryden is virtually detached from the main clause, so that there is a small syntactical surprise when we suddenly come upon Lavardin performing the main action of the sentence. But in Maimbourg the whole period conveys strikingly the effect of Lavardin, a center of order and experience both in the sentence and on the field, surrounded by disorder and inexperience he cannot eliminate, but only mitigate. Having lost some of this effect through his syntax, Dryden tries to recapture it by adding a clause: "as well as the disorder wou'd give him leave." Where

Dryden's syntax expresses movement through time and space, Maimbourg subordinates movement to a pattern of relationships he can scrutinize all at once.

To make his sentences flow pleasingly Maimbourg characteristically used the object of one relative clause as antecedent of the next. The subject shifts constantly, human agent replaced by his act, act in turn replaced by its cause or consequence. Attributes of men, their deeds and motives, become of equal syntactical importance with the men themselves. Dryden, it seems, instinctively maintained a focus upon human agent as subject. This difference between styles is plain in Dryden's reworking of an elegant simile. The irresolute Henry III's occasional gestures of decision were, says Maimbourg,

> semblables à ces foibles efforts qu'un homme encore demi-endormi semble faire pour se lever, & qui cedent aussitost aprés à cette force imperieuse du sommeil, auquel il se rend & se laisse par sa lascheté, & qui en un instant le fait retomber dans son lit. (pp. 73-74)

Maimbourg uses three subject: foibles efforts, un homme, and la force du sommeil. Dryden uses only one subject: " like those weak motions which men seem to make in frightfull dreams, when they rowze themselves a little, but immediately yield to the force of sleep " (p. 119). Dryden makes his human agents his sole subject, and makes the simile more striking by substituting men startled half-awake in a nightmare for a man drowsily and indolently half-rousing himself in the morning. Maimbourg's version is certainly more appropriate to his characterization of Henry III, the man who, on mounting the throne, slipped into a long self-indulgence, from which he was infrequently and only briefly aroused by recollections of his former greatness as Duke of Anjou. Dryden's instinct for the telling phrase, " frightfull dreams," distracts from the point to be made here.

Those " frightful dreams " remind us that the vigor of Dryden's prose results not only from a focus upon human agents. Nor does it come solely from a preference for sequence over simultaneity, from an inclination to subsume analysis under narrative or drama, an inclination equally apparent in *The Hind and the Panther* and *Of Dramatic Poesy*. The vigor comes also from the pressure he puts upon words. It's hard not to be struck by the freedom with which Dryden moves between levels of diction, ranging from the coarsely familiar to the elegantly formal. Dryden's comedies show that he had, as much as his Augustan successors, a clear sense of dictions appropriate to different classes of society. His nondramatic prose, especially the polemical prose of the 1680's, shows that, unlike many of his successors, he was willing to sacrifice propriety to vigor by introducing the vulgar but powerful word into polite contexts.[28]

This difference between Augustan propriety and, let us call it, Restoration indecorum is nicely illustrated by the response of that representative Augustan, William Warburton, to Dryden's translation of Maimbourg. Warburton's copy of *The History of the League*, now in the Huntington Library, contains his autograph opinion of the work on the front fly-leaf. His opinion runs in part:

> This elegant translation is debased by a great number of cant or fashionable words & phrasis [sic] then in use at Court, and which slunk out of the language again before they had made any further progress in it. The dignity of historic narrative is further debased by familiar & comic expressions, which Dryden had accustomed himselfe to use in his political Pamphlets.

Instances of what Warburton disliked are not hard to find. Maimbourg's Henry III, angered by the declamations of a League preacher, " le fit mettre en prison " (p. 119); Dryden's Henry III " clap'd him up in Prison " (p. 180). The coarse vigor of " clapped up " is extended when Biron warns Henry III to beware of receiving a procession of penitents in Chartres Cathedral. Maimbourg's Biron " conseilloit au Roi de les faire tous arrester " (p. 255); Dryden's Biron " counsell'd the King to clap them up in Prison every Mothers Son " (p. 370). Unlike Maimbourg, Dryden is " hearing " an approximation of what the blunt Biron " said " to Henry III. If Dryden debases " the dignity of historic narrative " here, he also achieves a dramatic immediacy absent from his original. That same preacher who so angered the

---

[28] Edmond Malone sums up the eighteenth-century view of Dryden in his edition. His appreciation for Dryden's prose is set out in his advertisement, which ends by quoting Johnson's magisterial assessment (I, i, i-xix). But Malone's notes to the essays include some thirty corrections of Dryden's grammar, syntax and diction, drawing attention to Dryden's carelessness and undue familiarity: e. g., " this colloquial vulgarism . . . which was common in the last age, is now seldom heard but from the mouths of the illiterate." (II, 22).

king was once ironically complimented by the Duke of Joyeuse for his " si beau talent de divertir, [&] faire rire le Peuple en ses Sermons " (p. 119). In Dryden the preacher is complimented for having " so noble a Talent as to divert the people, and set them on the merry pin of Laughing at his Sermons " (p. 180). Warburton presumably did not read Dryden against Maimbourg, but he could have easily identified as Dryden's departure from Maimbourg that " familiar & comic " expression, " set them on the merry pin of Laughing."

Warburton was neither first nor last to find coarseness in Dryden; the charge has been made from Jeremy Collier to C. S. Lewis. But Dryden's coarseness shows not only or principally in his frequent recourse to the familiar and comic. No more does *The History of the League* supply the clearest evidence. Tacitus provides the proper contrast. We have already seen how Dryden will sacrifice restraint to achieve vigorous and pungent judgment. The result may be good Dryden, but it's certainly poor Tacitus, quite losing the effect of more meant than said, of phrasing whose unfailing elegance never conceals the emotion that pushed such observations together. We may take Tacitus at his finest, and see how Dryden fares with him.

In the year of Rome 768 Germanicus went back with an army to the forest of Teutoburgium, where, six years before, three legions commanded by Varus were caught in marshes and annihilated by the Germans under Arminius. Their bodies, it was said, still lay unburied. Tacitus recounts in order the advance upon Teutoburgium, the finding of bones, their burial, the vindication of Rome from six years' shame by the rout of Arminius and the Germans. It's a compelling sequence, likely, one would think, to move Dryden, who shared the Roman rather than the French sense of *patria*: *pietas,* not *la gloire.* Dryden expands freely, but nowhere more strikingly than in the climactic discovery of bones. Here is Tacitus:

> medio campi albentia ossa, ut fugerant, ut restiterant, disjecta vel aggerata: adjacebant fragmina telorum, equorumque artus, simul truncis arborum antefixa ora.   (I. lxi)
>
> (in mid-plain were whitening bones, scattered or heaped, as they had fled, as they had stood firm; nearby were lying fragments of spears and horses' limbs; and heads were fastened to tree trunks.)

What should a translator do? What but cobble a rude metaphrase and append a despairing *O, altitudo!* Dryden, alas, had more confidence in himself:

> The middle of the Field was strew'd with Carcasses, and white dry Bones, some scatter'd here and there, and others pil'd on heaps; by which might be observ'd, whether they receiv'd their Death in flight, or fell together in manly Resistance to the last. Every where were found their broken Pikes, and Javelins; the Limbs of Horses, and their Jaw-bones; and the Heads of Men, which were fix'd to the Trunks, or hung on the Branches of the Trees. (I, 121)

Dryden lingers over the scene, amplifying and explaining it, especially in the thirty-one-word rendering of *ut fugerant, ut restiterant, disjecta vel aggerata.* He says everything twice: " Carcasses ... and Bones " instead of *ossa,* " Pikes, and Javelins " instead of *telorum; artus* becomes " Limbs ... and ... Jaw-bones," while " fix'd to the Trunks, or hung on the Branches " renders *truncis ... antefixa.* In Tacitus the judgment, the measuring of act against principle, is clear, but withheld to permit concentration on event. If they were to die there, it was better that countrymen find their bones heaped with comrades', not scattered about. Tacitus does not tell us it was better, because he does not need to. Dryden, it's true, does not tell us either, not roundly, that is. But his diction, his amplification, marks the preference, forcing it insistently upon us. Instead of permitting us an emotion we have partly created for ourselves, Dryden, in effect, orders us to feel it. " Manly Resistance " is sentimental. With Tacitus we have our work to do, and do it instantly. From the evidences he presents we must recreate the end of Varus and his legions, the mingling of actions, courage and weakness, the confusion of men with beasts and things, the shame and pain of heads on trees. We run through successive apprehensions, our own and those of Tacitus, Germanicus and his legions, Varus and his. With Dryden our work is done for us, the scene now busy, filled with evidences of many acts, gruesomeness elaborated into Gothic horror. Event is typified into the appropriate scene for a massacre, any massacre, the scene generalized through greater specificity. Dryden's version might have figured in an allegorical romance; in a Tacitus it debases the dignity of historic narrative. " Chacun a ses aversions & ses inclinations dans le langage, aussi-bien que dans le reste" was no doubt wisely said, but these things must also be said.

One feature of Dryden's translation here, his saying everything twice, illustrates a preference which shows throughout the versions of Maimbourg and Tacitus. Cæcina, we are told, *Marsos . . . prœlio cohibuit* (I.lvi) (the Marsi . . . he subdued by battle). But in Dryden "the *Marsi* . . . were vigorously repuls'd, and entirely routed" (I, 113). Instances troop through the pages of *The History of the League.* "Prémedité" (p. 11) becomes "premeditated, and hatch'd" (p. 14); "meriter" (p. 22) becomes "to deserve and gain" (p. 29); "dissatisfi'd, and weary" (p. 30) renders "lassez" (p. 23); "suppress'd and rooted out" (p. 64) renders "exterminé" (p. 33); "alloit troubler" (p. 58) stretches into "tended to the confusion and ruine" (p. 98). Such synonyms may signal the difficulty of catching the suggestions of one foreign word in only one English word. But fondness for synonymous or nearly synonymous words and phrases also characterizes Dryden's verse and original prose. Repetition, I concede, is often no more than a careless way of achieving emphasis or balance. But, by dwelling upon action or attribute, it can also increase physicality. And Dryden's prose, as much as his verse, is full of men doing things.

This physicality is also increased by another of Dryden's preferences in diction, a preference for the live over the dead or half-dead metaphor, an inclination to add a word or two in order to complete the action of a metaphor. Instances of this preference in the translations, while frequent enough, are not striking, but nonetheless suffice to illustrate a crucial feature of Dryden's original prose. At one point Maimbourg notes that "si l'Estat n'estoit pas encore tout à fait tranquille, on n'estoit pas du moins dans l'agitation d'une violente tempeste" (p. 4). But for Dryden, "if the State was not altogether in a Calm, yet at least it was not toss'd in any violence of Tempest" (p. 5). Admittedly, the voyage of the ship of state is a metaphor lying so close to anyone's hand as scarcely to be worth using. But we should note that Dryden's "in a Calm" and "not toss'd in" make a continuous sequence, a vicissitudinous voyage, of what in Maimbourg are disjunctive conditions associated with different subjects. The words of Dryden's clauses are more conscious, and more physically conscious, of each other than are Maimbourg's words. Later in the history Maimbourg describes the reaction of Henry III when the Duke of Guise, against the king's orders, returned to Paris and was tumultuously received. Henry decided to break the League's power in Paris and re-establish himself as master there. After receiving counsel, he " demeura ferme dans la mesme résolution, & ne voulut pas en avoir le démenti pour l'arrivée du Duc de Guise " (p. 239). In Dryden, the king " continu'd firm to the same resolution, and set up his rest to stand by it, in spight of the arrival of the Duke " (p. 347). Dryden's Henry, but not Maimbourg's, wagered his reserve stake, " set up his rest," loss of which ended the card game of primero. A Warburton could object that the image here is too familiar, a " cant or fashionable " phrase " then in use at Court." But the phrase catches well that note of risk, desperation, the gamble taken, which sounds throughout the confrontation of Henry III and the Guise in the hours before the Day of the Barricades.

III

When we apply the lessons of these translations to Dryden's original prose, we will look for the recurrence, not necessarily consistent, of other features than those we have learned, in recent years, to recognize there. We need not lose, indeed we should never forget, Dryden the father of English Augustanism, with a prose marked by conversational ease, urbanity, and a solicitude for correct English. But Dryden, as patriotic as Bouhours, was much more than an English Bouhours, and that more is focussed for us by the translator of Maimbourg and Tacitus. This is the Dryden of confident movement through time, space, or the points of an argument, the Dryden who, however rational his discourse, typically subsumes analysis under drama or narrative. This Dryden maintains an emphasis upon human actors, upon people doing things, so that the attributes of men, their thoughts, deeds, or gestures, become by metaphor men themselves. This Dryden presses upon words, restoring life to dead metaphors, and finds again and again the word not merely apt, but striking, the word not merely just, but lively, full of life. This Dryden combines the syntax of exploration, phrases made as needed, not fashioned in advance, with the diction of authoritative judgment. This Dryden, too, taking risks with language, sometimes pays the price with an imperfect construction or word strained too far,[29] a pointless repetition or vulgar elaboration of detail.

This Dryden is everywhere in the collections of Malone, or Ker, or Watson, but we ought to take him at his best, from that preface which he wrote to *Fables* after so many years studying and practicing the other harmony of prose. We need a paragraph:

> With this account of my present undertaking, I conclude the first part of this discourse: in the second part, as at a second sitting, though I alter not the draught, I must touch the same features over again, and change the dead-colouring of the whole. In general, I will only say that I have written nothing which savours of immorality or profaneness; at least, I am not conscious to myself of any such intention. If there happen to be found an irreverent expression, or a thought too wanton, they are crept into my verses through my inadvertency: if the searchers find any in the cargo, let them be staved or forfeited, like counterbanded goods; at least, let their authors be answerable for them, as being but imported merchandise, and not of my own manufacture. On the other side, I have endeavoured to choose such fables, both ancient and modern, as contain in each of them some instructive moral; which I could prove by induction, but the way is tedious, and they leap foremost into sight without the reader's trouble of looking after them. I wish I could affirm, with a safe conscience, that I had taken the same care in all my former writings; for it must be owned that, supposing verses are never so beautiful or pleasing, yet, if they contain anything which shocks religion or good manners, they are at best what Horace says of good numbers without good sense, *versus inopes rerum, nugæque canoræ*. Thus far, I hope, I am right in court, without renouncing to my other right of self-defence, where I have been wrongfully accused, and my sense wire-drawn into blasphemy or bawdry, as it has often been by a religious lawyer, in a late pleading against the stage; in which he mixes truth with falsehood, and has

---

[29] But Dryden was also conscious that his language lacked certainty and definition. See the dedication of *Troilus and Cressida* (1679) in *Prose Works*, ed. Malone, II, 49: "But how barbarously we yet write and speak, your Lordship knows, and I am sufficiently sensible in my own English. For I am often put to a stand in considering whether what I write be the idiom of the tongue, or false grammar, and nonsense couched beneath that specious name of *Anglicism*; and have no other way to clear my doubts but by translating my English into Latin, and thereby trying what sense the words will bear in a more stable language. I am desirous, if it were possible, that we might all write with the same certainty of words and purity of phrase, to which the Italians first arrived, and after them the French; at least that we might advance so far as our tongue is capable of such a standard."

not forgotten the old rule of calumniating strongly, that something may remain.[30]

The sentences in this paragraph, except the second and shortest, all seem slightly surprised at their own capacity for endurance. They appear uncertain at their setting forth of their precise destination or the stops they will make along the way. The matter of clause or phrase is determined less by the needs of the sentence as a whole than by the matter of the clause or phrase which precedes it. "Thoughts, according to Mr Hobbes, have always some connection."[31] Especially is this the case when thoughts are expressed in metaphors, because a partial metaphor clamors for extension until its action is completed. The painter not only touches "the same features over again," he also changes "the dead-colouring." The customs officer both confiscates contraband and taxes imports. The result is an unpremeditated syntax proceeding by accretion, clause added to clause with an emphasis upon co-ordinates. We can see from *The History of the League* that Dryden did not study for such a syntax, since, translating hurriedly, he used it there, often unsuccessfully, to render Maimbourg's premeditated syntax, where clauses and phrases are determined in length and position by the needs of the whole sentence. Dryden's Joyeuse, but not Maimbourg's, having proceeded, participially, from his lodgings to the battlefield of Coutras, finds to his surprise that he has nothing to do there but step aside in favor of the chief actor in the sentence, Lavardin.

One qualification should be made, and again the translations help us to it. The final clause or phrase, while still suggested by the preceding, also respects the needs of the whole sentence: it must end the sentence properly. Dryden's Sixtus V, changing his mind about Henry IV, traps himself in syntax, confusing objects with subjects, and extricates himself clumsily with a made-up, co-ordinate predicate. The predicate not only stretches into sufficient words to bear the weight of the preceding subjects, but also signals through partial repetition—" had open'd his eyes, and caus'd him to take much other measures "—that the sentence is coming to an end. Sentences like Dryden's, moving through

[30] *Of Dramatic Poesy and other Critical Essays*, ed. George Watson (London: Dent, 1962), II, 273-74.
[31] *Essays*, ed. Watson, II, 271.

the stages of an action or argument, ought not to end in midcareer, thrusting forward onto the next sentence. Accordingly, the movement can be slowed at the end by near or actual synonym, repeating argument or gesture, or seeing it again in a slightly different way. Sixtus V's predicate no doubt lingers on at least partly in the interests of cadence, but such is scarcely the case with the repetitions that conclude several sentences in the paragraph from the preface to *Fables*. By emphasizing the last detail in the scene, action, or argument that forms the substance of the sentence, repetition concludes the sense rather than the cadence. A prose of movement must know when and how to stop and restart, if it is to avoid fatiguing its reader with an endless point-to-point through a landscape whose features the reader is not permitted to pause over and appreciate.

What Dryden says, in the beginning of his preface, of his work on *Fables* is equally appropriate to the conduct of the preface and the individual sentences of which it is made:

> 'Tis with a poet as with a man who designs to build, and is very exact, as he supposes, in casting up the cost beforehand; but, generally speaking, he is mistaken in his account, and reckons short of the expense he first intended: he alters his mind as the work proceeds, and will have this or that convenience more of which he had not thought when he began. So has it happened to me; I have built a house where I intended but a lodge.[32]

Each of the sentences in the paragraph quoted earlier is a lodge which becomes a house, the mind changing as the sentence proceeds because the mind is so keenly aware of the way words work together. A designed metaphor proves to have unforeseen possibilities; a too bold assertion calls out for immediate qualification; and so clause is added to clause, realizing possibilities, modifying assertiveness, taking a slightly different view of the same matter. The unpremeditated syntax, always slightly surprised at itself, conveys (how could it do otherwise?) not the results of thought but the act of thinking. It conveys the reverse of the legislative or dogmatic mind, which needs to think its sentences out before writing them down. Dryden's prose expresses a mind naturally diffident and sceptical.[33]

[32] *Essays*, ed. Watson, II, 269.
[33] Preface to *Sylvæ* in *Works*, ed. Swedenberg et al., III, 11.

The *ignis fatuus* of scepticism flickers across almost the whole terrain of Dryden studies. How many questions with their attendant answers has it prompted? Was Dryden's scepticism real or apparent, dogmatic or probabilist; was he consistent or not? Is *Of Dramatic Poesy* a sceptical discourse, or a means whereby Dryden can legislate through the mouth of Neander? Can sceptics, or can they not, have a preferred point of view, while recognizing others? Such questions, with their answers, their distinctions, their refinements upon previous distinctions, usually derive from analysis which isolates ideas, intellectual positions, in Dryden's writings, often translating them into other terms, and then reads them off against a schedule of philosophical categories. If we restore Dryden's ideas to their context, responding to them in Dryden's words, the general problem disappears. Of course Dryden was a sceptic; the movement of his sentences declares him to be so.

But while Dryden's syntax expresses diffidence and scepticism, his diction expresses, sometimes authority, and always confidence. "If the searchers find any ['counterbanded goods'] in the cargo, let them be staved and forfeited." Or we may recall the case of Percennius and the Pannonian veterans, as described by Tacitus, as by Dryden. The speculative syntax checks the tendency of the definitive phrasing to sound arrogant; the definitive phrasing stiffens a syntax which might otherwise trap itself in nervous hesitation, modifying itself out of lucidity, out of existence. Our critical terms are sadly inadequate to account for the vitality of Dryden's prose. We are all condemned to drink blood and pass it on as water. But we can at least, without words, sense that blend of confidence and diffidence which is as clearly present in the opening paragraph of Dryden's first published essay as it is in the closing paragraphs of his last.

Some may object that Dryden's prose changes with the years, the occasion, and in accordance with the classical discrimination of styles. Of course it does; it would be surprising were it otherwise. Some may say—have said—that it is wrong to speak of Dryden's prose style rather than his prose styles. And here Johnson must answer: "Dryden is always 'another and the same.'"[34] The differences may be referred to changes in age, occasion, or circumstances of composition. The sameness is

[34] *Lives*, I, 418.

referable to the old maxim we have known so long that we have ceased to attend to it: the style is the man. When a man commands his language, his style will express, through syntax and diction, his sense of experience, of the way things come together or lie separate; it will express his priorities and preferences, his attitudes to other men, the depth and breadth of his thinking. Conversely, a man only commands his language if he has an interesting mind to express.

What catches the attention in the paragraph quoted earlier is the busy life with which it is filled, from the quiet deliberation of the studio to the disputes of the wharf and the acrimony of the law court. Maimbourg wanted to give history the delights of fiction while remaining zealous for truth.[35] Something similar is true of Dryden's criticism. Dryden tries, as Johnson put it, "to determine upon principles the merit of composition."[36] But the result of this endeavor is scarcely analytic. "I could prove," Dryden says, "by induction" that each of the fables contains "an instructive moral." But it's tedious and unnecessary to assemble examples in support of a proposition. In any case, an induction is a physical act, a leading in of someone, his reader, who must needs follow a route, must pass along "the way" to conviction, and all along the way the instances, like so many silly rabbits, "leap foremost into sight without the reader's trouble of looking after them."

In Dryden's essays men hunt, build, paint, trade, govern; men are lawyers and hangmen, physicians and clergymen; men sail and men fight. Four men take to the river in a barge and dispute the preeminence of ancients and moderns, English and French, rhymed and unrhymed verse. And as they do so, other men in ships of war dispute the pre-eminence of England and the Netherlands upon the seas. Both disputes are about the destiny of England and its civilization, are about its potential and actual greatness, which must be tested by international competition, in letters as in trade. The busy activity of Dryden's essays does not simply exist to enliven the critical discourse. It provides, rather, the proper social context for criticism. Writing literature and writing about it, talking about it, are activities which combine with many others to make up the quality of a civilization.

[35] *Histoires de l'Heresie des Iconoclastes,* 2nd ed., I, sig. ã5ʳ.
[36] *Lives,* I, 410.

The presence of other activities keeps Dryden's criticism, like his prose, in touch with civilization.

Arnold said in "The Study of Poetry," after reviewing some earlier styles,

> but when we find Dryden telling us: 'What Virgil wrote in the vigour of his age, in plenty and at ease, I have undertaken to translate in my declining years; struggling with wants, oppressed with sickness, curbed in my genius, liable to be misconstrued in all I write,'—then we exclaim that here at last we have the true English prose, a prose such as we would all gladly use if we only knew how.[37]

It takes an Arnold to find his touchstone in the postscript to the *Aeneis*, where Dryden for once seems like Arnoldian man, sad and alone. The passage, in fact, may remind us of Teutoburgium. There a scene, here a condition is elaborated into typicality, as Dryden generalizes himself into the old man out of office. We long for Tacitus and restraint, and if, like Johnson, we suspect ourselves of some partial fondness for the memory of Dryden, we may rather regret than applaud what Arnold exclaimed upon. Yet something of a better Dryden is here too. The strong participles—struggling, oppressed, curbed, misconstrued—check the easy slide of self-pity into the nerveless and querulous. So Arnold is partly right. We may want to use it otherwise, but this is prose such as we would all gladly use if we only knew how.

University of California
Los Angeles

---

[37] *Complete Prose*, IX, 179.

BIBLIOGRAPHY OF BOOKS AND ARTICLES BY EARL R. WASSERMAN

BOOKS

Elizabethan Poetry of the Eighteenth Century (Urbana, 1947).

Thomas Parney's *A Full Enquiry into the True Nature of Pastoral.* Ed. with intro. (Augustan Reprint Society: Ann Arbor, 1948).

The Finer Tone: Keats' Major Poems (Baltimore, 1953).

The Subtler Language: Critical Readings of Neoclassical and Romantic Poems (Baltimore, 1959).

Pope's Epistle to Bathurst: A Critical Reading, with an Edition of the Manuscript (Baltimore, 1960).

Shelley's Prometheus Unbound: A Critical Reading (Baltimore, 1965).

Aspects of the Eighteenth Century. Ed. (Baltimore, 1965).

Shelley: A Critical Reading (Baltimore, 1971).

ARTICLES

"The Scholarly Origin of the Elizabethan Revival," *ELH*, 4 (1937), 213-43.

"Pre-Restoration Poetry in Dryden's Miscellany," *MLN*, 52 (1937), 545-55.

"A Doubtful Poem in the Collins Canon," *MLN*, 54 (1939), 361-62.

"The Walpole-Chatterton Controversy," *MLN*, 54 (1939), 460-62.

"Henry Headley and the Elizabethan Revival," *Studies in Philology*, 36 (1939), 491-502.

"The Return of the Enjambed Couplet," *ELH*, 7 (1940), 239-52.

"The Source of Motherwell's 'Melancholye,'" *MLN*, 55 (1940), 296.

"Coleridge's 'Metrical Experiments,'" *MLN*, 55 (1940), 432-33.

"Collins' 'Young Damon of the Vale is Dead,'" *Notes and Queries*, March 16, 1940.

"Elizabethan Poetry 'Improved,'" *Modern Philology*, 37 (1940), 357-69.

"Moses Browne and the 1783 Edition of Giles and Phineas Fletcher," *MLN*, 56 (1941), 288-90.

"Rose Mary Davis's *The Good Lord Lyttelton*" (review), *JEGP*, 40 (1941), 424-26.

"Helen Hughs's *The Gentle Hertford*" (review), *JEGP*, 40 (1941), 426-27.

"René Wellek's *The Rise of English Literary History*" (review), *JEGP*, 41 (1942), 115-18.

"Early Evidences of Milton's Influence," *MLN*, 58 (1943), 293-95.

"W. J. Bate's *From Classic to Romantic*" (review), *JEGP*, 46 (1947), 224-25.

"The Sympathetic Imagination in Eighteenth-Century Theories of Acting," *JEGP*, 46 (1947), 264-72.

"The Pleasures of Tragedy," *ELH*, 14 (1947), 283-307.

"Coleridge's 'Metrical Experiments,'" *MLN*, 63 (1948), 491-92.

"Wilma Kennedy's *The English Heritage of Coleridge of Bristol*" (review), *JEGP*, 47 (1948), 204-07.

"Another Eighteenth-Century Distinction between Fancy and Imagination," *MLN*, 64 (1949), 23-25.

"The Inherent Values of Eighteenth-Century Personification," *PMLA*, 65 (1950), 435-63.

"Unedited Letters by Sterne, Hume, and Rousseau," *MLN*, 66 (1951) 73-80.

"Keats' Sonnet 'The Poet,'" *MLN*, 67 (1952), 361-65.

"Nature Moralized: The Divine Analogy in the Eighteenth Century," *ELH*, 20 (1953), 39-76.

"Marvin Mudrick's *Jane Austen: Irony as Defense and Discovery*" (review), *MLN*, 68 (1953), 258-61.

"Keats and Benjamin Bailey on the Imagination," *MLN*, 68 (1953), 361-65.

"*Adonais*: Progressive Revelation as a Poetic Mode," *ELH*, 21 (1954), 274-326.

"Shelley's *Adonais*, 177-179," *MLN*, 69 (1954), 563.

"Byron and Sterne," *MLN*, 70 (1955), 25.

"Myth-Making in *Prometheus Unbound*," *MLN*, 70 (1955), 182-84.

"Chester Chapin's *Personification in Eighteenth-Century English Poetry*" (review), *JEGP*, 55 (1956), 651-54.

"Dryden's 'Epistle to Dr. Charleton,'" *JEGP*, 55 (1956), 201-12.

"René Wellek's *A History of Modern Criticism*; vol. I: *The Later Eighteenth Century*" (review), *PQ*, 35 (1956), 274-75.

"*Shelley's Prose*, edited by David Clark" (review), *MLN*, 71 (1956), 154-56.

"*Coleridge's Collected Letters*, edited by Earl Leslie Griggs" (review), *MLN*, 72 (1957), 136-37.

"Harold Bloom's *Shelley's Mythmaking*" (review), *Yale Review*, 48 (1958), 609-11.

"The Meaning of 'Poland' in 'The Medal,'" *MLN*, 73 (1958), 165-67.

"Milton Wilson's *Shelley's Later Poetry, a Study of his Prophetic Imagination*" (review), *Yale Review*, 48 (1959), 611-12.

"Pope's 'Ode for Musick.'" *ELH*, 28 (1961), 163-86.

"The Twickenham Edition of Pope" (review), *PQ*, 41 (1962), 615-22.

"Shakespeare and the English Romantic Movement," in *The Persistence of Shakespearean Idolatry: Essays in Honor of Robert W. Babock* (Detroit, 1964), pp. 79-103.

"The English Romantics: The Grounds of Knowledge," *Studies in Romanticism*, 4 (1964), 17-34.

"*The Natural*: Malamud's World Ceres," *Centennial Review*, 9 (1965), 438-60.

"Shelley's Last Poetics: A Reconsideration," in *From Sensibility to Romanticism: Essays Presented to F. A. Pottle* (New York, 1965), pp. 487-511.

"The Limits of Allusion in 'The Rape of the Lock,'" *JEGP*, 65 (1966), 424-44.

"Collins' 'Ode on the Poetical Character,'" *ELH*, 34 (1967), 92-115.

"New Criticism and the Intentional Mind," *English Notes*, 3 (November, 1968), 8-13.

"Johnson's *Rasselas*: Implicit Contexts," *JEGP*, 74 (1975), 1-25.